WESTPAC
THE BANK THAT
BROKE THE BANK

WESTPAC

THE BANK THAT BROKE THE BANK

Edna Carew

DOUBLEDAY

SYDNEY • AUCKLAND • TORONTO • NEW YORK • LONDON

WESTPAC: THE BANK THAT BROKE THE BANK
A DOUBLEDAY BOOK

First published in Australia and New Zealand in 1997 by Doubleday

National Library of Australia.
Cataloguing-in-Publication Entry

Carew, Edna, 1949– .
    Westpac: the bank that broke the bank.

    Includes index.
    ISBN 0 86824 664 6 (pbk.).

    1. Westpac Banking Corporation. 2. Banks and banking–
    Australia. I. Title

332.12230994

Doubleday books are published by

Transworld Publishers (Aust) Pty Limited
15–25 Helles Ave, Moorebank, NSW 2170

Transworld Publishers (NZ) Limited
3 William Pickering Drive, Albany, Auckland

Transworld Publishers (UK) Limited
61–63 Uxbridge Road, Ealing, London W5 5SA

Bantam Doubleday Dell Publishing Group Inc
1540 Broadway, New York, New York 10036

Typeset in 12/15 pt Times by Midland Typesetters
Printed by Australian Print Group

10 9 8 7 6 5 4 3 2 1

To Hoffers: for his enduring sense of the ridiculous

*And to my parents: for providing a good education
and an inheritance of stamina*

*And to everyone who has said, at some time, it's as good
as money in the bank*

CONTENTS

PREFACE

Writing an account of Westpac's activities since the early 1980s is a task that calls to mind the renowned Japanese film *Rashomon* in which an examination of four conflicting yet equally credible accounts of the same event becomes a tantalising analysis of the nature of truth.

Researching this book involved absorbing a great many differently coloured accounts. The number of people interviewed ran into hundreds, the documents, papers and reports examined are countless. Distilling the information that emerged was complicated by the fact that many of the participants have personal agendas very much alive. I was grateful to be able to call on the experience and information gleaned during twenty years of observing the Wales/Westpac institution.

Structuring the book was frankly a nightmare. Crucial events and developments intertwined and overlapped; 1986, for example, was brimming with euphoric activity, later in the 1980s and into the early 1990s Westpac was twisting and turning, beating back bushfires on several fronts. A time-line is provided as a reference to the many strands of the narrative, as is a guide to key characters, the last, if nothing else, an unintentioned pointer to the blokiness of Australian banking.

The overwhelming volume of activity in the fifteen years under review in the book has necessitated some selectivity in coverage, some reluctant pruning of peripheral events that will, it is hoped, be recounted elsewhere. In reality, several books compete for these pages. Australian Guarantee Corporation, for example, is a story in itself, as are the foreign-currency borrowers. Westpac's experiences in just one year—1992—could fill an entire volume.

As the 1990s unfolded, and post-mortems of the 1980s multiplied, there was an increasing tendency to try to sheet home responsibility for what went wrong in Westpac. Where did the seeds of its problems lie? Why did the Board not ask more questions? But a board only gets answers to what it asks, and in any large organisation information is filtered through layers of management before it reaches the directors. And in an organisation the size of Westpac, with its several spirited subsidiaries, and staff that peaked at 46,600, it is not possible to identify any single source of the bank's difficulties.

Many people helped greatly in my search for information; some, regrettably, declined to contribute so their views are not recorded, and a few were unfortunately impossible to locate. It is a tribute to the sense of identity that has endured about the bank that so many were willing to discuss, at length, with energy and even passion, the events that shaped much of their working lives.

Most who have contributed preferred to do so ano- nymously, so it would be inappropriate to identify those who felt otherwise. My heartfelt thanks to everyone who cooperated, particularly where discussions led to further meetings and follow-up conversations, and to those who responded cordially and helpfully to my requests for additional information, for elaboration of technical details or a verification of recollections. My special thanks go to the handful who read selected chapters and also to those who cheerfully continued to make themselves available during the final stages of editing and checking the manuscript. I am hugely grateful for their enthusiastic and unstinting support.

There came a time in the research when courtesy suggested that Westpac be told this project was under way. It was my hope that access to staff in the bank—the few remaining with extensive memories and the newcomers now in charge—would help in rounding out the story. Westpac's

x

reaction was interesting, reflecting what appeared to be its twin but irreconcilable desires to exert control over, but at the same time distance itself from, a project that was going ahead whether cooperation was achieved or not. The response was curiously defensive, giving the almost comical appearance of timorous paranoia combined with schoolyard bullying.

Westpac's desire not to be seen as in any way endorsing the book was matched by my own. This is not an authorised account. Westpac went so far as to attempt to require a disclaimer, words which would in any event have found expression because they clarify the position: that the bank allowed me access to staff but that the views and opinions in the book, while widely shared, are mine.

Only a few inside the bank chose not to participate in this 'allowed' access. The interviews, conducted generally in the presence of a minder from the Westpac bureaucracy, had overtones of prison visits, a situation made all the more ludicrous because many of the subjects had been known to me for years. To those in the bank who went out of their way to be helpful, in the interests of seeing the story told as accurately as possible, my sincere thanks.

I would like to say how much I appreciated the spirit and support of Transworld Publishers, particularly Shona Martyn, Maggie Hamilton and Jude McGee; thanks also to Geoff Rumpf for his patience and to Judith Curr with whom the idea for the book was first discussed.

The Westpac story encapsulates much of Australia's ambitions in the 1980s when the financial community, indeed the country, was fired by a new energy and a conviction that it could forge a greater role for itself in the world. The story is a salutary reminder of the management challenges confronting large institutions as they try to grow larger; it highlights issues of corporate governance and raises many questions relevant to bank supervision which are even more pertinent in the wake of the Wallis Committee's report on the Australian financial system. It underscores the role of a corporate 'culture', an intangible but vital element in the health of any large organisation. And it illustrates how staff, the faceless but loyal footsoldiers in a corporate army, keep the business going from day to day while their leaders search for solutions to crises that threaten its existence. Quite simply, it is a story that had to be told.

DRAMATIS PERSONAE

Tony Aveling: joined Bank of New South Wales in 1963; after a variety of roles in corporate and retail banking, became general manager, Europe 1990; chief general manager, technology 1991; head of AGC 1992; head of regional bank integration 1995; chief executive of mortgage processing centre 1996; chief executive, business and private banking 1997–.

Peter Baillieu: Westpac board member 1974–97.

Peter Chan: joined Bank of New South Wales in Wellington in 1966; moved to Sydney as chief foreign exchange dealer in February 1983; left Westpac 1987, returned 1989 as chief manager, sales and distribution; chief manager, international and central bank relations 1992; chief manager, Hong Kong 1993–.

Frank Conroy: joined the Bank of New South Wales in 1960; held senior positions in Australia and overseas, including general manager, corporate in early 1980s; general manager, Asia, based in Hong Kong, 1986–88; chief general manager, retail financial services 1988; chief operating officer and director 1990; managing director 1991–92.

Stan Davis: joined Westpac through CBA merger, general manager, finance 1982–85; head of global treasury 1985–89.

Philip Deer: joined Westpac as general manager, Asia, 1983–86; general manager, corporate banking, Sydney, 1986, chief general manager, corporate and international until 1989; managing director, Partnership Pacific Ltd 1986–89 and chairman of PPL 1988–89.

Rob Douglass: joined Westpac 1983, general manager, merchant banking 1983–86; managing director, Partnership Pacific Ltd 1984–86.

Terry Dunne: joined Wales 1955; chief legal officer 1983–93.

Adrian Fletcher: joined Bank of New South Wales in 1980, head of group strategy 1980–87; head of investment banking, London 1987–89.

Sir Noel Foley: director of Wales/Westpac from 1964; chairman 1978–87.

Sir James Foots: director of Wales/Westpac from 1971; chairman 1987–89.

Stuart Fowler: joined Bank of New South Wales in 1949; assistant general manager, international business, 1978; head of corporate and international and board member of PPL 1984–86; head of retail 1986–87; managing director 1987–91.

Pat Handley: chief financial officer of Westpac 1993– (formerly a senior executive with Bank One, Ohio, US).

Vern Harvey: joined Westpac as head of strategic planning 1989; chief general manager, regional offshore banking group 1992–93.

Gary Hett: joined Westpac 1983 as deputy general manager, Americas division, a position held until 1993.

Derrick Heywood: after 20 years with a major international corporation, working in several countries, joined AGC in 1980, financial controller 1980–89; chief financial officer of Westpac 1989–94.

Professor Warren Hogan: Westpac board member 1986–.

Bob Joss: managing director, Westpac 1993– (formerly a vice chairman, Wells Fargo).

Warwick Kent: joined Bank of New South Wales in 1953; general manager, domestic business 1983; head of retail 1984–86; head of corporate and international and chairman of PPL 1986–88; head of credit 1988–89.

Ian Matheson: joined Bank of New South Wales in 1941; deputy managing director 1982–86; chairman of AGC 1987–88; chairman of Partnership Pacific Ltd 1984–86; chairman of BLE Capital 1987–90.

David Morgan: joined Westpac from federal treasury as deputy managing director, Westpac Financial Services Group 1990, managing director, WFSG 1990–91; chief general manager, Asia-Pacific 1991; head of retail 1992; head of institutional banking 1994–.

Sir Eric Neal: joined Westpac board 1985; deputy chairman 1987, chairman 1989–92, chairman, AGC 1988–92.

Sir Robert Norman: head of Bank of New South Wales 1964–77; board member 1970–84; deputy chairman of Partnership Pacific Ltd 1969–71, chairman 1971–84.

Barry Robertson: joined Bank of New South Wales in New Zealand in 1965; chief manager Singapore 1986; deputy general manager, corporate and investment banking in New Zealand 1988; chief general manager of ACG 1991; group executive, asset management 1992; group executive, commercial banking and property finance 1994; head of retail in Victoria, South Australia, Tasmania and Northern Territory 1996–.

Rob Robson: managing director of AGC 1983–89.

Iain Thompson: general manager, Westpac corporate banking, 1985–91.

John Uhrig: joined Westpac board 1989; chairman 1992–.

xv

Owen van der Wall: joined Bank of New South Wales in 1963; held a number of senior positions in Australia and overseas, including chief manager, New York 1986–89; general manager, global financial markets, Sydney 1989–91; chief general manager, institutional banking 1991–92; head of retail 1994; head of retail, NSW 1996–.

Tony Walton: joined Westpac 1983 as head of the Americas division, a position held until 1993; head of Americas and Europe 1991–93; Westpac director 1991–92.

Bob White: joined the Bank of New South Wales 1940; managing director 1977–87; board member of AGC 1977–90; board member of Westpac 1987–90.

TIME-LINE

1977: Bob White appointed managing director of Bank of New South Wales.

1978-80: Reddin management experiment.

1980: Adrian Fletcher recruited as head of corporate planning replacing Geoff Thompson who was working on special projects.

1982: Merger between Wales and CBA creates Westpac; Ian Matheson deputy managing director and a director of Westpac; assets $31 billion; reported after-tax profit $215 million.

1983: $A floated, exchange controls removed; Westpac buys 75 per cent of gold bullion dealer Mase Metals; recruits Tony Walton in New York, recruits Philip Deer in Asia, Rob Robson as head of AGC, Rob Douglass as head of merchant banking activities; assets $34.5 billion; reported after-tax profit $222 million.

1984: Westpac buys 50 per cent of stockbroker Ord Minnett: Stuart Fowler chief general manager, corporate and international; Warwick Kent chief general manager, retail financial services; assets $40 billion; reported after-tax profit $306 million.

1985: Sixteen foreign banks licensed to operate in Australia; Westpac is the first Australian bank to open a branch in Tokyo; Bob White nominated Banker of the Year by *Australian Business*; Westpac acquires 100 per cent of Partnership Pacific Ltd and Westpac Merchant Finance in New Zealand; Sir Eric Neal joins Westpac board; assets $49 billion; reported after-tax profit $368 million.

1986: Buys Johnson Matthey Bankers in the UK; buys primary dealer William E. Pollock in the US; forms Westpac Life; AGC launches Westpac General Finance in the UK; Westpac lists on Tokyo Stock Exchange; Fowler and Kent swap jobs; assets $60 billion; reported after-tax profit $400 million.

1987: Adrian Fletcher moves to London as head of global investment banking; Westpac takes 100 per cent of Ord Minnett; stockmarket crash; Bob White retires, joins Westpac board, Stuart Fowler becomes managing director; Sir Noel Foley retires, Sir James Foots becomes chairman, Sir Eric Neal deputy chairman; assets $70 billion; reported after-tax profit $409 million.

1988: Australia's Bicentennial; Westpac revalues its properties, holds rights issue; buys 100 per cent of AGC; assets: $84.6 billion; reported after-tax profit $693 million.

1989: Sir James Foots retires, Sir Eric Neal becomes chairman; lending problems appear in Westpac Merchant Finance in New Zealand, in PPL; Rob Robson retires, Peter Wilson appointed head of AGC; Westpac buys Banque Indosuez branches in the South Pacific; lists on New York Stock Exchange; Warwick Kent, Philip Deer leave, Vern Harvey recruited as head of strategy; assets $108.6 billion; reported after-tax profit $801 million.

1990: David Morgan joins as managing director designate of Westpac Financial Services Group; Westpac Pollock closed; Westpac General Finance in the UK closed; CS90 technology project wound down; Bob White quits board; Australia officially in recession; assets $107 billion; reported after-tax profit $684 million.

1991: 'Westpac letters' revealed, parliamentary banking inquiry; Westpac forms alliance with AMP Society to create AMPAC Life; Stuart Fowler retires, Frank Conroy becomes managing director; staff peaks at 46,600; assets $106 billion; reported after-tax profit $476 million.

1992: Westpac turns 175; Sir James Balderstone and Bob Johnston join Westpac board as AMP representatives; annou—ncement of half-year loss of $1.6 billion (about half attributable to AGC); more than $2 billion in assets written off; investors spurn rights issue; Sir Eric Neal resigns with four other directors, John Uhrig becomes chairman; Kerry Packer buys into Westpac, Packer and Al Dunlap join the board; Frank Conroy resigns; assets $110 billion; reported after-tax loss $1,562 million.

1993: Packer and Dunlap quit the board; Bob Joss appointed managing director; Lend Lease buys Packer's shares in Westpac, gains two board seats; sell-off of assets in the US and Asia: assets $105 billion; reported after-tax profit $39 million.

1994: Consolidation and recovery, efficiency ratio improves, home lending increases; AGC's and regional offshore banking group's non-core assets sold, Mase Westpac and Ord Minnett sold; assets $94 billion; reported after-tax profit $705 million.

1995: Buys Challenge Bank in Western Australia; assets $105 billion; reported after-tax profit $947 million.

1996: Adelaide mortgage processing centre opens; Westpac buys Trust Bank New Zealand; end of alliance with AMP, Westpac Life re-emerges; strategic alliance announced with Standard Chartered in Asia; assets $121 billion; reported after-tax profits $1,132 million.

1997: Longstanding board member Peter Baillieu retires; Westpac makes a successful bid for Bank of Melbourne; Wallis committee reports on the Australian financial system; reported after-tax half-year profit $638 million.

Let us possess the public confidence so long only as,
by a faithful discharge of the honourable trust reposed in us,
we may show ourselves worthy of it.
Whenever any one man may say with truth
'the bank has broken faith with us',
be then our ruin, and ours only,
the immediate consequence.

INSCRIPTION ON THE EARLY BANK OF NEW SOUTH WALES BANK NOTES

Fall of the Giant

Westpac squandered billions of dollars of its shareholders' money in less than half a dozen years. How it did that is a story of hubris, greed, vision, arrogance, ambition, fear and incompetence. The bank turned 175 years of business leadership into an unprecedented financial disaster that left its shareholders alienated and its customers disgusted, its reputation in shreds and its board and management in shock. And almost everyone—except the bank itself—had seen the cataclysm approaching.

Westpac had been an unquestionably sound bank, the biggest in Australia, a 'people's bank' respected by customers, shareholders and the business community. That stature, earned largely by its predecessor, Australia's oldest company, the Bank of New South Wales, was reduced by 1992 to a pitiful position as one of the world's weakest banks, relentlessly reviled in the media. The fall of this commercial giant is a tragedy of errors: the story of a bank that wanted to be bigger and better. In the attempt it all but crippled itself.

Opinions differ about the onset of the malaise that felled Westpac. Some put the source of its problems in the awkward attempt to 'unfreeze' the bank by experimenting with new theories of modern management; this attempt to build efficiency through decentralisation created instead a family of independent-minded subsidiaries that became ungovernable. Others pinpoint the merger in 1982 that created Westpac out of the old Bank of New South Wales and the Victorian-based Commercial Bank of Australia; others blame Westpac's over-reactive response to the perceived threats from financial deregulation, and the competition from major international institutions that followed. Dominance in its home market was seen as Westpac's best defence against foreign rivals and expansion overseas was seen as crucial to servicing, and thus retaining, an increasingly international customer base.

Westpac's strategy, in riding the rapids of the banking industry in the 1980s, was based on the assumption that growth was essential. So it set about vigorously building assets—which in its most simplistic sense means making loans—and seizing market share. It was not until later in the decade that the focus shifted to important criteria such as return on equity. Meanwhile, the bank spent hundreds of millions of dollars on acquisitions and on technology, much of which was wasted.

A major source of Westpac's near-fatal difficulties in the early 1990s was the explosion of growth in the late 1980s when, against a background of a booming economy, the bank's assets expanded by more than 50 per cent over two years. Westpac became infatuated with the idea of becoming 'Australia's world bank'. But the worldwide rush to lend in the overheated years of the late 1980s inevitably entailed picking up marginal business. A time-bomb was ticking. That no-one heard it was largely due to the absence of a centralised reporting system to monitor group-wide lending. Moreover, the fabric of the finance and investment markets was changing: 1988 was a year of euphoria in Australia, with Bicentennial celebrations, and the worldwide financial community, cushioned by ample liquidity from their central banks, was congratulating itself on having weathered the 1987 stockmarket crash and embraced a safer source of profit—property.

The property market boomed—and then collapsed. When it did so it left lenders shockingly exposed, a situation exacerbated for Westpac by a critical structural flaw: the group extended into the market through subsidiaries which a weak corporate centre had allowed to seize excessive power and independence. Despite being represented on their boards, the bank seemed unaware of critically menacing developments in its own subsidiaries.

Westpac's finance company Australian Guarantee Corporation, AGC's merchant bank Bill Acceptance Corporation, and its UK offshoot Westpac General Finance, Westpac's Partnership Pacific Ltd and New Zealand merchant bank Westpac Merchant Finance and Westpac itself were all lending into the same market, sometimes to the same borrower. All wound up over-exposed to a moribund property sector.

Inadequate group coordination and control reflected a misplaced belief by Westpac—one shared by many other banks at the time—in the synergies between banks and non-banks. This had led to the establishment or acquisition of diverse arms. Of these, Westpac Financial Services was a success but others, such as PPL and Pollock, the primary dealer in the US, brought problems and losses. Westpac seemed incapable of capitalising on the potential opportunities offered by its stockbroking arm, Ord Minnett, or its gold bullion dealer, Mase Westpac.

While Westpac's overseas strategy was criticised for a seeming lack of cohesion, that was not what brought the bank to its knees, but lethal mistakes in its bread-and-butter business: lending. Westpac failed to manage the challenges of a deregulated market, including the conflict it presented between credit and growth. Many banks leapt into international expansion in the 1980s and most had to curtail their overseas operations because they were weakened by bad-debt problems in their neglected home bases. Westpac was one of them.

In the early 1990s Westpac was forced to shift its focus from growth to improving internal controls and accountability. By 1992 it was blindingly clear to Westpac that as growth increases the complexity of the business, management controls and skills must keep pace if devastating consequences are to be avoided. In Westpac's case, the realisation came too late.

No other Australian financial institution had seized on the opportunities presented by the wide canvas of the 1980s with the same enthusiasm as Westpac. It grew enormously and rapidly in size, measured by assets and staff; it expanded overseas and diversified into new businesses. For the first time in its history it recruited senior executives from outside the bank. The newcomers brought fresh ideas and energy, but dangerous tensions developed between them and the bank's 'lifers'. Much of the energy was dissipated in rivalries and resentment.

Banks found during the tumult of the 1980s that they were being freed of regulations which had circumscribed their activities in exchange for an environment that called for judgment. They had chafed at the earlier controls, but events showed that many were not prepared for survival without them.

National Australia Bank, while not innocent of faults, serves as an example of what many banks were not. Castigated by its rivals in the 1980s for becoming sterile, merely a 'retail' bank in Australia, it emerged to dominate in the 1990s. It had prepared well for deregulation and resisted chasing new business for the sake of market share. It thought early and hard about technology, and how much it wanted to spend, and developed efficient centralised systems. It had a credit bureau that operated well away from the 'line' lenders and closely monitored different industries and graded loans. NAB operated with a tight, decisive team and enjoyed strong management and well-trained staff, leaving the board free to concentrate on strategy.

Banks that recognised the shift from processing to decision-making, and trained their staff accordingly, passed the test of the 1980s. Most banks did not, and Westpac failed miserably. Pulling the bank back from the brink in the 1990s was a huge turnaround and was achieved at huge cost in terms of staff numbers, businesses that had been nurtured with an eye to the future, and customer relationships. Westpac had recovered financially, but in a form far from the giant it had once wanted to be. The sacrifice was staggering, and questions endure. How much of it was necessary? How much better could it have been handled?

CHAPTER ONE

THE BIRTH OF WESTPAC

Four seminal events combined to set the stage for the dramas that embroiled Westpac Banking Corporation in the 1980s: Bob White taking over as chief of the Bank of New South Wales in 1977, an experiment in organisational change inspired by the credo of 'management by objective'; the merger in 1982 of the Wales and the Victorian-based Commercial Bank of Australia (CBA) which formed Westpac; and the opening up of the Australian financial system to new players which exposed a staid and protected banking industry to the exhilarations, and quicksands, of real-world competition. In the end, Westpac's frenzied response to this looming competition, and its purblind determination to fend off the newcomers at any cost, magnified the threat beyond its reality.

The appointment on 22 April 1977 of Bob White as chief of the bank brought in someone who was determined to shake the Bank of New South Wales awake and prepare it for the changes he identified as inevitable. The Wales, founded in 1817 by a group of Sydney businessmen, was Australia's oldest bank and oldest company. In its early years it was known as the 'people's bank'. In the late 1970s it had an overweening pride in its leading position in Australian banking and was a self-satisfied, even arrogant, institution, mindful of its heritage and role in the history of Australia, particularly New South Wales. Such was its dominance of

Australian banking that, in the 1930s, it had unilaterally devalued the Australian pound. Other banks fell into line, as the Wales knew they would, and they included the Commonwealth Bank, then the country's central bank. In the 1940s, the Bank of New Wales had led the fight against bank nationalisation. The Wales was seen by its peers and rivals as a bank puffed up by its own self-importance and, even more irritatingly, entitled to be so. It was a powerful institution.

The Bank of New South Wales had already spread its tentacles overseas. In 1853 it was the first foreign bank to establish in London, in 1861 it began what became a wide network in New Zealand, it had several points of representation in Papua New Guinea from as early as 1910 and it had operated in Fiji from 1901. Domestically, it had extended into savings banking, had a majority-owned finance company, Australian Guarantee Corporation Ltd, one-third of a leading merchant bank, Partnership Pacific Ltd, and minority holdings in other institutions. It was Australia's largest bank, in terms of assets and profits. By the late 1970s, though, the Wales's pre-eminent position was coming under challenge as its banking competitors gained ground and non-banks ate into the banks' territory.

White took over the helm from Sir Robert Norman, who had been chief of the bank for thirteen years and was the first Wales executive to be appointed to the board. Until Norman instituted a change to weekly meetings, the board had met twice a week, every Tuesday and Friday, a clockwork arrangement that reflected the bank's reliance on its traditions. Norman continued as a director of the bank after his retirement. White's affable and low-key approach contrasted with the more formal demeanour of his predecessor, whose manner doubtless suited his times. White had a sincere and enduring interest in the wellbeing of staff and, while some remember him as autocratic, others credit him

9

with creating a team approach to management, pushing authority and accountability down the line, although with mixed results. White's view of the future affected bank policy through much of the 1980s. He was convinced that Westpac had no choice but to respond to the forces of deregulation—which included welcoming the biggest names in world banking to Australia—by expanding its financial markets and treasury operations, aggressively but, he would argue, judiciously lifting corporate lending, and building its market share. However, the consequences of that response were more eventful than he could have foreseen.

Bob White had joined the Wales in 1940, aged 16, at its branch in Echuca, Victoria. The bank was then strongly dependent on the rural sector and many of its customers were large pastoralists. Says White: 'The Wales grew up following the development of the pastoral industry. Farmers were its main customers and lending for business came later.' Army service interrupted a career that otherwise spanned 50 years with the institution and included stints in London in the 1950s and 1970s—which White has called the 'highlights' of his banking career—and New Zealand, before his elevation to head of the bank. His career path was typical of his generation: join a bank straight from school, learn and train on the job, acquire banking qualifications as soon as possible but no university degree or exotic MBA. Married with no children, White was accustomed to working twelve-hour days, often into the weekends, and his chief diversion was his garden. He was conscious of the need to keep fit while holding a sedentary, desk-bound job, and followed his own exercise routine long before the advent of trendy city gyms. Friendly and approachable, though something of a loner and with a strong ego but a distaste for confrontation, White overcame an innate shyness to acquire an almost statesmanlike stature in Australian banking.

He inherited a rigid and bureaucratic structure with, he says, a woeful lack of planning. The bank suffered from deeply entrenched attitudes and traditions that left it inflexible and unprepared to cope with change. But the Wales was going to have to change. The Commonwealth Bank was becoming a serious rival in deposits, while the ANZ and National Bank were closing in on profits. Shortly after taking over as chief, White said: 'I am determined to put us back undisputedly as Number One in Australian banking and finance ... We can only do this if we put behind us the complacency and the bureaucratic behaviour that was appropriate when we were Number One ...'

Already in the late 1970s change was in the wind. Banks were feeling the nip of competition from less strictly regulated non-banks, such as building societies, credit unions and, in wholesale finance, the increasingly aggressive and entrepreneurial merchant banks. In 1979 the then federal treasurer, John Howard, commissioned a review of the financial system—the first in 40 years—which would lead to the removal of many controls over banks and open the banking system to new entrants. The Wales would have to move with the times. White brought in a catalyst, Bill Reddin, a UK-born, Canadian-educated behavioural scientist specialising in strategies for changing organisations, who would 'unfreeze' the bank.

Geoff Thompson, chief manager of research and planning, was instrumental in bringing White together with Reddin, whose work had impressed Thompson a great deal. Thompson agreed about the need to change the Wales, to transform it from a rigid, myopic bureaucracy and force it to address the real world. In a memo to White in 1977 Thompson had highlighted some deficiencies in the bank:

> We are no longer producing enough well-rounded trained executives for all key jobs becoming available.

11

> Indeed, we have difficulty in producing managers who
> can lend prudently and tellers who can balance their
> cash ... various studies ... show that our reputation
> for service is not as high as it ought to be ... we are
> encountering staff hostility ... we have become
> bureaucratic.

Thompson also wrote that a high proportion of staff were promoted without sufficient training, resulting in poor-quality service, costly errors and a failure to understand the bank's overall operations.

Reddin was recruited in 1978 and over the ensuing two years helped the Wales 'thaw'. White took a bold step in committing $1 million to a management change program that received only lukewarm support at board level, but he was convinced that it was an essential step in a campaign to bolster the bank against its competitors. At the heart of Reddin's strategy was 'management by objective'; that is, delegating power down the line and focusing on a job's outputs rather than inputs. A series of off-site staff conferences were held, involving perhaps 50 at a time, often at Leura in the Blue Mountains, west of Sydney. Many remember these as 'brainwashing' sessions involving long hours of self-assessment as groups of eight to ten evaluated their own and others' performances. Some found the experience quite confronting and disturbing; it brought out a sometimes unwelcome degree of honesty in colleagues' comments. Others felt liberated. Communication improved. The process produced a great release of energy as authoritarian clamps were removed. People were encouraged to think outside of the rule book. Bank managers were to become salesmen. A major cultural shift was occurring, intended to bring about a rethink in the Wales's middle ranks, to change doctrinaire administrators, wedded to a hierarchical style, into managers. The approach was not

12

sympathetically greeted by the traditionalists whose resistance, while not overt, would be a constant test of White's leadership abilities, as would the independent ambitions of some who were brought in to give the bank new energy.

Concurrent with overseeing the Reddin experiment, Geoff Thompson, as chief planner for the Wales, was eyeing the larger canvas. Technological change was looming, competition growing and the financial system inquiry, widely known as the Campbell inquiry after its chairman Keith (later Sir Keith) Campbell, was going to usher in fresh challenges. Thompson's duties expanded: he was coopted to draft the Wales's submission to the Campbell inquiry, and behind the scenes was exploring opportunities for expansion. The Wales considered it had three options for defence against the competition that would come with deregulation: it could become lean and hungry like the ANZ under its chief Mac Brunckhorst (known as Mac the Knife), it could merge with an international bank, or it could merge with a domestic bank, increase its presence in states where it was weak and use its domestic strength as a springboard for international growth. The Wales decided on the third option, but with an undertaking to incorporate some of the first. The transition to lean and mean did not eventuate during the 1980s.

In August 1980 Thompson transferred from his role as head of corporate planning and, under the cloak of working on the Campbell submission and with the title of chief manager, development projects, was to devise a merger strategy, codenamed 'Bermuda'. The Wales needed a new head of group planning. In White's view, Thompson had been the first to take the planning role seriously, and he shared Thompson's opinion that the Wales did not have the requisite skills in-house. The 'unfrozen' Wales wanted a fresh resource. They turned to the headhunters. The recruitment experts found Adrian Fletcher who, with a background in management and corporate planning in South Africa and

13

Australia, struck White as the right candidate. The appointment in late 1980 of Fletcher, educated in Britain, with degrees in physics and management science, broke new ground: an outsider, and a non-banker, was recruited to the Wales at a senior level with access to (later to become a member of) the executive committee. Fletcher found the prospect of orchestrating change at the Wales excitingly challenging. He recalls that many in senior management were eager for action.

With marriage in mind, the Wales, Australia's largest and most profitable bank, set its sights on the Commercial Bank of Australia, the country's fifth-largest. A merger of the two banks had been mooted as far back as 1962 and seriously proposed in 1968, but foundered largely because of the difficulty of bringing the CBA's pension scheme up to the more generous level of the Wales. Further, the management of the CBA had not been receptive to the idea of a merger which would have surrendered its identity to the dominant Wales. The Wales was reluctant to make a hostile bid. Business logic took a back seat. But the earlier foray meant that the Wales had done its homework on the CBA. And this time the Wales was willing to change the name of a merged entity. White, although proud of the name Bank of New South Wales, had been convinced during his years in London that it was not appropriate for a bank with an active role throughout the Pacific region and increasingly wide international representation.

The CBA, founded in 1866, had developed a solid base in Australia's southern states which would lift the Wales's representation in Victoria and South Australia. The Wales board decided to act. From October 1980 the bank began stealthily acquiring shares in the CBA. In 1981 it made an approach to the CBA, but was rejected. However, fate intervened. The chairman of the ANZ, during a lunch with his CBA counterpart, expressed interest in talking about a union and handed over a piece of paper which included some draft terms and conditions as background to a further discussion. The CBA interpreted the details as price-sensitive information and, being a listed company, felt obliged to make a public statement through the stock exchange. This took the Wales by surprise and for a time it appeared to have lost its place in the contest. But it was well positioned to increase the pressure. And working in its favour was a view in the CBA that the ANZ was a ruthless, 'take no prisoners' predator. The Wales was seen as more sympathetic and White was anxious for a friendly union. On 14 May 1981 White, Ian Matheson, general manager, merging and planning, chief accountant Graham McCorkell and Geoff Thompson flew to Melbourne to put their final proposition to the CBA board and top management. After a nerve-racking wait while the matter was deliberated, they were told their merger proposal had been accepted. The Wales's offer included a statement of its willingness to adopt a new name to cover both banks in a merged entity. This was welcomed by the CBA board members, and helped seal their agreement to the merger.

15

It was an unusually active time in banking in Australia. As well as the Wales's pitch for the CBA, the National Bank of Australasia had made a successful bid for the Commercial Banking Company of Sydney which, for an outlay of $446 million, created the National Australia Bank. The mergers reduced the number of large, nationally operating banks in Australia from six to four—Westpac, NAB, ANZ and the then government-owned Commonwealth Bank.

The Wales's offer of two shares plus $1.50 for each CBA ordinary share and $20 for each preference share valued the CBA at about $699 million. It was a high price, some eighteen times the CBA's 1979/80 earnings of $38 million. White was elated—he had pulled off the deal of his life. Later, the Wales was often criticised for having paid too much for the CBA—certainly more in real terms than it would have had to shell out in 1968—but White's retort has always been that if the deal had not been made, the cost in forfeited market share, status and opportunities would have been far greater. The merger, and the Reddin program, found particular favour in one corner, becoming the basis for a case study used by business management courses at IMEDE, a leading European business school for executives, based in Lausanne, Switzerland.

The merger date was set for 1 October 1982, leaving a tight sixteen-month preparation time. The Wales signed a nonredundancy undertaking promising that no CBA employee would lose his or her job, banned the word 'take-over' and introduced a new wardrobe ('uniform' was also stricken from the bank's lexicon) devised by top-drawer couturiers Adele and Peter Weiss. The Wales, mindful of the sensitivities of the Melbourne heavyweights on the CBA board, wanted to demonstrate that the CBA was not merely a junior partner. However, cynics on both sides knew that the 'partnership' was largely cosmetic. 'We tried to manage the amalgamation with some feeling,' Ian Matheson later said. A new name had to be found. Pieter Huveneers, a high-profile creator of names and logos, who had devised the strikingly successful big red W symbol for the Wales, was recruited to develop a new identity. He conceived the name Westpac (Western Pacific, reflecting the new bank's main area of focus), which enabled it to retain the familiar logo. The new name attracted considerable criticism and not inconsiderable ridicule from some directors, staff and the public. To some Wales directors, burying the proud old Wales name was nothing short of vandalism. The CBA buried more than one hundred years of history too. Selling the fresh identity to shareholders was not easy but its proponents were determined. Presiding over a meeting of several thousand 'proprietors', as Wales shareholders are quaintly known, was one of the finest hours for the bank's chairman, Sir Noel Foley.

It was a tense meeting, with many older shareholders object-
ing strenuously to the new name, but Foley handled it
smoothly, patiently fielding questions, offering explanations
and encouraging people to have their say. Westpac was officially launched on schedule, on 1 October 1982. It was Australia's largest financial intermediary, with a board of
eighteen directors, so big an increase from the previous ten
that a new board table had to be bought and a loudspeaker
system installed in the boardroom. The bank ran an extensive
television and print advertising campaign proclaiming:
'Competition is open.'

White is convinced that the earlier Reddin experience,
despite having its detractors in the old Wales, had been inval-
uable in paving the way for the merger. However, the CBA
had not been through a similar reorganisation and arguably
its 'unreconstructed' management diluted the Reddin influence in the merged bank. In the longer term, a legacy of the
experience was a degree of decentralisation that weakened
coordination and head office control over the aggressively
independent and competing arms of the Westpac group. A
further legacy was the strength and status of group planning
in Westpac. And the legacy of that legacy was to be a litany
of grand plans that turned sour.

An inevitable outcome of the merger was branch rationalisation, although critics contend that it did not take place
to the extent that efficiency dictated. But a number of small
towns which, until 1982, had boasted a Wales and a CBA
branch, found that instead of two banks they now had only
one—Westpac. White was acutely conscious that, in the
wake of a merger, banks tended to lose market share. He
was determined that the Westpac experience would be different; the CBA had cost a tidy sum and White was intent
on making the merger a success. His message to staff and
divisional managers was that Westpac's priority was to
maintain market share through judicious but vigorous

lending, a policy for which the bank nonetheless paid dearly a few years later as write-offs in 1985 and 1986 increased substantially.

The Bank of New South Wales's merger with the Commercial Bank of Australia not only created Australia's largest bank; it brought together the two banks' finance company subsidiaries. The Wales's AGC Ltd, using funds advanced by the bank, took over the CBA's 100 per cent–owned finance company, General Credits Ltd—whose market sobriquet was 'Generous Credits'. Westpac had to enter into a warranty agreement with AGC to protect it from future losses in General Credits. The merger also brought Westpac the CBA's 51 per cent–owned New Zealand subsidiary, CBA Finance, chaired by CBA and General Credits executive Tim Marcus Clark and with budding New Zealand entrepreneur Allan Hawkins as its chief executive. Westpac's growing family also included one third of the merchant bank Partnership Pacific Ltd, which the Wales had formed in 1969 in partnership with the Bank of America and Bank of Tokyo, as well as minority holdings in a number of other financial institutions in Australia and overseas. Shortly after the merger, in November 1982, Westpac launched Business Loans and Equity Capital (BLEC) Limited, a specialised lender to small and medium-sized business, owned 60 per cent by Westpac and 40 per cent by a UK financier, Finance for Industry.

Within two years White was able to say that he was pleasantly surprised at the speed with which the merger had settled down. A contributing factor, he said, had been the decision to split Westpac into virtually two banks, wholesale and retail, which gave it more flexibility.

Westpac had been busy bedding down the merger against a backdrop of impending upheaval in the Australian financial system. The Campbell committee, which had been reviewing the system since 1979, handed its final report to the federal government late in 1981. Its recommendations, which mirrored thinking in many other economies busily removing outdated controls from their financial markets, were regarded as a blueprint for the future. These included removal of government controls on bank interest rates, so that banks could charge and pay what the market required, freeing banks from a number of regulatory constraints that left them at a disadvantage compared with non-bank competitors, such as the need to place a portion of their deposits with the Reserve Bank (on which they earned minimal interest) and their inability to pay interest on short-term deposits, opening up the Australian banking system to new foreign and domestic entrants, allowing the value of the Australian dollar to be determined in the market (to float) instead of being set by the Reserve Bank and Treasury, and removing exchange controls so that funds could flow freely into and out of the country.

Westpac, with $30 billion in assets, earning a healthy 16 per cent on its shareholders' funds, the pre-eminent bank on the Australian scene with 24 per cent of the country's banking business, already well represented overseas, felt it was prepared for this brave new environment. It was ready to take on the world.

CHAPTER TWO

WESTPAC GOES GLOBAL

As Westpac sought comfort in its larger, new identity, it was trying to strike a balance between change and continuity, and between vision and tradition. Fletcher set about establishing management systems—motherhood notions in the 1990s but almost audaciously adventurous in the early 1980s—and improvements in management information. The unwieldy fourteen-strong executive committee, a compromise to accommodate competing Wales and CBA egos, did not facilitate a workable bank structure. A more streamlined structure was brought in during 1984, comprising domestic banking under Warwick Kent, corporate and international under Stuart Fowler, management services under Peter Douglas and planning under Fletcher.

A seed of a future problem had been sown, however; in its embrace of change, at first tentative but with growing enthusiasm, Westpac was beginning to confuse activity with sound management. In the years to come, the activists in Westpac increasingly gained the ascendancy, breeding an environment where to question action was interpreted as obstructing progress.

With the groundwork laid, Westpac could turn its attention to a longer-term vision. The Bank of New South Wales had long had an international presence—as well as operating in London, New Zealand, Papua New Guinea and Fiji and the Pacific Islands, it had had an office in Tokyo since 1969 and a New York representative office since 1970. Its finance subsidiary, AGC, had been in Malaysia since 1963. In the US, Westpac began building a business in the 1980s. In London, it was increasingly concentrating on wholesale and international, rather than retail, banking.

Asia

Bob White was a fervent ambassador for the Asia–Pacific region. He was baffled by what he saw as a lack of awareness of the western Pacific which, he said, was 'unquestionably the market of the future'. He comments in his memoirs, *Cheques and Balances*: 'If I had a mission in life, apart from promoting the bank, it has been to promote the western Pacific as the growth area of the future.'

Consistent with its name change and its identification with the Asia–Pacific region, Westpac set about extending its operations, opening new offices in Manila (although this closed in 1984) and Seoul which, with offices in Singapore, Hong Kong, Tokyo, Jakarta and Beijing, brought it representation in seven Asian countries. In 1983 the bank recruited former Morgan Guaranty executive Philip Deer, an Australian with experience and contacts in the region, to beef up its Asian operations. Later, in 1986, Deer moved to Sydney as general manager, corporate, swapping roles with Frank Conroy, who became general manager of the Asian division and, based in Hong Kong, continued to build on what Deer had begun. When Conroy returned to Australia in 1988, he was succeeded by Darcy Ford, who had previously worked in Japan and Hong Kong. Westpac developed an Asian business that included financial markets activities, centred chiefly in Tokyo, Singapore and Hong Kong, and corporate banking in those and other centres. Westpac's Asian operations achieved a high profile, by the early 1990s accounting for 7 to 8 per cent of its assets. The business was profitable, particularly in treasury and capital markets, and was backed by sound interbank relationships. In 1985 Westpac became the first Australian bank to open a branch in Tokyo, and that year it also listed on the Tokyo Stock Exchange and opened an office in Taipei. Its Hong Kong operation was upgraded to full branch status. *Asiabanking* in that year awarded Westpac top billing in the Asia–Pacific region for syndicated loans management. Throughout the 1980s Westpac's operations in the various Asian centres were seen as businesses that, with careful nurturing, would reward the bank with growth and profits. They were businesses for the future.

London and Europe

In the late 1970s, more than a century after opening its London branch in 1853, Westpac opened another point of representation in Europe with an office in Frankfurt. The European division was restructured in 1984, with a new branch in Jersey, a big promotional thrust into Europe and expanded capital markets activity. London was seen as the global centre for Westpac's interest-rate and currency swaps business.

The Wales's London office for years operated to service travellers and trade. In terms of a City profile it did not rank. Then, in 1979, at a time when other Australian banks were revamping their London operations, it came under the wing of David Murison, a director of the prestige London merchant bank, Schroder Wagg. Murison and his team under chief manager Peter Brind, an Englishman who had joined the Wales in London in the 1950s, progressively developed a spread of banking relationships in Europe and took Westpac into the euromarkets. Brind, who had twice been seconded to the Wales in Australia for training and experience, made a key contribution to the evolution of the bank's London business, and in 1986 succeeded Murison as head of its operations in Europe. By the mid-1980s Westpac had significantly lifted its profile, participating in several hundred eurobond and euronote issues, often as a lead or co-lead manager. In 1985 the bank featured in *Institutional Investor*'s list of leading underwriters in the international bond markets.

Murison had first joined the Wales's London advisory board in 1962. After a few years' absence when seconded by Schroder Wagg to its Australian subsidiary, Schroder Darling and Co, he returned to Schroder Wagg in London in 1970, becoming chairman of the Wales's London advisory board in 1974. In 1979 he resigned from Schroder Wagg to become executive chairman of the Wales advisory board and chief executive of its London business with responsibility for European operations. The Wales had secured the services of an experienced London merchant banker with a comprehensive background in company finance and management and a thorough working knowledge of investment and commercial banking. His appointment, with a brief to compile a strategy for the Wales in London, was a recognition on the part of the bank that its operations there were anachronistic, with no effective market penetration, and were managed simply as another, if far-flung, branch. The business chiefly comprised a tiny dealing room, a legacy from an earlier, more active trade finance operation, some banking business, and 'travel' business which mostly related to looking after visiting Australians' needs—and their needs had changed markedly. In earlier days travel had been a leisurely pursuit, generally undertaken by fairly affluent retirees, but it was now dominated by economy-conscious backpackers with little need of banks.

The London advisory board dated from the nineteenth century and owed its origins to Australia's growing trade with Britain in wool, grain and gold in an era that did not

23

enjoy modern communications. Australian banks were comforted by the thought that their representatives in London were under the supervision of local mentors. An oddity of the Wales board was that it was composed of men from institutions which, in many cases, were direct competitors of the bank. But, gentlemen all, they dealt with conflicts of interest. Generally, those on the Wales advisory board were significant City players with connections and interests in Australia. Members changed over the years but the calibre was always high; for example, the board at one stage in the 1980s included Tim Bevan, chairman of Barclays Bank PLC, Christopher Reeves, chief executive of Morgan Grenfell, John Prideau, chairman of National Westminster Bank, George Preston, an eminent officer of the Bank of England, and Peter Costain, chief executive of the engineering firm Costain Ltd.

Murison formed a credit committee to oversee credit decisions; this was not a board committee but a management process, and approval for amounts in excess of his limit still had to be sought from Sydney head office. The London board did not become involved in lending decisions. Murison expanded the office's operations in foreign exchange, recruiting Reg Barham, who had been head of the London dealing operation of Morgan Guaranty, and appointing George Preston as foreign-exchange consultant. While Westpac's London operation was an international business, it had virtually no activity in the domestic market, unlike the bank's business in the US which grew into a domestic corporate banking operation with several branches.

Australia opens its doors

The year 1983 was a watershed in Australian financial history. In December, the federal government announced that the Australian dollar would float; its level would be set by supply and demand in foreign-exchange markets instead of being announced daily by the Reserve Bank. At the same time, the government removed the exchange controls which had prevailed since the second world war, when they were introduced for reasons of national security. Foreign currency brought into Australia no longer had to be immediately converted into Australian dollars. Australians could hold foreign-currency deposits, and borrow in foreign currencies if they chose.

Westpac, in common with the other banks, had a foreign-exchange dealing business. Until 1983, restrictions on the foreign-exchange market limited its usefulness, although it was extremely profitable. Only those who had worked overseas had experience of trading in a free foreign-exchange market. However, in anticipation of a freer market in Australia, banks had sent staff offshore to learn the ropes. Westpac, with its operations in the key financial centres of London, New York, Hong Kong and Singapore, could build on the experience gained in these overseas markets. Following the float of the Australian dollar the Reserve Bank in 1984 authorised 40 non-bank foreign-exchange dealers, so that the Australian foreign-exchange market expanded exponentially and, within a couple of years, the Australian dollar had leaped from obscurity to become a widely traded currency. Everyone involved was on a steep learning curve.

Financial deregulation was bringing down other barriers. From August 1984 banks could pay interest on funds in short-term deposits and began operating cash-management trusts where depositors' money could be placed at 24-hour call and earn a level of interest rate otherwise available only to professionals in the wholesale money markets. Advances in technology were enabling the first tentative steps to be taken in electronic banking. Australian banks were discussing the possibilities of electronic funds transfer at point-of-sale (EFTPOS) but Westpac believed it already had the technology. Peter Douglas, head of management services, and Alan Hohne, general manager, information systems, conceived the idea of breaking ranks and launching a trial. Hohne was the driving force in developing the system while Douglas secured board approval. During 1984 Westpac announced the world's first national electronic banking system, following that with the installation of Australia's first EFTPOS network which, in 1985, operated through a number of retail stores and service stations.

Deregulation of the stock exchange brought negotiable commission rates and enabled stockbroking firms, which had operated as partnerships, to incorporate. To meet the brokers' need for capital and get a foothold in broking themselves, several merchant banks and banks formed partnerships with broking firms. Westpac bought a half share of the leading stockbroking firm Ord Minnett, a step that was intended to give Westpac customers access to the broker's investment services through any of the bank's branches. Westpac was embarking on its push to offer 'something for everyone', a financial industry philosophy that was gaining ground in the 1980s as banks likened themselves to financial supermarkets, offering a range of off-the-shelf products to the consumer. By this stage Westpac owned 60 per cent of its merchant bank subsidiary PPL, as Bank of America, in line with its world-wide policy of relinquishing minority holdings, had sold out to focus on its own merchant bank, BA Australia Ltd.

Floating the Australian dollar—enabling its value to be determined by market forces, but with some Reserve Bank intervention to smooth erratic movements—had been one of the many recommendations of the Campbell report, commissioned by the Fraser Liberal–Country Party government. The Labor government which gained office in March 1983 established its own committee of inquiry, under former banker Vic Martin, to review the findings of the Campbell report. The Martin review group reported in February 1984 and broadly endorsed the earlier recommendations. Foreign banks would be allowed to operate in Australia, and domestic banks were in a lather of anticipation about both the challenges ahead in the Australian market and the opportunities that would open for them overseas. Many countries had been out of reach for Australian banks because reciprocal arrangements were not permitted. Removal of the barriers to foreign banks establishing in Australia would open up the world for Australian banks. Westpac, enthusiastic about extending its empire, was also mindful of the implications of the big names in world banking, such as the aggressive Citibank from the US, setting up in Australia. But Westpac identified the admission of foreign banks to Australia as an opportunity for it to spread its wings further overseas. It wanted to be recognised throughout the world as 'an international bank of the highest standing'.

Sixteen foreign banks were admitted to Australia in 1985, virtually doubling the number of banks in the country. Merchant banks, building societies, credit unions and finance companies added to the weight; it was evident that Australia was over-serviced with competing financial institutions. Australian banks, accustomed to the protection of a regulated system, imagined foreign banks cutting a swathe through their industry. Genuine and, as it turned out, unnecessary fear and trepidation abounded. The Australian banks were well entrenched, with huge branch networks that no foreigner could easily emulate; moreover, the average Australian customer was not likely to rush to open an account with an unknown foreign bank. But logic was submerged by apprehension. Westpac was anxious to defend itself. It was nervous that its best staff would be poached by foreign banks offering seductive salary packages not known in the hierarchical Australian banking industry, although common in

27

merchant banking. Westpac called in an outside consultant to help design a salary structure that would make key executives reluctant to leave. The advice to Westpac was to pay a premium to retain valued staff at risk of being poached. However, rather than discriminate, Westpac blanketed the bank with pay rises, lifting costs across the board. White had been particularly anxious that branch managers should feel valued and had insisted that the consultants revise their initial proposal and include more branch managers in the salary package reassessment.

Deregulation enabled further rationalisation in the finance industry because banks, previously permitted to hold only a part-interest in a merchant bank, were able to own a merchant bank outright. As part of White's plan to streamline and add punch to Westpac's merchant banking activities, the bank took full ownership of Partnership Pacific and of its merchant banking operations in New Zealand. Merchant banking activities were to be amalgamated under the management of Rob Douglass, one of White's early 'outside' recruits who would bring fresh ideas to Westpac. Douglass left Bankers Trust in London in 1983 to orchestrate Westpac's capital markets and merchant banking plans. Douglass said at the time that the amalgamation would enable Westpac to exploit synergies by bringing all of its major fee-generating activities into one tightly managed area.

The mid-1980s saw Westpac at its gravity-defying zenith. While critics pointed to its bloated cost structure and high staff numbers, and some observers questioned the cohesiveness of its grand design—it had goals, but did it have a credible strategy to achieve them?—the bank revelled in accolades such as being identified among the 40 most innovative financial institutions in the world. It entered the list of leading underwriters in the international bond market and it was the first Australian bank to arrange and lead-manage a euronote issue—a five-year, $US220 million facility for

Bell Resources Limited. It was ranked outright winner in the business magazine *BRW*'s annual foreign-exchange poll and Bob White was nominated banker of the year in a survey by *Australian Business*. In 1985 its assets were $49 billion, up 22 per cent on the previous year, making it the 68th largest bank in the world. It could boast an 18 per cent return on shareholders' funds and profits were healthy although dented that year by a 45 per cent rise in the charge for bad and doubtful debts, a charge that leaped by a further 90 per cent in 1986. As was the case with other Australian banks, Westpac had a very low exposure to third-world debt, a problem that was plaguing many US banks.

White and Fletcher felt that Westpac was faced with a pressing choice: it could be content to remain as the largest piggy-bank in Australia or it could go thoroughly global, building on what it had in Asia and expanding in the US. Should the bank make a dash for the international big league? It was well-capitalised but not in the coveted top 50 banks in the world. In 1985 Adrian Fletcher's strategic planning team began working on a set of options to be considered at an off-site executive committee workshop in March of that year. Under discussion were 'small steps' such as buying an Asian branch, or big leaps such as a major overseas takeover, against a background of the challenge of building a profitable international presence to service an increasingly international corporate customer base. One proposal that drew no argument was the expansion of Westpac's Asian network. Westpac began to examine banks which had a good Asian presence, and was attracted by Seattle-based Rainier Bancorp, a leading bank in the north-west Pacific with assets of $US7.1 billion—around one-quarter of Westpac in size— and operations in a number of Asian countries.

Fletcher and Westpac general manager Reg Humphrys flew to New York to discuss possibilities with J.P. Morgan, whose mergers and acquisitions team had just been launched under

29

Roberto Mendoza. The Morgan team knew Rainier well and agreed to sound out the bank on Westpac's interest in the Asian arm of the business, and offered to find out whether the bank itself was for sale. Fletcher was very attracted to the idea. 'It would be a marriage made in heaven between two strong commercial and corporate banks with international experience,' he says. 'But mindful of my mandate, I had to say no, let's just inquire about the Asian network.'

Fletcher recalls that before the meeting ended, he and Humphrys were given a long discourse by Mendoza on the benefits of acquiring a US primary dealer (one of a select group of companies licensed by the US central bank, the Federal Reserve, to trade in government securities). 'It wasn't a throwaway remark,' says Fletcher, 'but a long reasoned statement about the critical importance of a presence in the biggest government-paper market in the world.'

Events took a different twist when Rainier responded that it was not prepared to hive off its Asian network but would offer itself for sale in its entirety. Fletcher enthusiastically reported to the Westpac board, and recalls one director saying: 'Seattle? It's hardly on the way anywhere, is it?' And there were concerns about the Washington state economy and its reliance on defence. Someone mentioned that it was home to an infant software industry, with new companies like Microsoft. Discussions ensued, but it was evident that Westpac felt the proposition was too big and too risky. Fletcher believed it would have been a 'stunning deal'. But Westpac turned down the idea. Says Fletcher: 'It is the only real regret of my time at Westpac that I did not pursue this project more aggressively, although I think it is fair to say that even if I had, the chance of success was extremely low.' Early in 1986 Westpac's name was also linked, though rather more tenuously, with the UK's Standard Chartered Bank in which Westpac had expressed an interest, particularly in its Asian network. However, although Fletcher and Ian Matheson had discussions in London with Bank of England officials and Standard Chartered, the proposition drew minimal board support and came to nothing. Speculation about a takeover was revived, though, in September of that year when Westpac leaped to take advantage of new Reserve Bank rules which allowed banks to include subordinated debt as capital and raised $US500 million in perpetual floating-rate notes. Westpac quashed the rumours that it had Standard Chartered in its sights. The capital raising was the outcome of months of preparation and discussions with the Reserve Bank. Westpac and other banks had been arguing in favour of the RBA relaxing its rules in this way, which brought Australian banks into line with their counterparts in the UK and Canada. A significant advantage in raising subordinated debt was that while it ranked as capital, it was about half as expensive as equity because its servicing cost was tax deductible.

Westpac stopped short of Seattle but elsewhere Bob White's ambitions for growth were being realised. In 1986 Westpac was promoting itself as 'Australia's world bank'. Assets were $60 billion, up 50 per cent in two years. New treasury dealing rooms were opened in Sydney, London and Wellington, while in Taipei Westpac bought the business of the Seattle First National Bank (Seafirst) which gave it 50 new staff and a business base. The representative office in Seoul was upgraded to a branch and Westpac bought selected assets from Morgan Guaranty Trust Company in South Korea. Operations in Hong Kong were also upgraded to branch status. Back in Australia, Westpac added a new dimension with the establishment of Westpac Life Limited, a life insurance and fund management operation. In his managing director's statement in the bank's 1986 annual report, White said that the success of the bank's long-term strategy for growth was now becoming apparent.

This strategy centres on three basic and mutually re-inforcing streams: cost-efficient development of base markets in Australia and New Zealand; selective expansion in the Pacific region; and development of a stronger presence in the major capital markets of New York, London and Tokyo.

Messing about in boats

Fortune seemed to be smiling on Westpac and it was not difficult to overlook early evidence of the bank's propensity for getting things wrong. During 1986 Westpac embarked on a public relations venture that turned into a financial fiasco. With the America's Cup twelve-metre yacht races scheduled to be held in Fremantle, Western Australia, early in 1987, Westpac came up with the idea of chartering a luxury cruiser for the three months of challenges and leasing the cabins to overseas and local VIPs keen to watch the races at close hand. The *Sea Goddess,* a 58-cabin ship which had been cruising in the Mediterranean, was chartered to come to Australia. Westpac deputy managing director Ian Matheson travelled with his wife to Tonga to sail in the ship back to Australia. They were between Fiji and New Caledonia when they encountered a cyclone which brought gigantic waves that sent the ship violently listing before it righted itself, and two passengers were injured, including Matheson, who broke two ribs. For some time all contact with the *Sea Goddess* was lost and the captain was unsure of its position. But it reached Sydney, where it stopped for a couple of days before continuing to Fremantle. A few Westpac executives took the opportunity while the ship was in Sydney to go on board. No formal function was organised; directors had been fairly cool about the idea, which had been promoted to them as good public relations support for an Australian effort. Bob

White chose not to go aboard. White had not opposed the costly charter but he was not entirely comfortable with it.

The *Sea Goddess*'s ill-starred voyage was just the start of Westpac's problems. Enthusiasm for sea-borne recreation had been deflated by the recent hijacking of the cruise liner *Achille Lauro* in the Mediterranean, where a passenger died. Westpac believed that the opportunity to watch the yacht races had not been promoted as effectively as promised by the *Sea Goddess*'s owners. Not a cabin was leased. Further, the charter was to be paid for in US dollars and the $A had fallen to record lows against the American currency, sending Westpac's costs soaring. The bank retained the ship for only a couple of months, filling the cabins with guests instead of paying customers. Moreover, the *Sea Goddess* was too big to moor sufficiently close for guests to observe the races so Westpac had to transfer them to its 90-foot cruiser *Tarquin*, bought earlier partly for the yacht races and partly for corporate entertainment on Sydney Harbour. The $10 million-plus cost of the *Sea Goddess* to Westpac was quietly trickled out in expenditure statements over the next two years. Sir Eric Neal, the sharp-eyed managing director of Boral Ltd, who had arrived on the Westpac board in 1985, was heard to express astonishment that a financial blunder of this order was not more closely queried by the board.

33

Gold

Late in 1983 Westpac had bought 75 per cent of an independent gold bullion dealer, Mase Metals Pty Ltd, subsequently known as Mase Westpac Limited. Mase Metals had been set up in 1980 as a specialist bullion dealing house by merchant banker Warren Magi and his Perth associate Ron Wise. Sydney had developed as a niche market in local gold in the late 1970s, with Hill Samuel (later Macquarie Bank) standing out as one financial institution that decided early to dedicate resources to gold. And the Sydney Futures Exchange had added to gold hedging facilities when it launched an Australian dollar gold futures contract in 1978. As a market-maker in the $US international gold market, helping fill the time-gap between the close of the giant gold exchange Comex in New York and the opening of the Hong Kong market, Mase Metals played a key role in the development of Sydney as an international dealing centre for gold. Mase Metals had particular expertise, having recruited a bullion trader, Lester Solden, whose London experience in gold trading complemented Magi's merchant banking background. Solden was brought in as an equity partner. He brought something that was unique in Australia at the time—experience of having operated in the international gold market.

34   By 1982 the company needed additional capital to expand its dealing lines and to acquire the financial credibility necessary to be able to deal with the big names in the gold market. Mase examined the possibility of a backdoor stock-exchange listing and discovered a shelf company which was available, a former Queensland drapery business named Rothwells Ltd. Solden was at his desk, expecting to hear the deal had been done, when Magi strode in and said: 'You won't believe it but we've been outbid out of left field by some guy called Laurie Connell.' Connell turned the drapery store into a financier which he labelled a merchant bank. It went on to lend enthusiastically before collapsing spectacularly, earning Connell a jail sentence and notoriety as one of the daring but doomed entrepreneurs of the 1980s. After some further investigation, Magi and Solden concluded that a diversified shareholding was not the best option from a credit point of view and they dumped the idea of a backdoor listing. They would have to sacrifice equity and go with a larger partner. They were encouraged by the outlook for the gold price and the potential for a significant expansion in

Australia's gold production. And Magi cherished an ambition to see Australia develop its own vibrant gold market.

Talks led them first to the ANZ bank and then, through stockbroker Peter Haines, a longstanding friend of Magi's, to Westpac. Reg Barham, the highly regarded foreign-exchange senior whom Murison had recruited in London and who was now in Sydney, confirmed the bullion dealing potential for Westpac. Stuart Fowler, as head of international, was also enthusiastic. Australia, with its small population, is a modest consumer of gold but historically it has been one of the world's major producers and exporters of bullion. No Australian commercial bank had recently ventured into gold trading. Westpac was the target of criticism for what some ridiculed as an inane diversification but its entry into the gold market through Mase was one of its more logical moves and, arguably, one that it ultimately failed to exploit fully. Most saw the acquisition as a natural extension of Westpac's international involvement in money markets and foreign exchange. And Westpac's links with gold stretched from the 1850s; the Bank of New South Wales had established its London office to help finance the colony's gold exports. The deal with Westpac provided Mase with capital and backing from a major bank that was on a global path. Warren Magi became managing director of Mase Westpac, with the bank's deputy chief, Ian Matheson, as chairman. Westpac paid $5.25 million by way of a capital injection for its 75 per cent of Mase, far less than it would have had to outlay had it tried to set up its own gold bullion dealing operation. Magi, Wise and Solden retained 25 per cent of the company.

The timing of Westpac's buying into Mase was exquisite. A matter of weeks after the acquisition, the Australian dollar floated and exchange controls were removed. This had a major impact on the gold dealing market in Sydney. Under the previous exchange controls, Australian dealers had to source dealing lines from overseas gold dealers because the Reserve Bank prohibited them from holding in London the stock which was necessary to clear trades. With exchange controls gone, Australian gold dealers were able to hold gold stocks in London and could trade in the international gold market on the same footing as other dealers.

By 1986 the gold market was strong. Australia's production had risen from 20 tonnes a year in 1980 to 75 tonnes. Mase Westpac had taken a leading role as financier to the numerous new gold-mining projects which were emerging in Australia. In May 1984 it pioneered the gold loan financing technique for gold mines and funded Pancontinental Mining in the development of its Paddington mine. Westpac was already a leading player in the gold market in Australia when another opportunity arose for it to take a much higher profile in the international arena.

In April 1986 Westpac beat some 40 banking rivals to buy the bullion, foreign-exchange and treasury-dealing assets of Johnson Matthey Bankers, a UK bank which the Bank of England had rescued eighteen months earlier from near-collapse. JMB's problems were unrelated to its bullion activities; rather, they were due to its poor credit controls in its non-bullion, commercial lending business. With the sale of JMB, the bad commercial loans stayed with the Bank of England and the bullion and treasury business went to Westpac. The enlarged Mase Westpac, with a staff of 350, now operated from Sydney, London, New York and Hong Kong. As part of the deal, Westpac bought out Magi, Wise and Solden's 25 per cent interest in the Australian operation, although Magi and Solden stayed with the company.

Westpac had an advantage in its bid for JMB. Bidding for the bank was coming from Hong Kong, New York, Zurich and elsewhere; however, the Bank of England preferred the business to go into suitably neutral hands. An Australian bank was ideal. The purchase, which cost Westpac

36

£67.5 million ($A138 million), being net tangible assets plus £17.5 million in goodwill, brought the bank the chance to become a force in the international gold market and with this, enhanced links with banks and central banks around the world, all of which to a greater or lesser extent held bullion as a reserve asset. The purchase was billed as complementing Westpac's pursuit of selected global niche markets.

With the acquisition of JMB, Mase Westpac Ltd became a London-registered bank and was the first non-English company with a seat at the exclusive London Gold Fix. No-one has ever put a figure on what that is worth. Only five banks participate in the so-called London Gold Ring which twice daily sets the price of gold. Although the price fluctuates through a 24-hour trading cycle, the London fix is the benchmark for gold producers and investors. Apart from JMB, the members were N.M. Rothschild & Sons, Samuel Montagu, Sharps Pixley and Mocatta & Goldsmid. Mase Westpac was by far the junior at the table; Mocatta had been founded in 1680, Rothschild and Sharps dated from the 1800s and Samuel Montagu opened in 1853. With London handling a good percentage of South African and Russian gold production, and undertaking extensive clearing and general dealing business, its status as a leading market was well established.

Magi, Solden and other key staff moved to Mase Westpac's head office in London, Magi becoming managing director of the new worldwide group and Solden dealing director, responsible for the group's global bullion trading. A third string was added to the executive management team in London with the appointment of Dick Gazmararian, who had wide experience in gold dealing with Mocatta in Hong Kong. David Murison, Westpac's chief executive in the UK and Europe, was appointed chairman of Mase Westpac Ltd. However, immediately after the acquisition was completed, Murison took ill and George Preston, who had been hired by Murison as foreign-exchange consultant and who knew the gold business inside out, became acting chairman.

Magi and Preston were like chalk and cheese. Magi, in his late thirties, was energetic, entrepreneurial, from a merchant banking rather than trading bank background. Preston, from a trading bank and central banking background, was in his seventies, deeply knowledgeable but conservative. Having been involved in the rescue of JMB, he had more than a passing interest in its continuing health. Difficulties emerged. Preston regarded Magi, Solden and Gazmararian as deal-makers, out of harmony with his own perception of a City bank. Magi believed Preston was trying to take an executive chairman role, overstepping his mandate. This was taking place against a background of the Bank of England's so-called 'four eyes policy' which required banks licensed in London, and Mase Westpac was one, not to allow executive power to be concentrated in any one individual. The position was resolved when Bob White flew to London and had discussions with the Bank of England and Magi. White advised the Bank of England that, as chief executive, Magi had the responsibility to run Mase Westpac and that the chairman's role was to keep an eye on Magi, not to be involved in the day-to-day running of the business. White advised Magi that he had to keep Preston fully briefed. Preston agreed to operate as non-executive chairman. Matters subsequently settled. Over the years, Preston became a great supporter of Magi at board level.

Between 1986 and 1988 Mase Westpac developed its London business as a source of funding for its financing of gold mines in Australia and North America. Its arrival in the City greatly influenced the market in the area of bullion treasury. Mase Westpac was also pioneering, with other Australian dealers, new gold-price hedging facilities for gold mines which, by enabling producers to protect against price fluctuations, have subsequently transformed the gold-mining industry worldwide. Between 1988 and 1990 Mase Westpac was ranked first among the top ten providers of gold loans and featured fourth in a list of the top ten arrangers of these loans.

Apart from its first year when it made a small loss, Mase Westpac was profitable, earning a satisfactory return on shareholders' funds. With its network of offices in London, New York, Hong Kong and Sydney, and branch offices in Perth and Denver, Colorado, Mase Westpac was an international institution in its own right and, as a gold bank, had an entrée to central banks and governments that could have been valuable to Westpac.

CHAPTER THREE

AGC: WESTPAC'S HEADSTRONG CHILD

Westpac, in common with the other major banks, had non-banking arms which were a legacy of the days when banks formed subsidiaries to undertake types of financing from which the more constrained parents were excluded. An outcome of the 1930s depression and the second world war had been a framework of government controls on the financial system, particularly on banks, and despite their hopes that in the aftermath of the war the federal government might relax its grip, this did not occur. The ensuing consumer boom of the 1950s reinforced the banks' view that, because of regulation and legislation, they were being denied access to increasingly lucrative business. Australians, hungry for new cars and household goods, embraced hire-purchase credit enthusiastically and the banks were keen to win some of this business. During the 1950s banks set up or bought into finance companies, which could undertake consumer lending in a 'riskier' segment of the market, and they also established merchant banks, often in consortia with foreign banks. Free of the prevailing restrictions applying to the banking parents, such as Reserve Bank ceilings on lending and interest rates, although subject to gearing (borrowing) restrictions under their prospectuses, these subsidiaries were able to flex their muscles in consumer lending and leasing, and in the more innovative forms of finance associated with money markets and capital markets.

Westpac—Bank of New South Wales as it then was—entered the consumer lending market directly in 1957 by taking a 40 per cent share in the finance company Australian Guarantee Corporation (AGC) Ltd, to which it had for some years been banker and provider of overdraft facilities. AGC, incorporated in 1925 and listed on the stock exchange in 1928, was established on strict guidelines. Its co-founder, Arthur H. Davies, wrote in the company's first annual report in 1928: 'The conservative and rigid policy adopted by the board, from the inception of the company, will be continued, and your directors do not anticipate any setback to the progress of the company.' AGC's business focused on financing motor vehicles, tractors and agricultural equipment before it expanded into personal loans. It raised the funds needed for lending from the general public, through regular issues of debentures and, from the 1970s, unsecured notes, which were sold through a registered prospectus. AGC continued as a major player in the lucrative hire purchase field; in 1978 that accounted for 34 per cent, and leasing 30 per cent, of its business. From the time that the Wales bought into the company it had a controlling interest which rose progressively from the initial 40 per cent until by 1980 it owned 76.7 per cent of AGC. As Bob White, chief executive of Westpac from 1977 to 1987, records in his memoirs: 'Under the agreement between the Bank of NSW and AGC, the AGC board was left to manage its own affairs, the exception being that AGC would ratify any major financial or policy changes with Westpac.' AGC was Westpac's subsidiary, but it operated at arm's length from its parent. Nonetheless, in the eyes of the investing public, the regular buyers of AGC debentures and notes, the presence of Westpac was important—despite the routine disclaimers in AGC prospectuses that the banking parent could not guarantee repayments of debentures or notes or interest due on them.

41

The empire had a further arm: AGC had its own merchant bank subsidiary, Bill Acceptance Corporation (BAC), run as an independent company, rather than as a division of AGC or Westpac, with its own board. Founded in 1965 by a consortium which included the finance company CAGA, stockbrokers Patrick & Co, MLC Assurance and Construction Finance Australia Ltd, BAC became a wholly owned subsidiary of AGC in 1977. BAC had by then made a name as a pioneer in the development of an active market trading in bills of exchange in Australia. BAC focused on money-market activities, bill-lending against property as security and other bill-based lending. Following a policy review in 1982—against the background of Westpac's own ambitions for growth and a world presence—it established a corporate advisory division and broadened its base, extending its services to Japanese and South-East Asian companies with interests in Australia and opening a representative office in London. In 1984 the merchant bank's capital base was boosted when issued capital was increased from $10 million to $15 million to enable it to expand into new businesses. With AGC already Australia's leading finance company, it seemed appropriate that BAC should be built into a leading merchant bank.

Australia's premier finance company entered the 1980s as a strongly managed, conservative lender which had weathered the ups and downs of the 1970s. During that decade, however, the company had been enticed into the prevailing trend towards diversification, taking 70 per cent of Budget Rent-A-Car, 51 per cent of the construction company Mirvac Pty Ltd, 45 per cent of Wyndham Estate wines, 30 per cent of ABE Photocopiers and a 50 per cent equity stake (later 100 per cent) of Kooralbyn, a 'quality lifestyle' resort and residential development in south-east Queensland. Stan Hamley, who joined AGC in 1972 as general manager of special projects, was charged with furthering the diversification program and at various times AGC also had substantial shareholdings in

Albury Brickworks, Visionhire, a television rental company, Paradine, a joint venture with the UK television personality David Frost, under which Frost was to bring prominent entertainers to Australia, and Viscount Caravans. Of these investments, Mirvac provided enduring success and Budget showed some profits; the returns on the others did not justify the cost. AGC's business focus, though, remained chiefly on hire purchase and personal loans, leasing and, to a much smaller extent, property and development loans. In the early 1980s the company in Australia was divided into four main operating areas: consumer, property and corporate finance, and general insurance. It also had a wide spread of interests overseas, having established in New Zealand in 1938, in Papua New Guinea in 1958, in Malaysia, Singapore and Brunei in 1963 and in Hong Kong in 1982. These operations were successful, as AGC was able to take established management systems and transfer them into less mature environments. The mid-1980s saw a further spread of overseas activities.

Under the stewardship of Ken Lambeth, group general manager from 1976 until he retired because of ill health in 1980, and then Keith Jack, AGC was a top performer. Jack's untimely death in 1982 at the age 55 from a hereditary heart condition was a blow to the company. Succession planning had not taken two such events into account. Jack was succeeded by Don Webb, himself about to retire. During much of the 1970s Webb had been general manager of the company's property division and his view was that the company could be either a lender or a property developer, but not both. That had kept AGC out of the worst excesses of those times. In the words of a former AGC executive, 'AGC straddled the finance industry like a colossus'—it was a highly successful organisation, tightly managed and with a strong credit culture. For example, AGC would not allow more than 30 per cent of total lending to be in property; the company operated with limits on how much property it should lend

43

on in each geographic area, and what type of property. Former staffers can recall a photograph hanging on the wall of the property manager's office showing the high-rise development on Queensland's Gold Coast and the manager saying: 'We financed about 80 per cent of all the buildings that you see there, but never more than one at a time.' In terms of assets and profits, AGC in the early 1980s was almost twice the size of its nearest competitor, Esanda, the finance subsidiary of the ANZ Bank. AGC staffers enjoyed none of the luxuries of, say, merchant bank or even bank employees; the company was run on disciplined, even spartan, lines which were reflected in its austere head office at 124 Phillip Street, Sydney, where the installation of air-conditioning was greeted as a luxurious indulgence.

Webb delayed his retirement to keep the seat warm until a new chief executive could be found. Robert Alick Robson, CBE, 56, was appointed in April 1983. With Webb went an important memory-bank of the property problems of the early 1970s. Robson's background was in mining and manufacturing rather than banking and finance, but he was to show himself to be a confident chief with firm ideas. His strengths were his intelligence and persistence; he was also noted for his ego and driving need to be the dominant person in any situation. Robson had been general manager of the pipe manufacturer Rocla Industries from 1970 to 1975, then managing director of Blue Metal Industries, a position he held until late 1982 when the company was taken over by Boral Ltd, then under the stewardship of Sir Eric Neal. Once head of an expanding company, Robson was now head of a division of Boral. Instead of retiring, he moved up again. By the time he arrived at the helm of AGC he had a high profile in the business community; he had been invited to participate in the 1983 Economic Summit held by the newly elected Hawke Labor government. Robson was a member of the Productivity Council and he became a member of the Business

Council of Australia. In 1986 he became chairman of Ciba-Geigy Australia Ltd, in 1986–87 he chaired the Australian Finance Conference and in 1988–89 he was chairman of Wormald International Ltd, at a turbulent time in its history. Robson's chief lieutenant was Peter French, group general manager and an alternate director, who had had extensive experience in the motor finance industry from 1956 before being appointed AGC's general manager of consumer finance in 1980. Australian lending operations, and so most staff, reported to French, who gained a considerable profile in the finance company industry. From 1985 AGC operated with six general managers: Brian Schuh, consumer finance; Arthur Burrows, property finance; Graeme White, business finance; John Deane, corporate finance; Don Crisp, insurance; and Ray Morley, international.

Robson took over as head of a company whose profits had increased in the 1970s by 20 per cent a year, compound, and in 1982 had reached $86.6 million. AGC had consistently achieved more than 2 per cent after-tax return on average assets, substantially ahead of its competitors. It accounted for less than a fifth of Westpac's assets but contributed more than a third of the bank's profits. At the time Robson became chief, every major loan went to the AGC board, which set the lending policy and guidelines, while minor consumer loans went before credit committees. Shelves in AGC offices creaked under the weight of large procedure manuals whose prescripts were rigidly followed. Compliance with policy and procedures in those days was a significant strength of the company. With the financial deregulation of the early and mid-1980s, though, this strength became a weakness because staff had been accustomed to solving problems by precedent, and deregulation rendered most precedent irrelevant. In 1983 AGC was chaired by Eric Tait, a former deputy managing director of Westpac and an AGC board member since 1973; the remainder of the board comprised Ian Matheson, deputy managing director of

Westpac, businessman John Blaiklock, former long-serving chief executive Geoff Carter, his successor, Ken Lambeth (who, before heading AGC, had been its chief financial officer), Geoff Hawley, a former managing director of the Export Finance and Insurance Corporation, Westpac chairman Sir Robert Norman, Bob White, an AGC board member until he retired in 1990, Stephen Kimpton, a former chairman of CBA, Rob Robson, and two alternate directors, the Westpac executives Stan Davis and Warwick Kent.

In selecting an outsider as chief of AGC the board had taken an unusual but deliberate step. AGC had to cope with the merger with General Credits and Robson brought with him considerable experience in acquisitions. He also brought an autocratic management style which caused some disruptions. Widely regarded as possessing a superior intellect, Robson favoured a rigorously analytical approach to AGC. He did not think that the diversification of the 1970s into businesses such as car rentals and wine companies was appropriate for a finance company, particularly as they were at best producing weak profits. He got rid of these without hesitation.

Robson's arrival, at a point when Australia was on the brink of wide-ranging reform that was to change the financial landscape, was a crucial event in the fortunes of AGC. Deregulation had brought widespread speculation that finance companies had had their day. A deregulated banking sector, which from 1985 would include sixteen new foreign banks—more than double the original estimate of six—was viewed as a direct threat to the finance company industry: it was widely forecast that finance companies, creatures of regulation, particularly those owned by banks and whose sole *raison d'être* had been to give the banking parent an entry to otherwise off-limits business, would disappear. That did not occur, but in the early 1980s finance companies believed they had a fight on their hands. Robson's answer was to look for business growth, and if that growth could not be found in Australia then it would be achieved overseas. International expansion was a mantra in the finance industry in the 1980s, and not just in Australia—banks and financial institutions around the world were spreading into new areas as barriers to entry fell. That finance companies survived owed a great deal to the differences between the market they serviced and that of their banking parents. Finance companies operated in a different, more spontaneous culture; their business network consisted of car dealers and brokers, their methods and business approach were far removed from the traditions of banking and their clients often people who might have uneasy relationships with banks. Finance companies dealt confidently at the riskier end of the market; banks generally preferred not to be in the business of repossessing cars. Further, a customer buying a car is often not interested in the source of finance and AGC, having been in the business of cultivating car dealers since 1925, was often the dealer's automatic choice when referring customers.

47

AGC was sure of its continued independence because it believed that no-one in Westpac could make a better fist of running the finance company business. The results spoke for themselves. By the mid-1980s AGC was making more than $100 million profit a year; it gave every appearance of having an accurate knowledge of its market and its competitors, and was building a stable of overseas businesses. Its strength was its dealer network and broker introductions, and its marketing was extremely effective.

In 1985, when AGC was 60 years old, a number of senior AGC executives, cognisant of the changing environment, undertook what was dubbed Project 2000. A team of people from the company went off-site for five days, inviting Dr Vern Harvey, a management expert from PA Consultants, to take part in an extensive analysis of problems facing the finance industry and where it would be in 2000. The project marked AGC as a forward-looking company, and Robson as a leader able to think ahead and to force people to think about the business they were in. Robson, convinced that the way forward depended on size, and with AGC already the largest financier in Australia, intensified his focus on overseas markets, exploring a possible acquisition in the UK and visiting the US to examine potential takeover prospects, some far larger than AGC.

While still successful, AGC's mix of business had been changed and its rate of profitability curbed by the absorption of General Credits, the Melbourne-based subsidiary of the Commercial Bank of Australia, about one-third the size of AGC, with $1.1 billion in assets on which it was earning a mere 1 per cent return. Westpac, having through the merger with the CBA forced the acquisition of General Credits on AGC, had provided $149.6 million for AGC to fund the takeover. The bank also provided AGC with a guarantee against future losses above a certain level (more than 0.62 per cent of receivables) that might stem from General Credits. Overall, the merger was seen as an event that had dulled AGC's management incisiveness. A condition of the marriage between the two banks had been that no jobs would be lost and in the process of fully absorbing General Credits' business and staff some of AGC's entrenched discipline was sacrificed. By default, AGC had been landed with some shaky business: General Credits had a greater involvement in property development than AGC, and had an 'intensive care unit' for problem loans, which absorbed a substantial amount of AGC management time. General Credits had $110 million in non-performing loans, mainly in property, of which $30 million was expected to be written off. The much larger AGC had $34 million in total non-performing loans. A particularly demanding problem brought to AGC by General Credits was the Avdev group, an airline operator to which General Credits had, in the late 1970s, lent $1 million, an exposure which had blown out to $12 million by 1983 and resulted in a loss of $9 million.

The mid-1980s were a watershed for AGC. By then it had largely recovered from the disruption of the merger but the tight controls had slackened and the predominance on its board of directors with wide practical experience in the finance industry was being diluted. Also, awareness was growing of the full consequences of financial deregulation— new players, increased competition, a tough fight to retain market share—but the drive to increase lending in Australia and overseas had not yet fully taken grip. Under Robson, AGC was changing course and values, taking a greater inter- est in property to achieve growth targets and, in a significant turning point in attitude, shifting from an unpretentious culture to one which accommodated a higher level of indul- gence, with lavish refurbishments at head office and more expensive cars. 'The company was starting to court disaster,' says one senior manager who left in 1986. Whereas AGC's head office at 124 Phillip Street had been plainly furnished, but imbued with an air of vitality, the new premises along the street at 130 were established in magnificent style, with a high-tech boardroom, a large rhomboid board table with a hollow centre replacing the former simple rectangular model, heavy, electronically operated curtains, elaborate remote- controlled projection equipment, three grand entertaining/ dining rooms—the Today, Yesteryear and Tomorrow rooms—and a board dining room complete with a vast cir- cular table, sufficient to seat fourteen and so capacious that the centre was cut out and another table seating eight con- structed out of it. The style was well beyond AGC's traditions.

AGC had always run its own race and had been highly profitable—and respected as a separate and aggressive company. At middle-management level, Westpac and AGC

49

were undisguised rivals. Internecine competition was a hall-mark of the sprawling Westpac empire, with, for example, the treasury arms of the bank, AGC, PPL and BAC, frequently bidding against each other in the professional money market for funds. While AGC had a department whose brief was specifically to liaise with Westpac and bring in business referred from the bank, there was considerable apathy and sometimes hostility from Westpac branch staff towards AGC. To the Westpac bankers, AGC managers were uncouth and ruthless, while the hard-nosed financiers, who saw themselves as dynamic business people, regarded Westpac as slow and bureaucratic. With 76 per cent of the company, Westpac had a controlling interest in AGC, but whenever the financier wanted to stress an arm's length relationship with its parent the 24 per cent minority shareholders were a convenient lever. For its part Westpac, while receiving 76 per cent of AGC's profits, tended to treat the financier as a competitor. According to Bob White, Westpac's legal advice was that it had no rights, other than through directors who were both AGC and Westpac directors, regarding information about AGC's exposures and clients. AGC was a separately publicly listed company with its own board and its own directors, and that was how it was run.

Robson had firm ideas and he was not shy about lecturing whoever was present, superiors or otherwise, about the direction of the economy, where deregulation was pushing AGC and the appropriate role of Westpac. In terms of incisiveness, ideas and aggression, he was a forceful voice at internal meetings with Westpac in the mid-1980s. At the quarterly joint Westpac AGC strategy meetings, usually held in Sydney's Sebel Town House, an observer could have been forgiven for thinking that Robson was head of a joint-venture company, not the subsidiary. Robson was clearly not going to be told by a bank parent how to run his company—and he backed his defiance by saying he had to look after the minority shareholders. Former AGC and Westpac staffers recall Robson 'playing the minorities to the hilt'. Independence and competitiveness between the two managements extended to a reluctance to share information about lending activities. Each was suspicious that the other would steal potential business. However, unwillingness to divulge exposures was often cloaked as a matter of client confidentiality. Says Robson: 'After 1988 [when Westpac took full ownership of AGC] the atmosphere was more cooperative but competitiveness remained an issue in some quarters, rather than high-minded notions of client confidentiality. No-one wanted to give a shopping list to a rival.'

In its mainstream business AGC rarely faltered but it stumbled badly when, from 1987, it plunged into large and long-term joint-venture property development deals. This involved a different kind of lending, and because in many cases the joint-venture partners defaulted, AGC involuntarily became a quasi-developer. But there was no shortage of omens for those who cared to look. AGC had early warnings of the problems that could emerge from lending related to major property construction: for example, in 1984 its merchant bank subsidiary, Bill Acceptance Corporation, had become entangled in loans guaranteed by shares in Sydney's Regent Hotel. In the early 1980s merchant banks, while enthusiastically spreading their wings and being seen as far more imaginative and entrepreneurial than their stolid and conservative banking counterparts, also felt vulnerable because of the new freedoms being delivered to the banks by deregulation. The merchant banks were keen to show they could fight back. BAC made a $20 million loan to a private overseas company, E.J. Ang, lending against the security of Ang's 59 per cent share in Ausintel Investments, whose subsidiary, Ausintel Management, held the lease to develop and operate the Regent Hotel. The loan was drawn down in a mix of $US and Swiss francs, to reduce borrowing costs, a factor that contributed to later troubles. Ausintel hit difficulties in the

51

form of cost overruns on the Regent and operating losses, and the $A plunged in 1985/86. By mid-1987 the amount outstanding on Ang's $20 million loan from BAC had risen to $A39 million. The funds lent by BAC to Ang were not intended for the Regent project but the only security BAC held against the loan was shares in the ailing developer Ausintel.

The prospect of a substantial loss on a doubtful loan of $39 million was a shock to AGC. The charge for bad and doubtful debts had barely exceeded $20 million a year in each of the previous three years. The company had never experienced a significant loss; rather, its bad-debt ratio had been something to boast about. AGC held a high-level internal investigation, carried out by its general manager, finance and administration, Derrick Heywood, and Vince Preston, executive assistant to Robson, to try to determine the basis on which the loan had been made, what had been presented to the board, what the board had said and whether the foreign-currency exposure had been managed as well as it could have been. It became apparent that there were serious deficiencies in the credit-assessment process at BAC, some statements had been taken at face value rather than investigated, and not all relevant information had been conveyed to the company's board. By the time the investigation was undertaken, the team which had organised the loan had left BAC. Overall, the group wrote off $10 million: through a risk-participation agreement AGC assumed $7 million of the loss, reducing BAC's loss to $3 million. The episode highlighted two risks: the uncertainties associated with construction and sale of major property ventures and the dangers of lending in foreign currencies to reduce borrowing costs. Neither warning was heeded.

While retaining its position as doyen, in terms of size, profits and assets, of the Australian finance company industry, AGC was also, in the mid-1980s, expanding its overseas network, opening in Indonesia and Fiji in 1985, in Thailand and the UK in 1986 and in Taiwan in 1988. AGC's expansion into Asia pre-dated the widespread 1980s obsession with 'going global'. The company had established a 60 per cent-owned joint venture in Malaysia in 1963 with Chartered Bank (later Standard Chartered), and from the early 1980s was keen to expand further overseas. To an observer, AGC's ambitions to internationalise might have seemed unnecessary and illogical, likely to lead to competition with its parent, given that Westpac was busily building abroad. However, in some instances AGC could move into markets inaccessible to Westpac because, until 1985, Australia had excluded foreign banks and Australian banks were in turn excluded from many countries. Expanding overseas was AGC's response to an increasingly crowded and competitive market in Australia. And by the mid-1980s AGC had a South-East Asian network that was contributing significantly to earnings. Its three subsidiaries—Credit Corporation Malaysia, the second-largest finance house in Malaysia, Credit Corporation Singapore and Credit Corporation Brunei—earned very healthy returns on shareholders' funds.

53

AGC spent considerable time examining growth prospects in the US and became interested in several potential takeover targets. To its banking parent this smacked of excessive ambition and Westpac, conscious of its own image in the US, and with some encouragement from Tony Walton, head of the bank's Americas division, finally put its foot down and told Robson to scale down his aspirations. AGC's attention was turned away from the large canvas of the US towards the UK, where it was felt there was greater potential for an acquisition. AGC made a pitch to take over a failed licensed deposit-taking company (a second-tier bank) in the UK; the bid did not succeed because AGC would require capital for the acquisition and Westpac adamantly declined to provide it. Further, a prerequisite for a finance operation in the UK was a licence from the Bank of England, and the UK's central bank had made it clear that, with Westpac already holding two banking licences in the UK, it did not intend to grant another to a Westpac subsidiary. A compromise was reached in late 1986 when AGC began operating in Maidenhead, Berkshire, through Westpac General Finance, a division managed by AGC executives and reporting to AGC in Sydney but with the business on Westpac's books in the UK. The intention was to get into motor vehicle finance, personal loans and property. However, Westpac General Finance, while enthusiastically increasing its number of branches in south-east England in 1987 and 1988, made little headway against stiff local competition in personal loans and motor vehicle finance and its emphasis fell increasingly on property, which was to prove its undoing.

Expansion continued elsewhere. In 1986 the Thai government invited AGC to take over a troubled Thai finance company. The acquisition cost AGC $17.1 million and brought it 80 per cent of the company, with the remaining 20 per cent held by the central bank of Thailand. In Fiji, AGC joined the Fiji Development Bank and the International Financing Corporation (a division of the World Bank) to establish Merchant Bank of Fiji Ltd, of which AGC held 30 per cent. By 1988 AGC's international operations extended to twelve countries, mostly around the Pacific Rim, and employed 1,000 people.

The lure of property

AGC's first sally into property development, as distinct from straightforward lending, took the financier into uncharted territory. In 1975 it became involved in the Kooralbyn project in Queensland, a joint venture with two entrepreneurs, Sir Peter Abeles and Sir Arthur George. According to AGC legend, the proposal for credit approval for the Kooralbyn project is the only recorded event where outside parties made a pitch directly to the board. Legend also has it that staff were surprised to hear that the board accepted the proposal. Management was not enthusiastic. Kooralbyn, a 5,670-hectare cattle station 95 kilometres south-west of Brisbane, was earmarked for development into a self-contained community of some 5,000 or 6,000 people living in a 'country club' environment with superior recreational facilities that would include two golf courses, an equestrian centre, a racetrack, tennis courts, lawn bowls and holiday accommodation. Abeles and George had acquired the land in the early 1970s, and in 1975 it had an ascribed value of $1.8 million. The project was expected to absorb $6 million in funding, with $2 million from Abeles and George and AGC providing $4 million. A significant element of the vision was that the project would become self-financing as land was subdivided and sold for private housing.

55

The vision was unattainable. By 1978 AGC had advanced $12 million. It was clear that Kooralbyn was not paying its way and probably never would. The partnership was dissolved and AGC took over the whole of the project. By 1982 AGC's contribution had reached $37.5 million. It had spent $16.5 million on land, infrastructure and subdivisions and had recovered $5 million through land sales, but it had advanced an additional $5 million to finance land purchases, spent $10 million on sports facilities and accommodation and incurred $11 million in operating losses. In 1982 a special investigation was mounted, handled by Derrick Heywood. Subsequently, Kooralbyn chairman Stan Hamley and general manager and consultant Graeme Evans left, and Heywood became chairman of the holding company, Kooralbyn Pty Ltd. The resort had been developed by then into a country club with an equestrian centre, golf course and high-quality villa and motel residential accommodation; later it boasted five swimming pools, two golf courses, a tennis centre and a bowling club. Heywood persuaded the regional general manager of Club Med, based in Hong Kong, to look at the resort, to determine if his company might buy it or operate it on AGC's behalf. But Club Med wanted a beach-side location in Australia.

AGC had a motto: *the first loss is the best loss.* Whenever it departed from that it ran into trouble. Kooralbyn is an example. In hindsight, that project should have been wound up in 1978, with AGC accepting a considerable, but not fatal, loss and certainly one substantially less than it ultimately incurred. The embarrassment would have quickly evaporated. Instead, AGC continued to pour money into the project, clearing bush land, sealing roads and building more facilities. Kooralbyn became a luxury resort, with a variety of lease-back accommodation in two-bedroom villas and one-bedroom units. 'The project was ahead of its time, trying to persuade people to live so far from Brisbane,' Heywood said later.

Part of the plan to develop Kooralbyn depended on encouraging light industries to establish there, creating jobs. An international school was built which, after a rocky start, became successful. A scheme to launch a film studio did not get off the ground. The setting attracted the attention of a successful and prominent private hospital developer, Doug Moran, whose Moran Health Care group had been a long-standing AGC client. In December 1982 Moran approached AGC with a proposal that it provide two hectares of land at the entrance to the Kooralbyn Valley on which Moran Health Care would build first a 50-bed hospital, and then a 300-bed 'hospital of excellence' modelled on the United States' Mayo Clinic, concentrating in one place world-renowned medical and health-care expertise, as well as research and training facilities. Wealthy Asians could travel there for specialist surgery for heart and liver conditions while their families could be accommodated at the plush hotel. Specialists would be flown in from the Gold Coast by helicopter. Correspondence early in 1983 between Moran and Kooralbyn Pty Ltd discussing the proposal reflected both Moran's enthusiasm and AGC's reservations about the proposed financing arrangements. Moran pointed out that he had a choice of sites but was very keen to build at Kooralbyn. 'It seemed pie in the sky to me,' says Heywood. Moran's proposal was rejected. In May 1984 Moran announced that he was building his hospital of excellence at Robina, on the Queensland Gold Coast. But those plans would later change.

In 1986, in a demonstration of increased board interest but with a brief to sell Kooralbyn, AGC board member Sir Harold Aston replaced Heywood as chairman of Kooralbyn Pty Ltd, with Heywood becoming his deputy, and the board was strengthened by two others regarded as having considerable experience in leisure and tourism—Sir Frank Moore, chairman of Queensland Tourism and Travel Corporation, and Sir Sydney Williams, chairman of Air Queensland. Golf had become Kooralbyn's trump card; its eighteen-hole championship course had been voted one of the top twenty in Australia.

In July 1987 AGC sold the Kooralbyn Valley resort to a Japanese company, Towa Kohmuten, a group involved in construction and management of golf and tennis resorts in Japan. Commenting on the $15 million sale, Robson said that AGC was a financier, not a resort manager. Kooralbyn had begun life in 1975 as a residential property development venture with extensive sporting facilities but the emphasis had changed in 1982 when it was extended—by default, because the property development side was not making progress—to become a resort and convention complex. Marketing studies in 1985 had indicated that the development would need further capital investment of between $20 and $25 million: for example, it would need a hotel if it were to attract tourists. AGC decided it could not afford to divert additional funds and management time into a project so un-related to its core business. Kooralbyn had its detractors—some recognised it as a white elephant—but the resort's opu-lence and promise had blinded many in AGC to the reality that it was remorselessly leaching funds out of the company. Over time, the project drained AGC of more than $50 million in operating losses, forgone interest on funds employed and capital expenditure not recovered in the selling price.

Joint ventures: the push into property

The push to increase profits from property intensified in the mid-to-late 1980s and AGC began to embark on a number of joint ventures with property developers. Margins in its traditional business of motor industry and consumer finance were being squeezed, and profitability was down in property finance, traditionally a good earner for AGC but weakened by General Credits' portfolio of non-performing loans. Against a background of limited prospects for natural growth, the company was looking for incremental profits and better returns on equity. Joint-venture financing offered an alluring prospect of great rewards, but was inevitably accom-panied by greater risk. The joint-venture structure involved forming a partnership, creating an off-balance-sheet asset and sharing profits or losses on a development. By taking an equity stake, a financier gambled on making a greater profit (or loss) than could be achieved by a mere lender. A typical AGC joint venture entailed a 20 per cent equity base con-tributed equally by the partners (normally the developer's land would count as its 10 per cent equity); and 80 per cent funding advanced by AGC, of which half was on its own account and half on that of the developer. AGC's policy of demanding a share of the profit was resisted by developers in the early 1980s, and at one stage the company was told it had lost business to other financiers which did not insist on an equity participation. However, AGC stood firm and by the late 1980s compliant developers were lining up at the financier's door, with AGC turning away four out of five applications.

In the second half of the 1980s AGC struck out in this way, engaging in fifteen major property joint ventures which tantalisingly promised a share of handsome profits. The downside—that if the project went badly, the financier, as joint-venture partner, also shared in the losses—was apparently not considered a serious likelihood. This reflected AGC's confidence in its credit analysis and its ability to monitor and control projects.

The foray into joint ventures began cautiously and successfully. Initially, in 1984, the AGC board had set a limit of $100 million in total exposure. That increased in April 1986 to $250 million—$100 million in joint ventures and $150 million in profit-sharing arrangements, the difference being that in a joint venture AGC shared profits and losses and, in the event of a developer's failure, might have to take over the liabilities of the partnership, whereas in a profit-sharing venture AGC shared in the profits but not the losses. Developers did not favour this arrangement because there was no downside, only upside, for AGC. After a year the $250 million limit on exposures was still in place, but it was now attributed entirely to joint ventures, with no profit-sharing projects. Buoyed by early successes, the board in September 1987 approved an increase in the limit to $400 million, and in December of that year to $500 million. However, reflecting the still-conservative approach of AGC, protection was put in place for the company in the form of provisions that in the event of a partner becoming bankrupt, AGC was not liable for its debts. Thus joint ventures changed from the initial partnership structure to unit trusts and corporate entities.

A typical initial joint venture undertaken by AGC in 1985–86 was a regional shopping centre, taking twelve to fifteen months from start to finish and involving around $15 million to $20 million in total lending. The first handful of these joint ventures produced returns of between 25 and 30 per cent a year, which compared very favourably with prevailing lending rates of 18–20 per cent. Relatively small joint ventures produced a profit of $10 million in 1985, followed by $8.5 million profit in 1986 and $22 million in 1987. To AGC, it seemed the nearest they could come to printing money. And Westpac was smiling benignly at AGC's contributions to its bottom line. In July 1988, after AGC had become a wholly owned subsidiary of Westpac, the Westpac/AGC board established a limit on approved commitments of $1,250 million, a move that contributed to AGC's property problems because, already committed, the company felt compelled to continue to lend against that limit, even when exposures were already in excess of the $500 million level established by board policy. A rather cavalier attitude to limits, and inadequate policing of them, seems to have compounded problems. Says Derrick Heywood:

> The whole concept of managing within the $500 million exposure limit was one of a kind of saw-tooth. Over time, drawdowns of approved commitments would take place up to the limit of $500 million and it was expected that the timing would be that these projects would be sold and loans repaid so that the limit was not breached. As loans were repaid, a new phase began and new loans made which would take exposures back close to the limit, then more sales would come in and so on. But the theory was that exposure was to be managed so that it would never exceed $500 million, over a range of projects.

AGC's first few joint-venture projects were fairly small and in some cases had been sold before construction was finished, comfortably locking in a profit. Then the projects started to become more complex, involving larger dollar amounts and a longer time frame. Whereas the early joint ventures might simply involve building a modest shopping centre, subsequent ventures included a five-star hotel, an office block, shops, a food hall and apartment buildings. And as the property market changed, it became difficult to achieve pre-completion sales. The operating and financial reporting systems at AGC in its traditional finance and insurance businesses were effective—many said they were far ahead of those at Westpac. Each month's results of loans, income, expenses and losses written off by each lending division were compared with budget and forecast, and with the same month of the previous year. Each month a fresh forecast would be made for the balance of the year, and that in turn compared with the previous month's forecast for the year, with a detailed explanation of variations in exposures, new business, net income and expenses. There was particular emphasis on credit and overdue accounts.

And AGC had a loan-grading system many years before Westpac adopted a similar system to rate loans according to creditworthiness. All the information was summarised in a familiar format and submitted to the board each month. The joint ventures, which represented a different line of business for AGC, with different constraints, reported as a separate part of the property finance division. In the case of joint ventures, no repayments were expected until the project was completed and sold. The company's conservative practice was to bring to account only the interest accrued on the 40 per cent funding advanced on behalf of the partner. As the amounts involved in the joint ventures rose, and the projects took longer to complete, it became harder to make an accurate assessment of progress, of costs yet to be incurred and of the prospect of selling the different components of a multi-function project on time; consequently, it was often not possible until close to completion to determine how much longer money could be tied up, and by that stage AGC had committed further funds to other projects.

And salesmen could always put a good spin on presentations to the board for approval of new proposals. Projections of profits from joint ventures were generally optimistic in AGC's annual plans—for example, $15 million in 1986 rising to $28 million in 1988. However, each year profits came in lower than expected, and later than forecast. But the AGC board was evidently content with the flow of information it received. There was no reason to probe for further details. AGC, with a reputation as a good project manager, was a profitable organisation. And the board had set strict limits for lending; it was not its role to be involved in individual commercial assessments, although it did intervene in decisions if the project exceeded the authorisation of the credit review committee. Generally, though, individual assessments were entrusted to AGC's executive team while the board was responsible for policy, which included avoiding an over-concentration of lending in any one area.

Between January 1983 and November 1989 AGC received 379 joint-venture applications for $23.8 billion of projects. It approved 67; in seventeen of those the other party decided not to proceed; by November 1989 AGC had 25 projects under way. Joint-venture approvals were bunched in the years 1986, 1987 and 1988 with most approved in 1987 and 1988. Of the projects listed in the table on page 64, totalling $1.6 billion, around $100 million was in 1986, $700 million in 1987 and $800 million in 1988. No warnings were sounding, despite the daunting aggregate exposure to property. It would appear that the AGC board should have become more questioning. The proportion of practical financiers who had been on the board in the 1970s progressively declined during the 1980s as the company became increasingly seduced by the heady prospect of rapid profits.

The first of AGC's major involvements as a property developer was the South Yarra project, later known as Como. It was not a joint venture and, as was the case with the Regent Hotel, AGC's involvement came about through its subsidiary BAC. The South Yarra project, initially unveiled in 1981 by its architect, the Asian property developer Jack Chia, and begun in 1985, was complex, involving a partnership agreement, legal arrangements requiring careful documentation and a number of lenders. Underwriting the project suited a property developer rather than a lender. It had been proposed twice to the Westpac board and twice rejected, the second time after Melbourne directors were requested, given the importance of the project to Victoria, to take a close look. Rob Robson says that, because of the arm's length relationship between the two companies, AGC did not know that Westpac had turned down the project. South Yarra was taken on by BAC which, keen to get into the limelight with a high-profile deal, would lead a financing syndicate. AGC's property finance people, Peter French and Arthur Burrows, were far from keen on the project. French, who was in China at the time the financing was announced, rang AGC in Sydney to register his resistance; he saw the deal as futuristic and liable to become a dead weight for AGC. Westpac's board, to whom the deal was presented as a *fait accompli*, and the bank's management were horrified to hear that BAC had taken it on. Boosting the deal's credibility was the strong support it received from the Victorian government, which passed a special act of parliament to give development approval to the project.

63

AGC's joint ventures

Joint venture	Date approved	Approved by
505 Little Collins St	May 1986	AGC board
Tugun Hospital	September 1986	AGC board
Mira Monte	1985–88	AGC loans committee
Citadel Towers	July 1987	AGC credit committee
Dockside	August 1987	AGC board
Exchange Plaza	August 1987	AGC loans committee
Oasis on Broadbeach	September 1987	AGC board
Runaway Bay	November 1987	AGC board
270 Pitt St	December 1987	AGC board
Australia on Collins	May 1988	AGC board
Elizabeth Street	July 1988	AGC credit committee
Southgate*	August 1988	Westpace/AGC board credit committee
	December 1988	Westpac/AGC board credit committee
Piccadilly Plaza*	December 1988	Westpac/AGC board credit committee
Village Fair Centre	March 1990	AGC loans committee
Total approved	$1.6 billion	

* After AGC 100 per cent owned by Westpac

BAC led a syndicate of banks and merchant banks which included the Bank of New Zealand, Barclays Bank Australia Ltd, Advance Bank Australia Ltd, CIBC Australia Ltd, Tricontinental Corporation Ltd and Kleinwort Benson Australia Ltd. The syndicate was to advance $100 million, including $30 million from BAC. State Bank Victoria was to contribute a further $50 million, with equity of $12 million coming from Jack Chia (Australia) Ltd and $5 million from the property finance division of AGC, in what was promoted to them by BAC as a 'passive investment' rather than a joint-venture involvement and which carried a 'guaranteed return' of 25 per cent. So the developers had access to $167 million to build the first stage of what was to be a $1 billion project. As with Kooralbyn, the idea was that money would be ploughed back as each stage was completed and sold. Jack Chia's dream was to build Australia's largest residential, commercial and retail complex. Stage one of the South Yarra project would include 69 residential apartments in a sixteen-storey block and 55 apartments in a separate building, a ten-storey office building, 6,000 square metres of retail space, a 139-suite hotel and three levels of car parking to accommodate 800 vehicles. When completed, the project would be a mini-city, built around a lagoon, accommodating 6,000 people in exclusive apartments who would commute to the city of Melbourne by way of a canal connecting South Yarra to the Yarra River. Early investors had tagged the project 'Little Venice'; by 1987 the concept was being derided by other developers as 'Dreamsville'. The highly publicised project, lauded by the government because of its potential to add to the state's economy—although there was opposition from Prahran council and local residents—became a sombre example of how grand plans could go off the rails.

65

The project went seriously awry in mid-1986. Drawdowns under the loan facility were around $60–$70 million when Melbourne suffered an unusually wet winter which inhibited construction work. Unexpected hikes in prices for materials and labour led to costs substantially overrunning budget. Demands from the construction industry flared into expensive industrial disputes. Changes were made in the architectural design even after concrete had been poured for the foundations. The objective that the project would quickly become self-funding was not going to be achieved. By late 1986 the monthly updates on expenditure were showing an alarming rise in the projected cost to completion.

Problems came to a head in November 1986. The banking syndicate, increasingly unhappy with the project, refused to advance more funds. The money originally allocated was almost exhausted but the builders needed more if they were to get even close to finishing stage one. Robson, out of action in October because of a severe gall-bladder condition, flew to Melbourne in November to try to get the project back under control. He spent several days interrogating contractors and others involved to determine the true state of the project and how badly it was behind schedule. In December 1986 AGC advanced $4 million on behalf of the other lenders and agreed to provide more later that month.

AGC's results for 1986 reflected the impact of high interest rates on its borrowers, with the financier reporting an increase of almost 200 per cent in net bad and doubtful debt charges to $39.3 million for the half-year to 31 March. While the Australian scene was troubled, with high interest rates lifting the number of bankruptcies in the small-business sector, tough times for rural communities and rising unemployment, AGC's international activities, which accounted for about 12 per cent of profits, showed an improvement. Depressed business conditions in Australia continued, resulting in AGC's loan loss provisions for the year to September 1986 more than doubling from 1985's $33 million to $73 million.

AGC attempted to inject a fresh perspective into the Melbourne project by employing new project managers, quantity surveyors and architects. In March 1987 a detailed report was given to the AGC board, and Chia was instructed that he would have to find top-up equity. If he could not provide additional funds he faced being taken out of the project. And the lending syndicate, meanwhile, was getting restless. It did not like the prospect of adverse media comment that would stem from being associated with a major project that had turned sour.

Chia could not find the money. In March 1987 AGC took over the South Yarra project. The banking syndicate had examined progress, future cashflows and the estimated cost to completion and did not like what it saw. It had been kept informed but the relationship between BAC and some members of the syndicate had become tense. The syndicate lenders, other than BAC, withdrew, but not without one, Barclays, threatening legal action against BAC for mismanagement. Theoretically, at that point AGC and BAC could have walked away from the project. But the AGC board was persuaded that the company should step in, on the grounds that leaving the South Yarra project an incomplete shell—a concrete monument to folly—would enormously damage AGC's public image. Normally it is the developer which is the butt of adverse criticism if a project flounders. But AGC felt it had no choice but to persist. Robson, known to revel in trouble-shooting, was in his element; stemming the damage in a highly visible project seemed to appeal to the engineer in him. Announcing its decision on 4 March, AGC said that the South Yarra project had suffered 'in the same way as a number of other construction projects in Melbourne from significant cost overruns due to external factors'. AGC, setting aside $30 million after tax—subsequently reduced to $20 million—to cover possible loss from the project, was caught by its own reputation: it had always said it would honour its commitments and it did. As had been the case with Kooralbyn, the South Yarra project was regarded as an out-of-character aberration.

AGC took out Chia, paid off the banking syndicate, and took complete control. Robson was doing more than merely taking over the South Yarra project; he was taking over Chia's company, which had tax losses from previous years which could be used by AGC. The manoeuvre cost AGC

67

$16.15 million, paid to Chia for his interests in stage two, for which he had bought land. In addition, AGC would have to fork out around $200 million to see stage one of the project to completion. In its statement at the time, AGC said that the project would not be completed for a further five years; group general manager Peter French said the project was a 'sound long-term investment' and that the $30 million provision would be the only one during AGC's forecast involvement. In May 1987, French said it was likely that the company would recover the funds. By then, AGC had re-assessed the project and felt more comfortable about its investment. Four months after AGC took over South Yarra, the project's name was changed to Como Properties Pty Ltd to mark the fresh approach, emphasise the end of the association with Chia, and to identify more closely with the area (formerly the suburb had been known as Como, named for a historic residence in the district).

It seemed that the Como project was over its crisis and that AGC could breathe a collective sigh of relief. Then Bob White received a call from Peter Costain, chairman of the engineering firm Costain Ltd, the builders at Como, who had disturbing news for the Westpac chief. His message was blunt: the project, arguably the highest-profile development in Australia at the time, was still in serious trouble and both Westpac, through AGC, and Costain were deeply committed. 'We'll have egg on our face, and you'll have egg on your face,' he told White. Costain invited White to fly to Melbourne to take a look at progress at Como, which he did, accompanied by Ian Matheson, chairman of AGC. They met Costain, the foreman and architect and other key individuals at the site. Costain and the architect said it would be essential to have someone from AGC on the site and that was agreed, with Don Nilsson, a former property lending officer of General Credits, then a senior AGC manager based in Victoria, being seconded to the project. Westpac and AGC were determined to see the Como project succeed. However it was badly flawed and, while the hotel concept had been defined, the retail side of the complex was still well behind target. And Costain's dour forecast proved right.

From 1987 Como was a cruel drain on AGC—over five years it became a $200 million exposure on the books, earning nothing and reporting operating losses. To generate funds and boost its bottom line, AGC sold a jewel in the company crown when it disposed of its 51 per cent share in the property developer Mirvac, collecting $27 million in a one-off sale of a major part of its business. Como was a sorry saga for AGC but in its 1988 annual report the company, in a burst of promotional rhetoric, said:

> The soundness of AGC's financial expertise and procedures was no more apparent during the past twelve months than in the company's handling of the giant Como development in Melbourne's South Yarra, Australia's largest urban renewal project. Aided by the high calibre of the consultants it had appointed to the site, the company completed, leased and opened 56 specialty shops, leased 10,000 square metres of office space to the ANZ Bank, completed and sold a block of residential apartments at prices which set new records for Melbourne, attracted one of the city's most prestigious restaurants, Maxims, to the site and managed to set the whole of stage one firmly on target for completion by the end of 1988.

Stage one was indeed completed by the end of 1988. However, opening of the Como Hotel and Promenade Shopping Arcade coincided with the pilots' strike of 1989 which flattened tourist revenue around Australia and badly affected the new complex. To help boost revenues, Westpac staff visiting Melbourne were dragooned into staying at Como. Then came the recession. Problems at stage two of Como, which never got off the ground, would have been compounded by AGC's inability to obtain approval from Prahran Council— never in favour of the original scheme—and subsequently the state government, to vary the original concept by increasing the density of the second stage of the development. Studies showed that stage two would probably have also been a major loser. AGC lost heavily on Como. In addition to the initial provision of $20 million, the cost to AGC by 1992 exceeded $200 million.

Como was not considered part of AGC's property finance portfolio and it was not regarded as a joint venture for AGC. The property finance division, against its wishes, had put in $5 million in equity as a 'passive investment' but the whole project had been instigated and directed by BAC. It seems remarkable that BAC succeeded in getting AGC involved, given that in 1987 the problems surrounding the loan to the Ang family involved in the Regent financing had barely been resolved. Como's problems came as a gigantic shock to the AGC and Westpac boards. AGC was not out of Como until 1993 when it sold the project—which by then included two office blocks, two apartment blocks, the Como Hotel and specialty shops and restaurants—for around $70 million to a group of Asian investors.

While the Como debacle was being played out, AGC's mainstream business had been running satisfactorily but profits were adversely affected by a rise in bankruptcies. AGC's contribution to Westpac's profits dropped from around one-third in 1983 to about one-fifth in 1986. The company's international operations, especially those in New Zealand, Hong Kong and PNG, continued to perform well. In 1986 and 1987, AGC enthusiastically entered into a number of high-profile property joint ventures, each underpinned by a strong and experienced partner. In May 1986 the AGC board approved an office block at 505 Little Collins

Street, Melbourne, and this was followed in September by approval for Doug Moran's hospital of excellence project, now to be established at Tugun on Queensland's Gold Coast. Moran, undeterred by the rebuff to his earlier proposal for a hospital of excellence at Kooralbyn, and lack of progress at his second choice, Robina, had resumed discussions with AGC, this time through its property finance division. In January 1985 Moran retracted his announcement of a proposed hospital at Robina, and in the following year AGC announced that it was forming a syndicate to provide $100 million to develop the hospital at Tugun. AGC would hold 40 per cent, the Japanese company C. Itoh 40 per cent and Moran Health Care Group, 20 per cent. Tugun Hospital was classed as a special-purpose project in that it was not a standard commercial or residential development; also, a hospital has limited alternative use. The original approval, granted in September 1986, was subject to a condition that AGC secure an agreement from two other financial institutions to underwrite the sale of the completed project. This protection for AGC was recommended by the property finance division and by the group credit committee, and endorsed by the board.

71

Early in 1987 Robson attended the annual world economic forum at Davos, in Switzerland, and visited a number of overseas branches of AGC. Neither he nor Westpac managing director Bob White was present at a board meeting in February 1987 when the requirement for the underwriting agreement regarding Tugun was removed. A revised profit projection showed the hospital as likely to be much more profitable, so that the condition was no longer considered necessary. In reality, despite extensive discussions, it had been impossible to obtain an underwriting agreement ahead of completion of the project. Robson found out about this later. The loan went ahead without the underwriting agreement and construction of the hospital began in May 1987.

By 1988 AGC was running advertisements proclaiming that 'AGC is now part-owner of a new private health scheme' with enthusiastic, even arrogant, text:

> Way back in 1956, Doug Moran first came to us for property finance. He had plans for a modest nursing home. We liked it and financed it. Since then Doug Moran has been back to us more than 40 times, with bigger and better Health Care developments. We financed every one of those. And in doing so, the Moran Health Care Group and AGC Property Finance have now become Australia's foremost experts in what is a highly specialised field. So naturally when Doug planned his dream hospital, the Moran Clinic–Hospital of Excellence, he came to us. Because we were his first choice for finance. Situated on a prime piece of real estate on the Gold Coast, it was a development opportunity we weren't going to pass up. In fact we were so impressed with the plans we not only financed it, we bought 40% of it ourselves. Cementing our working relationship that spans more than 20 years. And even more recently we assisted the Moran Health Care Group in the purchase of yet another 13 private hospitals. Making them the largest private hospital operators in Australia. If you've got a property development, no matter the size, give us a call. You'll find us in every state.

Tugun ranks in AGC's annals as another grand-scale vision that was unable to capture reality. Moran's record of successfully operating nursing homes seemed to seduce AGC; however, it was a big leap from running nursing homes to developing a large hospital of excellence, dependent as it would be on a steady flow of wealthy overseas patients. Tugun became famous for, among other features, a laundry large enough to service the Gold Coast as well as a lavish hotel for the families of patients. Moran added a note of strain to the relationship when in December 1986 he announced the provision of $500,000 by the joint venture as the basis for the Moran Portrait Foundation, the provider of Australia's richest portrait prize. This came as a surprise to some executives at AGC. AGC's involvement in Tugun ended in 1991 when the hospital was taken over by Health Care of Australia Ltd, a division of Mayne Nickless.

AGC had for some years been optimistic about Gold Coast property. Its investments there had passed the $500 million mark at the end of 1986, following its signing of a $120 million joint venture with the Ron McCaster Group to build the Bayview Harbour residential–marina complex. In October 1987, AGC took a 50 per cent interest in the $250 million Oasis on Broadbeach international hotel venture. In its 1987 annual report AGC said that the company 'maintains a firm policy of limiting both the sectoral and geographic spread of its property investments to ensure that it is not overexposed to one type of development or market'.

The worldwide sharemarket crash in October 1987 burst the bubble in equities but did not affect AGC's clientele; in fact, in the wake of the crash the investment community turned to the property market, which rose to giddier heights as funds flowed in. This was not an expression of faith in the property market so much as a reaction to disillusionment with shares. In this heady environment AGC plunged on with more joint ventures. However, the company had recognised the clouds gathering over the world's share markets and a couple of months ahead of the crash, on Robson's instructions, AGC Insurances disposed of its equities portfolio, generating $49 million in after-tax profit.

73

In January 1988 Westpac made a bid for the balance of AGC it did not already own. The takeover became effective in June, making the financier a wholly owned subsidiary at a cost of $280 million after Sir Ron Brierley's Industrial Equity Ltd, AGC's second-largest shareholder with 8.5 per cent of the company, pushed the cash component of the bid up from Westpac's original offer of $240 million. Westpac paid a premium to buy AGC, reflecting the market value of the business, although it had the advantage of buying the shares during a post-1987 market dip. The rationale for the purchase was that it made sense, from a control point of view, to integrate AGC into the bank. As full parent, Westpac could now have far greater say in AGC's business than was the case when the financier was a 76 per cent–owned subsidiary. Taking over AGC gave Westpac full control—and 100 per cent responsibility for its problems and losses. In November 1988 all Westpac directors became directors of AGC and Sir Eric Neal, deputy chairman of Westpac, became its chairman.

AGC, instead of operating with a board that until July 1987 had met fortnightly for half a day, became a thirty-minute item on the Westpac board agenda. According to White, this was a 'recipe for disaster': AGC was too big to be given so little attention. The new board gave AGC's loans committee, which was chaired by its managing director, a delegated lending authority of up to $100 million in group exposure to an individual customer; this meant that if Westpac had lent $50 million to a customer then AGC could lend only a further $50 million to that customer. Larger proposals up to $200 million group exposure went to the Westpac head office credit committee and even larger proposals to Westpac's board credit committee. Bob White, in 1988 no longer managing director of Westpac but a member of the bank and finance company board, spoke against the $100 million delegated lending authority, favouring tighter controls.

AGC was running up commitments which would eventually go far beyond the board policy of $500 million aggregate lending exposure to joint ventures. In 1988, at the height of the property boom euphoria and after Westpac had taken full ownership of AGC, the financier and Jennings Industries Ltd became partners in the $650 million Southgate Riverside Development project in Melbourne. They had bought the 2.4 hectare site for $11.3 million in 1985 and formed a joint venture company, Southgate Developments Pty Ltd. Their plan was to form a consortium of investors who would contribute long-term funds to build two large office towers, a 585-room hotel and an extensive shopping centre on the south bank of the Yarra, opposite Melbourne's central business district. Like Como, the Southgate project was born of an optimistic vision: the developers were counting on dormant areas being radically revamped by huge developments—and this was a vital element—attracting the shoppers and visitors whose spending would justify the enormous construction costs. The reality never came close to expectations and profits never matched projections.

AGC was also involved in the development of an office block at 270 Pitt Street in Sydney, a $235 million Dockside residential and hotel development at Brisbane's Kangaroo Point with joint-venture partners Girvan Group and Fricker Developments, and the $200 million Citadel Towers, two office blocks in Sydney's Chatswood, again with Girvan. In May 1988 AGC had become a joint-venture partner in the Australia on Collins with Citistate. In December 1988 it gave the go-ahead for the Piccadilly development in Sydney's central business district, which began in July 1989. Project values often quoted in the media, such as Piccadilly's $460 million price tag, represented the expected retail selling price, not the cost of the development or the size of AGC's loan; in Piccadilly's case, AGC had lent $120 million as its share of funding, plus a further $120 million as a loan to the joint-venture partner, and had provided $30 million in equity.

For the year to September 1988 AGC recorded a drop of 8 per cent in net profit before extraordinaries, despite lower provisions for bad debts and more favourable interest margins. The rate at which money was being poured into joint ventures started to overtake the returns from completed projects, although at first nobody seemed to become alarmed. Pre-tax profits from joint ventures plunged from $22 million in 1987 to $6 million in 1988—and in 1989 showed a loss of $21 million reflecting the write-off of $45 million in interest expense on AGC's share of funding the joint ventures. But in AGC's 1988 annual report the property finance division sounded confident, talking about building market share in a buoyant property sector: 'AGC's property interests as lender or joint venturer with experienced partners in prime sites spread across Sydney, Melbourne, Brisbane, the Gold Coast, Adelaide and Perth, include land for development, subdivision, hotels, shopping centres, commercial office buildings, residential complexes and industrial estates.' Within eighteen months one after another of these major projects would strike difficulties.

A problem had been cemented into the system when the board placed a much higher limit in terms of commitments (amounts agreed to be lent) than exposures (amounts actually lent). The generous level resulted in the company being able to agree to lend up to $1.25 billion but theoretically not being allowed by the board to have more than $500 million in loans outstanding at any one time. However, delays in construction and slow sales of completed projects, while funds were being advanced to new projects, resulted in AGC's breaking its lending limit. The earlier approach at AGC to property joint ventures had enforced restraint through having the same limit on commitments as on drawn exposures, and through limiting total property lending to 30 per cent of loans in Australia. Under this regime, new projects could not be approved once the limit had been reached, so delays in completion and sales could not push exposures beyond the limit.

Joint-ventures exposures policy had gradually crept higher: from $100 million in February 1984 to $500 million in December 1987—by which time commitments, or the total amount approved to be lent, stood at $600 million. Despite the crash in the sharemarket, the Australian economy was robust. During 1988, funds were flooding into property and, no matter what outlandish price was paid, an investor was confident of selling six months later at a profit. Potential seemed limitless. Robson and his executive team continued their aggressive lending on joint ventures. That they could do so showed that AGC's credit-assessment and diversity-of-risk policies were far from watertight. Total property loan commitments, which at some stage would become loans, and of which slightly more than half were joint ventures, peaked around $2 billion in early 1989.

Warnings that the commercial property bubble was about to burst had begun to emerge from the middle of 1988. An early, lone voice was that of economic forecasters BIS Shrapnel Pty Ltd, whose prediction that an oversupply of space would start to appear in 1989, with a classical down-turn in the commercial property market ensuing, was howled down by developers. But BIS Shrapnel's bearish forecast was endorsed in an address to a Sydney conference by John McCarthy, then general manager, Australian Fixed Trusts. McCarthy spoke of 'storm clouds gathering' for commercial property markets around Australia because of a looming oversupply of commercial space. In September 1988 Dr Ng Seek, managing director of Jones Lang Wootton Research Pty Ltd, told a Building Owners and Managers national congress in Brisbane: 'The current scenario has understandably brought back unpleasant memories about the most recent major property boom and bust in the

77

1970s, and raises concern about whether economic fundamentals have again been forgotten ... The lead-up to a collapse is when investment decisions get caught up in a market euphoria, with unrealistic expectations of a quick gain replacing careful analysis of final demand and risks.' The debate about how long the boom would run before a downturn took hold continued well into 1989.

Had the AGC board, as it was in the 1970s and early 1980s, been stacked with tough and pragmatic financiers instinctively suspicious of highly innovative and promising deals, particularly in such volumes, the story might have evolved differently.

A ground-rule set by the AGC board was that the financier would deal only with blue-chip developers but, as the economy subsequently deteriorated and asset prices fell, what had previously been a blue-chip developer often became a cash-strapped company. In almost every major joint venture, AGC's partner ran out of steam, leaving AGC to pick up the tab, thereby virtually doubling its exposure and taking the property in the joint venture as security. Many of the joint ventures also experienced overruns on costs. Because interest expense on AGC's portion of a joint venture loan funding was not capitalised during construction, the huge build-up of joint ventures became a mounting drag on profits. Further, AGC's property portfolio became increasingly unbalanced. By 1990 joint ventures accounted for 30 per cent of all property lending, a big leap from the strict geographical and sector constraints that applied in the early 1980s and a significant advance even on the 15 per cent that prevailed in 1987. By late 1989 and 1990 the economy was in a downward spiral and there was clear evidence of an oversupply of office blocks and five-star hotels. AGC's losses were increased by the need to sweeten rental agreements by offering inducements, such as 'rent holidays', to attract tenants.

One outcome of Westpac's move to full ownership of AGC was a decision to sell its merchant bank subsidiary BAC. It was now Australia's tenth-largest merchant bank but was seen as duplicating the services available elsewhere in the Westpac group. The bank was said to be looking for between $45 million and $55 million—about eleven times earnings, a price regarded by the market as unrealistic. There were few bids. The deadline for expressions of interest was extended by one month to 7 October 1988 but the one offer publicly made, from the State Bank of South Australia, was withdrawn. A late bid from General Electric Co of the US was also withdrawn in January 1989. BAC's business mix did not add to its appeal and the company had suffered adverse publicity over the Regent financing. Says Robson: 'There were unfounded fears about the quality of BAC's loans book. It was hard to sell the company in that environment.' Early in 1989, after five months on the market, it was withdrawn and in October 1990 BAC was absorbed into Westpac. Staff were assured that they would be accommodated in the group. Six months later about half of the former BAC staff were retrenched. Frank Conroy, then chief operating officer, described the sackings as 'regrettable', the result of Westpac's decision to contract the ongoing business of BAC and run down its book.

CHAPTER FOUR

A BANK WITHIN A BANK: THE AMERICAS DIVISION

In 1983, at a time when increasing competition was looming on Australia's banking horizon, Westpac, the country's largest bank, began lifting its profile in the United States. Plans to upgrade operations in the US had been germinating since the merger of the Bank of New South Wales and the Commercial Bank of Australia in 1981. The view within the merged entity was that because Westpac now accounted for around one-quarter of the domestic Australian market, global expansion was the only way to grow. Bob White told *The Australian Financial Review* in June 1984 that it would be impossible for Westpac to improve on the domestic share because of the increased competition that would come with the entry of foreign banks. 'The only way for real growth is to go outside Australia,' he said. And any bank serious about operating globally needed a firm foothold in the giant US market. Westpac, whose activities in the US dated from 1970 when the Wales opened a small New York office— upgraded to an agency in 1975—set out to transform what was essentially an overseas administrative office, clearing $A payments for Westpac globally and for other banks, into a substantial wholesale banking operation.

A first step was to recruit a head for this new Americas division. As with the appointment of Adrian Fletcher, Westpac broke with tradition and searched outside its own ranks. In October 1982 Tony Walton, a senior vice-president at Chase Manhattan Bank, was contacted by an executive recruitment firm asking whether he would be interested in an interview for the job of heading Westpac's activities in the US. Walton discussed the proposal with the recruitment firm, TASA, and with Jim Wolfensohn, who at the time was acting as unofficial adviser to Stuart Fowler, head of Westpac's international division, and to the bank's chairman, Sir Noel Foley. Wolfensohn, at that stage still considering whether he would take on the Westpac con-sultancy role that he was in fact to hold for nearly ten years, was a former Australian merchant banker turned Wall Street investment banker and consultant *extraordinaire*, at that time with the prestige Wall Street firm Salomon Brothers. He was later to form his own company, James D. Wolfensohn Inc, and even later to become president of the World Bank. In the early 1980s he was well known in Sydney financial circles and so had been asked to help locate a suitable candidate in the US.

Walton met Fowler in Chicago—the first meeting of an enduring close relationship—before flying to Australia in late November 1982 for a three-day visit to meet other senior Westpac executives, board members and managing director Bob White. What Westpac wanted—as it was expressed to Walton when he was recruited and what made the job an appealing prospect—was to capitalise on the opportunity to become an international bank of significance in the US. To Walton, it seemed to make a great deal of sense. He would be joining a bank with a top international credit standing and reputation and, moreover, one not saddled with the third-world debt that was a millstone at that time for many major US and European banks. Walton was attracted to the task of building an operation which, he was told, would be an important division of the bank. Westpac's senior management and the board would be receptive to an aggressive, well-thought-out growth plan for the US.

British by birth, son of a patent attorney attached to the British embassy in Washington and a naturalised American, Walton had grown up in Washington and the New York area. While he travelled a great deal between the UK and the US, he was educated in the US, attending high school, college and then Wharton Graduate School of Finance, University of Pennsylvania, graduating with an MBA. Before joining Westpac, he had spent sixteen years with Chase Manhattan, eleven of those in London, in a variety of assignments including head of multinational lending for Europe, Africa and the Middle East. In 1979 he had returned to New York to run Chase's global trade finance. By 1982, aged 42, he was ready for a move.

When he took on the role of head of Westpac's Americas division, the bank in the US had approximate balance-sheet footings of $US600 million, of which $US400 million was in interbank placements and the remaining $US200 million in loans to Mexico and Brazil. Westpac's role in the US as clearing house for the bank's global network gave it access to free funds which were then lucratively invested— in 1982 Paul Volcker, as chairman of the US Federal Reserve, was fighting inflation, and interest rates were in the 16–18 per cent range, so Westpac made a nice turn investing free funds. Although globally it ranked in size about equal to the twelfth-largest US bank, Westpac did not have a profile in terms of customer and market penetration in the US market.

The instruction to Walton from Westpac senior management in Sydney was: *We want you to build a wholesale bank in the US—how you do it is for you to work out and for us to approve.* The first step was to devise a plan that would encompass which customers Walton wanted the bank to service, which products it would sell and where in the US it would sell them, and whether the bank's reach should include Canada and Latin America. Walton worked on the plan with Jim Wolfensohn. Then Walton brought the plan to Sydney for approval by senior management and directors.

Walton came on board in January 1983 and a few months later was joined by Gary Hett, also from Chase Manhattan. Hett, a former medical school student who had joined Chase in 1972, was a retail banker by training, and later a branch manager. He studied at night, qualifying with a Bachelor of Science (Economics) degree from the State University of New York. After working in the retail branch network at Chase for three years, he moved to the personnel side of the business. He spent much of the next seven years working in human resources and staff functions, then went back into the business unit for three years as head of management services responsible for human resources, planning and financial control, working for Walton who had recently returned from Europe. When Walton, in his new role at Westpac, needed someone skilled in administration, he turned to Hett. The challenge of developing a new business appealed to Hett as much as it had to Walton.

83

The terms of Walton's employment and compensation contract were devised by the recruiting firm, with input from Wolfensohn and Fowler, who signed off on the contract, together with Westpac's head of human resources. A persistent rumour at the Sydney head office was that Walton's contract was structured so that increases in the volume of business written would trigger bonuses. Hett says that was wholly incorrect. The contract, he says, was related to three measures of performance: pre-tax profit, return on human resources, ie, the efficiency with which profits were produced, and return on assets. The widespread belief in Sydney that Walton's contract was based on volume was, says Hett, typical of the petty jealousies evident throughout the 1980s. Walton, as a non-Australian general manager recruited externally, was one of the first in Westpac to be categorised by other senior managers as a tall poppy. His compensation package, although in line with the New York market, went a long way towards explaining the resentment.

In 1983 Westpac ran a modest US business, with some 80 staff, including a small treasury operation of eight and a small lending operation which mainly serviced Australian companies or Australian-related companies in the US, with the remainder of the staff in back-office processing. Apart from its New York office, Westpac was represented in San Francisco—it had been the first Australian bank to move into the promising Californian market—and Houston. The merger with the Commercial Bank of Australia had brought Westpac an office in Chicago, and Barry Bint, a former CBA executive, had been sent from Australia to head the business there, now upgraded to a branch. Overall, in the US Westpac was operating a low-cost, break-even business, and the bank was not recognised as a force in a market that encompassed around 570 foreign banks as well as the leading US money centre and regional operators. Walton set about restructuring and upgrading the bank's operations. A new office was opened in Los Angeles, run by another Walton recruit, Sam Mills jnr, a career banker and former J.P. Morgan executive. Marketing staff was increased and efficiencies were improved as all Westpac's US offices—New York, Chicago, San Francisco, Los Angeles and Houston—came under Walton's supervision.

By this time Westpac, as part of its global thrust, was also lifting its profile in Asia. In May 1983, shortly after Walton took up the reins in the US, Westpac recruited another outsider, Australian-born Philip Deer, a former Morgan Guaranty executive, as head of its Asian operations. Deer in Asia mirrored Walton's moves in the US, bringing together under his control Westpac's operations in Singapore, Japan, Hong Kong and China. David Murison was already busy revamping Westpac's business in London and Europe.

Walton and Hett brought to the Westpac Americas division a rigorous annual planning process which stemmed from the fact that both came from the Chase environment where, they say, meticulous planning was ingrained. The Americas division reported monthly and quarterly to the Westpac management in Sydney, which then reported to the board. Walton says: 'My approach to management is basically to plan what you want to do very, very carefully, take it to your bosses and then take it to whoever they wish you to take it to, ie, the board if they wish, and receive approval for everything you want to do, repeat *everything*. So everything that we did was pre-planned and pre-approved as part of the annual planning process, or if we had to get involved in additional things during the year such as a one-off transaction there was an additional presentation.' A former Westpac executive comments: 'Tony had a mandate which he followed, and he reported quarterly to the board on the progress of what they had jointly agreed, and he was rewarded for that. If there was a quarrel, it should've been with the mandate.'

In its first half-dozen years, the Americas division performed well against head office targets, hitting plan in 1984 and in 1985 achieving 120 per cent above plan. In 1986, 1987 and 1988 it achieved 95 per cent, 100 per cent and 77 per cent above plan, dipping to 26 per cent above in 1989 and falling off to 1 per cent above in 1990 before recovering to 17 per cent above plan in 1991. Walton says that in excess of $US220–230 million was made in those years in the US. 'Profits were being made,' says Hett.

Shortly after the $A was floated in December 1983, Westpac sent Owen van der Wall to its New York office as chief manager and treasurer of the Americas division. The objective was to establish a more professional trading operation, build staff and develop a presence on the US West Coast to service the time zones. Van der Wall's role was to foster activity in Australian and New Zealand dollars with US-based companies and institutions. Over time, Westpac built a successful niche in foreign exchange in the US, particularly in $A swaps, and was also active in distributing $A-denominated securities to institutional investors. Van der Wall went on to run the New York branch, reporting to Walton, overall head of the Americas division, before returning to Australia in 1989.

In the early years of the operation in the US, Walton concentrated on the clear-cut Australian connections, Australian companies operating in the northern hemisphere. 'Unfortunately there were few of those, so the division quickly exhausted that as a possible market niche,' he says. 'We moved on to deal with American companies with actual or possible involvements in Australia.' Westpac's target market in the US included the US operations of Australian and New Zealand companies which were significant users of US bank credit, financial market products and advisory services, US companies with significant Australian and New Zealand operations, US companies with minimum sales of $US300 million and US industries such as electricity utilities, financial services and insurance.

A pertinent undercurrent in the early 1980s was that as Westpac expanded, the 'Pacific' connotation of the bank's name was becoming significant, and it was decided that the focus of the US operations should be on Australasian, not just Australian, relationships. The Americas division sifted through the elite companies in the *Fortune* 800 list and pinpointed those that had an Australasian connection. It created its own marketplace of about 470 large multinational names culled from the *Fortune* 800 that suggested opportunities to cross-market with the bank in Australia. Walton's approach identified companies that offered a combination of prospects for loans (with fees), treasury, and fee-based activities from which the bank could get the highest return on its capital. 'That was the message drummed home to marketing officers,' says Walton.

Walton had a strong aversion to lending to certain types of companies, those he regarded as high-risk, so Westpac in North America did not lend on real estate, shipping, the healthcare industry, casinos or entertainment—which made life difficult at the time because, in Westpac's own backyard, the gambling and entertainment mecca of Atlantic City was booming and banks, especially from New York City, were rushing to lend money. On six different occasions Westpac turned down invitations to finance a casino. The message to lending officers was that they should not waste the bank's time by analysing a loan to any of those sectors because the deal would not be approved. Overall, says Walton, the Americas strategy was: choose industries approved by the board of directors, make sure they had handpicked names, have the projects reviewed with Sydney, approved in Sydney, and then authorised to go, with very strict lending authority.

In America, Westpac selected industry segments which suited the bank's lending culture. One was utilities, a non-Australian-related industry, but Walton picked utilities because they were unusually safe from a credit-risk point of view; utility bankruptcies are extremely rare. Another dimension was gold lending, following the acquisition of the bullion dealer Mase Metals and later the British Johnson Matthey Bankers. With Mase Westpac Inc in the US, Westpac took a successful lead role in gold loan project financing. Later, in 1992, Mase Westpac Inc formed a modest boutique gold-lending business in Providence, Rhode Island. The initiative was made with the full approval of Westpac, and the opening of the business was attended by Walton and Westpac board member Professor Warren

Hogan, as well as the local mayor. However, Walton quickly became concerned that the operation was too downmarket. Within weeks, he recommended that Mase Westpac Inc withdraw from the business and, to the embarrassment of Mase Westpac Inc executives, the lending boutique was closed.

By 1986 Westpac had moved from its 1983 ranking of zero to the number 16 slot among foreign banks in the US, ranked on their ability to provide banking services to large domestic and multinational companies. By 1992 it was rated eleventh. The ratings were made by Greenwich Associates, a US consulting firm specialising in canvassing the opinions of US corporate treasurers. Greenwich ranked Westpac number one in the US for $A foreign-exchange products. It was a 'line bank'—that is, it had committed lines of credit—to more than 140 major US companies of which 35 were in the *Fortune* 500. By 1990 Westpac was rated equal fifth by its 'important' customers, and tenth by all customers, out of the top 30 foreign banks in the US. Bob White says: 'Tony Walton did an excellent job in establishing the Americas division. And he recruited some top people.'

On the lending side, Westpac ran a blue-chip book in the US. Later, in the early 1990s, when Westpac was forced to review its operations, the Americas division was criticised for making insufficient returns on capital. But Walton believed that lending to top credits was the only way to go, with additional efforts to increase ancillary income as much as possible. In the late 1980s, treasury and fee income generally accounted for about 60 per cent of total revenue of the division. Walton emphasises the degree of planning that went into the Americas division. 'It was highly planned,' he says. 'In fact I used to get heat from all my lending officers for being such a ghastly human being to work with in terms of planning programs. I insisted that everything be approved.' Adds Hett: 'Reviewing the planning process each year was known as "hell week" like in a college fraternity, where Tony and I would fly to each location and over the course of a full day, line by line, go through individual plans for the coming year.'

Walton and Hett contend, looking back, that three elements of those plans kept Westpac out of trouble in the US in the early 1990s, when many foreign banks were in difficulties: no real-estate lending, very tight controls on lending overall, and the strategy which gave Westpac regular fee income. The bank did become involved in a number of so-called highly leveraged transactions (HLTs, using debt to acquire companies) but only HLTs that conformed to the strategy, involving companies where there was a clear possibility of an Australasian link. HLT exposures created a great deal of concern among analysts in the late 1980s and early 1990s. Westpac's HLTs peaked in 1990/91 at about $US2 billion out of total assets of $US12 billion, or 17 per cent of the bank's US business. Also, Westpac in the US developed its own internal credit process to analyse cash-flow. Every Americas division officer had to undertake a two-week 'credit-modelling' program involving testing loans and potential loans under all adverse scenarios. Funds were lent only where the bank believed that income provided sufficient cover of debt.

The mid-to-late 1980s were years of peak performance for the Americas division, which was at all times a self-funding wholesale operation with no retail source of funds. In 1986/87 the profit performance of the division was $US40.9 million ($A56.7 million), 95 per cent over plan. In October 1988 Philip Deer, by then chief general manager, corporate and international, based in Sydney, wrote to congratulate Walton on the division's full-year results. 'Please convey to all in the Americas division that we regard the achievement as a first-class effort and that we recognise the level of personal commitment by everyone in your team,' Deer wrote, highlighting the division's 58 per cent increase over the previous year's results. By 1992, the Americas division had 670 relationships with different company names in the US, each of which had an average of three facilities, amounting to some 1,800 facilities of which about a third were loans.

Westpac extended its US network in 1986 when it opened in Columbus, Ohio. A reluctant Walton had been told that Australia was the largest trading partner of the state of Ohio, trading particularly in medical instruments, tyres and farm equipment and products. Ohio is also home to many of the big multinationals in the *Fortune* 500. Walton was resistant to the idea of opening there but his management committee persuaded him he was wrong. Westpac was the first foreign bank to open an office in Columbus; the opening was attended by the mayor and governor of the state. Westpac spent some $US300,000 in its first year in Columbus and in its second year made $US7.5 million, running a highly blue-chip portfolio. All the Westpac offices maximised the Australasian connection, although in New York and Chicago in particular the bank marketed itself as an international bank whose head office was in Sydney rather than as a 'foreign bank' in the US.

At its peak, Westpac had 575 staff in the US. Three times the bank examined the possibilities in Canada but was not convinced that it could make money there. Some 70 foreign banks were operating in Canada and, of those, a handful were profitable. Walton considered that a move into Canada would be too much of a diversion of management time, and the chances of making money poor. Westpac could monitor Canada adequately from New York.

Chicago, under Barry Bint, focused on business with corporates (*Fortune* 1,000) and energy utilities, and was a particularly profitable operation in one of the busiest banking markets in the US. The city accommodated some 150 foreign banks of which no more than 20 were real players and Westpac ranked among those. Over its ten-year life, the branch grew to $US8.3 billion in commitments and developed a customer base of more than 150 companies. Westpac in Chicago did not focus on lending (the companies with which it dealt could borrow more cheaply on the market in their own name) but rather concentrated on 'enhancements' such as letters of credit, commercial paper back-up lines, revolving credit facilities, asset securitisation, interest-rate risk-management products, project finance and equity for power projects. According to Greenwich Associates, Westpac's Chicago branch achieved coverage of 32 per cent of the midwest corporate market and 53 per cent of the national investor-owned electricity utilities market. 'Our aim, which we achieved, was to be among a company's principal banks,' says Bint. 'Many foreign banks simply buy a share in syndicated loans. Westpac was not one of these "stuffees", as they are known.' In the mid-1980s, Westpac was a lead member of a syndicate which provided the $US1 billion financing for an extension to Chicago's vast O'Hare international airport.

The Chicago branch was the most profitable corporate banking branch in Westpac's Americas division and, according to those who followed its fortunes, the business it had with the electricity utilities met so-called hurdle rates of return of any market. Bint says that had Westpac gone ahead with its plan to buy a retail bank in the US, that would have helped the Americas division's returns enormously. 'Retail banking in the US is very profitable and that would have locked in nicely,' he says, adding that Westpac looked at the prospect of buying Michigan National, a bank later bought by another of the major Australian banks, National Australia Bank. 'Westpac needed to buy a bank with retail products and we had plans about how to integrate that,' says Bint. 'But we were a bit slow, perhaps too picky, a bit scared of running a retail operation given that few foreign banks are successful in retail.'

The 84 staff at the Chicago branch were a well-qualified group and half of the management team of eight vice-presidents were women. When visiting the bank's US operations, Westpac directors and executives would include Chicago in their itineraries. Westpac's credit officers visited annually and maintained regular phone contact. One director, Warren Hogan, took such a keen interest in the Chicago branch that he was known as its 'godfather'.

The branch was particularly successful in its business with electricity utilities, a sector where it ranked among the top ten banks in the US, with $US2.73 billion in commitments. It formed Westpac Investment Capital Corporation (WICC) which took equity positions and held 24.7 per cent of the power plant developer Tenaska Power Partners. In 1990 Westpac Chicago was arranger and agent for a $US1 billion bridging loan facility for Kansas City Power & Light Company. The branch was also one of a handful of banks providing project finance to the alternative energy industry, developing resources such as wind power.

Westpac created Barton Capital Corporation in Chicago, a special-purpose securitisation vehicle to buy and finance receivables from Westpac's corporate clients. Barton accumulated $US1 billion in assets by 1992 and, thanks to a rigorous loan-grading system and portfolio monitoring, problem loans represented less than 1.5 per cent of the $8.4 billion commitments. The branch had three debtors in bankruptcy in its history; aggressive workout strategies resulted in a full recovery of principal from one of them, a customer with a $US33 million exposure, and the other two remained the only loans in the branch classified as non-performing.

Having turned down the prospect in the mid-1980s of buying Rainier Bank in Seattle, on the grounds that it was too big a proposition, Westpac was still on the lookout for a US acquisition. At that time, the bank's strategists were hungry for growth in global investment banking, rather than retail, and they snapped to attention when the opportunity arose to buy a US primary dealer in government securities. Primary dealers operated in the largest and most liquid capital market in the world, which also was a dominant influence on eurobonds and other foreign markets. Owning a primary dealer had not been part of the original plan but it was seen as opening the door to worldwide financial activities, including investment banking in the major centres of New York, London, Hong Kong, Singapore and Toyko. Says Adrian Fletcher, then Westpac's head of group planning: 'On face value it offered a profitable and central "inner" position in the largest financial market in the world, a new customer placement franchise in the US, new products for distribution by Westpac's European network and the ability to supply in-house a critical component of the swap product.'

Westpac, particularly Fletcher—who orchestrated much of the bank's drive to establish itself as a force in the new vogue of global investment banking—was apparently influenced at the time by moves at the leading US banking house, J.P. Morgan, which was turning its back on commercial lending where margins were too thin to focus on investment banking. Westpac believed that any company serious about hedging and distributing securities had to be in the US government securities market, and distribution provided access to a range of other customers for an investment banking operation. Fusing the two cultures of investment and commercial banking, however, would not be easy. Bob White did not appear to be daunted, telling *Euromoney* in May 1987: 'I'm not so worried about the challenge of bringing the cultures together as maintaining our place in the world tables, in terms of balance sheet, profits and market capitalisation.'

In July 1986 Westpac struck an agreement to buy New York–based William E. Pollock Government Securities Inc, one of 35 primary dealers in the US and one of five still privately owned. Acquiring Pollock, which had 200 staff and offices in New York and other centres including Chicago, Boston, Atlanta, San Francisco and London, brought Westpac membership of a select club of dealers licensed to participate in US government securities auctions and to market US government paper. Westpac intended that the primary dealer would become the cornerstone of its international treasury operation—which by now had evolved into a full-blown global investment banking strategy.

Walton had come to hear about Pollock through a bank contact. He rang Fletcher, who in the course of one of his regular visits to New York met the Pollock principals. Westpac's head office was involved in strategic discussions about the acquisition, discussing terms and conditions with Pollock executives. In Sydney, enthusiasm grew rapidly among the executive committee, which included Bob White, Stuart Fowler, Warwick Kent and Fletcher. The acquisition was heralded as further evidence that Westpac was forging a real international presence. An agreement was negotiated, and approved by the Westpac board. Geoff Kimpton, Fletcher's right-hand man, flew to the US to run due diligence—analyse and check the business—on Pollock. (Kimpton met his wife Meg through Walton, for whom she had worked at Chase and then at Westpac; Walton was best man at their wedding.) Barbara Filipowski, at the time Westpac's vice-president for legal services in the US, handled the legal aspects of the transaction. Walton became chairman of Westpac Pollock Inc and Owen van der Wall joined the board; former Pollock principals Robert Meyerhoff and Mort Swinsky, no longer shareholders, became joint managing directors, with Meyerhoff also president and Swinsky executive vice-president.

94

Westpac now had a capital markets presence as well as its corporate banking business in the US. Its foothold in the US bond market would be a vital advantage in the embryonic but fast-growing swaps market. Warwick Kent, at the time Westpac's chief general manager, corporate and international, said: 'Buying William E. Pollock isn't just another acquisition; it's going to give Westpac a new dimension. We'll be involved in all of the major US instruments, and other capital market business will flow from that. Also, interest rates on US government securities are a major influence on international rates, and being close to the action will help our management in a number of ways.' Westpac explained the rationale:

> For Westpac, the acquisition of W.E. Pollock represents a major step forward in a carefully planned strategy of global expansion. Already firmly established as the largest financial intermediary in Australia, Westpac has for some time been committed to development as a global banking institution . . . In Westpac's view, participation and expertise in the US government securities market is an essential component of any global capital market strategy . . . As the globalisation of capital markets continues, it may well become impossible to compete seriously in international markets without being a primary dealer in the US government securities market.

The owners of Pollock set a price which was a non-negotiable 2.5 times book value, a level, says Walton, that was at market at the time. The British bank Barclays PLC had also been interested in buying Pollock but was deterred by the price, although Barclays contacted White to suggest a joint venture; White declined, a decision he later said he much regretted. Westpac paid $US115 million ($A180 million) for a company with a net worth of $US47 million, whose assets were essentially the people who ran it. There were ten principals in Pollock, of whom half-a-dozen were key players. Hett says of the terms of the acquisition: 'The principals of Pollock were taken on and paid within the terms of what prevailed in the US market on Wall Street, essentially an annual salary and a market-related bonus, based on performance targets. This was in line with what other government securities dealers were receiving.'

The Australian media greeted the Pollock purchase as a brilliant coup and Westpac's profile in the US soared. Adrian Fletcher, who shortly afterwards became general manager, global capital markets, based in London, emphasised that Pollock—whose turnover ranked it seventh among the US government securities dealers—was a central plank in Westpac's global strategy. During its first year as a bank subsidiary Pollock performed well, conforming to the pattern of government securities dealers making good money at that time, and returning an after-tax profit of $15.2 million. Westpac wrote off $108 million in goodwill on the purchase and also advanced a special loan of $US50 million for ten years at a concessional interest rate to enable Pollock to grow.

However, in 1987 interest rates began to rise, an unwelcome trend for bond traders. And, to the dismay of its architects in Westpac, the vision of a new dimension in global business began to dissolve. Within a year of Westpac's purchase of Pollock the US federal government, in response to pressure from would-be players, suddenly licensed a host of new, and in some cases very large, primary dealers, taking their number to a peak of 46. This slashed the market shares of existing firms. Some of the larger houses were cutting out smaller players in the government securities auctions; all primary dealers found their margins down substantially in their bread-and-butter business of buying and distributing treasury bonds. In October 1987 Walton wrote to Warwick

Kent about the savage deterioration in the US bond market: 'Since January 1987 the bond market turned in a worse performance than for any comparable period in recent history ... industry estimates are that some $US360 billion has been wrung out of the US bond market since 31 December 1986 ...' Westpac Pollock turned in a reduced profit of $5.7 million.

In buying Pollock, Westpac had thought it was acquiring a vehicle which could be expanded into a more general business in the US, originating, trading and distributing paper through its large customer base. The dealing house would be the conduit through which Westpac could place $A bonds and eurobonds. Pollock was never intended to be a stand-alone operation. But, instead of the company being a stepping-stone to wider activities, the business became stuck in its traditional, and shrinking, slot. Says Fletcher: 'In retrospect there were some critical issues which were not understood either by us in Sydney or by our people in the US. These were the impact of a change in the general interest-rate environment, the difficulty of blending a previously owner-managed business into the bank's management culture and the increase in the number of primary dealers which transpired to be just around the corner.'

If the price and salary terms for Pollock principals excited comment in Sydney, even more so did the 'golden handshake' delivered to the ten principals of the firm when, in 1990, conceding that the business had become too great a burden, Westpac liquidated it. In buying the business Westpac had agreed—as a non-negotiable part of the employment element of the purchase—to take over the obligations associated with life insurance policies, owned by the firm, over the principals. The bank retained ownership of the life insurance policies. Westpac's obligation over the course of fifteen years was estimated at $US10 million in pension payments, against a face value of the policies in 1995 of $US14 million.

The decision to liquidate Pollock was made on Walton's recommendation, supported by the management and board of Westpac. An initial attempt to find a buyer was abandoned, after two-and-a-half months and two aborted discussions with potential acquirers. Walton and Hett had the unhappy task of closing down the operation. By that time, Westpac Pollock had notched up two years of losses, $6.2 million in 1989 and $9.1 million in 1990, adding weight to Westpac's mounting problems in Australia. Walton says: 'It takes a lot of stomach if you have big problems in your home base to be concerned about a primary dealer. Frankly I felt that, at that particular time, it no longer met the bank's needs.' Three-and-a-half years on, the reasons that had justified the acquisition of Pollock no longer existed.

After Westpac closed down Pollock, interest rates began to fall and the bond market revived. A core group of 30 Pollock staff joined Fuji Securities; they were reported to have made $US30 million in their first year there and $US45 million in their second. The Pollock episode drew strident criticism, within Westpac and in the wider market, and the blame was often laid at Walton's feet. Hett comments:

> Success has many fathers, but failure is an orphan. Everybody was very willing to thump their chests when the acquisition of Pollock was made but, three years later, when the landscape changed, when the mood in head office was different, when head office's performance was hitting problems, when the whole market changed and the whole push in investment banking was abandoned, suddenly Pollock became something that Walton had initiated in New

York and that was never the case. Westpac Sydney was always closely involved.

Bob White, who had been impressed with the controls in Pollock, was taken aback by the absence of warning about the disastrous increase in the number of primary dealers. 'That expansion came as a complete surprise to me,' he says. 'Especially as we had highly qualified people on the spot to whom it was also a surprise.' Says Fletcher: 'It's easy to say later that those in the US should have known that the primary dealer market was going to expand, but in 1986 the US authorities were extremely protective about the "primary dealer club". And in an almost xenophobic atmosphere, particularly towards the Japanese houses, there seemed to be good reason to assume that increased competition of this sort was several years away. This turned out to be wrong.' Fletcher adds that Westpac's 'lack of understanding of the potential impact of a changed interest-rate environment was less excusable'. He says:

> It was true that when we looked at Pollock's figures they showed consistent increases in profits over the years in which the owner-manager team had been in place, but in hindsight this was not long enough to give a reliable picture of profit predictability, and we should have understood this. And a final point is that senior Westpac management did not understand how to blend an entrepreneurially-run business such as Pollock—or Ord Minnett for that matter—into the bank's culture and management system, or how to change the latter to become more effective in the new investment banking activities. In this they were no different to most other large commercial banks which had taken over dealers, stockbrokers and investment managers. Tony Walton tried very, very hard to

make it work, but the cultural barriers to effective interaction with Pollock and Westpac in Sydney were enormous.

While the Pollock venture had failed, Westpac went on to operate successfully in key world money centres. Its global financial markets group, which came together formally in 1987 under Adrian Fletcher in London, has been an enduring strength for the bank. Walton says: 'The profits generated by these centres were of great benefit to Westpac, especially during its lean years in the early 1990s.'

Westpac made progress in the US in a different direction, in 1989 listing on the New York Stock Exchange. The impetus for this move had stemmed from management in Sydney, with the board somewhat unconvinced that it would bring advantages. Getting listed on the New York exchange was a big event, involving an enormous effort, mostly undertaken by Barbara Filipowski. The NYSE listing was coincidental with a $US130 million American depositary receipt issue, the normal listing method for foreign companies in the US, which was also handled by Filipowski.

Against this background the basic business of the Americas division was, in the words of Walton, 'humming right along, earning $US40 to $US60 million a year'.

We were making money but I would like to have made more money in terms of some of the efficiency ratios, and we were getting to that but at the same time I would never compromise on credit, under any circumstances. That was always our number one thing. Credit is king. I used to drum that home time and time and time again. If in doubt, don't recommend it, because you can't afford to lose any money on bad loans when operating on thin margins. I would not increase the risk profile to improve returns because that is the death-knell for a foreign bank.

By 1989 Westpac in the US, having concentrated on building the business, was entering a second phase in its development entailing a greater focus on returns. Since the introduction of new rules on bank capital by the Bank for International Settlements, the Basel-based central bank for banks, efficient use of capital had superseded the growth targets that had dominated banking strategies earlier in the 1980s. In the three years since 1986 the Americas division had raised pre-tax profit by 473 per cent to $US47 million, an annual compound growth rate of 67.9 per cent; over the same period asset growth had been 39.1 per cent and personnel 22.3 per cent. Walton was aware that growth in the future was unlikely to match that of the 1986–89 period, but during this second phase he aimed to increase pre-tax profit to $US100 million, before provisions, over five years. This ambitious plan would take Westpac into head-to-head competition with major international financial services groups; already, the bank was competing with leading city and regional banks in the US. Other targets in the five-year vision, approved by head office, included building a retail/middle-market presence through an acquisition, doubling corporate 'line bank' relations, improving the quality of earnings, capitalising on the bank's and division's expertise in $A products, reducing dependence on bought money and achieving a return on risk-adjusted assets of 1 per cent. In five to ten years, according to Walton's vision, Westpac would rank among the top ten foreign banks in the US by profitability, market penetration and representation.

Westpac headquarters was once again examining possibilities for acquiring a retail bank in the US and it considered several medium-sized banks in 1989 and 1990, at a time when a US recession and a high level of corporate debt was depressing share prices. The process moved slowly, however, checked by a persistent view among some in management that this was too big a project. In hindsight, Westpac missed out on some bargains. The search for a bank occupied much senior management time in the Americas division. At least five possibilities were examined in considerable detail. Walton says the eventual decision not to pursue buying a bank at that time, given the issues confronting the Westpac group, was correct.

In March 1991 Walton was invited to join the Westpac board and, a few months later, in October, his responsibilities were widened to include Europe as well as the US. The chairman, Sir Eric Neal, was impressed with the way Walton had run the Americas division and Europe needed close attention, having hit problems and made losses on real estate, especially from AGC's portfolio in Westpac General Finance. As chief general manager, Americas and Europe, Walton had reporting to him Tony Aveling, general manager of the European division, the corporate banking Americas division which included Jim Coleman, head of the eastern region, Barry Bint, head of the midwestern region and Sam Mills, head of the western region, Gerhard Tarantik, head of the financial markets group of the Americas division, deputy general manager Gary Hett who looked after audit, financial controls, human resources, legal and strategic planning, and Bruce Daglish, in charge of the division's credit policy and control.

While Walton's elevation to board status and increased territory nettled some in management ranks in Sydney, there was also considerable admiration for his management skills. The Americas division was praised as an efficient, professionally run operation. Peter Davidson, general manager group credit from mid-1987 until he retired from Westpac in 1993, and a regular visitor to the US, says that from his point

102

of view the Americas division was the most professional in Westpac. 'I saw every proposal above $25 million from the Americas division, and the quality of their customers, of the credits, the way the credit portfolio was presented and managed, was first class,' he says, adding that Westpac's Sydney head office adopted the Americas division's model for cashflow projections and analysis.

The year 1990 was a disappointing one for the Americas division, with performance a mere 1 per cent above plan, compared with far more buoyant results in preceding years. Problem loans included those to the retailer Macy's and to the Canadian property developer Olympia & York. Westpac was far from alone in facing these difficulties; the international syndicates lending to these companies included virtually every major bank in the world. Hett says that Macy's was a 'problematic, rather than problem', loan which was classified as a problem because difficulties in Westpac head office's own loans book had caused the bank to become rigidly unforgiving in its approach to borrowers.

> There was an informed view in this market that Macy's was 'money good', that the underlying business, which we knew well, was good. Macy's expanded too quickly, and had taken on too much debt, but they could work through their problems, albeit with some arrangements with banks along the way. But ultimately the principal was money-good. We had other motivations at the time, because the bank had some problems, so we were asked to be far more critical of loans that were problematic than we would normally be. As it turned out, the other banks which stayed with Macy's earned back all of their principal, interest and fees. They received equity for a portion of their principal in the restructuring. Westpac took a provision at the time and then sold

the debt for an amount greater than the provision level. Westpac had advanced $US100 million to Macy's, took a $US30 million provision then sold the loan for $US72 million.

Olympia & York was also experiencing problems in 1991 because of expansion and cashflow difficulties and problems in some subsidiary companies. As with Macy's, the Americas division believed that, over time, the company would recover but the division was obliged to follow Westpac's critical line. 'We provisioned 25 per cent of the $US100 million O&Y loan and sold the remaining debt at the provision level of $US75 million,' says Hett.

With Westpac taking a close look at where immediate returns were being generated, rather than maintaining a long-term view of its overseas operations, the Americas division came increasingly under fire for failing to produce an acceptable return on capital employed. It was deemed a 'value diluter' (in common with the European division and AGC's property activities). Value creators included Westpac's consumer and commercial banking, banking activities in New Zealand, AGC's retail business, and Asia–Pacific and Australian corporate banking. By the early 1990s Westpac was focusing on how to maximise returns, and any area that did not meet 'hurdle rates' was doomed.

A review of global corporate banking operations in 1991 showed Australian assets of $10 billion employing $550 million in capital on which the return was 21 per cent, while the Americas division's $13.6 billion in assets absorbed $597 million in capital which produced a 6 per cent return. Europe returned 8 per cent and New Zealand 19 per cent. Australia had the advantage of being able to spread costs over a bigger market share and broader product range. Higher returns had been the objective of Westpac's aborted plans to acquire a retail bank in the US. Had the Americas division encompassed a retail arm, as well as treasury and corporate lending, then comparison with Westpac's operations overall in Australia could have been more realistic. Part of Westpac's global corporate plan in 1991 was to reprice assets in the US or reduce them by $2 billion, and to shed some 100 staff; a similar plan was mooted for the UK operation. In 1991 and early 1992, the measure commonly used shifted from return on equity (ROE) to return on economic equity (ROEE), a more sophisticated measure which takes account of the riskiness of assets. The target for the Americas division was 14.6 per cent. In September 1992 it was making 10.6 per cent, according to Walton, who says he had put in place in June 1992 a program to increase ROEE to the required target within two years. A memo to the Americas division officers from Hett in June 1992 stated: 'Given the results announced by Westpac mid-year [a loss of $1.6 billion and major write-offs] the Americas financial objective has become an absolute.'

Profitability and efficiency goals could be achieved by increasing fees, or cutting staff or cutting assets. The decision was to do all three, by restructuring the western region, reducing premises costs and corporate centre expenses and divesting or reducing low-revenue business. The activities were to be redirected towards fee income instead of lending.

But Westpac was facing a US market that had matured considerably since 1983. Walton told the magazine *BRW* in April 1993: 'You can develop fee-based products till the cows come home but it's mighty hard to cover the gap when you're running a wholesale operation.' In the early 1990s, when the Americas division was trying to raise its returns, the entire foreign banking marketplace in the US was in upheaval. The Bank of Ireland announced a $120 million pre-tax loss. Barclays Bank, a powerhouse foreign bank in the US, lost $380 million through bad loans in 1991, the year that Westpac in the US made $US43 million. Paribas lost millions. ANZ and NAB, though with smaller operations than Westpac, were not having a good year either. Says Hett: 'Westpac was trying to lift its returns when other foreign banks, which had been in the US for twenty and thirty and forty years, were drowning in red ink.' In the six months to 31 March 1992 the Americas division recorded a loss of $43.1 million and had gross non-accrual loans of $US300 million (chiefly Macy's and O&Y), with a $US90 million ($A110 million) provision.

'One has to make adjustments along the way,' says Walton. 'But the issue that we insisted on is never compromise on credit policy, or price. Now that made it difficult. There were easily five or six Japanese banks ahead of Westpac which were there because they were buying market share.' In the previous two years, in terms of profitability and returns, Westpac would have ranked in the top ten foreign banks. Says Hett: 'Westpac made money and had upper-end returns in the marketplace.' Though buoyant for most of its existence, the Americas division never satisfied its critics in head office in Sydney, a factor that weighed against it when, in 1992, Westpac's problems in Australia narrowed the bank's focus to one objective: survival.

CHAPTER FIVE

ANOTHER SUBSIDIARY, ANOTHER PROBLEM: PARTNERSHIP PACIFIC LIMITED

Partnership Pacific Limited, a frisky Westpac offspring that grew into a troublesome delinquent, was reportedly conceived in a bar at the Shoreham Hotel in Washington DC in the late 1960s during a conversation between the then head of the Wales and a senior vice-president of the Bank of America. The two were in the American capital for the annual conference of the International Monetary Fund and the World Bank, an elaborate talkfest never missed by any banker keen to be seen on the world stage. Consortium merchant banks were all the rage, and the bankers liked the idea of being part of a powerful entity, the growing Pacific Rim economic region.

If banks represented solid strength, merchant banks were supposed to reflect flair. Australian merchant banks did not closely follow the traditions of their UK antecedents, which did not lend funds but drew on their agile intellect to structure financial deals for clients using someone else's money. Rather, Australian merchant banks engaged in a considerable amount of lending, chiefly because they could fill the gap in that market left by the more constrained banks. As the shackles came off the banks in the 1980s, the merchant banks, later known in Australia by the American term investment banks, had to find alternative sources of revenue, such as fee-generating advisory work.

The Australian economy had maintained robust growth during the 1960s which attracted a number of foreign players interested in sharing in its development, particularly in the resource sector. Foreign banks could not set up banking operations in Australia so, as a second-best option, they established merchant banking subsidiaries, often in association with an Australian bank. In 1969 Bank of America and Bank of Tokyo secured a toehold in merchant banking when, with the Wales, they established Partnership Pacific Ltd, with each bank owning one-third.

PPL was incorporated on 25 February 1969 and in its first annual report, covering the sixteen months from the date of incorporation to 30 June 1970, it announced a consolidated profit of $A82,695. Its chief purpose was to provide financial assistance to develop natural resources and industrial projects in Australia, New Zealand, Papua New Guinea, Fiji and adjacent territories. It participated in two large development projects, Bougainville Copper and Robe River iron ore. During its first year, in September 1969, it established a financial subsidiary, PPBNV, incorporated in Curacao, Netherlands Antilles, as a vehicle to fund overseas loan requirements. And in May 1970 PPL Investments Pty Ltd was formed in Australia to make equity investments.

'Experience indicates that, in its present area of operation, there is vast scope for PPL in the field of natural resources and associated development,' said Sir Robert Norman, chief general manager of the Wales and deputy chairman of PPL. Rudolph Peterson, chairman of the executive committee of the Bank of America, was chairman. Sumio Hara, president of the Bank of Tokyo, was a director, as was A.W. Clausen, president of the Bank of America. General manager was the Wales's C.W.L. (Bill) de Boos, who said in 1971: 'We are not just lenders, we like to get a piece of the action on the basis that if our judgment is right, then the return to us is substantially greater.' It was a policy that was to bring problems later in the 1970s.

In 1971, when Sir Robert Norman replaced Peterson as PPL's chairman, some 50 per cent of the company's loans and equity support was directed to the mining sector. Directors commented: 'Consortium financial institutions in Australia with overseas connections are playing a vital role in linking local and international capital markets, and now arrange a significant portion of the overseas loans introduced to this part of the world. Few local companies have the ability to approach the eurodollar markets in their own name. However, by utilising organisations such as Partnership Pacific, they are able to tap this source of funds.' The concentration of consortium financial intermediaries in Australia was said to be second only to that in London and this, coupled with the influx of merchant banks into the region, made for keen competition.

PPL's 1973 annual report emphasised its role in property. By 1974, when Australia was undergoing tough economic conditions, with soaring inflation and interest rates, PPL's exposure to property rose to 22 per cent of total loans while mining dropped back to 16 per cent and corporate finance rose to 28 per cent. In the following year, when inflation had moderated to 14 per cent and interest rates were also lower, its prime activities included accepting short and medium-term deposits, providing bill of exchange facilities and lending to short, medium and long-term Australian borrowers, domestically or overseas, arranging and participating in syndicated loans funded in domestic or foreign currency and providing corporate advice. In that year, 1974, PPL made a loss of $8.5 million, after substantial write-downs of problem loans, nearly wiping out its paid-up capital. The partners had to inject new funds and the merchant bank returned to modest profits. The funds took the form of concessional-rate deposits from the Bank of New South Wales. However, prevailing exchange controls prohibited the other partners from easily lending $A to PPL so they injected money by way of transferring to PPL the income from high-yielding Latin-American loans which they were funding. The loans returned to haunt Westpac in 1987 when the bank had to make provisions of $75 million against its Latin-American debt, of which close to $20 million was attributable to PPL. Bob White, in 1974 recently returned to Sydney from London to be general manager of the bank, had to oversee PPL's first crisis, an experience that left him with a jaundiced view of the merchant banking subsidiary. In his view, its best contribution to the group was as a convenient conduit for short-term deposits which, until 1984, were not available to banks and, even after that, until the late 1980s, were subject to regulatory costs not imposed on merchant banks.

In 1980 Bank of America began streamlining its Australian operations, disposing of minority positions to focus on its own merchant bank, BA Australia Ltd. It sold out of PPL and the merchant bank became 50/50 owned by the Bank of New South Wales and Bank of Tokyo. Within a couple of years Bank of Tokyo was also forming its own merchant bank, BOT Australia Ltd, and it sold down its stake in PPL, enabling Westpac to move to 60 per cent ownership of the merchant bank which, in 1982, turned in record profits of $7.7 million. In the early 1980s Westpac had smaller shareholdings in other merchant banks: it had a 10 per cent stake in Schroder Darling & Co Ltd (later Schroders Australia Ltd) and an 11.3 per cent share in Australian United Corporation (forerunner of J.P. Morgan Australia Ltd). When the then Bank of New South Wales merged with the Commercial Bank of Australia to form Westpac, it gained interests in other non-bank subsidiaries. In 1984, after rules on bank ownership of merchant bank subsidiaries were relaxed, Westpac took 100 per cent control of PPL, buying out Bank of Tokyo for $25 million, and its minority share-holdings in other merchant banks were progressively unwound. PPL had its own board, composed of Westpac executives with no external directors. Although not required to do so, PPL for several years published its own annual reports which in some instances were lavish marketing documents.

In an attempt to bring together the disparate merchant banking arms of the Westpac empire, in May 1983 Bob White recruited an outsider, Rob Douglass, a vice-president of Bankers Trust in London, as general manager, merchant banking. Westpac's strategy was to establish a new merchant banking division based on the now wholly owned Partnership Pacific Ltd and embracing the various merchant banking arms of the group. It would provide capital markets products and services. Westpac could have simply subsumed PPL's activities and conducted them directly but the view was that it was better to acknowledge and keep separate the different cultures of merchant banking and bureaucratic retail operations. And PPL was a useful borrowing arm for Westpac. Further, merchant banking demanded highly paid entrepreneurial talent, so it was more convenient to have a separate subsidiary which was not constrained by the inflexible salary structure of a bank. Time was to show that a missing ingredient was strong control from the parent bank and a degree of corporate governance that would become *de rigueur* in the 1990s.

Rob Douglass, Australian, a graduate in law, had worked with Bankers Trust for twelve years, in Tokyo and then in London. He was attracted by White's vision for Westpac, and his own views of where merchant banking was headed seemed to capture the interest of White and his deputy, Ian Matheson. Westpac also wanted to breathe new life into PPL. As a consortium lending merchant bank it faced a limited life, given that banks were now freer to lend. Rather, PPL's future lay in developing merchant banking skills involving capital markets and fee-based activities. Westpac did not have in-house expertise to take it down that path.

Douglass was one of the early 'lateral recruits'—Westpac's quaint term for outsiders hired to senior levels in the bank. He became a member of the coveted inner circle at Westpac, the executive committee, reporting to Bob White. His immediate appointment to the executive committee ruffled a few senior feathers. At Bankers Trust, he was familiar with a forum where ideas were aired and discussed; at Westpac, he struck a less flexible organisation in which the old and the new did not always sit well together. The diehards disliked the newcomers, usually university-educated and with outside experience, whom they regarded as having been brought in to teach the older hands 'how to walk on water'. The 'lateral recruits' assumed that part of their brief was to shake up the organisation, and inevitably trod on toes in the process. In merchant banking, the intention was to have Douglass overseeing a stable comprising PPL, BAC and the New Zealand operation, all under the Westpac umbrella. Integration of the merchant banking activities was not plain sailing—rivalries persisted among the various entities in the group, boiling over when, in 1985, AGC's Bill Acceptance Corporation lost its corporate advisory team to Partnership Pacific.

An early problem confronting Rob Douglass emerged in New Zealand where Westpac had acquired the merchant bank CBA Finance through the merger with the Commercial Bank of Australia. CBA Finance owed its origins to Transvision Holdings Ltd, a television rental company which ran a small finance subsidiary. The CBA had been persuaded to buy into the company with the view of turning it into its finance company and merchant bank in New Zealand. New Zealand entrepreneur Allan Hawkins was in control of Transvision in 1978 and worked with CBA executive Tim Marcus Clark on CBA's purchase of its interest. Marcus Clark became chairman of the renamed CBA Finance, with Hawkins as chief executive.

When CBA Finance became part of the Westpac group, relations between Hawkins and Westpac executives did not mirror the harmony he had developed with Marcus Clark. Hawkins did not get along with Westpac's general manager in New Zealand, Geoff Thompson, whom Hawkins in his book *The Hawk* referred to as a 'doomcaster ... [who] believed in the inevitability of a New Zealand-wide Australia-wide or world-wide economic recession ...'. Thompson had been appointed to run Westpac's operations in New Zealand after successfully helping orchestrate the bank merger in 1982, and he was intent on keeping Westpac away from anything that smacked of risky lending. CBA Finance and Hawkins had a high and popular profile in their own market but Thompson took the view that their business style was too flamboyant to sit easily in the Westpac group. Rob Douglass, installed by Westpac as chairman of CBA Finance to replace Marcus Clark, also found Hawkins difficult to deal with. Westpac's unease about its new infant was so pronounced that the bank was unwilling to grace it with the Westpac identity; it remained CBA Finance while fruitless discussions continued about a new name. The friction between Hawkins and Westpac was insurmountable. Early in 1984 Hawkins was dismissed and Westpac bought his 15 per cent share of the merchant bank. Hawkins did not go quietly. In June of that year he floated his own company, Equiticorp Holdings Ltd, with Marcus Clark as chairman and 21 of his former CBA Finance staff on the payroll. The mass defection of these employees was a blow to Westpac and restoring the strength of its subsidiary took many months. It also resulted in acrimonious litigation, with Westpac suing Hawkins for alleged breach of contract and breach of fiduciary duty and Equiticorp suing Westpac for alleged interference with its business. After escalating claims and counterclaims, the parties reached a confidential settlement in 1987.

Without a chief executive and with the loss of key staff, CBA Finance was reeling. Douglass flew to New Zealand to determine how to resurrect the Westpac subsidiary. Brian Eggert, at that time heading BAC's money-market division, was sent to hold the fort until a new chief could be found for the merchant bank, which was operating with skeleton staff. Geoff Luck, a partner of the headhunters Spencer Stuart, who had brought Douglass to Westpac and found Philip Deer for the bank's Hong Kong operations, had the task of unearthing the right candidate. According to Luck it was not an easy assignment. The atmosphere in New Zealand was very much in favour of its local hero, Allan Hawkins, and unsympathetic to a big bank from across the Tasman. Luck came up with George Stoopin, a candidate with suitable merchant banking credentials—a former general manager of South Pacific Merchant Finance Ltd—who rebuilt the business as Westpac Merchant Finance. The new name signalled the parent's satisfaction that the subsidiary was now respectable, as well as reflecting its new direction, with less emphasis on hire purchase and an increased focus on treasury activities, corporate finance and advisory and commercial property finance. There was some irony in Westpac's discovery that the name Westpac Merchant Finance had already been registered, without the bank's knowledge, by Allan Hawkins.

In Australia, PPL's activities included lending and treasury, which encompassed domestic money-market trading and a currency hedging operation. Peter Purtell, with a strong background in foreign exchange, had been recruited from the

Commonwealth Bank in 1980 to a newly created position of chief general manager, international, to strengthen PPL's presence in this area and lift its profile in the currency hedge market.

PPL, through its Netherlands Antilles subsidiary PPBNV, had a longstanding group of clients in Australia who borrowed in foreign currencies. PPL had developed a practice of providing advice to those clients, especially after the currency hedging operation had expanded under Purtell, on which currencies to borrow, whether the borrowing should be single or multi-currency and, depending on the view of interest rates, whether the term should be for three or six months.

In December 1983, the float of the Australian dollar and removal of exchange controls exposed the Australian economy and financial markets to the full force of international competition. The removal of exchange controls freed access to offshore funds and products such as foreign-currency loans. These offered apparently cheaper sources of funds, enabling the launch of many projects that would not have got off the ground had Australian-dollar funding costs applied. 'Retail' lending in foreign currencies was a fairly new area for banks, widely regarded as potentially highly lucrative and, in many quarters, highly dangerous. To borrowers, it was extremely attractive: a chance to secure funds at a cost of, say, between 5 and 7 per cent compared with Australian rates of double that level or more.

Even before the $A was floated and exchange controls abandoned, competition for experienced staff in Australia's foreign exchange markets was fierce. In 1981, within a year of his arrival at PPL, Peter Purtell was poached by the Australian Bank Limited, Australia's first new bank in more than 40 years, to establish its foreign-exchange operations. In September of that year Louise Jackson was appointed assistant manager, international, at PPL. Jackson's background was in the international division of the Commonwealth Bank, where she had specialised in country risk and global limits systems for banks. PPBNV, PPL's Caribbean subsidiary, had a portfolio of high-risk loans to countries in central America which were performing dismally, and Jackson's experience with country limits was seen as very valuable.

The float of the $A brought greater volatility in currency movements, including the big risk that a movement in relative currency values could wipe out the interest-rate gain of a foreign-currency loan. Australians had to come to grips with the risks of foreign-exchange trading which were not widely understood for the simple reason that experience was thin. Few thought a drop in the value of the $A against low-interest-rate, strong currencies such as the Swiss franc could be of such dimensions as to completely eradicate a 10 per cent interest rate differential. But it did, and more.

In 1984 Jackson was nominated by PPL's managing director, Reg Humphrys—seconded from Westpac to run the merchant bank and familiar with her work—to set up and manage a proposed new foreign-exchange department. Following the lifting of Australia's exchange controls, PPL, in common with some 40 other non-bank financial institutions, had applied for and been granted an authority from the Reserve Bank to deal in foreign exchange. Jackson at that stage did not have experience of managing a foreign-exchange department, but in 1984 few in Australia did. However, she had worked in international banking for eight years, and was skilled in using international capital markets, monitoring limit controls on foreign-exchange dealers and providing advice to foreign-currency borrowers. And she had worked with programmers to design computer systems to improve banks' management information on international credit risks.

Now manager, international money markets, Jackson hired David Green as chief dealer and Peter Mihajlovic as senior dealer. Green, an Australian who had worked in the London foreign-exchange markets for many years, and Mihajlovic, who had several years' experience in the Australian markets, appealed because they brought a level of technical experience that was generally lacking in the markets at that time. The three made an effective team and by mid-1985 felt confident that they were operating a successful foreign-exchange department.

In October 1984 Rob Douglass became managing director of PPL, as well as general manager of Westpac's merchant banking. PPL was then Australia's largest merchant bank, and Douglass was responsible for its seven divisions: treasury, lending, credit control, project finance, capital markets, corporate advisory and leasing, and administration. The divisions reported to Humphrys, who remained as general manager of PPL's day-to-day operations until he retired in 1985. Towards the end of 1984 Douglass recruited another new executive, Brian Eggert, who joined as head of PPL's treasury from BAC's treasury after his period as caretaker of the New Zealand merchant bank. Westpac's policy of placing new blood side-by-side with older hands often had the effect of squeezing out the more traditional thinker. Shortly after Eggert arrived, PPL's money-market manager John Saunders, who had been with the merchant bank for ten years, left to join a competitor, PNC International Financial Services Ltd. The considerable harmony and good working relationships that had existed among Humphrys, Saunders and Jackson were not replicated in the new team. As 1985 progressed, Eggert and Jackson began to clash over most issues. The open personal dislike and distrust of her ability that Eggert displayed towards Jackson were in contrast to the generally high regard in which she was held. In return, Jackson made no secret of her low opinion of her new boss's approach to and grasp of the business. Disharmony extended beyond personal conflict, with enormous tension between the treasury under Eggert and the lending division under Tony Snape over the allocation of the cost of funds.

After Jackson's arrival, PPL's specialist service for PPBNV clients developed into the concept of borrowing in a basket of currencies, generally less risky than borrowing in one currency but still carrying a currency risk which was explained to clients. PPL's 1984 annual report described the services it offered in offshore borrowing, arranging borrowings in a single currency or in a basket:

> Borrowing uncovered in a single currency involves a considerable degree of risk. Borrowing in a basket of currencies tends to reduce the exchange risk while retaining some of the interest rate advantages of certain foreign currencies. Partnership Pacific's basket loans are structured to meet the individual requirements of borrowers, taking into account each borrower's attitude to foreign exchange risk and interest costs. Daily monitoring of the loans is also undertaken with borrowers being alerted to any significant beneficial or detrimental exchange rate/interest rate movements.

The report cited an example of successful offshore borrowing: a client borrowed substantially in Swiss francs, at an exchange rate of 1.97 Swiss francs to the $A. The exchange rate moved in the client's favour, to 2.12 Swiss francs. 'The effect of this movement was that the client was actually borrowing at a negative interest rate,' the report stated.

Early in 1985, Mihajlovic had taken the view that the $A was growing weak and Jackson's team advised PPL marketing officers and interstate staff to alert their clients to the need to hedge their exposures against a fall in the value of the local currency. Some marketing officers took the advice and some did not. After the $A had plunged against the $US, the Swiss franc and the yen, those clients who had not hedged were facing losses. Jackson's team began to suggest strategies to extricate these borrowers as far as possible and many were happy to listen to any advice offered.

At that stage PPL had no formal risk-management product and no discretionary powers over clients' accounts, and had to wait for clients' instructions before carrying out any dealing on their behalf. The strategy that Jackson's team suggested was that clients should hedge their exact exposures, including interest payments, to the next rollover date but should unwind the hedge cover for short periods if it seemed possible to take advantage of short-term favourable swings in exchange rates. Deals were not pooled and, mindful of the volume of paperwork necessitated by this personal service, trading volumes were carefully managed to avoid undue pressure on settlements staff and systems. Clients, who were typically property developers, were generally hedged except for short periods. PPL took a spread between buying and selling currencies—the foreign-exchange trader's 'fee' on a deal. Like the mark-up between retail and wholesale in any commodity, be that wine, clothes or money, the spread can be at a normal commercial rate or it can be set at a level that squeezes extra profits out of the customer. PPL's clients were happy to deal with it because they got a better rate than was available from banks, given the amounts in which they traded.

The strategy was successful and word spread. Based on demand from clients who were already in deep trouble following the drop in the value of the $A which began late in 1984 and broke into a gallop early in 1985, PPL decided in mid-1985 to formalise the foreign-currency risk-management service, something that was offered by only a handful of financial institutions. PPL's approach was to charge clients a flat $10,000 fee, with marketing officers exercising their discretion to increase the fee for larger exposures. Clients who accepted this service had their positions managed, and were freed from having to follow markets themselves.

Rob Douglass did not like the risk-management product and is believed to have said so in a memo in mid-1985 to Brian Eggert, asserting that it was being introduced against his, Douglass's, wishes. The product went ahead. Clients agreeing to take the risk-management service were required to sign a power-of-attorney document which gave PPL authority to manage their foreign-exchange dealings on their behalf. The document was drawn up by the law firm Allen Allen & Hemsley.

By the second half of 1985 many of the foreign-currency borrowers were already in dire trouble, with effective borrowing costs of more than 40 per cent a year because of the drop in the value of the $A. The objective of PPL's risk-management service was to wind that cost back to a less punishing level. With the new power-of-attorney system in place, PPL did not have to contact clients using the service to get their instructions before dealing, a considerable advantage in a fast-moving market when a client might be out of reach and so miss opportunities. The PPL team under Jackson's management, with the technical approach developed largely by Mihajlovic and the timing of the dealing decided by Green, felt they had developed a successful niche with benefits for their clients. Jackson undertook a series of internal seminars to explain to staff and clients the operation of foreign exchange and its associated risks. Some clients were apprehensive about the workings of the product; how could they be sure that PPL's traders were working for their customers' benefit and not the merchant bank's? They were given reassurance that, in the case of a dispute, they could have access to PPL's daily returns to the Reserve Bank.

PPL's new foreign-currency risk-management product was trading well, suggesting that borrowers were satisfed. Clients were informed each month of how they were faring, with their performance compared with borrowing costs had they borrowed in $A, or had they not agreed to have the foreign-currency positions managed. The January 1986 monthly accounts for PPL showed that the foreign-exchange department had generated trading profits of $1,213,000 in the first four months of 1985/86 and $116,000 in advisory fees, against a combined budget target of $440,000. The results were more than satisfactory in Jackson's view but, according to her, she and Green came under pressure to increase the profits. She felt insufficient facilities were in place to handle an increase in business.

When Jackson returned from a week's leave on 10 February 1986, she was immediately called to Eggert's office. The company secretary, Russell Hooper, was also present. Jackson says she was told she was being dismissed. It was a bolt from the blue. She asked for a reason but was told that was not required; when she insisted, she was told it was because of her management style. Jackson was given a choice: either resign or be sacked. She chose not to resign. She returned to her office where Green was waiting to discuss his own decision to quit, which he had reached while Jackson was on leave. Green, uncomfortable with senior management at PPL, had considered resigning several times; with Jackson gone, there was no ally between him and a management with which he could not agree, and that clinched his decision. He tendered his resignation that day and left the company, even though he had no alternative job lined up. Morale among some staff took a battering as news went round the company of Jackson's fate, partly because an executive widely respected as competent—although some said headstrong—had been shown the door and partly because the foreign-exchange department was seen as one of PPL's chief strengths. Jackson packed up and left the building. The company had lost two key people in one day.

On the following day, Jackson's secretary was dismissed, which eliminated a third person with knowledge of the department's administration. Those remaining with a grasp of the risk-management system were Mihajlovic and the settlements manager, Julie Cleary. Jackson was replaced by Andy Fedas, an American who had recently been recruited to PPL from Saudi Arabia, and who had international but not Australian experience. Another dealer, Haniff Abu Bakar, was an enthusiastic interbank foreign-exchange trader but he had no knowledge of, or involvement with, client management service. Arguably, the Reserve Bank, which authorised foreign-exchange traders, should have taken a keener interest in staff movements among those whom it licensed to trade because having adequate experienced staff was a condition of a foreign-exchange licence.

Jackson's departure coincided with a planned shift to a new mainframe computer system on which she had been collaborating with a software design company. Since the system was still in a trial stage, no-one else in PPL was familiar with it. The system was to replace an earlier procedure where the managed clients' information was processed on a spreadsheet but that was inadequate for the increasing volume of business. At the time of Jackson's dismissal, PPL had started to promote its management service to Westpac for the bank's foreign-currency borrowers, which at that stage totalled close to 900. The new computer system would have better handled the increased volume but, at the time Jackson left, it had not been determined how this would be done. Nor had the problem of credit risk been addressed: how PPL should handle foreign-exchange exposures of Westpac clients when Westpac held the clients' securities.

Flying blind

The operation of PPL's foreign-exchange department changed radically after Jackson's departure. The foreign-exchange risk-management service offered by Westpac through PPL was, in her view, misrepresented, with the service being vigorously marketed when neither staff nor systems were adequate to handle it. As he left, David Green had predicted that, with Jackson and himself gone, PPL would not have the capacity to handle the product. A few weeks later he emphasised his concerns in writing to PPL general manager Graeme McPherson, pointing out that if Mihajlovic left, there would be almost no-one in the company familiar with the product. Green felt that McPherson seemed to share his concerns. Mihajlovic left on 1 April. On 4 April Jackson wrote to Douglass, pointing out that he would have to accept personal responsibility for the consequences of his decision to back Eggert (over her departure). While Douglass acknowledged in a letter dated 10 April that she had written in the best interests of PPL, he confirmed his decision to support Eggert and accept the consequences.

PPL continued to offer the foreign-currency risk-management product, despite having lost the staff who had devised it, and with a shortage of experienced staff to run it, and despite the existence of a cancellation clause in the power-of-attorney document under which PPL or the client could give seven days' notice to terminate the management agreement. Moreover, twenty-two borrowers were transferred from Westpac to PPL, to take advantage of the merchant bank's management service. That took PPL's total of managed loans to more than 50. The consequences for borrowers were disastrous, because the $A plunged between April and July 1986. A deterioration in Australia's terms of trade (exports had fallen and the lower currency was forcing up the price of imports, widening the gap) was compounded by what became known as the then treasurer's 'banana republic' statement in which, on radio, Paul Keating outlined the doleful state of the world commodities market, vital to Australia's economic wellbeing, and forecast that if Australia did not adjust, its economy would deteriorate to the level of

123

a third-world country. Keating's words made headlines and the $A immediately dropped four cents against the $US and continued to decline against the Swiss franc and the yen. It was a body-blow for all banks, including Westpac, involved in foreign currencies.

Jackson was immediately offered a job by her former boss, John Saunders, with PNC International Financial Services Ltd. David Green and Peter Mihajlovic later joined her. It was evident from the records of one client who subsequently followed the team to PNC from PPL that his foreign-currency position had been left unattended for some time.

As 1986 progressed, several managed clients were becoming dissatisfied with their service from PPL. A managed borrower, Charles Spice, who had been happy with the service he was receiving from Jackson and Green, had become increasingly agitated as his position had deteriorated after their departure. He was one of several who began writing critical letters to the merchant bank. By Christmas 1986 Spice was thoroughly unsettled, and anxious to find out how profits had been turned to losses. PPL, it seemed, could not provide him with a satisfactory explanation.

The volatility of the $A during the year had intensified clients' concerns about their positions. Many had exercised the mutual seven-day termination clause under the power-of-attorney and ended the management contract with PPL. Closing out their positions often crystallised losses and, except in cases where the borrowers were skilled in foreign exchange or had sources of good advice, often resulted in their being unhedged at inopportune times and then again seeking cover. Unless they chose the right moment, that could result in further losses. Most clients found the monthly reports inadequate and many were demanding a daily update of their position. Internally, criticisms flew as complaints prompted a rush of defensive responses. In June 1986 PPL's

WA manager wrote a memo to senior PPL management highly critical of the way borrowers were being managed; this was followed by an equally censorious memo from the Sydney primary marketing officers to Graeme McPherson, to whom Eggert reported. Early in July 1986 McPherson sent Eggert a memo critical, among other things, of Eggert's handling of the managed borrowings. Eggert responded by dealing with each issue in a way that, he felt, resolved the concerns. At a mid-year management planning conference Eggert, whose unease over the risk-management product had increased over the year, was adamant that PPL should discontinue the product because it was becoming too difficult to manage. Reflecting growing tension between the lending side of PPL, headed by Tony Snape, and Eggert's treasury, he was fiercely opposed by lending and marketing officers who claimed that their clients liked the product. The opinion of Stan Davis, Westpac's global treasury head and a member of the PPL board, was sought. His view was that, given PPL's small market share and provided staff had the skills, the risk-management product had a role, because sensible foreign-exchange action could minimise a borrower's exposure. However, the remainder of 1986 was characterised by continuing client losses and dissatisfaction and a serious lack of effective communication among the various hostile factions in PPL.

By the end of the year, PPL treasury clearly felt that the risk-management product it had been saddled with was an administrative nightmare. Much of the problem stemmed from the growing number of transactions and the inadequacy of administrative resources to cope with them. Pooling transactions seemed a logical solution from an administrative point of view because it helped reduce the volume of paperwork but, when the clients subsequently learned of this, it raised doubts in their minds about the fair allocation of transactions not just among clients but between clients and PPL's

125

house account. Despite the problems, the marketing officers continued their vigorous opposition to the proposal to abandon the risk-management product, claiming this would do nothing to appease dissatisfied customers.

In 1985, when the service was introduced, PPL's board had included Ian Matheson, deputy managing director of Westpac, as chairman, Stuart Fowler, Westpac's head of corporate and international, as deputy, Frank Conroy, Rob Douglass, Frank Ward, Westpac's general manager, credit, and Reg Humphrys, with Bob White as an alternate. Within a year Matheson had retired and, following a job swap imposed on Fowler and Warwick Kent early in 1986, Fowler replaced Kent as head of retail, and moved off the PPL board, while Kent took his role as head of corporate and international.

A different view of the world

126

Late in 1986 Westpac's executive committee (at the instigation of Kent who, on Matheson's retirement, became chairman of PPL) called in a UK firm, LEK Management Consultants, to help decide the future of the bank's international capital markets strategy. Westpac, in common with other large banks, was confronting a dilemma: how far and how much to commit to investment banking—should it spend time and energy trying to take on the giants such as Nomura and Goldman Sachs? Kent, with a background in traditional retail banking, had found himself presiding over a large and disparate portfolio of activities: Westpac's capital markets activities in New Zealand, the US, Europe and Asia as well as its aggressively independent merchant bank, PPL, and Westpac's own financial markets division, also vigorously independent. Struggling to come to grips with this widespread empire which, under Stuart Fowler, had been billed as the area that would launch Westpac as a world bank, Kent turned to outsiders for some direction.

LEK was given three months to report. In December 1986 it made its first presentation to the Westpac board. Kent attended the meeting. LEK's conclusion was that Westpac was simply not large enough to be an effective competitor in the full range of international capital markets. The bank would have to rethink its strategy. This advice came at a time when the bank had just acquired Pollock, the US primary dealer, which was to be an integral part of the global investment banking strategy. In the UK, it had extended its bullion dealing with the acquisition of Johnson Matthey Bankers and its Asian operations were ticking over comfortably. The New Zealand problem had been attended to. The diverse Westpac board, never known to be overly communicative, was moved to learn more. Many queries came from Warren Hogan, who had joined the board in August 1986 and who began, as he was to continue, asking questions.

It was a shock to the board and management to be told that the global capital markets strategy did not make sense. LEK met some resistance from the architects of the strategy, Adrian Fletcher and Geoff Kimpton, who lobbied to have parts of it left intact, particularly the centralisation of capital markets in London. The board agreed not to dump the entire strategy; London remained on the agenda. Kent was apparently unimpressed with the business philosophy of the Americas division and its focus on good corporate loans at fine margins but Walton was regarded as competent, hard-working, aggressive and articulate, if perhaps generously remunerated, and he had not made a major error. The Americas division was left alone. In Australia, Douglass was enthusiastically doing what he thought he had been recruited to do and was busily fostering a high profile for Westpac's merchant banking thrust. He had big plans for PPL and in June 1986 brought in a new recruit, Paul McCullagh, from New York, to head a proposed new originations department.

This proposal never came to fruition and McCullagh left early in 1987.

Kent was having difficulties getting a clear picture of what was going on in PPL, a common problem for Westpac executives who, when asking questions, felt they were brushed off as 'yesterday's men' by the new breed of merchant bankers. Kent felt uncomfortable that he could not claim categorically to know every movement and deal in PPL's treasury and was left with the unnerving sensation that an area under his command was veering out of control. He was not prepared to continue with a unit about which he was not wholly comfortable and this, coupled with LEK's advice, gave weight to the case for integrating PPL with the bank by merging the two treasuries. LEK's view was that PPL did not offer anything additional and, if the merchant bank had problems, it was better to handle those within Westpac. Douglass, having been brought in by Bob White to integrate Westpac's merchant banking and capital markets activities— no easy task given the turf-wars, power plays and ego struggles within the Westpac group—seemed to his peers to believe himself in a strong position, with a hotline to the Westpac managing director. But, to some, it was becoming obvious that White had cut the cord. The LEK conclusions were the writing on the wall for Douglass.

Kent, with White in the background, broke the news to Douglass just before Christmas 1986: he was out. Philip Deer, general manager, corporate banking, and a director of PPL since early that year, became head of the merchant bank, with the task of steering it through an enduring identity crisis and the challenge of reconstructing a viable investment banking business in an entity whose treasury was about to be merged with its parent's. Deer's vision had none of the grandeur of Douglass's but he saw possibilities for exploiting synergies between Westpac's corporate and merchant banking activities; having the two under one guiding hand could foster beneficial interdependence, he said at the time. However, the cultural and salary-package differences between the bank and the merchant bank were always an obstacle.

A mismatch of expectations had developed from the outset between Douglass and Westpac. Geoff Luck believes that Douglass thought he had a stronger mandate than he did. Douglass had been led to expect that he would join the boards of Westpac Asia and of AGC. Neither appointment eventuated. Energetic, enthusiastic and flamboyant, Douglass came across to the Westpac lifers as overly self-confident. 'Rob did some good deals at PPL,' says Luck. 'A difficulty was that he could not get PPL into the shape that he wanted, or get the calibre of people he wanted. Time got lost.' Under Douglass's stewardship PPL managed Australia's first public float of an advertising agency when it advised on and underwrote the Monahan Dayman Adams (MDA) launch as a public company in 1984. In that year the merchant bank also helped in financing the successful musical hit *Cats*. Probably the best example of PPL's skills in structured and long-term project finance was its role in the $500 million funding package for the Sydney Harbour tunnel.

Over Christmas 1986, those in charge had to work out how to implement the integration of Westpac and PPL treasuries in the face of considerable hostility and resentment in the various divisions of PPL. A steering committee comprising Fletcher, Kent and Deer was formed for the task. Not least, the board had to be pacified about the scrapping of what had earlier been sold to them as a winning strategy. And Kent, overseeing the dismembering of a dream, was straining to hold together his empire—trying to subdue bubbling dissatisfaction in the stockbroking subsidiary Ord Minnett where the partners felt little synergy with Westpac, and calming uncertainty about an investment banking centre in London—while coping with mutiny in PPL. With anxiety growing about PPL's future, several staff responded with their feet. Eggert left early in 1987 and further departures followed. Eggert's exit line to his seniors at Westpac was reportedly: 'This thing [the foreign-exchange risk-management product] will bite you in the bum.'

In February 1987, with the worldwide financial markets boom still in full flight, Westpac centred its capital markets and related activities in a London-based investment banking group. Headed by Fletcher, the group embraced Mase Westpac, Westpac Pollock, Ord Minnett and the capital markets and mergers and acquisitions divisions of Partnership Pacific, as well as capital markets and treasury activities in Australia, New Zealand, North America, Asia and Europe. It was described to Fletcher by an observer as an 'excitingly impossible job'.

Westpac also announced that PPL's treasury would come under Stan Davis in Sydney. From January to June 1987 LEK played a role in merging PPL's operations with Westpac treasury. However, the British consultants were hampered by a bureaucratic glitch typical of the inefficiencies—internal and external—that dogged Westpac. Most had returned to the UK for the Christmas break only to find that their visas did not enable them to re-enter Australia for another year. So it was a smaller, weakened consulting team that was helping Westpac integrate a recalcitrant PPL. In March 1987 PPL stopped trading in foreign exchange and its operations were streamlined, with treasury and capital markets absorbed into the investment banking group. In July PPL's foreign-exchange licence was surrendered. Asset-based finance and project and advisory services were linked to Westpac's corporate banking division. PPL continued to exist because it was a useful fundraising mechanism for Westpac. Banks at that time had to lodge 7 per cent of their deposits with the Reserve Bank, on which they earned an irritatingly slender 5 per cent interest a year; there was no such requirement on merchant banks. From 1987

130

PPL focused more aggressively on lending, building an exposure to property that was to become another disaster. And the time-bomb of the foreign-currency risk-management product was still ticking.

The management vacuum

Westpac and PPL treasuries were physically merged in Westpac's dealing room, with PPL treasurer Garth Carter reporting to Westpac's global treasury head Stan Davis. The move, intended to put PPL's operations under efficient management, was a tragedy of paralysis. Carter, an experienced money-market operator, was candid about his lack of familiarity with foreign exchange. During the first quarter of 1987 Westpac's risk-management unit, under Agnes Wong, was given responsibility for supervising the managed borrowings. However, Wong could only advise. PPL still had a formal legal obligation to manage certain foreign-currency accounts, but the staff handling PPL's foreign-exchange clients after Jackson's departure had left. Mistakes were being made and reporting to clients had broken down. Legally, Westpac's foreign-exchange dealers could not manage the product directly until new documentation was in place. Management of the foreign-currency borrowers fell between two stools, in what lawyer Paddy Jones, a partner of Allen Allen & Hemsley, later described as a 'period of non-management'. Administrative delays resulted in the management vacuum continuing for several months. The formal transfer of the management of the foreign-currency loans to Westpac stalled, partly because the Westpac risk-management unit was nervous about what it was taking on.

A series of internal memos between officers of PPL and Westpac, subsequently leaked and circulated in March 1991 and read in federal parliament, showed an astounding breakdown in communication regarding the management of foreign-exchange risk and serious rifts between PPL's head office and branch managers. PPL's Queensland manager, Tom Booker, alleged that Wong, a Westpac employee, was managing the PPL loans pool without either the proper legal authority or the clients' knowledge. Concern was also expressed that when deals were written by Wong and her staff, they were handled as a bulk deal between Westpac and PPL and then PPL staff apportioned profits and losses to clients. An avenue open to Westpac to overcome the problem of legal authority would have been to second one or two bank foreign-exchange dealers to the staff of PPL, but no action was yet taken on this.

In May 1987 a PPL client of Booker's branch, Thomas Nominees, lost $450,000 (6 per cent of the face value of its loan facility) in six days. Booker complained that he had not been advised of this by PPL treasury in Sydney but had learned of the loss from his client. Booker also discovered that a South Australian client had lost only 2.5 per cent of the face value of his facility over the same period. On 5 June 1987 Booker sent a memo to PPL's treasurer, Garth Carter, with a copy to then managing director Philip Deer, who was also Westpac's general manager, corporate banking. The memo complained of the breakdown in communication and the client losses and asked how it was that Wong, a Westpac dealer, had been allowed to trade on behalf of a PPL client without the client's knowledge.

A Westpac diary note dated 12 June recorded a meeting of executives to discuss Booker's memo of 5 June. It was noted that if copies of the memo went into customers' files, and a customer were to bring either PPL or Westpac to court years later, the memo would be unearthed under court processes and would 'implicate the bank'. From a strictly legal point of view, Wong appeared to have acted without authority, although authority from PPL staff was implied, the note said. There was concern that copies of the memo might have travelled through PPL and Westpac; it could be too late to destroy it. But at least it could be kept out of official files. Rather, an official memo would be written for the files, to state that Wong had not acted without authority. Another diary note dated 15 June 1987 recorded an opinion from Allens solicitor Philip Cornwell that it would not be advisable to backdate Westpac staff's secondment to PPL, although 'something' should be written. The air was thick with defensive memos.

Letters of 18 June to two Westpac dealers recorded their secondment to PPL 'effective from 18 May'. On 29 June PPL terminated the foreign-exchange risk-management product and Westpac offered to assume management of PPL's managed clients. Thomas Nominees declined to continue being managed, but a handful of others transferred to the Westpac risk-management unit.

In July, PPL treasurer Garth Carter responded to Booker's earlier memo, stating that 'at no stage was Westpac managing the client's positions' and explaining that Westpac dealers had been seconded to PPL effective from 18 May, and from that time they managed the portfolio as employees of PPL. Booker's response was that it was regrettable that he had not been informed that Westpac dealers had been seconded to PPL as, if he had known, he could have told clients.

In August 1987 sixteen PPL employees, including Chris Lane, PPL's national manager of mergers and acquisitions, Bruce Fraser, national manager, group services, and Tom Booker left *en masse* to establish their own merchant bank, Campbell Capital Ltd, with offices in Sydney, Melbourne and Brisbane and financial backing from Ariadne Australia Ltd. Lane and Fraser were joint managing directors. A month later, Thomas Nominees and another Queensland client of PPL complained to Westpac's managing director about the administration of the risk-management product. The bank could not ignore these complaints. Westpac's in-house legal counsel, Terry Dunne, asked Martin Kriewaldt of Feez Ruthning, a Queensland affiliate of Allen Allen & Hemsley, to investigate. Kriewaldt reported to Dunne that he was most unsettled by what he was finding in PPL, that it was very hard to get a clear picture as accounts conflicted. Dunne suggested that Kriewaldt write a letter to Deer, with a copy to Dunne. When he received Kriewaldt's unexpected letter detailing perceived serious problems in PPL, a shocked Deer rang Dunne and also spoke with his immediate boss, Warwick Kent, head of corporate and international. Kent in turn sought Dunne's advice. It was decided a thorough review should be carried out and the person appointed to the task was Allens partner Paddy Jones. Jones, a litigation expert, was briefed by Dunne, and carried out a full documentary audit of PPL. Confidentiality of the project was emphasised. It was a major assigment even for Allens, whose work for Westpac each year represented a multi-million-dollar income. Jones's letters to Westpac, written on 26 November and 11 December 1987, in which he concurred with Kriewaldt's preliminary observations, were greeted with horror. The letters, written in colourful style, contained damning revelations, including reference to excessive point-taking (taking more profit than PPL was entitled to, at clients' expense and to its own advantage). The letters condemned what had gone on at PPL. The information in the letters, in unfriendly hands, could be dynamite; however, the letters were written under legal professional privilege to a client and it should have been possible to keep their content secret.

To compile his report, Jones and his team examined more than 50,000 documents, 1,500 in detail, and visited each PPL interstate office. They interviewed close to twenty PPL staff but deliberately chose not to interview former staff of the merchant bank, in the interests, as recorded in the letters, of keeping a lid on the problem. That potentially excluded vital evidence. Jones was assisted by Westpac's legal team under Dunne, and by Ashley Ayre, a Westpac corporate banking executive with overseas and foreign-exchange experience.

Jones's first letter charted the progress of PPL's treasury and specifically its foreign-exchange risk management, the staff conducting this, the deterioration in the department's morale after Jackson and her team left, the breakdown in communication among the various components of PPL and the clients, Westpac's move to take over risk management and the 'management vacuum' in the first half of 1987. He concluded that managed borrowers would succeed in any action against PPL. He commented on the unusually self-critical tone of the internal PPL memos and ended by re-commending that PPL keep 'as close and cordial contact as possible with all potential claimants'.

Jones concluded that Westpac should avoid litigation at any reasonable cost, get the borrowers out of foreign curren-cies and into $A loans as quickly as possible and essentially keep them happy with concessions and kid-glove treatment. And keep the whole matter under wraps. The second letter, written two weeks later, discussed whether PPL had any criminal liability through the point-taking and deal-switching which allegedly occurred in late 1986 or early 1987 (but decided that was a civil matter) and Westpac's conduct in managing foreign-currency loans.

Jones also advised on the management of the foreign-exchange portfolio: 'I think it important that the former PPL managed borrowers be kept fully hedged, unless and until there is a clear strategic appreciation of the $A against the relevant currency. A fully hedged client may not like the interest rates, but he is suffering no losses and he can't sue. A policy of ruthless conservatism is called for.' According to Gerhard Moser, manager of Westpac's risk-management unit after Agnes Wong left the bank in September 1987, Jones's advice—which reflected his role as a legal, rather than foreign-exchange, expert—was passed on as instructions to the unit.

A shell-shocked Westpac did not immediately think to query the accuracy of the letters, or dig more into their contents; the general thrust of Jones's letters reinforced Kriewaldt's findings. But both were based on documentary, rather than accounting, evidence. Jones commented in his first letter on missing 'suspense account books' and said: 'The absence of these books greatly hinders the unravelling of transactions and this difficulty and the difficulty in establishing when, in the course of the day's trading, a particular transaction took place, have prevented us from quantifying the profits which PPL made from point-taking.' Jones went on to say that, notwithstanding this, factors existed which led him to believe that a court would find that point-taking occurred. 'The loss of the suspense books makes it impossible to form a firm view about deal-switching,' he wrote. Westpac decided that client complaints should be dealt with as they arose. The board was concerned that customers might have suffered, and instructed Ashley Ayre to discuss any problems with them and rectify them, giving customers the benefit of the doubt. In subsequent evidence to the 1991 parliamentary banking inquiry, Ayre said his clear instruction was: 'Do not try to do the best deal you can for the Westpac group or PPL, give them [the customers] the benefit of the doubt so that you are comfortable that there has been a fair settlement.' Jones and Ashley Ayre travelled around Australia, dealing with complaints and settling with a great many borrowers.

Nearly three years later, at the end of 1991, it dawned on Westpac that it had been preoccupied with settling with clients without further investigating the conclusions in Jones's letters to determine whether the missing books held crucial evidence. During 1991, after the letters had fallen sensationally into the public arena, the bank had been receiving claims from former PPL customers and, in considering how to deal with these, it began to re-examine PPL's records. The bank appointed the accounting firm Coopers & Lybrand to conduct a detailed investigation of PPL's books. Whereas Jones, approaching the matter from a legal angle, had conducted a thorough documentary audit, Coopers & Lybrand looked at the accounting facts. Coopers, with resources and time not available to Jones—its examination took months—trawled through the dealers' positions sheets and the deal tickets to recreate the pooled deals and establish what was dealt on whose behalf and when, then matched deals with the Reserve Bank and other records of exchange rates on the day of the transactions to check whether or not clients received unfavourable terms. Coopers concluded they did not. Many in Westpac closely involved with the issues concluded from Coopers's reconstruction of PPL's records that the letters had presented an incomplete picture.

Jones's letters were written in response to what those in Westpac with concerns about PPL were seeking: to sound an alarm and invoke a sense of urgency. They were not written with publication in mind, and Westpac has never waived the legal professional privilege over the letters; even though they eventually became public, neither the bank, Allens nor Coopers & Lybrand will disclose further details of the investigation. Jones abruptly refused to discuss the matter with this writer. But the verdict of most in Westpac involved with the issue would appear to be that whatever went wrong in PPL in late 1986 and into early 1987 was due to incompetence rather than crookedness. A combination of inadequate resources, the speed with which foreign-currency markets were moving, bad communication with clients and sloppy documentation propelled overstretched staff, who were dealing with a complex product, into taking expedient measures, such as pooling clients' transactions. And a damaging hiatus occurred before the implementation of the decision to wind down PPL's treasury and absorb it into Westpac. When the move was made, it was against a background of inaction and infighting, with some of the people involved hindering rather than helping the merger.

Several former PPL staffers believe that Westpac was at pains to heap the odium on to PPL in a way that would exonerate the bank from any suggestion of mismanagement of foreign-currency loans. Point-taking—taking a spread on a deal—is legal; it is how foreign-exchange traders make their profits, with a wide gap for retail compared with wholesale clients. Because spreads vary from client to client, and are a source of profits, banks are coy about revealing them. The Westpac group, and especially PPL, was criticised for taking excessive points from so-called 'captive clients' (foreign-currency borrowers who could not easily take their business elsewhere because whatever credit lines they could muster were with PPL/Westpac). A better explanation of spreads, and of the fees and charges that borrowers might incur in foreign exchange, would have helped clear the air between bank and customer.

Foreign-currency loans which went bad represented a mix of greed by borrowers and greed by banks. There were genuinely tragic cases among the borrowers, many of whom grew bitter. A few were pitifully naive. Westpac was at pains to keep PPL cases out of court because, the bank claimed, litigation would have been long and painful. All PPL cases were settled, some at the eleventh hour. Many observers see another motive: the evidence aired would have been disastrously damning.

Depending on whom one believes, either PPL's managed foreign-currency borrowers in late 1986 and early 1987 were in the hands of well-intentioned if inexperienced operators desperately trying to service their clients with inadequate resources and in a volatile market, or the clients were under-informed and sorely mistreated. Either way, from around the middle of 1986 and into 1987, PPL would seem to have taken on more than it could handle, resulting in many clients being financially disadvantaged.

The letters written by Paddy Jones were to return to haunt Westpac.

CHAPTER SIX

Midnight Money

The worldwide financial markets boom of the 1980s spawned a whole new industry. At its best it helped companies and individuals better manage their funds, and at its worst it was personified by greed and more greed in the name of wealth creation. The arcane world of high finance was brought into the general domain with films such as *Wall Street* and *Trading Places*, and high-profile swindlers such as Michael Milken and Ivan Boesky did little for the image of the average trader. During the 1980s, people who might have thought buying a few shares an adventure suddenly found they could indulge in more complex financial strategies in exotic currencies. Financial markets, whose roots stretch back through the centuries to the traditional merchant banks which financed trade, took on a life of their own. Trading became an end in itself, fuelled by easy credit, willing buyers and sellers, borrowers and lenders, improved communications technology and increasingly deregulated financial markets.

A feature of the 1980s was the growth in what became known as the treasury area, also known as financial markets or capital markets divisions, of banks and investment banks. Whatever its name, the area encompassed trading in cash and securities such as bills of exchange and bonds, foreign exchange and, increasingly, including futures. As the operations grew, so did the dealing rooms, which handled business as a principal for the bank or investment bank, and also serviced clients through the corporate desk. After the $A was floated in December 1983 it rapidly became a highly traded currency, soaring from obscurity to rank in the top half-dozen most traded currencies in the world, partly because of its fluctuations which could provide good trading profits (or substantial losses) and also because Australia offered comparatively high interest rates which attracted foreign investors. Moreover, in the wake of the 1983 initiatives, Australia operated with fewer controls than elsewhere. In foreign exchange, in particular, the markets exploded far beyond the capacity of the control and reporting systems to monitor them effectively. But such was the pressure and the pace that everyone just kept trading, kept growing.

The forex game

At the time the $A floated, Westpac operated with some two dozen foreign-exchange dealers, mostly chosen from within Westpac ranks and mostly young. As demand for foreign-exchange dealers grew, the bank started to recruit from outside. Inevitably, given the novelty of floating exchange rates, experience in foreign-exchange dealing was scant, although some of Westpac's staff had worked for a few years in London and Singapore in preparation for an open foreign-exchange market in Australia. But, overall, foreign-exchange trading was a new game, and relatively inexperienced traders rose to senior positions, and high salaries, at a young age. They could afford an indulgent life and they revelled in flaunting it. Foreign-exchange dealers in those days returned profits that banks would kill for in the 1990s. Being good in the 1980s meant being seriously sharp, having the brass to outstare the other guy. Forex traders were cocky, in control, confident of making their fortunes. They worked hard and played hard. The pressures of the dealing room were frequently relived and relieved in a long lunch or after-hours drinks session. It was a macho world, where the codes of conduct that govern industry behaviour in the 1990s were yet to be formalised and enforced. New freedoms were being tested. It was a breeding ground for some kind of disaster, although most were intoxicated by the ride on the roller-coaster markets and oblivious to the dangers.

Westpac's chief manager, foreign exchange, Peter Chan, had been educated in Hong Kong and joined Westpac as a trade finance clerk in its Wellington, New Zealand, branch. He became involved in foreign exchange, and the bank moved him to its Sydney head office to beef up its trading. Chan, paraded unashamedly by the bank as its spokesperson on currency markets, oversaw what a *Sydney Morning Herald* article in December 1983 headlined 'Westpac's ulcer department'. The media sought him out for reportable information about his esoteric world and he obliged. He once said: 'I've got to psych the guys, I've got to motivate them. I want 100 per cent commitment. When I ask for their right arm, I want them to say "Take my left one too." ' Between 1983 and 1987 Chan was constantly in the public eye, featured as one of Westpac's most promoted show ponies, photographed in the bank's 1984 annual report striding along a moving walkway at Sydney airport. The bank had set out to establish itself as a leader in foreign exchange, through aggressive pricing and advice. It succeeded, reaping considerable profits from its trading. By 1985 Westpac had achieved star status in foreign exchange, emerging as the winner in the annual *BRW* poll on the industry and pipping the merchant banks which had romped ahead of the banks during the previous two years. Westpac was nominated as best for overall service and Chan rated among the top ten foreign-exchange personalities. He seemed at home in the frenetic world of a foreign-exchange dealing room, putting in a twelve-hour-plus day, coping with constantly ringing phones and wildly fluctuating exchange rates (the $A plunged from 85 US cents to 63 in less than two weeks early in 1985). He often pointed out that the foreign-exchange market moves quickly, not minute-by-minute but second-by-second. He attributed his ability to thrive on the tension to his early career in Hong Kong where savage competition meant only the best survived. In a newspaper interview in June 1985, he said he loved 'living on the edge'. At 40, considerably older than most in his team of dealers, Chan was a veteran.

Within a few years, Australia, particularly Sydney, became an important staging post in the 24-hour world of foreign exchange. The market opened in New Zealand, then progressively through Australia, the Asian centres such as Tokyo, Hong Kong and Singapore and into the European and London day and finally to New York and the US West Coast. Trading at times was chaotic. Record-keeping relied on a trader marking a trade on his or her daily position sheet and filling in a docket that went to the back office for confirmation and settlement. The largely manual system was slow and unwieldy. The profit for one month was not generally known until halfway through the next and even then all a manager received was an overall figure for foreign-exchange trading with no meaningful break-down of the currency portfolio and no system for checking individual dealers' books.

Such was Westpac's stature in the foreign-exchange markets that it caught the attention of a television producer who sensed the makings of a feature story in this exotic, high-speed, high-tension environment. Channel Nine's *Sunday* program approached the bank in late May 1986 proposing to document 'A Day in the Life of a Foreign-Exchange Dealer'. Feelings in the bank were mixed. Some thought the idea would be good for public relations. Mike Eastaway, then chief dealer, thought differently but was persuaded that it could only be of benefit to Westpac's image. The television crew filmed activity in Westpac's new high-tech dealing room over three days, beginning on Wednesday 11 June when the prime minister was scheduled to deliver a late-afternoon address to the nation. Speculation about the content of his announcement fuelled hectic trading. By comparison, Thursday was a quiet trading day after the frenzied session the day before; a convivial lunch at nearby John & Merivale's, a restaurant where the Westpac foreign-exchange dealers regularly dined at table 31, seemed a good idea. Charles Wooley, the reporter covering the story, and several of the dealers indulged in a long celebration that included generous quantities of champagne. Eastaway, normally a beer drinker, was filmed quaffing Dom Perignon. The film crew kept the cameras rolling as the lunchers became increasingly boisterous. Filming in the Westpac dealing room resumed on the Friday, when the release of the balance of payments figures triggered another bout of feverish activity in currency markets. The 'champagne cowboys', as Paul Keating had dubbed them, worked and played at high pressure.

The screening of the program on 15 June, including the restaurant episode, shattered the Sunday morning tranquillity at the homes of Westpac board members and senior executives. They were appalled that the bank's name should be associated with what they saw as sheer vulgarity, even from those *wunderkinder* in foreign exchange who were earning so much money for the bank. The board hit the roof. Complaints and criticisms flew. Senior Reserve Bank officers who had seen the program were also singularly unimpressed. Stan Davis, head of Westpac's global treasury, was told to do something about it. Davis lectured the traders about standards of behaviour. While he was less than happy about the fallout, his private view was that management had over-reacted. The video was true to the 1980s and could have been filmed in any market in any major centre at that time. But it hurt Westpac's image. The bank's sheer size had enabled it to dominate the foreign-exchange markets, and an antagonistic relationship was evident at times between Westpac and its competitors, with the bank resented as a bully. Its corporate customers had a love–hate relationship with Westpac; they did business with the bank because a good customer could get a good price, but Westpac sometimes treated them with arrogance. As other banks expanded and intensified the competition, Westpac's brute impact on the market diminished and it later came to be regarded as a 'good citizen' in foreign exchange. And during the bank's tough years in the late 1980s and early 1990s the treasury and financial markets activities underpinned the business with consistent profits and market share.

The reverberations from the television episode had barely died away when criticism of another kind arose over Westpac's dealing room. On 15 September 1986 Neville Miles joined the bank as head of corporate treasury, with a brief to overhaul its systems and financial controls. Miles had come to Australia from South Africa, where domestic markets had been deregulated in the late 1970s; he was well aware of the challenges and pitfalls. Identified as overly pessimistic by most of his peers, he prophesied potential for disaster in Westpac's dealing room, with its back-office and reporting systems that could not keep pace with market volumes. He saw it as out of control, and such was his concern that he put his views in a lengthy note to corporate and international head Warwick Kent, much to the irritation of Davis as treasury head. Among other criticisms, Miles cited slack reporting to the Reserve Bank and inadequate record-keeping. Events proved his gloomy predictions right.

The scam

On 12 January 1987 a discrepancy came to light that set in train a series of events that was to rock Westpac. Ken Vallance, the bank's treasurer, received a telephone call from a staff member of the merchant bank Kleinwort Benson Australia

145

Ltd—which employed a former Westpac senior dealer, Benny Choo—saying that he thought there was a problem: it appeared that Westpac was trading at off-market rates in a deal that benefited Kleinwort Benson.

Vallance immediately rang the chief foreign-exchange dealer, Mike Eastaway, to have him check the transaction. Eastaway examined the trade and related paperwork and found the exchange rate in the dealer's position sheet did not match the rate on the deal docket (which is transferred to the back office for processing and confirmation with the client). The trader who did the deal was identified as Naji Halabi, who had been recruited to Westpac's fledgling foreign-exchange division in August 1983. Investigations were to reveal that the bank was the victim of a multi-million-dollar scam.

Vallance asked Eastaway if he could find the tape of the conversation between Westpac's Halabi and Kleinwort's Choo. It was standard practice for telephone transactions to be tape-recorded for reference in the event of a dispute. Before moving to Kleinwort in late 1983, Choo—one of the first foreign-exchange dealers hired by Westpac from outside the bank—had at one stage shared the chief-dealer role with Eastaway. While at Westpac, Choo had recruited Halabi. After listening to the conversation between Halabi and Choo, Vallance called in Halabi and ordered him to take seven days' leave. More irregularities came to light over the ensuing week. On 19 January Halabi was dismissed from Westpac.

When the evidence of a foreign-exchange scam began to emerge, Westpac called in its legal advisers, Allen Allen & Hemsley, and referred the matter to the New South Wales Corporate Affairs Commission. The CAC began its own investigation into the matters involving Kleinwort Benson. A total of more than $200,000 in losses to Westpac was discovered in transactions involving Choo at Kleinwort Benson. These had taken place since June 1986, while Halabi had been trading on Westpac's corporate desk. Profits were found to have been

146

directed to money-market accounts held by Trans Pacific Investment Corporation Pty Ltd and Cashcount Pty Ltd, companies controlled by Naji Halabi's older brother, Ramzi. In March 1987 the CAC launched a prosecution against Naji Halabi and Benny Choo, extending that in August to include Ramzi Halabi. At that stage, not realising the full extent of the deals involved, the bank was investigating only transactions with Kleinwort Benson Australia Ltd. Later in 1987 more complex trades, involving Swiss Bank Corporation (SBC) in San Francisco, came to light.

Naji Halabi, arrested by fraud squad detectives in March 1987, was charged under Section 158 of the Crimes Act with making a false entry and misappropriating $9,000. Westpac also launched civil proceedings against Halabi in the New South Wales Supreme Court. He was released on bail, and his passport was impounded. As more investigations were undertaken, larger and more suspicious transactions were uncovered, and Westpac added to its claim, which by now totalled $215,000. Halabi faced further charges under the Companies Code. In June he was arrested for a second time over allegations that he was intending to leave Australia, using a false passport to travel from Cairns to Papua New Guinea. In September he was committed for trial on 96 charges relating to alleged fraud under the Crimes Act and the Companies Code. Ramzi Halabi was also committed for trial for conspiring to cheat and defraud Westpac.

Ramzi and Naji Halabi both had considerable experience in foreign exchange. Ramzi had been a senior dealer for First National Bank of Boston for four years until 1974 when he established his own foreign-exchange broking firm, Sarabex, operating in Bahrain and London. By 1982 Ramzi Halabi employed 136 staff, including his brother Adli, working in the London office. When Naji Halabi turned 21, in 1977, Ramzi arranged for him to gain experience as a trainee foreign-exchange dealer with Swiss Bank Corporation, in

Basel. In the following year, Naji began working for Ramzi at Sarabex. In 1982 he applied to Westpac to work in Sydney as a foreign-exchange trader. His referees were impressive, including Andy Schmits, a vice-president of Swiss Bank in Basel, Alexander Wood, an employee of Ramzi, and Peter Koestner, a former treasurer of Algemene Bank Nederland (ABN), Bahrain. Ramzi Halabi contacted an old friend, Benny Choo, then one of Westpac's chief foreign-exchange dealers, enclosing Naji's application. Choo recommended Naji Halabi to Westpac, citing his experience in foreign exchange and suggesting a starting salary of $20,550 a year. Naji Halabi began working for Westpac in August 1983, as a trainee dealer, then in November of that year he was appointed interbank dealer. By the late 1980s Ramzi Halabi, who had arrived in Australia with other family members in 1982, was a wealthy businessman in Cairns, Far North Queensland. Adli had remained in London.

148

The Halabi network seemed to circle the globe. While on Westpac's interbank desk Naji Halabi transacted a number of deals with SBC in San Francisco. These transactions dated from 1984 and were more sophisticated than the later deals done with Kleinwort Benson. One deal between Westpac and SBC had been transacted for $10 million but no mention was made of an exchange rate. Those investigating retrieved the deal slip and found Westpac had lost $50,000 on that transaction. The absence of any mention of an exchange rate set the alarm bells ringing. Funds were traced through SBC in San Francisco and the Bahrain office of the Dutch bank ABN in what was later dubbed a 'golden circle' of foreign-exchange dealers by the deputy governor of the Reserve Bank, John Phillips. It was helpful that the dealers' conversations were taped but with the Beirut-born, Swiss-educated Halabi speaking in a mix of English, French and Arabic the exchanges were hard to follow.

Westpac later claimed that between August 1984 and January 1987 Naji Halabi was involved in dishonest foreign-exchange deals amounting to $4 million. Most of the funds found their way to the Halabis through a series of complex arrangements involving a senior dealer at SBC in San Francisco, Larry Helzel, a Panamanian company set up in 1981 by Ramzi Halabi, Sonal Finance Inc, and one of Switzerland's largest private banks, Pictet et Cie.

Systems in foreign-exchange dealing rooms have been vastly refined since the late 1980s. A foreign-exchange transaction that appeared out of line with the market would now be immediately picked up. But in the 1980s banks lacked strong management controls. Westpac was no exception. Its system was open to abuse in an area where operations relied a great deal on people's integrity. Naji Halabi would have had a trader's knowledge of the gaps and shortfalls in Westpac's internal controls and how to exploit them to transact deals at below normal market rates, causing losses to Westpac and a profit to the banks with which he dealt. With the cooperation of dealers in other banks, millions of dollars in profits could be siphoned off into privately held bank accounts. Investigations found that Halabi was operating scams in four ways:

149

- Discrepancies, where one rate had been recorded on the dealer's position sheet and another on the deal ticket. A dealer acting in this way is capitalising on the absence of checking by a head dealer of the details on the two records.
- Deals not recorded—for example, a transaction with SBC was recorded on a deal docket which went to the back office but not on the dealer's position sheet which the head dealer examined each day to determine whether a dealer had made a profit or a loss.
- Overnight deals, in which a transaction would be recorded as the last deal on the position sheet of the previous day but appeared to have been written on the following

morning with the benefit of knowing how an exchange rate had moved overnight. This could be tracked down through telexes which carry the time of execution.
• Forward rates which were well out of line with the market.

In April 1987, a few months after Halabi was dismissed, Peter Chan was moved 'upstairs' into a marketing role at Westpac, with the title of product manager, foreign exchange, reporting to Australian treasurer Ken Vallance. The day-to-day operations in the dealing room came under Ian Town, senior manager, foreign exchange, international money market. Town had been brought in from Westpac's New York office earlier in the year, largely in response to the adverse reaction to the *Sunday* television program and specifically to smarten up the foreign-exchange dealing room. Flamboyant and outspoken when he chose, Town brought with him an unusual combination of dealing and administrative skills. He brought about an improvement in relations between Westpac and the Reserve Bank, and he orchestrated a greater involvement by Westpac in the industry's Forex Association, particularly on the training side. He and Mike Norton, brought in from Bank of America as chief manager, domestic money markets, and Paul Skerman, who joined Westpac from the Commonwealth Bank and brought the skills of a strategic thinker, introduced new policies and procedures to the dealing room.

A month later, in May 1987, Chan left Westpac to join the New Zealand investment bank DFC New Zealand Ltd as executive director, treasury. At the time he left, Westpac was ranked eighth in *Euromoney*'s survey of corporate foreign exchange services. Chan denied widespread speculation that he was leaving Westpac because of the changed role, or that he was being made a scapegoat for the 'golden circle' fraud. The decision to move to Wellington was partly influenced by the fact that his wife was a New Zealander. However, Chan said the departure from Westpac after more than twenty years saddened him and that he was leaving 'with a sense of regret'. He seemed genuinely torn about the decision, bidding an emotional farewell to Westpac chief Bob White. His comments did not wholly quash the view that he felt sidelined by his new marketing job; that Westpac, having made him a star, with a high public profile and internally a direct line to the chief executive, had sent out a clear signal that the star had dimmed. His peers remained convinced that Chan was paying the price of what had become known as 'Najigate'. Stan Davis emphasised that much of the rationale for moving Chan was a desire to keep separate those who were dealing on behalf of the bank from those advising customers. That meant partly dismantling the empire which, in earlier times, Westpac had been happy for Chan to build, but which was showing weakness. Davis made it clear that Westpac would always welcome Chan back and, indeed, was quick to rehire him in January 1989, as chief manager, sales and distribution, in Australian financial markets. Davis said that Chan's 'unique skills and presence would provide further impetus to Westpac's already strong position'.

151

Clive Alexander, who in 1987 was acting as deputy treasurer, foreign exchange, was appointed to undertake a thorough investigation of foreign-exchange transactions involving Naji Halabi, tracing transactions and comparing deal dockets. 'He did a magnificent job on that,' says Stan Davis. 'With his ferreting skills and attention to detail he built up a great story.' Alexander was spending most of his time on the Halabi investigation, working under the direction of Gaire Blunt, a partner with Allen Allen & Hemsley.

As part of his investigations, Alexander travelled to San Francisco, spending a week there with Swiss Bank Corporation. In October 1987 he went to Switzerland where, with Stan Davis, he visited SBC to discuss a detailed audit that had been carried out on its San Francisco office. ABN, whose Bahrain office was a party to Halabi's dealings, remained unwilling to cooperate in the investigation. Banks generally are not keen to reveal flaws in their systems. As he moved from financial centre to financial centre, Alexander found the banks retreating into secretiveness about potentially embarrassing disclosures of inadequate internal controls.

Alexander continued his investigations, painstakingly comparing and matching deals and tracking through the relevant paperwork. Sifting through tens of thousands of deal slips, and marrying their details with those on the dealers' position sheets, he found transactions involving other dealers in Westpac which he identified as potentially suspicious. These deals, transacted not with other banks but with Westpac customers, showed an exchange rate on a deal slip significantly different from the rate on the dealer's position sheet. Alexander felt he had uncovered a pattern of disparities—exchange rates discounted in the clients' favour. However, his investigations in this direction made little further headway and ultimately he was told that no further investigation into those deals was warranted. Alexander's suspicions did not come to light publicly until several years later.

In November 1988, after eighteen months of searching and investigating, Alexander was told by Westpac to stop his work entirely. According to Alexander, he was told that he was 'dangerous' because he 'knew too much' and the bank would never want him to stand in a witness box. Alexander was thunderstruck, and felt threatened by the assertion that he 'knew too much'. However, Westpac's legal advisers had indeed counselled against using Alexander as a witness because there was a danger that his evidence could be twisted by a wily cross-examiner.

According to Alexander, he had submitted to Westpac two handwritten, undated reports (the first, written in February 1988, ran to 66 pages; the second, which he was still writing in November 1988, was unfinished). Then, in a late-1988 restructuring of Westpac's treasury, Vallance became chief manager, special duties, and Alexander manager, special duties. Alexander was advised that the bank had a series of special tasks for him, but he regarded his new position as a demeaning downgrading of his status. He saw himself as neutralised, his 23-year career at Westpac over. In 1989 he left the bank. Alexander believed many at Westpac were happy to see the back of him, particularly among the traders who, as his investigations progressed, had dubbed him 'Inspector Plod'. They had offered little help to someone they saw as not part of the 'family'—not just of Westpac dealers but the wider dealer network which enjoyed considerable rapport. They believed that, even if well-intentioned, he was on a misguided mission which threatened to damage them. Alexander had been assigned to investigate the circumstances of Halabi's dealings, not to widen his inquiries to others in the dealing room and then form opinions that, they believed, were not backed by hard evidence. Alexander was distressed; he believed that he had properly carried out the investigations only to have his findings buried. He felt isolated, and feared that there was an element in the bank keen to discredit his work.

Naji and Ramzi Halabi and Benny Choo were charged with conspiring to defraud Westpac Banking Corporation through the Kleinwort Benson transactions. Ramzi was charged because the money had passed through his bank account. Choo had been paid a 10 per cent fee for his role in each deal. In total, close to $250,000 of Westpac's funds had been siphoned off in several deals. Committal proceedings were launched by the Director of Public Prosecutions in August 1988 and the three were committed for trial. The matter did not go to trial until mid-1991.

Further proceedings were instituted by Westpac against several members of the Halabi family over the SBC transactions. Under US federal law, Allens and Westpac were able to secure documents from SBC in San Francisco and representatives of the law firm, James Gibson and a junior counsel brought back 30 boxes of the bank's documents to Australia. Making sense of the documents required more than a legal eye and in August 1989 Coopers & Lybrand was called in to investigate. Coopers' brief included examining close to 400 transactions involving SBC. What was expected to take a few weeks took considerably longer. Coopers sifted through the volumes of information—deal tickets, dealer position sheets, telex confirmations and computer print-outs—to track the processes, and compiled an expert report which was handed to the trial judge, Justice Rogers, and to Ramzi Halabi's solicitors. Certain conclusions were reached regarding transactions between Westpac and SBC, for example, the exchange rates in certain deals indicated strongly that they were off-market and executed in a manner designed to conceal that fact. This provided crucial evidence in the civil case. But, despite an exchange of correspondence between Allens and the Swiss private bank Pictet, Coopers was hobbled by a lack of information from the private bank and an absence of cooperation from ABN. Ramzi Halabi's solicitors were also having difficulty prising documents from Pictet. Rogers concluded that the solution was for both sides to travel to Switzerland and talk to Pictet.

On orders in court from Rogers, the investigating team went to Switzerland in March 1991 but had no success in extracting information from Pictet. Ramzi Halabi and his counsel also travelled to Switzerland to try to inspect documents. They all but collided in the rarefied atmosphere of Pictet's offices, which reeked of an intriguing combination of establishment wealth and utter secrecy and were furnished with an arresting mix of valuable antiques and the latest in modern technology. Coopers partner Rahoul Chowdry, who was handling the investigation and had compiled the Coopers report, and his colleagues coincided with Ramzi Halabi and his legal counsel from Hunt & Hunt, who introduced him to Chowdry. The immaculately groomed and impeccably polite Halabi was unruffled. 'Mr Chowdry,' he said calmly and amiably. 'I have read your masterpiece.' Halabi always kept his gentlemanly cool. Later, in a court canteen in Sydney, he said to Chowdry: 'It would be good to meet under happier circumstances.'

By the time the civil matter involving the SBC transactions went to trial the principal claim against the Halabis, which stemmed from the work carried out by Coopers & Lybrand, was about $4.5 million, before interest; including interest and costs, the total was eventually around $13 million.

Australia's world bank

Westpac's status continued to grow. In 1987 the bank was operating in 23 countries outside Australia, global assets were $70 billion, up 15.8 per cent from the previous year. It was nominated eighth in the world in a survey of foreign-exchange dealing banks by the influential magazine *Euromoney*, the first time an Australian bank had ranked so highly. It acquired 100 per cent of the stockbroker Ord Minnett, and finalised the formation of its Australian Financial Markets Group incorporating the bank's treasury division, the treasury and capital markets activities of PPL and Ord-Westpac Fixed Interest which, with Mase Westpac and Westpac Pollock in the US, came under the umbrella of the London-based investment banking group headed by Adrian Fletcher. Investment banking activities in Asia were centred in Singapore, Hong Kong and Tokyo. In London Westpac secured the services of Kleinwort Benson's director of swaps, Duncan Goldie-Morrison, as part of its strategy of competing in European investment banking. That also formed the basis for a promising swaps team which considerably raised Westpac's profile in the London markets in the late 1980s.

During 1987 Westpac announced an ambitious program of technology investment which would provide an integrated system. The project, known as Core System 90 (CS90), was flagged as both revolutionising the delivery of financial products and keeping a lid on operating costs. Westpac forecast that customers would see the first benefits of CS90, developed by Westpac and the Federal Systems division of the giant IBM, in the second half of 1988. Total cost was estimated to be $120 million.

156

For the year to 30 September 1987 Westpac Merchant Finance, the former CBA Finance now wholly owned by Westpac, reported a 26 per cent increase in after-tax profits to $A15.5 million, providing an admirable 25.6 per cent return on equity. Its counterpart in Australia, PPL, made $27 million, with income boosted by fees for advisory work on projects such as the Sydney Harbour tunnel. Westpac's own profit, though, was hobbled by a rise in tax and a 62 per cent increase in bad-debt provisions, of which $30 million was attributable to the Como project and $75 million to an abnormal provision for Latin-American debt. Income tax expense rose because of an increase in the corporate tax rate from 46 to 49 per cent and the impact of fringe benefits tax. As a consequence of these developments, after-tax profit was virtually at a standstill at $409 million for the year to September, although pre-tax profit rose 21 per cent to $848 million.

In October 1987 the Westpac board ended considerable debate when it decided that Stuart Fowler would succeed Bob White as head of the bank. White, who had earlier been asked by the board to extend his term until October 1988, his 65th birthday, announced his retirement. He felt that once a successor had been named, it was best to leave. However, Fowler had not been his preferred choice. Fowler's appointment was announced in November with the bank's annual results. To minimise uncertainty regarding succession to the role of chairman, the board reinstated the position of deputy, with Sir Eric Neal nominated to that position and taking the place vacated by Stephen Kimpton who, being of a similar age to Sir Noel Foley, had retired with the chairman the previous year.

White's legacy to Westpac was one of growth and expansion: having inherited a bank with $10 billion in assets, mostly in Australia, he left Westpac with $70 billion in assets, of which 38 per cent were held offshore. In 1985 Westpac's total assets had grown by 21.6 per cent and in 1986 by 23.5 per cent, and in each of those years the bank's Australian assets had risen by around 11.5 per cent, so that around half of the growth had been overseas. Costs were a problem that Westpac had still not confronted in 1987. Bank analyst Richard Holdaway's research showed Westpac's expense ratio higher than that of ANZ or National Australia Bank; non-interest expense as a proportion of assets was 3.5 per cent for Westpac compared with ANZ's 3.35 per cent and 2.86 per cent for NAB. Westpac's profit per employee was also considerably lower than NAB's. Holdaway told *Euromoney* in May 1987: 'All my figures suggest that Westpac is overstaffed.' And he added that Westpac had been behind the more efficient NAB since 1982. White's vision, with contributions from a succession of influential planners such as Geoff Thompson and Adrian Fletcher, had taken the bank on to the world stage, through a series of acquisitions and the establishment of offshore offices. During the 1980s White had twice been crowned Banker of the Year. One aspect of Westpac, though, remained constant, and that was an almost naive belief in its invincibility.

An outcome of White's departure was a sharp decline in high-level support for Adrian Fletcher, now in London. Within a few days Fletcher was removed from the executive committee and during 1989 he left the bank. White's view of Fletcher as an intelligent and aggressive achiever was not shared by all in the bank; to several, he was a thorn in the side.

Warwick Kent, the other serious contender for the role of chief of Westpac and widely regarded as White's preferred candidate, had missed out. After Fowler and Kent had been forced to swap jobs in 1986, a move neither saw as a compliment, Fowler had taken to retail banking with the same enthusiasm he had applied to international business. Kent, on the other hand, was struggling to get a grip on an unfamiliar area that included the Americas division, London, Asia, PPL and Westpac's financial markets and corporate divisions.

It is a criticism of both the board and of White, chief executive for ten years, that no obvious successor had been prepared for the role. It has been suggested that White did not strongly support either of the two, Fowler or Kent, and had put forward other prospective candidates. These were scrutinised by various board members but, for one reason or another, such as age or lack of experience, were deemed unsuitable. Unkind observers have said that White was simply unwilling to leave, and cherished a notion of remaining with the bank as chairman, a vision that would have evaporated when Fowler and not Kent was appointed as chief executive. White joined the Westpac board, a move he has since said was a mistake. 'I would strongly recommend to anyone else in that position not to go on the board,' he says. 'You can't say things and what you do say is brushed aside.'

In the end, the extroverted Fowler was a far better salesman than the retiring and more thoughtful Kent. An exuberant man, with a long background in international banking, enormously loyal to the institution he served, Fowler could walk into a banking function anywhere in the world and probably know half of those in the room by name, many by their nicknames. Fowler was affable and outgoing, blunt and ebullient, avuncular to some and overbearing to others. He had joined the Bank of New South Wales at its Nedlands, Perth, branch in 1949, and in 1955 embarked on a London posting, igniting an enthusiasm for international banking that would endure for much of his career and see him appointed as chief general manager of Westpac's corporate and international division in 1984. He served on the board of PPL in 1984 and 1985.

Fowler took over at the helm of Westpac in January 1988, on the heels of a worldwide stockmarket crash and on the eve of Australia's celebration of the Bicentennial. The mood in Australia was euphoric. Westpac had contributed a 200-foot flagpole—one foot for every year—at Sydney's Darling Harbour as part of the Bicentennial commemorations.

While the sharemarket crash had wiped the sheen off equities, it had increased investors' appetite for property and, for the more security-conscious, bank deposits. Westpac, in common with other banks, benefited from the 'flight to quality' syndrome that saw money flood into bank accounts. At that time, caution might have suggested that Westpac embark on a period of consolidation, focus on improving controls and management and information systems, and review its business and credit policies against a shifting economic environment. Instead, it was inflamed with a desire for further expansion. The 1988 and 1989 annual reports carried the tag 'Australia's world bank' and the sails continued to be set for growth. During 1988 Westpac revalued its group premises by $1.3 billion and held a rights issue that raised $743 million, almost doubling the bank's capital base and so laying a foundation for an explosion in lending in what was to prove to be the wrong time in the business and property market cycle. As an example of the bank's ebullience and confidence, it had entered into a 25-year lease of extensive and expensive office space at 75 King William Street, in the heart of the City of London and a stone's throw from the Bank of England. At the time, the bank's existing premises in nearby Walbrook House appeared insufficient for its growing London presence. However, on making the move in 1989, Westpac found unexpectedly that there was no taker for the office space at Walbrook House. It had to bear the costs of both until a tenant could be found. Within a year or so London's overheated property market nosedived and, as Westpac's own activities in London began to scale down, it became obvious that it had taken on too much space at King William Street. The new premises were a lingering cost burden.

160

In June 1988 Westpac was ranked 54th by market capitalisation, the highest of the Australian banks, in a survey by *International Business Week*. It wanted to be in the top 50. Westpac believed it could look back with some satisfaction on having broadened its business outside of Australia, especially in the US, and having built a network in Asia and laid the base of a global capital markets operation in London. It had added a major business arm, the Westpac Financial Services Group, a combination of Westpac Life and the bank's investment division, which Westpac intended to become a force as a life office. Confident of results from its CS90 technology investment, Westpac was internally forecasting that it could develop another dimension over coming years, selling information services in Australia and overseas. Substantial investment in technology was justified as essential to give Westpac a competitive edge. Westpac was selling itself as having achievable strategic objectives. It would retain an Australian head office—its most valuable assets remained its customer base in Australia and New Zealand—

but, with a growing volume of its activities taking place overseas, it had to take an increasingly global view of its business.

At the close of the 1988 financial year, on 30 September, Westpac's assets were $84 billion, up nearly 17 per cent during the year, while net profit jumped 69 per cent to $693 million. Return on equity was a robust 15.5 per cent. Size was still regarded as critical for Westpac to achieve its global objectives, a point that Fowler emphasised in the 1988 annual report. He said: 'Westpac no longer has the option of remaining essentially a domestic bank. The group's strategy in expanding its business globally has been to build on its existing strengths and to complement them by carefully tar-geted acquisitions. To date, these acquisitions have been designed to boost the group's capacity to meet the invest-ment banking requirements of its international customers.' The global theme was reinforced in the annual report with statements such as: 'Every business day, in every time zone across the world, Westpac is at work.'

CHAPTER SEVEN

AGC: OUT OF A BLACK HOLE

In July 1989 AGC, now a wholly owned subsidiary of Westpac and sharing the bank's board, came under new stewardship. After six years at the helm Rob Robson retired, having extended his five-year contract by a year at the board's request to see the company through a difficult period. Robson later said that at the time of his retirement the estimated book debt exposure of joint ventures was at the policy level of $500 million, although he conceded, in an article which appeared in *The Australian Financial Review* in December 1995, that there was a 'known tail of written facilities but it is hard to reconcile them with the amount later written off'. The deep and protracted fall in the property market provided some explanation. Additional drawdowns under existing commitments took exposures to joint ventures from $480 million in March 1989 to $660 million in September of that year, when commitments of $840 million were in the pipeline. While no major new joint ventures were written after September 1989, existing commitments meant that the volume of loans being drawn down continued to climb, and many of those became black holes, eventually to be fully owned by AGC/Westpac. Although retired, Robson continued his involvement with the Como project. That suited everyone because no-one else at AGC wanted to be closely associated with Como, which was widely regarded as Robson's problem. AGC hoped, vainly, to be able to sell the unfinished project some time in 1990. At the request of the joint Westpac/AGC board, Robson and Ian Matheson—until 1988 chairman of AGC—remained on the Como board, Matheson as chairman, to provide continuity, both leaving in July 1991. Westpac director Jim Scully was also on the Como board until he indicated that Westpac representation was no longer necessary.

Robson is remembered as independent, strong-willed, determined and articulate. His intellect and intelligence were never doubted but many questioned his abilities as a lender. Coming from outside the finance industry, he was seen as someone who lacked the 'streetsmarts' and sixth sense that make a good finance company lender. He and Peter French, to whom Australian lending operations reported, were seen as being strong in sales and marketing rather than in the analysis of a deal. Says Derrick Heywood: 'Robson was highly autocratic, but if you stood up for your rights and argued with him, and were correct, he respected you. And there was a great deal of justification for his attitude because firm discipline had been a major factor in AGC's continued increase in profits. There were no problems until the financier departed from its main business and got into the joint ventures that became such problems in the early 1990s.' AGC operated with a strong head office and a set of rules that everyone unquestioningly followed (Westpac's head office was, by comparison, weaker, issuing orders which tended to be queried rather than followed). And the buck indisputably stopped with Robson. He says his maxim in business life has long been: 'The one who delegates becomes captive of those whom he or she empowers. I give people the authority to make mistakes. And they do. This is the price of developing experienced staff.'

Robson's successor was Peter Wilson, who had joined AGC in June 1987 after a 41-year career with the Commonwealth

Bank of Australia. Wilson, widely tipped to become head of the Commonwealth Bank, lost the chance for the top job when the then federal treasurer, Paul Keating, appointed Don Sanders, previously deputy governor of the Reserve Bank. Wilson had been dissuaded from retiring by the prospect of running AGC, initially joining as chief general manager, subsidiaries and equities. A thorough gentleman who at the Commonwealth Bank had held a series of senior positions as chief economist, financial controller, general manager of the savings bank and, ultimately, chief general manager, retail banking, Wilson was a newcomer to the rough-and-ready finance company world. It is doubtful whether at that stage he could have done anything positive to alter the disastrous course of AGC, which needed a firm, even dictatorial, hand on the helm. In 1989 AGC's joint ventures had been committed if not started, and would have been difficult, but not impossible, to unwind, although the rate of lending could have been slowed.

Wilson's involvement in AGC was brief but covered a critical period. The property market had been overheated but at that stage no-one had seriously thought that even when the market fell, CBD buildings would be worth less than their replacement cost—and impossible to sell. But a powder keg lay waiting. By the beginning of 1990 the profit projections in monthly forecasts were deteriorating and the increasing exposure to joint-venture development projects was causing fluctuating financial returns. Sales of completed projects, which would determine when AGC could record its portion of the profit and interest as income for the period, were taking longer as the property market slumped. AGC's accounting policy complied with two basic principles: as a financier, interest expense on development projects was not capitalised and neither a profit nor interest income could be earned until a transaction with an independent third party had been completed. This contrasted with the practice of property developers who capitalised interest on the funding of projects. AGC could have adopted the accounting policies of a property developer only if the board decided to change the focus of the company—a move that, in the prevailing environment of a dismal property sector, would not have been well received by the market, investors and ratings agencies. Had AGC not operated as it did, income would have been reported which in subsequent years would have had to be written off, increasing losses in those years.

By late 1989 it was clear to the Westpac board that restoring AGC to profitability must be given priority. The recovery would be slow, given the drain of funding the still-incomplete Como and the increase in the loans to the joint ventures whose protracted construction periods would result in no profit or interest income being realised in 1989/90. The impact of the joint ventures was beginning to emerge.

Determined to secure a clearer picture, in November 1989 Sir Eric Neal, chairman of AGC since November 1988, appointed a subcommittee of the board, headed by Sir Llew Edwards, a consultant with Jones Lang Wootton, and comprising Rod Cameron, a high-profile accountant, and businessman Bruce Reid, to review AGC's prevailing policies and exposures in commercial property, with special emphasis on joint ventures.

In January 1990 the Westpac board received minutes from an AGC loans committee meeting held during the previous month which had approved a loan for an $88 million development in the burgeoning Sydney commercial suburb of St Leonards. The minutes included a note recording that one person had disagreed with the proposal. He was Westpac's representative on the AGC loans committee, Peter Davidson, the bank's general manager, group credit, who had also served as an alternate director on the earlier AGC board credit committee which had been disbanded when Westpac took full ownership of the finance company. At the AGC committee meeting on 19 December 1989 Davidson was accused of not understanding AGC's methods of lending—his critic was the AGC executive who had introduced the proposal, and it could be argued that his presence on the review committee was improper. Davidson's views were deemed irrelevant and the loan was approved. One of Davidson's concerns was that St Leonards was one of several areas identified in a recent review of Westpac's property exposure as vulnerable to a downturn in demand for office space. The ratings agencies were already expressing concern at the level of Westpac's exposure to property development.

Davidson spelled out his criticism on 21 December 1989, two days after the loans committee meeting, in a report to his boss, John Chatterton, who brought it to Stuart Fowler's attention. Chatterton had taken on the role of acting chief general manager, group credit policy and control, for a few months between the resignation of Warwick Kent and Harvey Garnett's taking over the position. He had already advised Fowler of his and Davidson's unease over the $88 million loan. Davidson outlined the unattractive features of the proposal: the $88 million would be a loan, secured by a non-cash-producing asset (a hole in the ground), to a company which had no income or equity, with the funds lent to pay out the existing lender. This was not prudent, he wrote. The ongoing development of the site was not yet finalised, so there was no assurance it would go ahead. That left the lender overly reliant on security, which was essentially the lease on the land. The lessor, State Rail, had the right to cancel the lease without refund if construction did not begin within a certain period, which placed the value of the security in doubt. Davidson's objection was that the valuation for the loan was based on the development being completed; if the developer collapsed, the value of the land was a fraction of the $88 million advanced to cover the cost of the 99-year lease. In his view, the issue of the security being leasehold was of secondary importance. Moreover, the loan was dependent on guarantors for servicing, and it was not unknown for guarantors in general to cry poor when the heat was applied. Davidson concluded that the transaction contained unacceptable risks, and noted that while his views had been expressed to the committee, its chairman, Peter Wilson, the managing director of AGC, had exercised his prerogative and approved the loan. Davidson was concerned that a representative of Westpac was on the AGC loans committee but that AGC was apparently not required to pay attention to his views. He was also uneasy with the $100 million delegated lending authority extended to the AGC loans committee after the 1988 takeover, and had discussed with Chatterton the prospect of reducing the authority.

The minutes of the AGC loans committee were tabled at board credit committee meetings, as well as before the board, and at least one director rang Westpac's company secretary, John Wilson, asking for further information and giving notice that at the forthcoming January board meeting there would be a couple of questions regarding an AGC loans committee matter. Davidson's memo was tabled before the Westpac board meeting on 18 January 1990 as an item for discussion. By that stage the deal had been approved so the board was hearing about why it had gone ahead rather than discussing whether it should have been approved or any powers of sanction. Had the board reversed the decision, AGC would have had to welch on the deal. Davidson was painted as the uninformed party, a traditional banker who did not understand property lending. For his efforts, Davidson received a reprimand from the chairman, Sir Eric Neal, for having exceeded his authority, delivered by a reluctant Chatterton who was familiar with Davidson's credit skills. Boardroom convention prescribes that a chairman will support a managing director over a less senior executive, and

Neal had a reputation as a stickler for convention. Moreover, it was said to be up to the managing director to judge the appropriate level of exposure to property, not Davidson.

Davidson, his caution dismissed by Neal and Fowler as a failure to understand AGC's policy of lending against lease-hold security, was in fact a highly experienced credit officer with arguably a better grasp of the risks involved than those who chose to ignore his advice. He had cited sensible reasons not to lend.

The instance was one out of many problem loans and, on this occasion, the Westpac representative went out of his way to speak against a proposal. Davidson was proved correct. The developers dug a hole in the ground and then ran out of funds. Within months the loan was on the doubtful debt list. Ultimately Westpac wrote off nearly $80 million. In 1996 the St Leonards project was still a hole in the ground and the site sold for $15 million, to be developed as a mix of residential and commercial real estate. Habitual adherence to boardroom etiquette and deafness to sound professional executive advice proved expensive to Westpac and its share-holders, when a loss might have been avoided by adherence to good credit standards and a sharper curiosity.

In June 1990 the board received the report of the sub-committee it had established six months earlier under Sir Llew Edwards to review AGC's exposures in commercial property and particularly through joint ventures. The task should have required the directors to make a rigorous inves-tigation of the business—arguably beyond their purview—but the resulting report, containing as it did mostly broad recommendations, was not an incisive document. It exam-ined the scale and growth of lending and concluded that they were within company policy. However, the committee reported that commercial property loans had risen signifi-cantly since 1987, from $950 million to $2,130 million by

March 1990, an increase of 124 per cent in two-and-a-half years, and over the same period property joint-venture exposure had grown from $134 million to $830 million, or 519 per cent; delays in completion and sales left some exposures overdue and bad debts had increased. Undrawn commitments were a concern. The committee's conclusion was that clearly there were problems in AGC, that exposures were high but under control, although management needed to be vigilant, and that some sales should be attempted because it was preferable to take losses in some instances to avoid continuing holding costs. The report said provisioning was satisfactory but there was potential for significant loss if the property market deteriorated further. AGC was to undertake no further joint-venture lending until it had worked out existing projects. This was repeating the obvious, since the managing director had said a year earlier that AGC would not enter into any more joint ventures. The last approved had been Piccadilly, in December 1988. The question of future joint ventures should be left open until the market recovered, and if any further ventures were undertaken they were to be kept under strict review. Overall, the committee commented that it was impressed with the breadth of experience in AGC's property personnel, to the extent that it canvassed an idea that had been floated before, but had never reached maturity—that there might be advantages in greater integration with Westpac's own property activities, so that the bank could benefit from the experience and expertise in AGC. The report should have set a red light flashing.

Had AGC complied with the $500 million limit on joint-venture exposure, with no more than 30 per cent of assets in property and a planned geographical spread, then a lid could have been kept on the problem. As it was, AGC had too many large commitments too close together, so that the slightest downturn in the property market, or rise in costs to complete, would send it over its limits. While only a slight tremor was required to tip the balance, what transpired was a veritable earthquake as the property market dived and stayed down. By September 1990 actual exposures were $920 million against commitments of $1.5 billion as the slump in sales strangled the inflow of proceeds.

It was clear the AGC properties were not going to sell or be fully let until the economy turned around. Meanwhile, it was in Westpac's interest to wait in the hope that when the property market recovered and the rate of inflation began to rise, values would increase as they had in the past and demand resume. In a better climate the bank might be able to sell a building for, say, the $150 million it cost to build instead of the $30 million it might bring in an immediate fire sale. There was a precedent for this approach: in the case of the Regent Hotel, AGC had hung on and eventually, after several years, recovered all but $10 million of the loan it had advanced against the security of shares in the hotel. However, the property market decline of the early 1990s was far more widespread and already longer than had been expected, given the experience of previous downturns. And while 1990 had ended with treasurer Paul Keating asserting that Australia was in the grip of a 'recession we had to have', and many commentators were talking optimistically about a 'soft landing', the economy in fact endured a protracted, extremely hard landing that lasted eighteen months.

But expectations at the time suggested that recovery, with an upturn in the property market, was around the corner, so that AGC could escape relatively unscathed. In December 1990, when almost every joint-venture project was indicating a loss, several of AGC's executives were optimistic that Piccadilly and Southgate, two major projects, would be sufficiently profitable not just to cover all losses but to provide an overall profit. It was a misguided optimism, because nearly all joint-venture projects became substantial losses.

And warning signs were there: the estimated increase in costs for only nine major projects, because of delays in construction and sales, was $440 million. Board approval was required, but with the projects well advanced, the board felt it had no option but to give the nod. Of the $440 million, $200 million was interest, $65 million for additional construction costs, $150 million in lease incentives and about $20 million in incentives to obtain vacant possession so that construction could begin. While some AGC executives were unwilling to believe that the property market would deteriorate further, others were concerned about the increasing problems in the joint ventures. The positive view prevailed until March 1992, to the cost of AGC and Westpac. Meanwhile, AGC continued with business as usual in its other activities, maintaining its high profile as a consistent borrower from the public. A major concern was to protect the inflow of cash from debentures, AGC's chief source of funding. This was successful as, despite the mounting problems, and even when these later became public, AGC did not experience a grievous drop in the rate of renewals for debenture subscriptions.

171

In January 1991 Westpac established a special unit to manage group property exposures, with its principal focus initially on major AGC property loans, including joint ventures and the Como project. Headed by Howard Dudgeon, general manager, group property finance, the unit—which later grew to become the asset management group—went through AGC's loans, especially those related to property, with a fine-toothed comb. AGC customers felt the winds of change; there were reports of longstanding customers receiving unprecedented harsh treatment, while any loan in doubt was summarily dealt with. AGC managing director Peter Wilson publicly confirmed that the management of AGC's property joint-venture portfolio had been passed to Westpac, as had supervision of most of AGC's other property loans, totalling about $2 billion. AGC's independence was definitely over. Wilson pointed out that, following the full ownership of AGC by Westpac from 1988, there was logic in bringing AGC's credit policies more into line with those of its banking parent.

However, the changes took their toll on AGC's image with borrowers and developers. A dispute with private hospital mogul Doug Moran, a longstanding customer, was seen as a sign of AGC's changed business relationships. Moran, sponsor of the hospital of excellence at Tugun on the Gold Coast, took his joint-venture partners AGC and C. Itoh to court to break a costly deadlock that had brought construction to a standstill in September 1990. Neither lender would advance additional funds but the hospital needed equipment. A year later, in November 1991, Westpac and C. Itoh took the Moran Health Care Group out of the grandiose Tugun development—purpose-built and hard to sell—after prolonged litigation. The final settlement included a binding agreement that neither side discuss the project. Eventually Westpac and Mayne Nickless completed the hospital and Westpac sold its share to Health Care of Australia Ltd, a division of Mayne Nickless. AGC, ultimately Westpac, lost close to $100 million on the hospital project.

Of the other joint-venture projects, AGC had been trying to sell Capital Hill, Brisbane, for two years; it was also trying to sell West End Centre in Melbourne which was mostly vacant, having been finished two years behind schedule. AGC had agreed to complete the $235 million residential and hotel development at Dockside in Brisbane, following the collapse of its joint-venture partners, Girvan and Fricker Developments. With Girvan also involved in the $200 million Citadel Towers in Sydney, it was left to AGC to oversee that project which, in mid-1991, had only one tenant. Generous incentives had to be offered to induce others into the completed but almost empty building. An

Bob White, 1985: managing director of the Bank of New South Wales/ Westpac, 1977–87, he was the architect of Westpac's advance into global banking.*

Sir Noel Foley: as last chairman of the Bank of New South Wales and first chairman of Westpac Banking Corporation, he oversaw the demise of the Wales and the birth of Westpac.

*All photographs and illustrations courtesy of Westpac Banking Corporation, except where otherwise indicated.

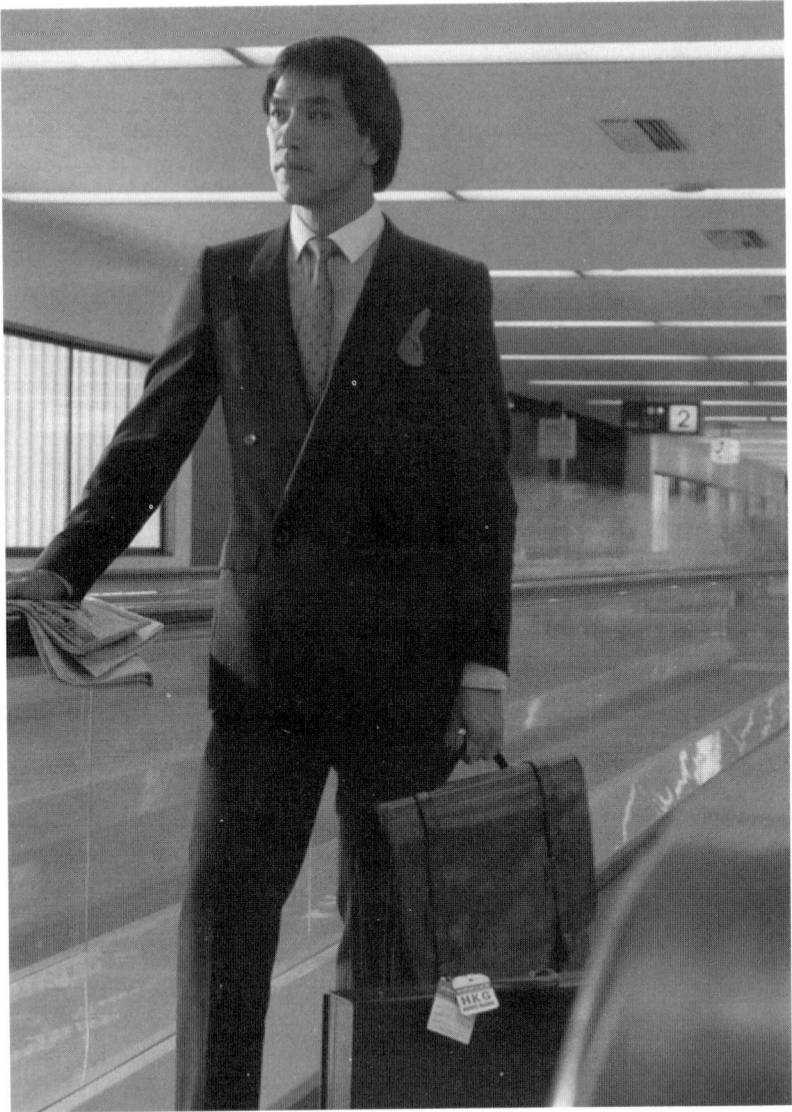

Peter Chan: a symbol of Westpac's transition from a domestic to a 'world' bank, Chan ran its aggressive foreign-exchange department, dubbed the 'ulcer department'.

Westpac's 1985 annual report captured a meeting between Gary Roberts (left), group financial controller, and Michael Kent (centre), finance director of The Adelaide Steamship Company Ltd, a longstanding client of the bank, and Barry Robertson, group account executive, corporate banking. The relationship with Adsteam, which dated from the turn of the century, was sorely tested when the sprawling, debt-mired empire later hit problems. In the 1990s, Robertson—after serving as the bank's Mr Fix-It in Singapore and New Zealand—launched into a new career as Westpac's bad-debt trouble shooter before moving to take charge of Victoria, Tasmania, South Australia and the Northern Territory.

Warren Magi, managing director of Mase Westpac Ltd. A chance relationship brought Westpac an entry to the heart of the world's bullion trading market and gave rise to a promising subsidiary which was cast off in the rationalisation of the 1990s. (Photograph courtesy of BRW magazine)

Then Westpac chairman, Sir James Foots, and managing director Bob White at the 1987 Expo, a year when Westpac was riding high and a satisfied White was on the brink of retirement after ten years at the helm.

The board of Partnership Pacific Ltd, Westpac's wholly-owned merchant bank subsidiary, in 1987: (standing, from left) Tony Snape, David Braidwood, Ron Thomsen, Peter Davidson, Tony Battle, Stan Davis; (sitting) Frank Ward, Philip Deer and Warwick Kent. PPL was an energetic, headstrong Westpac child which brought its parent considerable trouble.

The board of AGC in 1988, after Westpac had taken full control of the finance company. Westpac directors became directors of AGC so that the two operated under the one board and a common chairman. AGC matters were dealt with as an item on the crowded Westpac board agenda: (top left, from left) Sir Frank Espie, Rod Cameron, Sir Neil Currie, Sir David Zeidler, Bruce Reid; (top right) Rob Robson; (centre left, from left) Sir Eric Neal, Sir James Foots, James Scully; (centre right, from left) Ian (Jock) Harper, Bob White; (bottom left, from left) Peter Baillieu, Stewart Macindoe, Warren Hogan; (bottom right, from left) Sir Llewellyn Edwards, Stuart Fowler, Sir Harold Aston. (Photographs courtesy of Westpac Banking Corp and AGC Ltd)

Stuart Fowler in 1988: Fowler succeeded Bob White as chief of Westpac. He aimed high for the bank he had served for almost forty years—but the profit element of his cherished trifecta of $1 billion in profit, $100 billion in assets and 100,000 shareholders eluded him.

office block at 270 Pitt Street, Sydney, was leasing, but slowly. And AGC had taken out C. Itoh from the $275 million Oasis on Broadbeach. The $650 million Southgate project, though, was to be Westpac/AGC's biggest loss.

AGC and its now extinct merchant bank subsidiary BAC, with their combined bad debts of $218 million, mostly related to property loans, accounted for some 40 per cent of Westpac's bad and doubtful debt provisions in the half-year to March 1991. Far from contributing to Westpac's bottom line as it had in the past, AGC had become a severe drain. Its non-accrual loans (those on which interest due had not been received) had jumped from $262 million to $1 billion. Several joint ventures would require additional funding. AGC recorded an 82 per cent drop in net profit for the first half of 1991 to $9 million, despite the benefit of $48 million through a 'risk participation agreement' with Westpac. Under this arrangement, Westpac agreed to fund $1.25 billion of AGC's property exposures, interest free, with the bank assuming responsibility for losses on AGC's joint-venture projects. In return, Westpac was entitled to future profits, which did not eventuate. The question of the agreement was discussed with the Reserve Bank which, alert to the circumstances, agreed to the arrangement but was not very happy about it. The central bank's approach is that a bank should not stand behind a subsidiary to the extent that investors in the subsidiary believe they have an investment akin in safety to a bank deposit. Westpac's 'life-line' to AGC blurred the distinction between parent and subsidiary.

Westpac's action delayed AGC's slide into the red. In May 1991, announcing AGC's $9 million result, Stuart Fowler said that the financier would confine its activities to core consumer finance business and would quit property finance, although not necessarily forever. Nonetheless, this was an undignified exit of a major non-bank operator from the property market. Fowler's brief remarks reflected the savage impact of AGC's property portfolio on its banking parent. He added that no improvement in the commercial property market was expected for a further eighteen months to two years.

Peter Wilson retired in May 1991 and in June Barry Robertson was placed at the head of the finance company. Robertson was tagged Westpac's 'troubleshooter' because of his success in solving the bank's problems in New Zealand, having already tidied up a number of foreign-currency lending difficulties in Westpac's Singapore branch.

At his first board meeting he had the unenviable task of having to confront the board with the news that AGC was in serious trouble regarding its prospectus. AGC was a continuous borrower from the general public through debentures and unsecured notes. The most recent prospectus, dated 28 March 1991, stated that AGC's results for the year would be substantially below those of 1990 but a profit was still expected. Now the company was internally forecasting a net loss of $120 million. Westpac publicly defended the earlier statement, saying the continued deterioration in the economy and in the property market had changed the situation. A supplementary prospectus was brought out. Instead of: 'The results for the year to 30 September 1991 are expected to be a profit but will be substantially below the level achieved in the financial year ended 30 September 1990', the new prospectus stated: 'Continued deterioration in the property market in Australia and absence of any signs of sustained recovery in the general economy have resulted in the need for a further re-assessment of the group's portfolio. The directors have decided, as a prudent measure, to establish additional significant provisions, particularly in the property portfolio. Consequently, current indications are that the group's results for the year will be an after-tax loss in the order of $120 million.' A far-reaching review of AGC was carried out. Bank analysts were critical of Westpac for having sent out misleading signals because, in their view, the property market had not significantly altered since the earlier announcement.

In July 1991 Westpac injected $150 million in preference share capital to help keep the finance company afloat. The bank concluded that AGC required major restructuring, a reduction in staff and a thorough review of its role, which would at the same time preserve its particular skills and strengths. On Friday 16 August 1991 the board issued a statement confirming that AGC's business focus would be more modest, focusing on its traditional core activities of leasing, consumer, motor vehicle and equipment finance and factoring. The statement made no mention of the four general managers who lost their jobs that day: Peter French, group general manager and Rob Robson's right-hand man, Graeme White, general manager of property finance, Ray Morley, general manager of retail lending, and John Rumble, general manager of group marketing. The four were told at lunch-time, following a Westpac board meeting, that their positions had been 'made redundant'. French, rarely ill, was at home with a bout of flu; he received a call from Westpac, insisting that he come into the office. He arrived and was told he was no longer needed. These decisions confirmed Robertson's reputation as a hard-nosed, take-no-prisoners fixer.

With the nature and extent of AGC's property problems becoming increasingly clear, relations between Westpac directors and the Westpac executives appointed to manage the property portfolio became correspondingly more strained. Westpac directors, having brought in Westpac executives to run AGC, then ripped into them and often fought with them. Directors' confidence in the executives plummeted; language in the boardroom grew blunt, with verbal exchanges at times acrimonious.

The Westpac executives were accused by the directors of lacking the expertise to manage property and handle promotion and sales. The executives resented criticism from directors who, in their view, did not understand the business. Reports that a director had suggested that all that was required to sell a particular motel in Australia and recover the loan was to give it a coat of paint left executives unimpressed about directors' grasp of the seriousness of the problems in the property market. Some directors, dismayed by the turmoil, engaged property consultants and appeared to be trying to take over management functions. For their part, Westpac executives disliked having to shoulder problems created by others in AGC, BAC and PPL. They had the difficult task of unscrambling legal tangles and conducting often hostile discussions with joint-venture partners. Several directors took increasing responsibility, including Sir Eric Neal and the anointed 'property expert' Sir Llew Edwards, who together visited construction sites in Melbourne, Brisbane and the Gold Coast. They also travelled to Indonesia, Singapore, Taiwan and Hong Kong to promote the attractions of Australian property. By the middle of 1991 values in the Sydney central business district, Australia's leading market, had dropped by around 40 per cent from their late-1989 peak. Pressure was on valuers to provide realistic property valuations; auditors were taking a tough approach to what was a 'true and fair' value of an asset on the balance sheet. The major accounting firms, backed by the revamped Corporations Law, were emphasising to directors the focus on current market value, rather than historic or future intrinsic value.

For the year to September 1991, against the background of a woeful economic climate, AGC as predicted recorded its first loss in its 65 years of operating, $114 million after tax. This was despite booking abnormal profits of $70 million before tax through bringing to account an actu-arially assessed surplus in the staff superannuation fund and a $16.7 million tax credit through altering accounting policy for the general provisions. AGC group non-accrual loans had nearly doubled, from $603 million to $1,095 million. The Westpac group's non-accrual loans had risen by 50 per cent to $3.68 billion. AGC and its badly bleeding UK offshoot, Westpac General Finance, were responsible for more than 43 per cent of Westpac's $1 billion charge for bad and doubt-ful debts. In 1991 office vacancy rates in the UK were appallingly high and the property book of Westpac General Finance nosedived. Having failed to make headway against the local competition in motor vehicle finance and personal loans, Westpac General Finance had been lending heavily against commercial property. Much of the business was broker-introduced, in a market where it was vitally important to be able to distinguish the brokers who brought good busi-ness from those who did not. Westpac General Finance's growth had been rapid: at its peak it employed 100 staff, based in the Maidenhead, Berkshire, head office and in seven branches opened over three years around the south-east and in Bristol, Newcastle, Birmingham and Manchester. By now, having lost $96 million for the year, WGF was no longer writing business. Tony Aveling, Westpac's man in London since March 1990, was persuaded to take control of the busi-ness and was winding it down.

AGC's problems in New South Wales, Victoria, Queens-land and Western Australia came home to roost in 1992. Sir Eric Neal said that AGC was expected to make a loss similar to the $114 million recorded in 1990/91. Westpac clearly faced a huge challenge as the factors that had tipped AGC into the red, such as falling property values, bad debts and record non-accrual loans, continued to deteriorate. AGC's exposure to joint ventures well exceeded its capital. It had

177

now become impossible to sell projects at sensible prices and exposures had ballooned to $1.7 billion. Additional draw-downs on new projects had proceeded even though existing projects were not sold. Caution would have argued in favour of withdrawing from lending in the face of the ruinous drop in the property market and the mounting surplus of com-mercial property and hotels. But AGC continued to honour its commitments. Gallant, perhaps, but fatal.

In May 1992, when Westpac revealed its results for the 1991/92 year to March—detailed in chapter 13—it became clear publicly to what extent AGC had damaged its parent, losing $719 million in the six months to March, on top of the loss in the year to September 1991—and that was despite Westpac's relieving AGC to the tune of $92 million under the risk-participation and funding agreement struck in March of that year. In the full year to September 1992 AGC lost $726.1 million after tax, off a shareholders' funds base of $1.1 billion. Had AGC not received a capital injection of $850 million from Westpac in May, it would have been in breach of its trust deeds which could have led to the trustees having the right to demand repayment of all debentures and notes, virtually putting the company into liquidation. AGC had enjoyed a succession of what seemed golden years in 1987, 1988 and 1989, when profits were robust, but these in fact had been substantially boosted by asset sales and changes in tax rates. The high level of reported profits added to the mood of euphoria and helped fuel the burst in lending—assets rose in those three years by 48 per cent.

By late 1992 Westpac had taken control of Como, Citadel Towers and Perth's Exchange Plaza. Joint ventures in Mel-bourne had emerged as major problems, with AGC commit-ting to lend more than $700 million on three projects: Como, where troubles had preceded the property slump, Southgate, and Australia on Collins. Queensland was another source of AGC's woes: the company's enthusiastic plunge into the

Sunshine State's buoyant property market had created another sword in Westpac's side, through the property joint ventures at Dockside in Brisbane, Broadbeach on the Gold Coast and the Moran hospital at Tugun. Westpac and AGC were also bigger property owners in Western Australia than they would have wished, as developers there, too, were hit by the early 1990s slump. Even as late as November 1989 AGC had been forecasting in board reports that profits from the sale of joint ventures would be $31 million in 1991 and $68 million in 1992, assuming all projects were held to completion. Of an estimated $500 million outstanding in Perth, the group's largest exposure was the Exchange Plaza office tower in the city's business district. Exchange Plaza cost around $240 million and in May 1992 was still seeking tenants. Westpac, on behalf of AGC, bought out joint-venture partners C. Itoh and Shimizu Construction in 1991. Westpac had also invested some $200 million in various developments in and around Perth.

AGC's problem loans for the half year to March 1992 totalled $1.8 billion. AGC and its related activities—Bill Acceptance Corporation, Westpac General Finance in the UK and the support arrangements provided by Westpac—accounted for $1.1 billion, or two-thirds, of the $1.67 billion loss announced by the bank in May 1992. The tone of the directors' statement was in sharp contrast with earlier comments and forecasts. In an interview with *The Australian Financial Review* on 11 March 1992, Frank Conroy, by then Westpac managing director, had said:

> What AGC did was two things wrong. They were traditionalists ... a consumer finance company, leasing and personal loans ... They also used to do smaller type development projects. For example, they would lend to a builder who would buy five acres of land and build a lot of houses, and provide

virtually the bridging finance, and they did that well for years. And then suddenly in the late 1980s, from about 1987 onwards, they took two steps. First of all they went into these individual large company loans, $1 billion at a time, really big stuff . . . big, big stuff, big lending, they had never done before. And the second thing they did wrong was the joint ventures where they went in for part of the development and actually selling them. Well, that went wrong because you can't sell them.

According to the *Financial Review*, Conroy's view at the time was that Westpac did not have to write down to current market value the assets backing its problem loans because it was a big institutional provider of finance and a long-term holder of property. 'We don't just slash values and dump property,' said Conroy. 'So you have just got to be big enough and strong enough to sit on it.'

Conroy would have to change that view.

As the year wore on Westpac, under the risk participation agreement, took more and more AGC joint ventures under its wing, taking Jennings out of Southgate, Citistate out of Australia on Collins, Pidgeon out of Dockside and Capital Land Corporation out of Piccadilly. Had Westpac chosen in 1987 to redevelop rather than sell the former CBA head office at 335 Collins Street—a sale that netted a profit of $95 million—it would have owned a large development on each side of Collins Street. Westpac could not walk away from AGC. And, because Westpac took its financier's problems on the chin, AGC's name escaped otherwise unavoidable tarnishing. At the end of 1992 Westpac's $10.9 billion exposure to Australian property included $4.5 billion in problem assets and AGC could claim responsibility for about half of those. AGC's half-developed properties continued to make a mockery of the $500 million maximum exposure limit; the company's shares of the Southgate project in Melbourne and the Piccadilly venture in Sydney would on their own have taken AGC well past the limit. The $650 million Southgate project was eventually sold in early 1994 to the Victorian government's Transport Accident Commission for $310 million. The office block at 270 Pitt Street in Sydney sold for $40 million. Later in 1994 Westpac disposed of Piccadilly Plaza, one of the last projects to be sold in its clearance of property assets inherited from AGC's joint ventures, for $140 million. The slump in property brought bargains for buyers: during the year Westpac off-loaded eight hotels and a clutch of retail complexes to Singapore's Thakral Group for $263 million, providing the diversified family empire with an instant chain of hotels.

AGC's problems stemmed from a combination of circumstances but the primary cause was that it became overly involved in major property joint ventures which were taking longer and longer to complete—at a time when the property boom was starting to wane. AGC crossed a line when it became not just a lender but a de facto developer, involuntarily having to lift its equity stake in joint ventures because of partners' problems. And within the Westpac group fiefdoms prevailed, a trend that was not unusual in the 1980s when management thinking encouraged the notion of internal rivalry as a performance incentive. But increased operational autonomy should signal tighter centralised financial controls. Events showed that central control in Westpac was weak and each fiefdom—AGC, PPL, BAC, WGF—went its own way. Market share had become the Holy Grail and, in the pursuit of business, deals got through the system that warranted far greater scrutiny and caution.

There was also a considerable element of corporate ego in AGC. The company flaunted its involvement in highly visible projects such as the Regent Hotel, Como, Southgate and Tugun. In 1983 the absorption of General Credits had brought a different mix of business, with a greater emphasis on property lending, much of it in 'intensive care'; deregulation had sparked a rush for growth; not for the first and probably not for the last time in history the appeal of property was irresistible. Within the Westpac group, AGC was seen as entrepreneurial and spirited. It marketed itself stridently, in 1987 commissioning a video, *Building Atlantis*, which featured several of its property developer clients including Girvan Group chairman Paul Petersen, Sid Londish, Doug Moran and Ron McCaster. In the video, Petersen praised AGC's support, which helped Girvan grow from a small company to a major construction group undertaking projects worth hundreds of millions of dollars. 'Without their help we would not have been able to do what we've done.' Sid Londish, a client of AGC since the 1950s, spoke of the 'great rapport' he had with his financier. That rapport came to an end in November 1992, when Westpac appointed a receiver to three properties of Londish's company, Comrealty Ltd, prompting Londish to put the company into provisional liquidation.

The board should have been more cautious and inquisitive when confronted by enthusiastic staff who insisted that a profit would eventuate next year, or the year after, that it was merely a matter of timing. Management tends to judge board members by the quality of the questions they ask. A board response—inadequate but all too common—is that directors can only ask questions if they have adequate information so that they know what questions need asking. Poorly monitored management can get away with being selective in what it tells a board. Those with mounting doubts about optimistic forecasts of occupancy rates or rentals would try to draw attention to the size of an exposure by regularly providing information on progress and outlook so that the board could make a judgment. But bullishness about property was hard to shake. By the time the Westpac/AGC directors began querying aspects of the company's business, they got answers that shocked their socks off. Every rock they turned over seemed to reveal a new death adder.

Despite the trauma, the brand name of AGC held up well during the early 1990s. Investors knew that Westpac could not state that it guaranteed AGC's debentures but they nonetheless saw the bank supporting AGC in some way—as in the end it did. Australia's corporate history offers plenty of examples of banks, to their cost, supporting their finance companies. An extreme example is Finance Corporation of Australia which, in 1979, brought down its parent, the Bank of Adelaide, to the point where the governor of the Reserve Bank instructed the Bank of Adelaide to put itself up for sale. The bank was bought by the highest bidder, the ANZ Bank. So the Westpac parentage was enormously important to AGC investors. Throughout the early 1990s AGC's debenture book was mostly stable, even modestly growing, with support continuing from third parties such as brokers who did not stop recommending AGC. The perception of the public that Westpac, despite the stiff denials in the prospectus, stood behind its finance company, was strong enough to preserve their loyalty.

When the prestige British bank Barings PLC was ruined in 1995 by an out-of-control and under-supervised derivatives trader in its Singapore branch, a universal shiver went down banking spines. Could Australia experience a similar disaster? The similarities that can be drawn between Barings and AGC are striking: AGC in the 1980s was allowed to run its own race, profits were being generated so no-one was asking too many searching questions, it was active in an area of business not wholly familiar to its parent and volumes were growing rapidly. The Barings trader was left pretty much to himself while profits were being generated but his position in the market grew so monstrously that when the market moved against him he was destroyed. AGC took a dangerously big position in property but, unlike Barings, it did not collapse when the market moved against it. AGC, whose losses all but wiped out its shareholders' funds, was rescued by its banking parent's injection of $1 billion in new equity. Barings was taken over by a foreign bank. For its parent, AGC produced negative returns on equity in 1991 of 10.97 per cent and in 1992 of 64.71 per cent.

The year 1992—by which time Westpac ranked as one of Australia's largest property developers and arguably its largest hotel operator, having shouldered most of the dead weight of AGC's troubled joint ventures—ended with the axe falling on a quarter of AGC's staff, who were to be phased out of the shrunken finance company over eighteen months. Barry Robertson, in a major reshuffle instigated by Westpac chief Frank Conroy, was elevated early in November 1992 to head Westpac's asset management group. Robertson had been keen to stay in AGC which, with most of its problems taken over by Westpac, was now returning to a profitable business, with good staff who knew how to price and sell. But perhaps he had done his job too well as a fixer. He was brought back into Westpac where he would be working on the rehabilitation of many of the poorly performing assets he had earlier transferred from AGC to the bank. Tony Aveling, who had proved his abilities in downsizing at Westpac General Finance and in Westpac's technology division, replaced Robertson at the head of AGC. Despite the earlier forecasts to the contrary, finance companies continued to prosper, separately branded from banks.

Much of the turbulence was over when Aveling became head of AGC. As was the case with Westpac, while the top echelons of the organisation were concerned with the drama of survival, underneath the staff went on working at their regular jobs, keeping the organisation ticking over. In a sense, staff had been on remote control, working without the support and investment that they rightfully expect from the centre. Aveling arrived to run a recovering company with a strong balance sheet and high credit standards whose focus was on areas where it had shown expertise—and he had a brief to steer clear of major property deals. It was acknowledged that AGC had a good grip on a client base which would never deal with Westpac and which, if the finance company were to be folded into the bank, could be lost to the group.

AGC's annual report for 1992 contained an optimistic prophecy from John Uhrig, who had replaced Neal as Westpac chairman, that the company would return to profitability in 1992/93 (under the risk participation agreement, which ran until June 1992, AGC's non-accrual loans were funded by Westpac). The group still had more than $1 billion of non-accrual loans at the end of the 1992 financial year but significant progress had been made in reducing the level of problem assets. 'A revitalised AGC will continue to focus on specialist finance company activities of consumer and motor vehicle financing, factoring, leasing and equipment finance and small, mainly residential, property development finance,' Uhrig said.

The loan portfolio of AGC (Advances) Ltd—essentially some of the joint ventures and a few large property loans— went to Westpac when the bank bought the company, which boosted AGC's results in 1993 because it had fewer loans to fund and avoided further provisions for loss. In 1993 and 1994 AGC completed the sales of its Asian assets, in the teeth of considerable internal resistance to selling good businesses which had not produced any major loan losses. But the disposal was in line with Westpac's recovery plan of retreating to 'core' activities. And Westpac's new boss, Bob Joss, no fan of grand offshore strategy, was in favour of the sales. Westpac's Vern Harvey, now chief general manager, regional offshore banking, and charged with getting rid of the group's Asian network, worked with Standard Chartered PLC on the sales program. Standard Chartered, apart from its high profile in Asia, was also a joint shareholder with AGC in the consumer finance companies Credit Corporation (Malaysia) Berhad, a vehicle and equipment leasing company established in 1963, and Credit Corporation Singapore. In fact, during 1992 Standard Chartered had approached AGC with a proposal that it float its Asian operations, retaining 50 per cent. But Joss was adamant that they remain on the block. Westpac sold its 85 per cent share in the Indonesian bank Westpac Panin to the ANZ Banking Group, and wound down its branch in Seoul. In December 1993 AGC Finance (HK) Ltd, a well-run company with a solid range of business and no bad loans and which attracted more than 50 potential buyers, was sold to AT&T at a profit of $48.9 million. The profit on the disposal of AGC (Thailand), a promising joint venture with the Bank of Thailand, was $32.5 million. The sale of AGC Taiwan brought a loss of $1 million. In February 1994 AGC's share of Credit Corporation (Malaysia) Berhad was sold, netting about $34 million for Westpac. Because Singapore's monetary authorities insisted that Credit Corporation Singapore be run by a bank, it rejected the blue-chip regional names keen to buy and CCS was taken over by Standard Chartered. During the year AGC repaid $500 million to Westpac, being the redemption of the preference share capital injected during 1991 and 1992. AGC was producing a healthy 9.4 per cent return on equity, with a staff in Australia of just under 2,000 compared with the 3,300 of four years earlier. Overseas staff totalled a mere 36, compared with the previous 847.

In the eight years to 1993 AGC reported a cumulative net loss after tax of $104 million, a figure that would have been much greater had results not been bolstered by a series of favourable transactions: profit on the sale of its investment in Mirvac, the sale of the AGC (Insurances) share portfolio, the benefit of a change in the tax rate, the sale of AGC (Insurances), a one-off change in the basis of recording deferred income on loans (to bring AGC's income recognition into line with that of Westpac), two consecutive surpluses in the pension fund, a subsidy from Westpac in the form of the risk participation agreement and the benefit of Westpac's capital injections.

Westpac's lifeline to AGC

Westpac's rescue of AGC had progressed in stages. From October 1990 a concessional rate of interest applied to a $1.3 billion loan from Westpac to AGC to fund joint ventures and property loans, with the amount subject to a Reserve Bank-imposed cap which limited Westpac's exposure to a subsidiary; under the risk participation agreement, Westpac took responsibility for Como, several joint ventures and large property loans, amounting to assistance of $1.1 billion which provided a benefit to AGC of $48 million after tax in the first six months of 1991; in June 1991 Westpac injected $150 million into AGC in the form of preference shares; this was modified in June 1992 when the risk participation agreement was cancelled and $850 million in equity contributed by Westpac. In October 1991 Westpac bought two properties from AGC, 270 Pitt Street and Citadel Towers, enabling AGC to reverse provisions for losses and recover interest previously deferred on its equity and loans to the projects, after the partners' equity was bought out at a discount of 30 per cent. In November 1992 Westpac bought AGC (Advances) for $1, removing most of the joint ventures and property portfolio from AGC's balance sheet and significantly improving its gearing.

The asset sales and the assistance from Westpac amounted to hundreds of millions of dollars of benefit to AGC; remove them, and AGC's after-tax loss over the eight years to 1993 would have been around $550 million and AGC would not have been able to pay dividends. Had AGC been an independent company, rather than a wholly owned subsidiary of a major bank, it would almost certainly have joined the list of casualties of the 1980s, companies which sorely misjudged how to respond to changed business and economic conditions.

CHAPTER EIGHT

BIG BAD BUSINESS

Between 1989 and 1991, as persistent high interest rates took their toll, the Australian economy sank into recession, bringing widespread business failures, rising unemployment, shrinking demand for bank finance and a level of misery and uncertainty in the general community not seen for decades. The property market bubble burst; investors evaporated and many central business district developments were unsellable. Westpac became increasingly introspective and defensive as it tried, often in a flat-footed way, to fend off its critics. Westpac had never been through a period like this. Tensions between board and management increased. It was no secret that Sir Eric Neal was greatly irritated by what he saw as shortcomings in Westpac management. They in turn resented his manner, which engendered considerable dislike, and they resented what they saw as his lack of knowledge of banking. The board generally became less passive and more questioning as problem after problem came to light. They queried management about lending policies and credit controls, and the bonus system which rewarded corporate lending staff regardless of the performance of the loan. To the board, some of the lending officers appeared more like advocates for the borrowers than officials of the bank. To the credit officers trying to supervise the recovery of troubled loans, board criticism smacked of shooting the messenger. In the earlier rush for business, it seemed everyone had forgotten a basic tenet of banking: will this loan be repaid? Directors Peter Baillieu and Warren Hogan won a fight to boost the status in the bank of the group credit policy and control division by having its head made a chief general manager and a member of management's powerful inner circle, the executive committee.

Strategy had become less clear-cut, although the bank, for a time at least, was still enthusiastic about making an acquisition. The board considered buying Yorkshire Bank in the UK and looked at several propositions in the US. Domestically, Westpac made an unsuccessful tilt at State Bank Victoria which in 1990 went to the Commonwealth Bank, even though Westpac had bid $55 million more in cash than the winning offer of $1.6 billion.

In January 1989 Sir James Foots had presided over his last annual general meeting as chairman of Westpac, having served on the board since 1971 and been chairman since 1987. Age had dictated that Foots, in his seventies when he had taken over from Sir Noel Foley, be a temporary chairman. Foots expressed his conviction that Westpac would continue to grow 'as a significant financial services group, developing in selected global markets while maintaining its strong base in Australia, New Zealand and the South Pacific'. Foots was succeeded by Sir Eric Neal, a board member of Westpac since 1985 and deputy chairman since 1987. Neal's appointment was not without controversy. Towards the end of 1988 a meeting of non-executive directors was called, chaired by the outgoing Foots, to discuss the matter of a new chairman. There was considerable disagreement over the choice, with Bob White vigorously opposed to Neal's nomination, and the meeting was adjourned. A subsequent meeting was organised for the following week; it was suggested to White that, because of his long association with management, he should not attend. White and Stuart Fowler were at a Returned Servicemen's League annual dinner on 16 November when Fowler was called to the telephone.

He returned to tell White that Neal had been unanimously voted in as chairman of Westpac. By any measure, his was a swift rise to the top board slot.

Neal, managing director of Boral Ltd from 1973 until he retired in 1987, had been knighted in 1982 for services to industry. He habitually worked a twelve-hour day, six days a week, and expected similar dedication from those around him. At Boral, where he had spent most of his working life and fourteen years as chief executive, he presided over un-interrupted profit growth in the quarrying, road surfacing, building supplies and energy group. For Boral, the 1980s was a decade of expansion, much of it through acquisition, when assets, sales, net profit and debt all grew by more than 100 per cent. Neal gained a reputation as a 'hands-on' chief, and at Westpac he went on to become similarly involved—many said interfering—an executive chairman in all but name. He was known to be shrewd, hard and proud, charm-ing but stonily impenetrable when being interviewed. He was acknowledged as an excellent systematic thinker, one of Australia's best corporate managers. Capable of being avun-cular, and equally able to be ruthless when he chose—he was dubbed 'the smiling piranha'—he had run Boral with an iron fist. He admitted that, when at the helm, he could be very firm, even tough.

Since his arrival on the Westpac board in 1985 Neal had been disturbed at what he perceived as the lack of account-ability in the bank. It irked him that the episode of the *Sea Goddess*, a financial fiasco which had cost Westpac millions of dollars, did not prompt an intensive grilling by the board. Accustomed to a constant flow of information from around the world at Boral, he encouraged Fowler to upgrade West-pac's accounting and reporting systems.

Born in London in 1924, Neal came to Australia at the age of three when his father began working for the South Australian Gas Company, and started his own career at

Broken Hill, in NSW, as a junior engineer. Trained as a mechanical and electrical engineer at the South Australian School of Mines, Neal had followed in the family footsteps when he joined the gas business; he was working with the Ballarat Gas Company when it was taken over by Boral in 1963; ten years later he was chief executive of Boral, succeeding Sir Elton Griffin. Neal had worked his way up from the shop floor to management and then to the boardroom, acquiring considerable social status along the way. He juggled the demands of corporate life with outside interests such as patronage of the arts and membership of several government committees. The punishing schedule left little time for leisure but he enjoyed an evening walk with his wife, Joan, and an occasional game of golf. He found time for frequent visits to the theatre and became an expert on maritime history. Although he remained a member of the Boral board for five years after his retirement, the chairmanship of the company he had served for 30 years eluded him. However, when he joined the Westpac board, aged 61, Neal was also a director of Wormald International Ltd, vice-president and director of the Business Council of Australia and coordinator of the Duke of Edinburgh Award scheme in Australia. He later added directorships of John Fairfax Ltd and Atlas Copco Australia. In April 1987 he was appointed chief of three commissioners who took over responsibilities of the elected representatives of Sydney City Council, following the dismissal of the councillors, with the three holding office until the end of 1988, steering Sydney through its landmark Bicentennial celebrations.

In April 1989, not far into Neal's term as chairman of Westpac, he gave a demonstration of his style which left no-one in doubt about who, in his view, called the shots. He had come to feel that there was a negative perception of the board among the executive committee. It added to his view that Westpac's executive team did not understand the role of the board. His response, justified in the eyes of some fellow directors who believed that the executive committee had acquired too much authority, was to summon the committee—themselves regarded as demi-gods—and read them and a handful of senior staff a lecture about, among other items, the quality of Westpac's board. Neal stood at a lectern, flanked by several board members, and sermonised to the assembled group about the calibre of the board, its responsibilities, and how management should revere the board members' experience and their talents and encourage a positive view of these men. Monty Hilkowitz, managing director of Westpac Life, turned to a fellow executive and muttered: 'That's it for me, mate.' Hilkowitz, a former managing director of Liberty Life Association of South Africa Ltd and a Fellow of the Institute of Actuaries in London, refused to be spoken to like a schoolboy. Shortly afterwards he left Westpac, much to the dismay of Stuart Fowler who had hired him specifically to lead Westpac Life, the bank's successful subsidiary that was intended to make Westpac a power in the insurance and superannuation industry. Under Neal, the power of the executive committee was reduced in favour of a shift in power to the board.

The year 1989 had hardly got under way when problems began to bubble, initially concerning Partnership Pacific in Australia and Westpac Merchant Finance in New Zealand. In March, Stuart Fowler was the unwilling recipient of the news that Partnership Pacific and Westpac Merchant Finance would be swelling Westpac's loan provisions in that half-year. It could be said that 1989 was the year in which Westpac began to reap the results of folly. In the six months to March 1989, Westpac's specific bad debt provisions and write-offs were 73 per cent higher, at $226 million, than they had been in the first half of 1988. Partnership Pacific accounted for $77 million specific provisions and Westpac Merchant Finance wrote off $48 million through ill-advised lending in the woeful New Zealand economy. WMF's bad debts were mostly property related, reflecting the 45 per cent crash in the country's property values. Barry Robertson, sent to New Zealand late in 1988 as deputy general manager with a brief to merge WMF into the newly created corporate and investment banking division of Westpac, found himself fixing problems in the troubled merchant bank. From early 1989 he was relaying warnings to his fellow executives in Sydney about the ravages caused by a sharp boom-to-bust in the property sector. Fowler candidly said that the latest reporting period had been a disappointment. Intensely loyal to Westpac, Fowler would always try to put out bushfires himself rather than involve the board in management issues. But as the 1989 financial year went on, the profit element of his cherished trifecta—$1 billion profit, 100,000 share-holders and $100 billion assets—looked increasingly in doubt. However, at this stage the bank's focus was still on growth, on being in the world's top 50 banks; the domestic retail franchise, seen as a cashcow underpinning the expansion overseas, suffered from an unjustified belief in the bank that it was so sound that no adjustment was needed. This was a dangerous oversight because it threatened the very strength of the bank. Asset quality was not yet recognised as a growing problem. But deadly threats were emerging on the home front.

In mid-1989 several directors undertook a series of overseas visits to acquaint themselves more closely with Westpac's offshore operations. Ian (Jock) Harper, in Europe for a conference, wrote a lengthy report about the London advisory board which prompted a visit to the UK by Neal, Sir Neil Currie, Stuart Fowler, Peter Baillieu and Bruce Reid. The visiting directors queried the necessity and composition of the advisory board, and questioned its continuing value for Westpac. In their view, two members of the board faced a conflict of interest. Moreover, since 1986 Westpac also operated with the Mase Westpac board in London. Fowler, who had remained longer than the others in London, received a directive from Sydney instructing him to fire the London board. Having served with Westpac in London, Fowler knew all the board members well and found the situation highly embarrassing. But the London advisory board was summarily dismissed. Letters advising each board member that his services were no longer required awaited when they arrived for the next scheduled board meeting. They were also informed that their presence would not be required at a forthcoming conference of offshore directors, to be held in Sydney. Bob White, who agrees that he might have a bias in favour of the London group, having relied on its advice and support from time to time, was critical of the unceremonious dismissal of a board that had served the bank since its London office opened in 1853. To him, it was another regrettable break with the past.

195

During the 1980s lending binge, practices had changed as banks, local and foreign, rushed to secure market share. Credit was there for the asking. Lending officers virtually threw money at the market, egged on by incentive schemes which paid bonuses in proportion to the volume of business they brought in. The 1987 stockmarket crash failed to curb excessive optimism. The Reserve Bank and other central banks around the world ensured there was plenty of cash in the financial system to prevent a post-crash meltdown, such as had occurred after the cataclysmic stockmarket collapse in 1929. This fuelled a massive property market boom before that sector too went into a calamitous plunge, arguably the worst in a hundred years, as borrowers, investors, developers and business generally succumbed to punishingly high interest rates.

Hooker

In July 1989 Hooker Corporation Ltd, Australia's second largest property company and a customer of Westpac for decades, collapsed with a total debt globally of $2 billion, some $200 million of which had been lent by Westpac. A further 75 banks were owed money. Hooker employed 10,000 people and had 13,000 shareholders.

The company had changed character in 1986 when it came under the stewardship of George Herscu, and took a new and more adventurous direction. At the time of Herscu's takeover, Westpac's exposure to Hooker was $86 million and, following the takeover, requests for additional funds were treated gingerly. But pressure from Herscu for funds was constant; while Westpac declined his requests for additional finance in March and April 1986, it agreed to advance a small amount when he next applied in May. During 1987 the debt progressively increased in response to Herscu's requests for various 'bridging' facilities. Whereas the National Australia Bank had walked away from Hooker in 1987, taking the view that Herscu was trying to achieve too much too quickly in the US, and was paid out the $30 million owed, Westpac had increased its exposure to the company, despite mounting concern on the part of the bank's credit committee about the rising debt. In three years Hooker had four successive Westpac account officers and, by the time a provisional liquidator was appointed to the company in 1989, Westpac's group exposure was $288 million—$203 million to Westpac, $65 million to AGC and $20 million to PPL.

Funds had bled out of Hooker into Herscu's ambitious but doomed US operations—and Westpac, and the other banks, had failed to staunch the flow. Hooker was Westpac's first serious bad loan in Australia. The bank had been trying, earlier in the year, to run down its exposure to the developer but the attempts were tentative, the approach too soft, and thus fruitless.

Hooker Corporation first struck a reef in the 1961 credit squeeze and was rescued by Keith Campbell. It hit problems again in the mid-1970s, but under Campbell, its chairman from 1974, the company prospered. At the time of Campbell's death at the age of 55 in 1983—after he had not only steered Hooker into calmer waters but also chaired a ground-breaking inquiry into the Australian financial system—the company was in good shape, a well-regarded property company with a valuable land bank.

Given its activities and status, the conservative Hooker had appeared underpriced and was vulnerable to predatory forays, carried out by Consolidated Press and TNT in 1984, and the entrepreneur Alan Bond in 1985. Hooker then fended off Lee Ming Tee's Sunshine Australia. But the man who succeeded in grabbing the prize was George Herscu, a successful property developer himself, with personal wealth estimated at hundreds of millions of dollars, according to the annual *BRW* 'rich list'. Herscu had arrived in Australia with the great wave of migrants following the second world war. He took whatever job he could before finding his niche in property development and founding Hersfield which, although fairly small in terms of staff, grew to be a major Melbourne-based developer. Herscu epitomised the legend of the penniless migrant rising to business magnate and, nearing 60, he was still enthusiastic for further adventures in development and wealth.

Herscu, financed by the ANZ Bank, bought into Hooker, acquiring the maximum 20 per cent allowed without having to make a formal bid, then launched a takeover offer through his company GSH Finance Pty Ltd. In September 1985 he announced he had acquired a block of 44 per cent at an average price of $2.44 a share. Hooker resisted initially then, after two major shareholders said they would accept Herscu's offer, finally conceded. Many other shareholders scrambled to exit. Herscu now had control of Australia's second-largest property company which operated nationwide, chiefly in land subdivisions but also building home units, office blocks and retail developments. It also had some small developments in the United States. With a staff of thousands, it was a far larger entity than Hersfield.

After Herscu and his team took over the company early in 1986 nearly all Hooker directors walked out. Barry Glover, the company's chief executive, stayed—and lasted ten days under the domineering, volatile and irascible Herscu before quitting the company for which he had worked for 25 years. Herscu appointed himself chief executive; he liked the status and under his entrepreneurial hand Hooker expanded into more speculative property developments. Herscu was growing not only in Australia, but also enthusiastically in the US. To do this, over a period of three years and through various banks, the company borrowed some $800 million in Australia, most of which found its way into the US by way of a daisy chain of corporate entities; borrowings and loans were steered through a complex string of tax havens until the funds arrived in the US as equity— which could then be used as a platform for further borrowings to invest in properties. Unchecked, a further debt of close to $1 billion accrued in the US.

Herscu threw money away. He bought the department-store chain Bonwit Teller for $108 million, which was far ahead of the next bid and more than double the company's worth. Two years later Bonwit Teller was in bankruptcy. He also bought a series of retailers which were not performing well and so were readily available to a keen buyer with easy access to funds. Herscu was building Hooker into a large retailing company in the US, with the retailers under the company's umbrella being installed as foundation tenants in the lavish retail centres the company was developing and running. Analysis was not one of Herscu's strengths and he had great difficulty reading financial statements; his early substantial successes had been a result of good instincts but in the late 1980s they lost their potency. Circumstances were against him: first came the sharemarket crash in 1987, then the high interest rates·of the late 1980s and the recession of the early 1990s. A combination of high rates, a collapsing property market and the dismal results from the under-performing retailers Herscu had bought, plus the sheer unattainability of his expensive ambitions, brought him undone. What had been a risky strategy, a potential time-bomb, was detonated by the downturn in the worldwide economic cycle. In Australia, Hooker's long-serving management team had protected the company from the level of destructive excesses that sent it over a cliff in the US. Hooker in Australia remained mainly in the company's traditional business of home units and land, with only a moderate involvement in commercial developments, and left thus would have survived.

By late 1988 there were signs of strain between Hooker and Westpac, and several other lenders were becoming anxious. Westpac was keeping a close watch on developments in Hooker. At one point, in mid-1989, a group of Westpac directors—Sir Eric Neal, Sir Frank Espie, Peter Baillieu, Rod Cameron and Jock Harper, essentially the board credit committee—and Frank Conroy were in Papua New Guinea, visiting the Ok Tedi mining development and other projects to which Westpac was lending. Conroy, with the group because the PNG office reported to him, was regularly ringing Iain Thompson, general manager, corporate banking, in Sydney to get blow-by-blow updates on the state of affairs at Hooker. Baillieu, head of the board credit committee, was receiving his own version of events, which he could test against Conroy's news, through frequent briefings from Sydney. The calls kept pace with Baillieu as the group moved from place to place and, straining to catch the news through bad telephone connections, he was far from comforted by what he was hearing.

Westpac, on behalf of the banks lending to Hooker, turned for outside help to Sean Wareing, a principal of the consultants Gatfield Robinson Wareing Ltd, who, with a background as a Lend Lease executive, understood the property business. Wareing was to attend many meetings at 60 Martin Place with Iain Thompson—the man who had to front up to the board with the bad news on loans—and Stuart Fowler. Wareing's first call from Thompson came in July 1989. The situation had deteriorated dramatically.

Wareing was enjoying an evening at the opera when, walking into the foyer for a drink at the interval, he was surprised to find his secretary waiting with a message: Iain Thompson at Westpac wanted to see him in his office at 60 Martin Place that night. It was 9 pm. The message had a note of urgency. Wareing sacrificed the last act of the opera and strode up to the bank's headquarters, taking the lift to Thompson's office where he found the Westpac executive conferring with a legal adviser. Hooker was in default and the banks were extremely concerned about their position. Westpac, a major lender, was trying to see what could be done on behalf of all lenders. They were uncertain at that stage whether Hooker was viable. At a subsequent meeting, Sir Eric Neal, who took a keen interest in the Hooker situation, looked Wareing straight in the eye and demanded to be told whether Hooker could be saved. At that stage Wareing did not know.

A strategy was hammered out. An initial plan was to install as chief executive at Hooker an outsider in whom the lenders could have confidence. If Wareing were to take on this role, he would need a clear mandate that he, not Herscu, was in charge. There had been pressure for some time from the banks to have Herscu step back into the chairman's role, making room for someone with more managerial experience as chief executive. Wareing met Herscu at the entrepreneur's lavishly appointed apartment in Sydney's Quay residential tower to discuss the proposal. After some fruitful conversation, which left Wareing with the impression that Herscu had complete confidence in himself and did not regard a default as a serious issue, Herscu invited Wareing to dinner. The jovial evening ended at 1 am. Wareing subsequently met the Hooker board and they devised the basis on which he would become chief executive of Hooker and operate with a free hand. Wareing was able to report to Thompson that he felt they had an arrangement, subject to an indemnity to protect Wareing. But negotiations stalled. An alternative was suggested: Wareing could act in an advisory capacity rather than an executive role. A deal was made. Wareing began what he thought would be a year-long assignment, for a fee of $750,000. It took one week to discover that Hooker was flat broke. The banks could keep it alive only if they were prepared to put in the $130 million needed just to service existing liabilities.

A board meeting was held in late July by video link-up between Wareing in Sydney and Herscu and the Hooker board in Melbourne. Wareing delivered his message: 'George, I signed on as your adviser, but I never said that you would enjoy the advice I'd give you. Hooker is hopelessly insolvent. The legal advice is that you must seek to have a receiver/liquidator appointed.' Herscu told Wareing he was fired, overlooking the fact that it was not his prerogative to dismiss the banks' appointee, and walked out of range of the camera. Hooker adviser John Dahlsen, a consultant to the legal firm Corrs, moved on to the screen and Wareing ran through the numbers. Hooker was indeed hopelessly insolvent. Herscu dug in his heels but was urged again to call a board meeting so that, as the law requires in the case of an insolvent company, the board could pass appropriate resolutions transferring control from directors to a receiver/liquidator. After heated arguments, the meeting was called and an application made for provisional liquidation, with John Harkness and Richard Grellman of KPMG Peat Marwick appointed joint provisional liquidators.

Within a day KPMG's team was installed at Hooker, with Harkness, Grellman, three other partners and close to 30 staff handling what was a major challenge—Australia's largest bankruptcy. The Hooker executives were exhausted. Wareing's assignment appeared to be over. However, such was the dimension of the collapse and the amount of money involved that he was asked by Harkness and Grellman to stay on. KPMG began an arduous analysis of where the funds had gone. It took until December 1989 to determine the flow of funds between Australia and the US. And Hooker had by then also defaulted in the US. Tracking down the money flows and unravelling the problems in the US took until mid-1990.

Westpac, as a large lender, was up for more than $200 million. A further large group of banks and a number of syndicates had also advanced funds to the company in Australia, unsecured, under a negative pledge. The list read like a bankers' directory: in addition to Westpac, the Commonwealth Bank and State Bank of NSW, State Bank of South Australia and ANZ had lent funds, while overseas names included Citibank, Mitsubishi Bank, Bank of Nova Scotia, First Chicago, Manufacturers Hanover, First Fidelity, Citizens & Southern National Bank, PNC International and Barclays Bank. As was often the case in syndicate lending, smaller players relied to a considerable extent on the due diligence and analysis they thought the larger players had carried out—if it was okay for Westpac, it must be okay for others.

In July 1990 Herscu and his wife Sheila declared themselves bankrupt. Their debts of nearly $500 million provided a record for personal bankruptcy in Australia. Earlier that year Herscu had been charged with bribing Queensland government minister Russ Hinze; he pleaded not guilty but was convicted and subsequently went to jail. He was released in 1993.

Westpac's full-year results to 30 September 1989 showed a net operating profit of $791.1 million (subsequently revised to $800.7 million), a rise of 34.3 per cent, with assets up by 28 per cent to $108.6 billion and much of the increase coming from home loans, reflecting Westpac's acquisition of Defence Service Homes Corporation's loan portfolio. Westpac's bottom line in 1989 benefited from a strong performance in the retail bank, a drop in the corporate tax rate from 49 to 39 cents, and from tax write-backs following a tax audit that had been in full swing when White retired at the end of 1987.

Not all the news was good. Total bad debts and provisions for doubtful debts for the Westpac group more than doubled to $562.9 million, mostly because of lending problems in Partnership Pacific and Westpac Merchant Finance. As a damage-control step, lending business in both merchant banks was folded into Westpac, leaving the subsidiaries to pursue fee-generating activities such as advisory work. Fowler told a media conference: 'Asset-based merchant banks are creatures of regulation.'

PPL's involvement as a lender to Tasmanian property developer Bob Hosken led to Westpac's having to take over three properties there, the most valuable being a 165-room hotel in Launceston, estimated to have cost $44 million to develop. The hotel, the largest private development in Launceston for 50 years, had been opened by the state premier amid pomp and ceremony, only to fall victim to the prolonged airline pilots' strike which badly affected tourism in all parts of Australia and virtually ended business and holiday travel to Tasmania. The hotel and other assets of the Hosken group of companies hit financial problems. Such was the impact of the strike on the tourism industry that the prime minister, Bob Hawke, had written to banks and financial institutions asking them to take a sympathetic approach to cash-strapped tourism businesses affected by the strike.

Je ne sais quoi

Overseas, Westpac had listed on the New York Stock Exchange and late in 1989 expanded its network with a deal to acquire 44 branches and some $900 million in assets from Banque Indosuez in New Caledonia and French Polynesia. Westpac was now represented in 27 countries. The idea to buy the network from Banque Indosuez had apparently arisen during a chance conversation in 1988 between Fowler and Jean François Lepetit, head of the French bank, when the two were attending an international conference. Negotiations became more official in June 1989 when prime minister Bob Hawke was in Paris and raised the subject with his French counterpart, Michel Rocard, who, in Australia a couple of months later, discussed the matter with Fowler. Lepetit followed this by formally calling on Fowler in Sydney and discussing the proposal with him and Frank Conroy. Banque Indosuez was looking to offload its South Pacific network, which was a considerable distance from head office, was peripheral to the bank's main operations and was not bringing in profits. When the matter arose for discussion at an executive committee meeting, the only voice against the proposed acquisition was that of Warwick Kent, who pointed out that Westpac did not have the skills to operate in a foreign-speaking environment and different culture. Conroy and Fowler are remembered as being keen: the South Pacific network sat at Westpac's door—the bank was already in Fiji—and surely, they

204

argued, among Westpac's 44,000 staff could be found a handful with French-language skills. Time was to prove Kent correct. In the meantime, the only executive proficient enough in French to attend a ceremony to mark the takeover from Banque Indosuez was Derrick Heywood, who had moved to Westpac during 1989 as general manager, group financial control, after nine years at AGC. Heywood flew to Tahiti early in November to officiate at a handover ceremony. John Stone, general manager of Pacific operations, attended the opening in New Caledonia. It was not until January 1991, when Fowler and Heywood visited New Caledonia, that Westpac's managing director had a chance to review operations on the islands. An outcome of Westpac's $120 million acquisition of the 44 branches in the French territories was that it had to seek a banking licence in France. France's central bank, the Bank of France, insisted that a bank operating in a French country must have a licensed office in France, with executives reporting to the Bank of France. Westpac offered to have a representative fly regularly from London to Paris but that did not satisfy the Bank of France. Westpac opened its Paris branch in 1990, rationalising that the move would strengthen the bank's presence in Europe, where it was not well represented, ahead of the single European market scheduled to start in 1992. However, when the Paris branch opened, Westpac closed its representative office in Frankfurt, opened in 1974, a move that ruffled the Germans. There was pressure not to close the office: the Australian ambassador in Germany rang prime minister Hawke in Canberra, who called Fowler to persuade him against the move. But Westpac could not justify retaining the Frankfurt office.

Westpac had organised a two-day conference of offshore directors to be held at the bank's training centre in Ingleside, in Sydney's northern suburbs, in September 1989, as a forum to review the bank's performance and strategies for the 1990s. The erstwhile London advisory board had been 'disinvited' but present were directors from New Zealand (where a local board had been retained), Mase Westpac directors, including Keith Halkerston, directors from Westpac Asia and from PNG, Tony Walton as head of the Americas division, American adviser Jim Wolfensohn, executive committee members and several senior executives as well as the main board of the bank.

The final session was an assessment of Westpac as a world bank and the implications of that ambition. It was suggested that Westpac could either have major operations around the world with substantial but smaller operations in Australia, or it could be dominant in Australia with operations around the same size as those in Australia in one or two major financial centres such as London and New York. The proposition that Westpac might choose to build substantial operations around the world raised the question of where the bank would find the capital to fund this. Another question was whether Westpac had the management and technological resources to support such an operation. Various views were put forward during the discussion before a summary was provided by Jim Wolfensohn who quietly but firmly outlined the full implications for Westpac of its aspirations to be a 'world bank'. Westpac would require a great deal more capital, and would have to appoint international executives to its main board which, with the bank, would be located in the US, not Australia. Australia would operate with a local board. He pointed out that Westpac had no internationally skilled directors or executives. Japanese banks, on the other hand, with an eye to the international arena, had been sending executives overseas to gain experience for the past twenty years. Westpac had taken steps towards internationalising but essentially it was an Australian bank. It would have to decide whether

it wanted to be an international bank, and if it was genuinely prepared to accept the consequences of trying to
meet that objective. Wolfensohn's verdict silenced the
room. Some in management, especially those with overseas
experience, had privately assessed Westpac's international
aspirations as beyond its reach, but many in the audience
looked crestfallen. The chairman, Sir Eric Neal, wrapped
up proceedings by emphasising that directors were aware
of their international responsibilities, that several had
already made trips to review offshore operations and that
the full board would meet in the US in April 1990.

But Wolfensohn's message sank home. That, combined
with changed economic circumstances, forced Westpac to
lower its sights. The tag 'Australia's world bank' which featured on annual reports and other marketing documents in
the late 1980s did not survive past 1990.

207

Late in 1989 Westpac put in an indicative bid for the UK's
Yorkshire Bank, which had been put up for tender by its
four UK banking parents in October, generating considerable
interest. Westpac carried out partial due diligence on Yorkshire and held discussions with its management in the UK.
Westpac's management recommended the acquisition to the
board, and met little enthusiasm. Lively discussion ensued,
until management was stumped by the question: if we buy
this bank, what do we do next? Westpac had wholesale operations in the UK and it was now looking at buying a retail
bank. There was no synergy. Board concern about the bank's
growth strategy found a voice through at least two members,
Warren Hogan and Bob White. The board gave the proposition the thumbs down, based on a view that Westpac could
not justify the price or the costs of managing such a distant,
stand-alone operation. Yorkshire was taken over by NAB, at
a cost of $2 billion, strengthening NAB's existing UK
network.

In December 1989 Vern Harvey, recently appointed general manager, strategic development, and responsible for coordinating Westpac's relationships with the ratings agencies, together with Derrick Heywood, Harvey Garnett, incoming head of credit, and two executives from the credit department, Doug Ferdinands and Howard Dudgeon, attended a meeting in Sydney with the leading New York ratings agency Moody's Investors Service. Moody's fired some probing questions about the credit classification of the loans portfolio and asked for other information which was not forthcoming from the Westpac executives. Heywood and Harvey gradually became uncomfortably aware of the paucity of Westpac's information. Westpac simply did not have the type and detail of data the agency was seeking about the make-up of the bank's loans portfolio, especially total exposure of $11.2 billion to commercial construction and property. This figure was 44 per cent higher than its level at the end of 1988, at a time when property was coming off a boom and Sydney and Melbourne CBD office vacancy rates were being forecast by Westpac's economists to increase alarmingly in 1990. Moody's was also concerned at Westpac's 150 per cent increase over the previous year in non-accrual loans to $923 million. And Westpac's loans had exploded by 27 per cent over the 1988 level, and by 47 per cent over 1987.

The Moody's representatives spoke at length about property-related banking problems in Norway, which left the Westpac team bemused. The relevance of the Norwegian experience became clear later, when they had done some homework. Moody's had highlighted three areas of concern that had parallels in Norway: Westpac's property exposure was up when the property market was falling, its non-accrual loans had increased and its loans book had ballooned. But at the time of the meeting there was still an aura of invincibility around Westpac—at least in the minds of its management and board; the bank's loan book had never been queried before, so why now? However, the meeting sowed the seeds of doubt: the executives left feeling that they ought to know the answers to the agency's questions, but the information about loans was simply not sufficiently marshalled across the group, which included not just Westpac's corporate and commercial lending but the business of AGC, PPL and BAC.

The new year opened on a bleak note. From January 1990 Westpac endured a series of loans turning sour: Abe Goldberg's Linter Group, Russell Goward's Westmex Ltd and the property developer Girvan Corporation Ltd. Greetings Group, Australia's eighth-largest hotel operator, to which PPL was the major lender, owed $20 million. More corporate clients would fall before the year was out. A variety of factors lay behind the collapses, ranging from background influences such as a weak economy and high interest rates to greedy, over-zealous expansion on the part of ambitious company chiefs. For example, Linter—and a later problem, Adsteam—involved a baffling web of associated companies where the structure was hard to clarify. With Hooker, the warning signal had been the flight of senior executives when Herscu took control as a one-man band, followed by another red light: rapid geographic expansion which was not sufficiently critically evaluated. Girvan, an experienced developer, nonetheless over-rapidly expanded into property. The Greetings Group troubles involved lending to a company that may have been over-reliant on the tourism industry, and the problems with Westmex related to Westpac's lending against the security of shares in a bull market. A source of relief for Westpac was that Frank Ward, head of credit until he retired in 1988, had kept the bank clear of high-flying 1980s entrepreneur Christopher Skase, whose Qintex group went into receivership in late 1989.

The Linter Group's connection with Westpac developed through the bank's relationship with National Textiles, a client of Westpac's since the 1950s, which became part of the Linter Group in 1985. Also, Goldberg had a relationship with PPL dating from the early 1970s. Before he got control of Linter, Westpac's exposure was $52 million, but by 1990 when receivers and liquidators were appointed, total group exposure had risen to $160 million. In the intervening years, Linter's account had been handled by a succession of Westpac account managers, suggesting that an absence of continuity contributed to the failure of the evaluation process. Westpac, uncomfortable with the adequacy and reliability of the information it was receiving about the company, had been trying unsuccessfully for months to reduce its exposure to Goldberg. When Westpac asked Linter for a repayment of funds in September 1990, Goldberg fobbed it off, and the bank gave him an extension until Christmas. Says a former lender to Goldberg: 'He knew that all we banks were waiting for our money and he didn't have it. We were all screwed.'

Goldberg ranked among the migrants-made-good. He arrived in Australia in 1949 with his family, Polish survivors of the second world war, and continued the family tradition of earning a nice living in the textile trade. Goldberg increased his wealth through a number of takeovers and mergers, along the way taking control of a former finance company, Development Underwriting Ltd, later Entrad. By 1984 he was dubbed the Godfather of the Australian rag trade, having won control of Bradmill Industries and ownership of some of Australia's best-known brand names— King Gee, Stubbies and Actil. Through a complex series of transactions and share purchases, Goldberg in 1988 took over Linter Group Ltd, floated in 1985 as a timber and textile business. The empire expanded into what Trevor Sykes in *The Bold Riders* described as 'a complex web'. Concerns about Goldberg began to circulate late in 1989 and between

Christmas and New Year 1990 his bankers appointed KPMG Peat Marwick to look at the company. Sykes recounts:

> What [KPMG] uncovered was one of the biggest rats' nests of the 1980s. The Goldberg empire comprised a web of companies, trusts, partnerships and individuals. Money had been shuffled around in it untraceably. The total debt was far larger than anyone had thought—to the horror of the banks—and was hopelessly in excess of the value of the assets. The Godfather of the rag trade was broke several times over. On 24 January 1990 the bankers voted to appoint receivers to Linter Group. It was the end.

The list of lenders to Linter was long. Westpac featured prominently, with an exposure of $105 million. A further shock for Westpac, and one that highlighted the inadequacies of group control, was that Partnership Pacific had lent another $15 million and Bill Acceptance Corporation $40 million, taking Westpac's group exposure to Linter to $160 million. Goldberg was declared bankrupt in July 1990 but by the time the necessary papers were drawn up he had left Australia. He went on to travel in style, through the UK and the US and Europe, and early in 1992 moved to Poland, a country that does not share an extradition treaty with Australia. Goldberg claimed he was on the financial skids but his lifestyle argued against that. A warrant issued for his arrest lay idle, useless unless he returned to Australia.

Westpac was learning some harsh lessons. From 1990 until 1992, it worked on extending a loan-grading system throughout the bank which would make it better able to manage its credit portfolios. When the first major problem loans occurred in 1989 there was no group-wide application of a loan-grading system—or a system of tracking how the loan portfolio deteriorated—which would later classify loans as A (blue chip), B (high quality), C indicating a satisfactory risk, D signifying a commercially acceptable risk of loss, E or F if on the watch list and G, H or I if problems were apparent. Nor were the lending officers familiar with how to treat a loan when it went bad; they froze—there was no section dedicated to the management, recovery and work-out of impaired loans. And the freeze went up the chain; staff and the board at that stage were reluctant to take action which might lead to foreclosure of a borrower.

CHAPTER NINE

WATCHING TELEVISION

In January 1990 Sir Frank Espie retired from the Westpac board after twelve years as a director, and in the following month Frank Conroy, the bank's chief operating officer and heir apparent to the managing directorship, joined the board. Westpac's annual report, released ahead of the annual general meeting, revealed that problem loans had almost doubled in the 1989 financial year to $2 billion.

The flood of corporate bankruptcies and insolvencies which surfaced in January 1990, making senior Westpac staff nervous about opening a newspaper, highlighted worrying deficiencies in Westpac's control and reporting systems, particularly regarding overall group exposure. It also under-scored earlier inadequacies in preparing staff for the changed lending environment of the 1980s, in which assessing risk and pricing accordingly had become paramount. Westpac's experience of bad debts was a dimly recalled exposure to Gollins in the 1970s. The bank was poorly prepared for the snowballing confusion that can occur when bad debts start to mount, especially when this is set against a deteriorating economy and falling asset prices. By now there were second thoughts about the quality of loans made in a wave of expansion that had seen assets rise exponentially. The bank had cause for worry but it had not shaken off its preoccupation with growth, although there was increasing recognition at board level that property-related problems were brewing. However, there was still a belief by the board, with the chairman its champion, that the acquisition of a medium-sized retail bank in the US would round out Westpac's operations there, providing the 'third leg' to a stool that already comprised corporate and financial markets activities. Jim Wolfensohn's firm was searching for likely targets. Following up on Wolfensohn's recommendations, the chairman and managing director had looked at several potential acquisitions during 1988 and 1989.

In February 1990, Neal, Fowler and Harvey were in the US, sounding out the potential of a selected target, Meridien Bank in Philadelphia. With them were Paul Volcker, former chairman of the US Federal Reserve and now chairman of James D. Wolfensohn Inc, and Tony Walton, Westpac's chief in the US. Returning to New York in a limousine, the group debated how or whether Westpac should forge ahead with the acquisition. That evening Fowler received news that took his mind off Meridien Bank: a fax alerting him to the collapse of the Linter Group. He discussed the matter with Harvey later that night, after learning that Westpac could lose tens of millions. By the following day Fowler had received word that because of the Westpac group's exposure, the loss had grown to around $100 million—and would be even higher. Fowler was shattered by the dimensions of the loss, and the revelation that the bank was not fully protected by the securities it held or charges over the assets. As the realities of the recession took hold, Fowler increasingly retreated from the notion of acquiring a bank in the US, although Westpac was still considering listing in Paris and Frankfurt.

On home ground, spending continued as Westpac seized the chance to buy 7.5 per cent of the ANZ Bank from The Adelaide Steamship Company, which was selling down its investment portfolio to concentrate on mainstream operations. Westpac paid $6.10 a share, outlaying $416 million. There was considerable argument about the price but those in favour of the purchase, Fowler reportedly among them, regarded it as a good opportunity for Westpac to make a strategic investment in a major bank; moreover, there was an expectation on Fowler's part, although this was not made a condition of the purchase, that Adsteam chief John Spalvins would use the funds to pay down Adsteam's debt to Westpac. This did not occur. The analyst Bill Shugg, frequently a critic of Westpac, pointed out to two directors at a private meeting a few months later that the bank could have waited and acquired the shares progressively on the market, saving close to $70 million. However, Westpac was insistent about the value of the strategic holding in the light of a proposed merger between the ANZ Bank and the insurance giant National Mutual Life Association. The merger, to Fowler's delight, was ultimately vetoed by the federal government.

The recession continued to send out ominous signals which evidently failed to reach some in the Westpac boardroom. In March 1990 Vern Harvey, in a strategy presentation to the board, suggested that the economy was going to take longer to recover than had been thought, and that the bank must take this into account. Part-way through his presentation, Harvey was asked by the chairman to stop. Neal, after apologising for the interruption, said that the people chosen to sit around the Westpac board table were leaders in their fields and he would like to take a moment to ask their views. None voiced support for Harvey's bearish outlook. But Harvey was right.

In April 1990, the board of Westpac for the first time in its history made a mass offshore visit, traversing the US from west to the east. Thirteen directors—White and Conroy remained in Australia—visited all of Westpac's points of representation—San Francisco, Chicago, Columbus, Houston, Los Angeles—before finishing with a dinner hosted by the New York Stock Exchange. In a militarily precise operation, the board separated into five small groups, each accompanied by a senior executive of the Americas division, that spent two days visiting Westpac branches and representative offices and meeting bank customers before reassembling in New York. A meeting was held in the board-room of the New York Stock Exchange, where Jim Wolfen-sohn addressed the directors about the implications of trying, at that time, to acquire a retail bank, what potential targets were available, and what the cost might be. Tony Walton and Wolfensohn delivered several hours of presentations, going over all the possibilities. The fundamental fact even-tually emerged that Westpac had changed its attitude and was not, after all, ready to buy a US bank.

The visit by the board drew criticism for its reported cost of around $1 million—according to Gary Hett, deputy general manager of the Americas division, a more accurate figure was about half of that. But details of the trip, which included several dinners hosted by Westpac, and directors being ferried about in limousines and chartered jets, were splashed in the Austra-lian press in the context of Westpac's disastrous first-half results and a subsequent drop in the bank's share price. Walton defended the expense. At the time, many foreign banks were promoting their profiles through advertising and public rela-tions campaigns. A full-page advertisement in the *Wall Street Journal* would have cost $US125,000 and, in Walton's view, a better way to spend money was to have the board visit the US, see the bank's operations and meet customers. 'We worked them very hard,' says Hett:

> It was a meticulously planned itinerary, involving meetings with hundreds of Westpac customers. We brought the board out to do something, to call on customers; we had them at working lunches, break-fasts, dinners, as well as individual customer calls. They arrived in San Francisco, then broke into smaller groups to visit other offices. We worked them for more breakfasts, one given by the Chamber

216

of Commerce in Columbus. They had dinner with several bank and corporate chief executives as well as correspondent bankers. This was not some junket to the US, as it was written up in a few Australian press articles. This was an opportunity for the Americas division to access hundreds of customers at senior levels using the bank's main board directors, which leverages you up when you make customer calls. It was very effective. We held a dinner in New York for 100 customers. The visit created tremendous goodwill and considerable profitable business with customers and with correspondent bankers, and we know that because we tracked the business that resulted from those meetings.

As the board members were stepping onto the US-bound aircraft, an issue of the weekly magazine *BRW* appeared containing an article titled 'What's wrong with Westpac', in which a Westpac director was quoted as saying that 'anyone would have to have rocks in their head' to believe that the board was satisfied with Westpac's performance. The article went on to detail the bank's low credibility with the Australian investment community, its own staff and the Australian Bank Employees Union. Analysts were reported as describing Westpac as a 'rudderless ship', obsessed, from board-level down, with being the biggest bank, and reiterating concerns about Westpac's $3 billion portfolio of highly leveraged transactions, most of them committed through the Americas division. There were increasingly frequent comments that chairman Sir Eric Neal, rather than managing director Stuart Fowler, was calling the shots in the bank, although both as usual were at pains publicly to deny any absence of harmony. Outwardly mutually supportive, the two had plenty of arguments privately. 'They fought like cat and dog,' said one former Westpac executive.

Following the US trip, the chairman called a meeting of all non-executive directors, demanding to know who had spoken to *BRW* reporter Ali Cromie. In his pursuit of a confession—which his supporters said was prompted by a desire to assuage Fowler's sensitivities about being undermined by the article—the chairman neglected an opportunity to delve into why directors might be dissatisfied with the bank, a more important issue than who had spoken to the media. White suggested an off-site meeting to discuss the situation. But the matter went no further.

The directors had not returned home to good news. On 4 May the credit-rating agency Standard & Poor's downgraded Westpac, largely because of the bank's dubious loans to the Australian commercial property sector and to many highly geared companies. This followed earlier downgradings by Moody's. The bank announced a 58 per cent drop in pre-tax operating profit to $249.7 million for the half-year to March 1990, before bringing in $325 million in abnormal profit from a surplus in the staff superannuation scheme. Following actuarial reviews which found group super schemes over-funded by around $1 billion, Westpac took $650 million from the surplus, with $325 million going to the bank and $325 million promised as additional benefits to employees. After subtracting the bonus of $325 million from the after-tax profit and allowing for tax on the super fund transfer, the net profit for the half-year was left at a mere $156 million, down by 59 per cent from the previous year. Write-offs and provisions for bad and doubtful debts, totalling $586 million compared with $226 million a year earlier, had eaten into returns. The transfer from the super fund was unsuccessfully challenged by the Australian Bank Employees Union.

The wheels were coming off. During the 1980s, in its efforts to compete head-on with the world's big players, Westpac had been preoccupied with growth, expanding overseas into corporate banking and investing in the latest technology, and justified the costs associated with this by rationalising that it was building the business. The bank had to recognise that that approach was no longer feasible. Reality had caught up with Westpac. It had to trim its workforce and lift profit per employee. Running a costly but overly labour intensive bank had been a risky strategy throughout the 1980s, but it was no longer sustainable because the bank was not making the requisite profits. Addressing an in-house executives' forum in May 1990, Stuart Fowler said that Westpac had 'an insatiable demand for technology that has given us an information systems cost structure that I understand is higher than that of NAB by some $70 million per annum'. Fowler added that Westpac's overseas offices were included in cost-cutting plans. 'Our New Zealand business has been a disappointment for the past two years and Pollock [in the US] is a totally unacceptable drag on profits.'

Westpac was now confronting an unprecedented rise in bad and doubtful debts, reflecting the poor quality of its loans portfolio. And the bank could not look forward to a breathing space because the economic downturn was taking its toll on second-tier companies and the property market. Westpac's performance was being criticised in the media, and the downgradings by ratings agencies would affect the cost of its fundraising in world capital markets and its ability to transact foreign-exchange business. Australian shareholders were growing restless. The drag of non-performing loans meant that the bank had to earn additional pre-tax profit before it could hope to lift its return to shareholders. Westpac had demonstrated that it could fare well in times of prosperity; now it had to prove that it could also manage under adverse economic conditions. That was shaping as a considerable test and those watching included shareholders, customers, staff, ratings agencies and analysts. Their reactions were all relevant.

Lifting profits meant trimming expenses, increasing returns on corporate loans and reducing asset growth. Cost-cutting measures included a ban on executive bonuses unless these were part of a contract, and on international travel unless authorised by the executive committee. The curtain fell on an era of generous hospitality. *Tarquin*, the 90-foot cruiser that Westpac used to entertain clients on Sydney Harbour, was mothballed, and all but one box at the Sydney cricket and football stadium sold. Sponsorships and the use of outside consultants were reviewed. Westpac had to shift its focus from growth to the bottom line. The bank's 68 per cent growth in assets from $70 billion in September 1987 to $118 billion at March 1990, and 60 per cent rise in loans over the same period, had clearly been excessive, and at the wrong time in the business cycle. The bank, traditionally heavily padded with people who regarded a job with Westpac as a job for life, was now faced with the prospect of shedding staff, a task that Fowler found particularly hard to embrace. His preference was to cling to the convention of gradually reducing staff numbers through retirement and people leaving, rather than show loyal staffers the door. But attrition was too slow a process. Employee numbers, which reached a peak of 46,600 in May 1990, were reduced to 42,430 during the following year and were 39,253 by the end of 1992. Some senior people were leaving of their own volition: Warwick Kent, having been bypassed for the top job, had been head-hunted and resigned in late 1989 to take up the post of managing director of the Rural & Industries Bank of Western Australia, later BankWest. And Philip Deer, chief general manager, corporate and international, quit Westpac to be head of National Westminster Bank's office in Australia, later running NatWest divisions in Hong Kong and London.

In June 1990 Westpac closed down its US primary dealer, Westpac Pollock, and negotiated the sale of Westpac Travel to Australian Airlines. Westpac was beginning to appear as an institution able only to react to bad news rather than one taking the initiative. And pressure was increasing from all directions.

Adelaide Steamship sinks

In May 1990 Westpac had become nervous about the situation at The Adelaide Steamship Company, a sentiment that was reflected in the wider market. Early in July 1990, amid mounting concerns about Adsteam's financial health and with the company's loan facilities due for renegotiation, Westpac called a meeting of senior representatives of the other major banking lenders. Adsteam, a longstanding client of Westpac with a relationship dating from the turn of the century, was founded in 1875 as a shipping company but had since diversified and expanded exponentially. By 1990 its empire, which included David Jones Ltd, Tooth & Co Ltd, Industrial Equity Ltd and Woolworths Ltd, spanned a broad range of activities in retailing, hotels, wine, food, property development, timber and civil engineering. Since 1981, Adsteam had been under the stewardship of John Spalvins, a Latvian who migrated to Australia in 1950, aged 12, and went on to train as an accountant. He had joined Adsteam in the early 1970s, rapidly rising through the executive ranks. When Spalvins added Industrial Equity Ltd to Adsteam's burgeoning corporate domain he was hailed as Australia's most forceful entrepreneur; six months later, in mid-1990, he was struggling to keep Adsteam afloat, desperate to buy time while he restructured the business.

Concerns about Adsteam's convoluted structure and its level of debt had been growing all year. Westpac's own concerns were evident when, in May, the bank had struck a deal with the company under which further financing would be available only if Westpac were permitted to have one of its corporate managers inside Adsteam to examine its books. While this was little help in untangling the Adsteam maze, it did reveal that the company's debt was much greater than had been thought. At the July 1990 meeting chaired by Frank Conroy and attended by Iain Thompson, Westpac's general manager, corporate banking, the four major banks discovered, to their mutual horror, that their combined loans to Adsteam totalled at least $4 billion, while overall debt was more than $6 billion—an impossible burden for a company with shareholders' funds of some $1 billion. The banks demanded that Adsteam quickly sell some assets; it responded by disposing of Westpac and National Australia Bank shares. Nervousness was increased by the publication of an analysis of Adsteam's corporate structure by a leading analyst, Baring Securities' Viktor Shvets, which said that a realistic valuation of Adsteam shares was between $3 and $4, far below their market price of $5.50—and their 1989 peak of $7.50. By November 1990, the shares had dropped to 50 cents. Adsteam went into an informal receivership and work began on restructuring, with the components of the empire being taken over by the four major banks. The burden of keeping the Westpac board informed about the faltering client companies, including Adsteam, fell mostly on corporate banking chief Iain Thompson, who was closely involved in the work-outs. On one occasion he was reporting to the board credit committee about Adsteam, a problem with which he was living daily, and took no file notes into the meeting. Thompson had no need of them; he was all too familiar with the details of the case. Conroy encouraged him to take a file next time, if only for appearances.

Westpac's exposure to a combination of Adsteam, Tooth and David Jones featured at the top of the bank's twenty largest problem loans in 1992, around $340 million.

A corporate banking review prepared in July 1990 confirmed for the board what it by then already suspected:

222

there were serious flaws in Westpac's approach, not least in the medium-term business plan for the corporate and international division which had set an objective of 100 per cent growth in assets over the three years to 1990. In 1989 Westpac nearly made its annual target, with total assets growing by 28.4 per cent, admittedly against a background of a 28.5 per cent expansion in the money supply and at a time when all banks were vigorously lending. In 1989 National Australia Bank's assets jumped 22 per cent, from $76 million to $93 million, while ANZ's assets rose 16 per cent from $85 million to $99 million. Westpac's aggressive growth target, though, did not take account of the credit implications—the more enthusiastically a bank lends, the more likely it is to collect a growing proportion of dud loans—or the 'ripple' effect of the growth which was reverberating by the middle of 1990. The report also cited inadequate central controls of group exposures, which enabled subsidiaries to go their own way in lending with no-one adding up the total. And a policy of 'rewarding' those who brought in business encouraged a drive to complete deals rather than carefully analyse potential risks. Overall, analysis of companies' cashflows and industries was often inadequate. Frequent turnover of the bank's relationship managers resulted, in several instances, in relatively inexperienced staff handling large exposures—a particularly dangerous practice in the late 1980s given the aggressive nature of some of the borrowers and, in some cases, the complexities of their corporate structures.

In August 1990, after nearly three years as a director, former managing director Bob White quit the Westpac board. White had been growing more and more uncomfortable about the bank's approach to customers, its mounting problem loans and bad debts and its ability to manage them. Under White and his team, Westpac had reacted to the threat of competition from the world's biggest banking names by broadening its base into wholesale banking. But as White drove Westpac towards its place on the world stage, the institution over-stretched its own ability to manage not just the increased volume of business but the associated increased complexities. And by 1990 some chickens were coming home to roost, such as the losses in the US primary dealer Pollock, the mounting bill for the grandiose CS90 technology project, which was not yet producing the promised results, and problems in headstrong subsidiaries which, under ambitious leaders, had been determined to run their own race. White recounts in his book that he felt 'increasingly isolated' at the Westpac board table. His relationship with the chairman was far from harmonious. Professionally, White felt he was no longer being heeded, but being frozen out. On the personal side, he was needed at home: his wife of 40 years, Molly, was seriously ill. He submitted his letter of resignation to the chairman on 16 August 1990:

Dear Sir Eric

With deep regret and after a great deal of consideration I have come to the conclusion that I must submit my resignation as a Director of the Bank.

For some time now I have felt increasingly at odds with the general approach of the Board under your leadership and this raises in my mind a growing anxiety that my continuing membership of the Board might well be perceived by the proprietors, customers and staff as an endorsement of the current approach. By itself, that is a worry but because I retire by rotation at the end of this year, it would seem to be inappropriate, if not a neglect of my responsibility to the proprietors, to allow my name to go forward for re-election without some qualification. I think it is preferable that I face the issue now.

White went on to cite two reasons: the manner in which the *BRW* article, critical of the bank, was handled earlier in the year, where the board concentrated on 'who said what and substantially ignored the more important content of the article'; and his perception of a 'gulf between the Board and the Executive of the Bank'. White wrote:

> This is for me a new development not hitherto appar-
> ent since I first entered the boardroom on a full-time
> basis over sixteen years ago. In a service industry,
> and particularly in one of our size, it is a prime
> responsibility of the Chairman and the Board to
> develop and maintain a working relationship of
> mutual trust and confidence between the Board and
> the Executive.
>
> The absence of such a relationship inevitably pro-
> motes a demotivating influence at senior levels
> which is likely to cascade down through the organ-
> isation. It is of course difficult to make a judgment
> on the overall impact of that, and even more difficult
> to measure its significance on the quality of service
> to the customers. However, you will recall that I
> raised, at the last Board meeting, my concerns about
> the impact on our customers of our current approach
> and I continue to be greatly worried by what I per-
> ceive to be a rising level of customer dissatisfaction.

An undisguised gulf already existed between White and Neal. To some on the board it seemed that White, still close to many in management and sympathetic to customers of the bank, was too wedded to the past. They were tired of the

225

friction between him and Neal. White was later critical of the dash for growth of the late 1980s, saying in October 1991 in an article 'Banking in the 1990s—Back to Basics' in *The Australian Banker*: 'It follows almost as night follows day that a bank which is rapidly increasing its market share of loans will finish up with a big share of the "left-overs" and will see the average quality of its loan portfolio decline.' The comment raised a thin smile among those who had watched Westpac's pitch to lift its market share in the mid-1980s, when its assets rose 50 per cent between 1984 and 1986 to $60 billion, at a time when total credit growth was around 21 per cent a year. In an address to the Securities Institute of Australia in 1991, Reserve Bank deputy governor John Phillips said: 'We seriously overestimated the capacity of banks, their managers and their boards to cope with the changes unleashed by deregulation.'

Westpac's media relations department was instructed that no press release should be issued to announce White's departure. Tony Benner, Westpac's head of media relations, made a fruitless trip to the chairman's office to argue that Westpac should appear gracious about the departure of the man who had given his life to the bank. But he was told that White had received sufficient acknowledgment of his contribution to the bank when he left the role of managing director and that the resignation of a board director was of little consequence. The appropriate notice was sent to the stock exchange. White was subsequently informed that the board had accepted his resignation with regret.

Channel Ten: A television drama

Westpac, banker since the late 1970s to Northern Star Holdings, a small but growing regional media company based in Lismore, northern NSW, came to be a major lender to

226

Channel Ten when Northern Star's ambitions took it beyond regional and into national television. In the media merry-go-round of the late 1980s, television stations and newpapers changed hands at a staggering rate, and at even more staggering prices. In 1987 Northern Star bought Channel Ten. The deal was financed partly by backing from a growing investment company, shopping-centre king Frank Lowy's Westfield Capital Corporation, then a 45 per cent shareholder in Northern Star. The new owners paid $842 million for Ten. After three years of struggle to lift ratings and revenue and cut costs, Lowy concluded that his team was never going to turn the network around. Desperate to exit from his loss-making television venture, he cast about for a buyer. In September 1989, in a complex deal using funds advanced by Westfield, Broadcom Australia Ltd took control of Northern Star. Broadcom—a private television production company controlled by Steve Cosser, a former radio and television reporter, former merchant banker John Gerahty, a director of the entrepreneurial investment company AFP Pty Ltd, and leading business journalist Max Walsh—took a 19.9 per cent stake worth $30 million which gave them Channel Ten stations in Sydney and Melbourne. The network's stations in Perth, Adelaide and Canberra were sold to businessman Charles Curran's Capital Television for $185 million. Gerahty, chairman of Broadcom, became chairman of Northern Star.

Westpac was a major lender to Ten; others included a bank syndicate which had provided a $154 million facility of which about one-third was advanced by Citibank, and the Commonwealth Bank. The sale of the Ten network to Broadcom was not Westpac's preferred outcome but there seemed to be no alternative. Citibank, bankers to AFP, knew and supported the Broadcom team and encouraged the sale. Broadcom in fact paid nothing. The $30 million loan from Westfield to enable it to buy control of Northern Star was non-recourse. Broadcom soon discovered that the cost of overseas program contracts, particularly a deal struck with the US production studio MCA, were millstones around its neck. The potential cost of these contracts was frightening; under the onerous deal with MCA the Ten network was obliged to take everything the studio offered. The details of these contracts were not understood by Broadcom until too late. Broadcom also discovered that Northern Star was far more debt-burdened than had been thought. This was some-thing of a revelation for the banks, too, which, it could be argued, should have known more about the company's finan-cial position. For Cosser, buying control of Ten had been easy; making it work was much harder.

From the start Broadcom, which had a ten-year contract to provide facilities and local programs for the Ten stations, worked closely with the lending banks, and regular discussions continued, with Northern Star executives providing a running report on the company's performance. Cosser cut staff by 25 per cent and reduced costs in a battle to turn the stations around but the burden of debt, combined with the high cost of overseas contracts, weighed heavily. He succeeded in renegotiating the contracts except for the largest, that with MCA. Other suppliers were more amenable, preferring to cut a deal to sell products at a lower cost to a viable company. Northern Star continued to lose money. Not only were its operating costs higher than Broadcom had anticipated but the television advertising market was soft. By March 1990 its shares were worth 17 cents. In June 1990 the banks agreed to provide Northern Star with an additional $50 million until the end of August. They would not commit for a longer period until they could assess the network's cost projections.

At a licence renewal application hearing on 13 June, West-pac's corporate banking chief, Iain Thompson, assured the Australian Broadcasting Tribunal (ABT, later Australian Broadcasting Authority), which has to approve a new station

228

owner, that the banks would not act precipitately to endanger Northern Star. The syndicate was considering whether to extend Northern Star's three-year $415 million debt facility which would expire in October 1992. Thompson told the ABT that while an interim facility was in place, the syndicate would examine Northern Star's medium-term needs. Thompson's dilemma was that he did not want to say or do anything that might jeopardise renewal of the licence but he wanted to keep his options open and not make firm promises of additional long-term funding. He had to tread a fine line. The banking syndicate by then had doubts about Broadcom's ability to manage the network and to service the debt, but was not saying so openly. To protect their own position, the banks had to maintain the confidence of suppliers, creditors and regulators in the existing management team at the Ten network. 'The banks will attempt to negotiate a medium-term supplementary facility to help Northern Star trade out of its current difficulties,' Thompson said to the hearing. He said the group's long-term financing would depend on its achieving performance forecasts:

> We need time to review the needs of Northern Star, to agree on the required financing and to obtain approval from our respective internal authorities, including, in the case of Westpac, the approval of the board. In the longer term ... banks could be expected to maintain support if management's performance were in accordance with projections. That presumes full exchange of information, constant monitoring of revenue and expenses, and continued confidence in management.

Westpac was particularly apprehensive because of the softening in the advertising market which was having a serious impact on an already debt-burdened Northern Star. It had already called in the accounting firm Ernst & Young to monitor and report on Ten's finances. Cosser proposed a solution to KPMG Peat Marwick, receivers of Channel Seven, another beleaguered network: Ten and Seven could merge. The suggestion infuriated Kerry Packer, owner of Channel Nine, who rang Cosser from his London hotel, bellowing down the line that the government would not allow it and he would do everything he could to prevent it. A combination of Seven with its monopoly on broadcasting the Australian Football League, and Ten with Rugby League, would have left Nine trailing. Packer's message to Ten was always the same: learn to like coming third out of three.

Cosser had cut Ten's costs by 20 per cent and reduced its losses and its debt but he still needed to get the network into the black. Debt was the chief problem; the company was making money but not enough to cover the $70–$80 million annual interest bill. Money was leaching out at a rate of at least $1 million a week. That had to be staunched. Cosser told *BRW* in June 1990: 'The options for further debt reduction through the disposal of assets are limited. From now on it will have to come from profits or, at some point, an injection of equity. But I don't believe the climate is right for the latter at this stage.' By September Northern Star's financial position had deteriorated further. For some months Broadcom had required approval from either Westpac or Ernst & Young before issuing cheques of more than $25,000. The company was to announce its annual results at the end of the month and it would have to confirm in adopting the annual accounts that it was a going concern.

Thompson, nervous that the continuing friction among the bankers in the syndicate could lead to a damaging breakdown, had decided that having an enthusiastic and skilled bulldog as a negotiator on his side was desirable. Westpac appointed Turnbull & Partners as consultants to help restructure Ten. It is a rare syndicate that works in complete

230

harmony but the banks lending to Northern Star were increasingly out of step. Citibank, which had a closer relationship with Broadcom, was more and more at odds with Westpac. The appointment of corporate lawyer turned investment banker Malcolm Turnbull, given Turnbull's former close relationship with Kerry Packer, became a problem for Westpac, feeding Broadcom's growing concern that the bank was not playing with a straight bat.

Broadcom's relationship with Westpac was becoming tense. An earlier press report that Westpac had put Ten on credit watch, although unconfirmed, was very damaging to the network. Whether intentional or otherwise, Westpac was emitting differing signals over its approach to Northern Star and there appeared to be conflict within the bank about how it should be handled. Broadcom directors would be told one thing then read a different version next day in the press. Or one Westpac executive would play rough, so Broadcom would plead its case higher up the line, and be given more concessional treatment. On one occasion, in September 1990, Cosser had left a meeting with Conroy with a sense that at last someone in the bank was listening sympathetically and that he could feel reasonably confident of Westpac's support. Conroy, while willing to listen, believed he had been fairly non-committal about support. On another occasion, Stuart Fowler commented to other lenders that he had not yet met Cosser and he scheduled a lunch to rectify this. Thompson tried strenuously to dissuade Fowler from hosting a lunch at a point when Westpac, while as yet undecided on a course of action with Northern Star, was acutely aware that clouds were gathering. A convivial lunch— and lunches with Fowler were always convivial—hosted by Westpac's chief executive could send out the wrong message about the bank's commitment to Ten. To Fowler, the lunch was social; Thompson emphasised that it would be interpreted in a business context. The lunch went ahead. To everyone but Fowler, it had tremendous significance.

231

Inconsistencies in Westpac's approach inevitably led to problems. Differing views about whether Ten could be rescued, and mounting mutual distrust caused the relationship between Westpac and Broadcom to deteriorate. The beleaguered Broadcom believed it had reason to suspect Westpac's impartiality, given that Packer's Consolidated Press was a large and longstanding client and two Westpac directors, Peter Baillieu and Jock Harper, were on the Consolidated Press board. And speculation in the media that Broadcom was milking additional fees out of Ten for management and supplying facilities was undermining both it and the network; Broadcom laid the blame for the mischief at Westpac's door.

An infuriated Max Walsh wrote to Fowler on 13 October 1990:

> I write to register my distress at another round of destabilising and erroneous reporting ... The canard that has been placed in the media against Broadcom is that it has ripped off Northern Star through its production agreement. This has been very damaging to Broadcom and, let me say, to its directors ... You will be the first to realise that the media people who are being used to destabilise Northern Star and in the process destroy its market value do believe that Westpac is a singularly duplicitous institution; a judgment I believe will gain wider circulation in the community. Just why any senior Westpac executive should see any rationality in undermining the financial viability of a television network which owes Westpac more than $250 million eludes me.

The angry Walsh subsequently visited Fowler and Conroy and left them in no doubt that Broadcom believed damaging misinformation was emanating from the bank. Fowler and Conroy were not convinced.

Walsh later wrote in his regular *Sydney Morning Herald* column:

> A few years back I was a director of a public company, Northern Star, put into receivership by Westpac. There was no quarrel about this. From the time of taking control the new board recognised it was acting as a *de facto* receiver dependent on bank support to survive. What was galling about the episode was the behaviour of Westpac, which had a representative at each board meeting. The board was repeatedly assured it did indeed have the confidence of the bank. Yet we found ourselves the subject of destabilising speculation fostered in part by claims attributed to Westpac executives. At one stage, the company chairman presented a statement to share-holders that had been approved by the bank only to have Westpac's spokesman put out an official denial. Perhaps the most frustrating aspect of the situation was that we could not identify the bank's agenda. Naturally, there were all sorts of conspiracy theories ... Just what was going on inside Westpac, who was pulling the strings or calling the shots, remains a mystery to me still.

By September 1990 Northern Star owed its bankers $455 million, more than half of it, around $255 million, to Westpac. The debt had become one of Westpac's biggest head-aches. And Westpac also had a $70 million exposure to Capital Television, controlled by Charles Curran, which had bought Ten's three regional stations. With the banks agreeing to cap-italise the interest, the debt was growing. Westpac's second-half profit would be severely depressed if Northern Star were placed in receivership because provisions would have to be made for the entire amount owed. The debt would not be written off at this stage because of the possibility of recovery.

Amid continued reports of dissent among the banks, at 4.30 pm on Friday, 14 September, they appointed James Millar and Robert Dunn of Ernst & Young as receivers. Fowler said that the banks had moved because of speculation about the viability of Northern Star. They believed Cosser had been given enough time and latitude and had failed in the job of turning around Ten. Cosser bought some time by persuading the banks into a 'cooperative receivership', leaving him nominally in charge of Ten. He was still chief executive but financial control of the network rested with Millar and Dunn. On that evening, over a drink with friends at the Australian Youth Hotel near Ten's Ultimo offices, Cosser said Northern Star was pleased that the banks had agreed to a 'friendly receivership'. The receivers more or less followed a plan that had been devised by Turnbull & Partners to trim Ten into a 'no-frills' cheap-and-cheerful station. They cut $100 million out of Northern Star's cost base between September 1990 and January 1991 and went on to run the network for several months.

Four weeks into the 'friendly receivership', on 16 October 1990, Cosser was out. Gary Rice, a former Channel Nine executive, was put in as chief of Ten, reporting to Millar. Ten then suffered another body blow. An opportunity had arisen to renegotiate its most valuable program contract, the rights to broadcast Australian Rugby League. Discussions ensued over what Ten was prepared to pay and, before a satisfactory conclusion was reached, the contract lapsed. The rights to broadcast Rugby League were picked up by Channel Nine.

In October 1991 most of the assets of Ten—the television licence, staff and certain contracts which enabled the business to continue—were sold to a wholly owned subsidiary of Westpac, Television and Telecasters Limited. No other buyer could be found. Westpac, with the most to lose, believed that the best way to get Ten on its feet was to take over the station. The bank discussed the proposal with the Reserve Bank which, although not very happy because it did not want to create a precedent, accepted it in the circumstances. The other banks were paid out, pro rata, although the Commonwealth did provide some financial assistance to Westpac.

Television and Telecasters operated Channel Ten until November 1992, when the network was sold for $240 million to a consortium headed by a Canadian communications group, CanWest Global Communications Corp. Says Turnbull, who was recruited by Westpac to handle the sale of Ten: 'Westpac's desire to sell Ten at the time they did was really driven by a wish to have Ten off their balance sheet. It was a very high-profile reminder of a very bad loan and in the atmosphere of the time it was better to be seen to be clearing the decks.' In early 1997 analysts valued the Ten network between $1.1 and $1.3 billion.

Ten was among Westpac's biggest corporate write-offs, sharing the star billing with Hooker and Linter. Westpac had not realised what it was lending to in Ten and, once it understood it, hated the investment and the surrounding publicity. Broadcom had brought bad news to the bank at one of the worst times in its history, when an uncomfortably high level of loans had turned sour and when it faced property problems around Australia and was suffering from an unusual degree of internal disharmony. Westpac was hobbled by appalling internal communications problems— no-one wanted to speak openly about the disasters. Max Walsh, in his SMH column in June 1993, referred to an organisational disease called 'the snake pit of organisation politics', saying that Westpac was not unique in suffering from this affliction.

The cover-up routine is not confined to the top of the organisation. All employees soon learn that ... communicating to superiors should be done on the basis that new news is bad news. In the cover-up process messengers are highly vulnerable and expendable. When I complained to Westpac's chief executive, Stuart Fowler, and his then deputy, Frank Conroy, that the bank was behaving in a duplicitous manner, especially in providing false and misleading information to the media, they undertook an investigation. I wasn't surprised when they reported back to me that my claims were without substance—that despite the fact unnamed Westpac executives had been quoted in a number of newspapers and on television, nobody had spoken with the media. Fowler and Conroy were unquestionably honest; they may have simply been snowed.

Exposures to fallen high-flyers such as Hooker, Adsteam, Linter and Northern Star were compounded by problem loans to less well-known, medium-sized companies. Fowler later said of those dizzy years: 'It was not always easy to get a complete handle on some companies' borrowings. Banks were at fault in not insisting on tighter credit standards at the time, but they were very competitive times and a bull market was running.'

Westpac's Harvey Garnett, who became chief general manager, group credit policy and control, following Warwick Kent's resignation in 1989, told *Australian Business* in October 1990 that corporate account managers in 1983 attended a course on 'relationship management', an initiative that reflected Westpac's big push to train relationship managers and build its loan book. The course included lectures by professors of finance from the prestige Harvard University, focusing on, among other things, how to make financial evaluations of companies. Later in 1983 Frank Conroy, then deputy chief manager, corporate banking, chaired a relationship management task force whose objective was to boost Westpac's efforts in corporate banking by matching valued corporate accounts with the more skilled corporate bankers who were paid and treated differently in the bank. The recruitment early in 1985 of Iain Thompson from Bank of America as general manager, corporate banking, was part of the drive to lift Westpac's profile in this sector. The bank later, in its 1985 annual report, emphasised the importance of corporate client relationships when it featured photographs of Westpac senior staff with executives of prized customers such as Adsteam and Bell Resources. Garnett was later quoted: 'We had very material rewards for business written that gave very little focus on the quality of the credit.' Westpac was not the only lender in the 1980s guilty of that approach. Garnett also said that a mistake made by all banks was not to track where the money was going. 'You don't lend into a bottomless pit,' he said. 'As a banker, you lend for a specific purpose.'

Westpac was by now, in late 1990, confronting a problem of a different kind and one that was bedevilling several banks: a technical breach of the Credit Act. Borrowers were not financially disadvantaged but Westpac was in breach of the act for failing to disclose details of commissions on insurance sold with its loans. Under the new and complex legislation, lenders forfeited their right to credit charges if full disclosure of fees due was not made in a contract. Westpac had its personal loan documentation reprinted and subsequently agreed to refund some $2 million to customers. The episode was another blow to Westpac's image. In April 1991 Reg Barrett, a partner with Allen Allen & Hemsley, was appointed as secretary to the board, replacing John Wilson, who retired after 44 years with the bank.

Barrett also took the newly created position of general counsel, with responsibility for legal matters and compliance. He had dual reporting lines: to the chairman on board matters and to Fowler on management business. Barrett's appointment was interpreted as a reflection of board determination to raise the quality of specialists in support functions at Westpac.

In November 1990 Westpac announced a 45.6 per cent fall in pre-tax profit to $589 million for the year to September, excluding the impact of the $325 million return of superannuation fund surplus reported earlier that year. This was a sharp drop from the 1989 pre-tax profit of $1,083 million and, in fact, was less than the bank had earned, if similarly calculated, in 1985. Operating profit had peaked at $1.1 billion in 1988. Bad and doubtful debt provisions were $1.2 billion, about twice those of the previous year, and a figure that left it with a higher proportion of its loan book in trouble than its private rivals, NAB and ANZ. Non-accrual loans were $2.5 billion. Profits had been badly affected by failures in the large corporate sector, but the rate of increase in corporate bad debts appeared to have levelled out. Against this, there was a deteriorating trend in overdue accounts in the consumer loans business of AGC. The bank said that increased resources had been dedicated to supervising loan portfolios. Meanwhile, the bank's return on equity reflected the brunt of the loan losses, dropping from 13.4 per cent to 10.1 per cent.

These results forced Sir Eric Neal to warn shareholders at the January 1991 annual general meeting of a dividend cut because of the blow-out in problem loans. Frank Conroy, whose appointment as a director had to be confirmed by shareholders, came in for some direct criticism when the analyst and outspoken critic of Westpac, Bill Shugg, said he would oppose his appointment. After the dismal 1990 results Conroy, addressing the Westpac retired officers' club, had

238

said that the bank's results were a disgrace. Neal supported Conroy at the annual meeting, saying Conroy had been correct, the results were a disgrace. The property market in early 1991 was looking grim but it was hard to read. In its 1990 annual report, released on 4 January 1991, the bank said that it was putting its strategies and operations through a 'thorough reassessment', with increased emphasis to be placed on credit control and the performance of core businesses. Inadequate control over subsidiaries, a longstanding issue, had contributed to the problems, as had the lack of group-wide credit policies. From 1990, the responsibility for group credit policy and control was extended over the entire group, and around the world.

Businesses were now identified as either in the category of 'value creators'—consumer and commercial banking, global financial markets, Westpac Financial Services, retail banking in New Zealand and, as borderline cases, AGC's international operations, Asia–Pacific and Australian corporate banking and New Zealand's corporate and international—or 'value dilutors' which were Europe, the Americas division and AGC's property. The Americas division represented a collision of goals: Westpac wanted a presence in the US and the division needed to grow and generate increased revenue to cover the expansion and make profits, but growth demanded a capital investment which, in the early 1990s, had not reached its 'hurdle rate' of at least 14.6 per cent return on equity.

Westpac was reaping the consequences of the 1980s, when the bank had deliberately chosen to lift its share of corporate banking aggressively and, in common with other banks, in Australia and around the world, had taken on more than it could handle. Under Bob White, the bank had embarked on a succession of overseas expansions into major and highly competitive markets in the US and the UK at a time when it was still coming to grips with how to operate in a domestic

239

market which had been deregulated more rapidly and broadly than had been expected. White had correctly discerned that major changes were afoot in Australian banking in the 1980s. In a sense, in his far-sighted drive to extend Westpac's reach, he had been trying to effect two revolutions when even one would have been daunting: increase the volume of business, which placed a strain on management and, even more challengingly, convert a traditional Australian bank that had existed since the early nineteenth century in a protected environment, offering a limited range of products, into a global, diversified financial services group. One bright outcome of the 1980s expansion was the global financial markets area, with Westpac consistently dominating the foreign-exchange field in *BRW*'s annual forex poll. Another saviour for Westpac was its strong but increasingly neglected retail base. But the bank needed to sharpen its focus and eliminate duplication. The possibility of acquiring a small regional bank in Australia was still in Westpac's sights, because that would strengthen its home base. But it had to kill off relationships that did not generate sufficient profits, and forget about cross-selling financial products to subsidise corporate lending at fine margins. Overseas, the strategy of expanding corporate banking assets, which had been Westpac's main thrust, was no longer sustainable. Westpac simply did not have the fat in its core business to subsidise the expansion undertaken in the 1980s. Write-offs, bad debts and the burden of non-accrual loans were increasingly sapping its strength.

These were truths. But a dangerous thread of disbelief continued to run through the Westpac group: a supreme self-confidence blinded it to its errors. Delays in recognising mistakes compounded its problems in the early 1990s.

CHAPTER TEN

THE LETTERS, THE TRIALS AND THE BORROWERS

Naji Halabi's impact on Westpac went far beyond the millions of dollars he is said to have creamed off the bank in foreign-exchange trading. Westpac first got wind of a looming crisis in September 1990, several months before the Halabi trials, when its chief legal officer, Terry Dunne, was contacted by the Lebanese consul in Sydney, Gilbert Aoun, and invited to lunch at the consulate. As the meal drew to a close, Aoun told Dunne that he was representing the parents of Naji and Ramzi Halabi and he wished to try to settle litigation between the family and Westpac. The consul, apparently acting independently of his diplomatic role, handed Dunne a sealed brown envelope and, according to Dunne, said: 'Mr Dunne, you should not have gone to the police. We have ways to settle these matters.' Back at his office, Dunne opened the envelope, which contained an invitation for the bank to settle, proposed terms of settlement and a number of other documents including a copy of the second of what were to become known as the 'Westpac letters', written to the bank in November and December 1987 by Paddy Jones, a partner of Westpac's legal advisers, Allen Allen & Hemsley. Jones's letters, until then strictly confidential, were a legal expert's response to the bank's concerns following complaints by customers about mismanagement of foreign-currency loans by its merchant bank subsidiary, Partnership Pacific Ltd, in late 1986 and 1987. Westpac was left in no doubt about what was intended by the proposition: settle the case against the Halabis or risk potentially devastating publicity to itself, or the possible embarrassment to clients, that would follow from the damaging letters being made public. Westpac characterised the approach as blackmail. Dunne rang Aoun and said that Westpac did not do business in this manner. A subsequent fax from Aoun disclosed that the Halabis had many thousands of pages of Westpac and customer documents, and suggested a further meeting outside Australia to discuss the matter.

It was news to Westpac that Jones's letters and other documents were missing. The dates on the letters, November and December 1987, showed that they had been removed from the bank several months after Naji Halabi had been dismissed. Westpac turned to the police but the NSW fraud squad, citing lack of resources, was unwilling to handle the matter; nor were the federal police prepared to take it on. Westpac felt there was no alternative but to pursue the matter itself, to find out what other documents were in the Halabis' possession.

Dunne then received an overseas call from a solicitor, Maurice Sellier. Born in Trinidad, working in London and in the Middle East, Sellier had replaced Aoun as negotiator; a further meeting was discussed. In November 1990 Dunne was making a routine visit to the UK on behalf of Westpac and he arranged a meeting in London with Sellier and a longstanding friend of the Halabi family, Alexander Wood, a Scottish banker who had worked in the Middle East. They met on 13 November at a three-storey house at 44 Green Street, in London's classy Mayfair. Dunne was accompanied by Mark Hyde, a solicitor from Westpac's London lawyers, Clifford Chance. They were astounded to be shown two plastic laundry baskets stuffed with bound volumes, documents and deal slips. They were told there was more. As an indication of what the baskets contained, they were again shown the letters written by Paddy Jones. Following the meeting, Sellier twice wrote to Dunne during November, outlining terms of settlement. The Halabis would pay Westpac $1 million and return all documents if Westpac dropped the case; the Halabis also undertook not to talk to journalists or parliamentarians. Westpac declined the offer to settle. Early in December Dunne went to the British courts to secure a civil search warrant for 44 Green Street, and for the homes of Sellier and Wood, but nothing was found. The documents had gone, and were not seen again until copies were anonymously mailed to some 200 recipients early in 1991. The bank's anxieties were twofold: the potential damage to its own reputation and possible breaches of customer confidentiality.

Within Westpac's legal division there was some discussion about whether to go public about what was happening. Some advisers thought that if customer information were in danger of being published, and customers could be justifiably angry, Westpac should take the initiative and reveal what had occurred. Undecided about what course of action to pursue, the bank sought outside public relations advice. At a meeting in mid-December in Dunne's office on level 15 of Westpac's headquarters, attended by outside consultants as well as Westpac's internal head of public relations, Tony Benner, it was decided—far from unanimously—that the bank should keep silent for the time being. Fowler later said that the issue would be re-examined after the Christmas break. However, preparation for the annual general meeting in January diverted attention on to other matters.

The letters

A few days after the January 1991 annual meeting came the bombshell: envelopes postmarked in Belgium began landing on desks around Australia, their explosive contents mailed anonymously. The Paddy Jones letters, written to Westpac in confidence in 1987, were now in the hands of a wide range of journalists, politicians, companies and bank clients. The only clue to their origin was the Belgian postmark. On 29 January extracts of the letters were published in *The Sydney Morning Herald*, in an article by investigative journalist Anne Lampe, headlined 'Westpac arm could face forex lawsuits'.

Westpac had missed its chance to control the damage and was on the back foot from then. Probably nothing either before or since in Westpac's history so tarnished its image with the general public as the 'letters affair'. The board had to be informed about the issues. Dunne prepared a statement for Fowler which he presented to a startled board. One director lightened the mood with a comment that the amazing tale would make an exciting mini-series which could lift the flagging fortunes of Channel Ten.

Within 24 hours Westpac had obtained injunctions from Mr Justice Young in the NSW Supreme Court to stop publication or use of the letters. The injunctions were against John Fairfax Group Pty Ltd, David Syme & Co Ltd, Anne Lampe and, a few days later, Naji Halabi. In the High Court of New Zealand injunctions were obtained against two New Zealand newspapers. In Westpac's view, the letters were confidential communications protected by legal professional privilege between solicitor and client.

John Fairfax and Syme lost a Supreme Court application to have the injunction set aside. Counsel for Fairfax, Steven Rares, had argued that the documents could no longer be considered confidential, given the wide distribution of both *The Sydney Morning Herald* and *The Age*. 'The cat is out of the bag,' he said. In dismissing the application, Justice Powell said he was 'far from satisfied' that the information in the letters could be regarded as being in the public domain, nor was he satisfied that there was sufficient evidence to prove the documents had been 'deprived of confidential quality'. Justice Powell described the media coverage of the events surrounding Westpac's attempts to preserve the confidentiality of the letters as 'unbridled hysteria'.

An element of farce relieved the drama: while the injunctions were being upheld in the Supreme Court, newsagents outside were selling the left-wing newspaper *Tribune*, which had reprinted the full text of the Westpac letters. Westpac staff passing newsstands in Martin Place, near the bank's head office, bought up remaining copies of the *Tribune*.

Westpac, determined not to take any action that, in its own view or in the view of its legal advisers, might jeopardise the outcome of the forthcoming Halabi trials, resolutely refused to comment on the letters, explain their origins or suggest why they had been leaked. Westpac did not want to say anything that might be construed as obstructing a fair trial. Attempts to identify who had stolen the letters and other documents initially led nowhere. Ramzi Halabi later confirmed under cross-examination by Charles Sweeney, QC, during proceedings in February 1991, that in August or September 1990 he had received a bundle of documents, including some originals and advice from Allens to Westpac regarding its prospects against the Halabis, but denied any knowledge of their source. Ramzi Halabi said he had given the material to his solicitor in October 1990. Westpac surmised that the documents had been stolen by a former employee and sent to Adli Halabi in Europe, who had then mailed them to journalists and politicians in Australia.

Tension mounted in Westpac as arguments flew back and forth over how best to contain the damage. Some in the bank were angry that Paddy Jones had expressed his concerns so vividly in writing. But Westpac's headlong flight to the courts had been a disastrous tactical error. Under pressure to act

245

swiftly, the bank followed its legal advice and obtained injunctions which turned what might have passed as a one-day burst of adverse publicity into a protracted drama that tainted Westpac's name in an unprecedented fashion. The true origins of the 'letters affair' were complex and involved arcane legal and foreign-exchange issues of little interest to most people. It was far more titillating that Westpac, Australia's largest bank, was trying to stifle a story about allegations of mismanagement of clients' affairs in its merchant bank subsidiary. Public relations experts agreed that Westpac had provided a textbook example of how not to handle a crisis and had succeeded only in ensuring widespread coverage of the more salacious aspects of the story.

Fowler was grappling with that when *The Bulletin*, which had obtained an internal Westpac document, revealed criticisms of the bank's group credit policy in a review prepared for the board. The *Bulletin* article summed up the review: 'In essence, it says that Westpac has not really understood how to go about its mainstream business of lending money.' The leaked document zeroed in on the bank's lack of portfolio management as a key factor in its problem loans and recommended establishing a portfolio management system. The review pointed out that Westpac's problem loans had been much in line with those of the National Australia Bank in the late 1980s but had recently deteriorated and were closer to the level of ANZ, whose performance had been adversely affected by its acquisition of the UK bank Grindlays PLC. The Westpac document noted:

> Westpac had no such external influences. Its problems must therefore have been driven by a drop in the quality of the loan portfolio in its base business ... Westpac has performed worse than the market. Westpac is presently underperforming shareholder expectations as a result of a reduction in loan quality. The general reason is that the credit risk

management process has not yet made the transition from operating in a regulated environment. The specific reason is that Westpac has not been practising portfolio management ... Management of credit risk is presently carried out through a combination of management of individual credits and a procedures-oriented approach to credit policy. The dominant concentration is on the approval process for individual credits. The theory behind this approach is that if individual credits are good, then the sum of the individual credits must also be good.

Westpac was enraged to see the internal criticisms publicised, and made forceful attempts to check the source of the leak. The ripples reached the higher echelons at Consolidated Press, publishers of *The Bulletin*, because at that time Westpac was the company's main banker. But the storm blew over.

Adding to pressures, and despite the injunctions, on 20 February the leader of the Australian Democrats in South Australia, Ian Gilfillin, read out substantial sections of the letters in the state parliament, so that they were recorded in Hansard. This went against the stance taken by the federal Senate which had earlier rejected an application for the letters to be tabled. The president of the Senate, Kerry Sibraa, had said the letters should not be tabled because the matter was *sub judice*. Later, Australian Democrat senator Paul McLean, a vocal crusader against bank lending practices, was granted leave to table the letters. He had already distributed some documents outside Parliament House.

Its campaign to suppress the contents of the documents clearly fruitless, Westpac decided in late February to try to publish as much of the story through newspaper and magazine advertisements as it could without breaching any sensitivities. The team working on the wording of the bank's statement gathered in Stuart Fowler's office and included representatives from Allen Allen & Hemsley as well as Westpac's Dunne and his assistant Barbara Filipowski. The group formulated a series of advertisements headed 'Westpac Confidential Letters—the facts':

> Westpac is dismayed that certain parties have ignored the rulings of the courts with regard to the Westpac Confidential Letters.
>
> Westpac is concerned that certain individuals approach the administration of justice as a game in which they use their best endeavours to evade the rulings of the courts.
>
> The reading of the documents in the South Australian Legislative Council we believe is a clear breach of a fundamental parliamentary convention and has jeopardised several principles which are cornerstones of our society.
>
> Westpac is also disappointed that Senator McLean appears to have ignored the spirit of the ruling by the President of the Senate by distributing the documents outside the Senate chamber ...
>
> Westpac is unable to reveal or comment in any detail on the confidential letters since they remain the central issue in a number of legal cases, both recent and longstanding, before the courts ...
>
> But Westpac wishes to have the public record set straight about the circumstances in which the letters were written.
>
> The letters in question are letters of advice sought by the bank from its external solicitors in November and December 1987. They relate to the management by Partnership Pacific Ltd (PPL) of foreign currency exposures for a small number of clients ...

There is no doubt that the letters contain opinions critical of the way in which certain activities of PPL were conducted ... PPL has now been merged into the bank.

The legal position which the bank has taken in relation to these two letters has been endorsed by the courts. It is very important to note that Westpac in each of its actions against:

—John Fairfax Group Limited (receivers & managers appointed), David Syme & Co Ltd (receivers & managers appointed) and Anne Lampe

—the Australian Broadcasting Corporation

—Federal Capital Press of Australia Ltd, publishers of the Canberra Times

—Naji Halabi and Others

has been granted injunctions restraining the disclosure of the contents of the two letters.

In the proceedings Westpac has brought against Naji Halabi and five other members of his family, the judge ordered all defendants to detail the circumstances under which copies of the letters came into their hands. Mr Naji Halabi swore an affidavit in which he claimed that he could not comply with that part of the Court's order because to do so may tend to incriminate him. In the course of argument in Court Mr Halabi's counsel handed up to the judge a document listing a number of criminal offences for which his client could potentially be liable, as the bases for declining to provide the information required by the judge's order ...

One of the constraints placed upon the bank and its advisors is that it has not been free to comment extensively on all relevant matters surrounding events of the past month because of the pending criminal and civil trials set down for April and June ... The bank is unwilling to take any step (by

public comment or otherwise) which might be preju-
dicial to a fair trial . . .

The bank has on five separate occasions issued
press releases to explain why it was taking the court
action it has pursued. The bank's press releases have
been ignored entirely or in large measure by the
media, although some journalists and others appear
to have no hesitation in making use of documents
obviously obtained unlawfully . . . a quantity of bank
documents have been stolen. They have been copied
and distributed in such a way as to cause the bank
maximum embarrassment . . . regardless of the quite
irresponsible criticism levelled at the bank in the
media Westpac has not succumbed to nor will it ever
succumb to threats to pervert the course of justice.
That is the larger issue confronting the bank.

In February 1991 Westpac began proceedings in the NSW
Supreme Court against a former employee, John McLennan,
who had become a consultant to disgruntled foreign-currency
borrowers. In December 1990 McLennan had made a submission to the government inquiry into the banking industry
and was to be called as a witness in connection with foreign-
currency loans. Westpac sought, among other things, to find
out what documents McLennan had, and how he had come
to be in possession of them. McLennan wrote to the committee that he considered this a 'blatant attempt to intimidate'
him over his well-publicised submission to the inquiry.
Westpac managing director Stuart Fowler later denied that
the bank had tried to intimidate or gag a witness appearing
before the inquiry. In his statement to the inquiry in March
1991, Fowler said that the press reports that John McLennan
had been gagged were described by a judge of the Supreme
Court as 'a gross distortion and fanciful'. In May 1991
McLennan launched a counter-claim, suing Westpac and

Fowler for defamation and abuse of process. The dispute between Westpac and McLennan—whose legal costs were said to total $140,000—was eventually settled on a confidential basis in June 1992.

Backed by his knowledge of Westpac's systems, McLennan felt he was able to assist and motivate the borrowers, who felt that the banks should bear responsibility for the foreign-currency loans they marketed—particularly, they claimed, when bank officers had not given adequate warnings about potential losses or had not managed the loans properly. While in early court cases borrowers had often been hobbled by insufficient evidence, McLennan, who had worked as an efficiency auditor during his banking career, was able to guide them on what documents to request for their court battles so that, armed with the necessary paperwork, they were far better able to fight their damages cases. McLennan claims that he was harassed from May 1990, by electronic and other forms of surveillance and two break-ins at his remote NSW farm. During that time Westpac had been writing to McLennan to ascertain how he had come to possess certain documents, but had had no response. The bank appointed process servers to deliver the correspondence but they had difficulty tracking down someone who had no listed address, an unlisted phone number and who claimed he had operated virtually out of the boot of his car. Says McLennan: 'There was no team, just myself, a phone and a fax machine. I was living on the edge for two or three years. I passionately believed that the banks were screwing a lot of people. There was a great deal of complacency, and very few people prepared to fight. Westpac was never sure what I had, it thought I had lots of documents. I became the anti-Christ to Westpac.'

During court proceedings, McLennan had suggested that the confidential Westpac documents he had received might have come from Rob Douglass, the former managing director

251

of PPL, the merchant bank at the heart of the letters' fiasco. Douglass publicly refuted involvement in their distribution. In a statement to the media in March 1991, Douglass said he was not in possession of confidential letters from the bank, nor had he sent letters to Australian media organisations and politicians. Paddy Jones's letters, with their criticisms of PPL and comment about 'a tradition of weak management' in the company, did not reflect well on Douglass. In his statement he said: 'Everyone knows I left Westpac about a year before the confidential letters were written. I was totally unaware of Allen Allen & Hemsley's investigation. It may seem odd, but my views were never sought by the writer of the confidential letters before he wrote them. If he had, I am sure he would not have reached such specious conclusions.'

The banking inquiry

252

The 1991 parliamentary inquiry into the Australian banking industry, chaired by Stephen Martin, then Labor member for Macarthur, was prompted by community concerns during 1990 about banking policies and practices and provided an opportunity for an assessment of the consequences of the first decade of financial deregulation. Such was the controversy over the Westpac letters that Martin considered it was diverting attention from the central issues of the inquiry. On 6 March 1991 he contacted Stuart Fowler asking him to consider tabling the letters before the committee. By then, the committee had received its own copies of the letters in a plain brown envelope posted in Belgium. Westpac agreed to appear before the committee on the following day. Its legal team worked late into the night preparing Fowler's statement. The bank chartered a private jet to fly Fowler, Terry Dunne and Jim Dwyer from Allen Allen & Hemsley to Canberra. In what the committee's report, *A Pocket Full of Change*, described as the most dramatic episode of the inquiry, Fowler appeared before a special hearing in Canberra on 7 March and confirmed that Westpac would not object to the letters being tabled. Their release represented a complete reversal in attitude by Westpac, which had spent the previous six weeks vigorously trying to suppress the letters. Fowler said: 'The bank was told on a number of occasions, both in Australia and overseas, that if it did not discontinue certain civil litigation brought by the bank to recover very large sums allegedly misappropriated from the bank, the documents in question would be made public. The bank was not prepared to submit to this blackmail and will not do so.' Fowler lashed out at the media, the Democrat senator Paul McLean and others who had been 'prepared to traffic in stolen documents'.

Stephen Martin commented at the hearing that 'some people who are separate from the inquiry and who may be perceived to have their own political agendas, as well as some media organisations, have raised these documents to a level of significance that is possibly beyond their actual contents'. He added: 'The public perception that Westpac's approach to this whole matter has been to suppress and restrain public debate and discussion has not assisted in defusing the issue. Many people would agree that as a public relations exercise this has been a disaster.' Westpac agreed to the withdrawal of court orders restraining media publication of the letters. However, the bank has never waived its claim of legal professional privilege.

Fowler told the committee that the so-called 'Westpac letters' related only to PPL. 'It is unfortunate that they have become known as the Westpac letters as they do not relate to the conduct of the bank itself,' he said. He went on to say that it was not until mid-1987 that Westpac executives became aware that two customers had lodged complaints about PPL's management of their foreign-currency exposures. In his evidence to the inquiry Fowler referred to

253

aspects of concern regarding PPL's management of foreign-currency exposures for clients 'particularly during a two-to-three month period in the first half of 1987'—the period of the hiatus when Westpac treasury was attempting to take over, however informally, the management of PPL's loans. This is at variance with the time-frame referred to in West-pac's February press advertisement, where the bank said that the letters related solely to limited activities of its wholly owned subsidiary, PPL, in the period 'leading up to 1987'. The advertisements, written hurriedly to a deadline, were an attempt to quarantine Westpac from the problems in PPL. The time-frame cited in Fowler's statement presented a more accurate picture.

Giving evidence to the committee, National Australia Bank chief Don Argus weighed into the debate with a defence of the banks: 'There was a greed factor there and a lot of these customers now crying foul went into these things [foreign-currency loans] with their eyes wide open,' he said. John McLennan conceded there was a greed factor but argued that did not relieve the banks of their responsibility. 'Even PPL, with all its resources, could not protect the loans,' he said. But the extent of the collapse of the $A also took borrowers and banks alike by surprise.

The banking inquiry committee examined the question of foreign-currency loans in subsequent hearings.

Halabi trials

Westpac v Halabi involved a succession of court proceedings. Criminal charges were heard in April 1991 in the NSW Supreme Court where Naji Halabi was accused of conspiring, with his brother Ramzi and Benny Choo, an employee of Kleinwort Benson and former employee of Westpac, to defraud Westpac. On the first day of the trial, Ramzi Halabi pleaded guilty to nineteen charges of aiding and abetting Choo in improperly using Choo's position to gain financial advantage for another. Choo pleaded guilty to charges of making improper use of his position as associate director of Kleinwort Benson to gain a monetary advantage for another.

The Crown alleged that Naji Halabi defrauded Westpac of some $250,000 in the six months between July 1986 and January 1987 when, as a Westpac foreign-exchange dealer, he entered into nineteen foreign-exchange transactions with Choo at dishonest off-market rates and the deals caused a loss to Westpac and a profit to Kleinwort Benson, with Choo effecting a transfer of the profits to Ramzi Halabi's account. Naji Halabi pleaded not guilty. During the three-and-a-half-week jury trial in Sydney's old criminal courts in Taylor Square, presided over by Mr Justice Grove, crucial evidence was presented on behalf of Westpac by Mike Eastaway, its former chief foreign-exchange dealer. Eastaway, who had left the bank in July 1987, painstakingly explained the practices used in Westpac to record interbank foreign-exchange transactions in 1986 and early 1987.

The jury had to come to grips with complex technical issues. Eastaway was on the stand for two-and-a-half days. Peter Hely QC, for Naji Halabi, put to Eastaway a number of transactions, carried out by various foreign-exchange dealers, from subpoenaed Westpac documents. In several cases, the transactions were entered on deal slips but omitted from dealer position sheets, in others there was a note 'no exchange of funds'. Eastaway provided reasons for the discrepancies in most deal dockets but could not find an explanation for the discrepancies in dockets written by Naji Halabi. During the trial, Halabi's lawyers pushed Eastaway to concede that Westpac had breached Reserve Bank rules by carrying out 'parking' transactions—where a bank deals with an offshore associate to reduce its overnight exposure—to conceal the fact that the bank was over RBA-imposed limits on foreign-exchange deals (limits which were a constraint for all banks). Reference was also made to the suspicions raised in Clive Alexander's report suggesting wrongdoing on a wider scale in Westpac's foreign-exchange dealing room. In his second day of outlining the case against Naji Halabi, Crown prosecutor Ian Lloyd, QC, said one reason that fraud was able to occur was business practices that did not keep a complete check.

The jury took four hours to find Naji Halabi guilty of conspiracy to defraud Westpac. He was sentenced to eighteen months' periodic detention in jail. In handing down sentence, Justice Grove described speculative foreign-exchange trading as 'a form of gambling' and said Naji Halabi had taken advantage of a 'background of disorder' by disguising the losses on the nineteen deals as part of daily profits and losses in foreign-exchange trading.

Naji Halabi had lived in a style well beyond the means of a junior foreign-exchange trader, in a well appointed penthouse apartment in Tewkesbury Avenue in the inner Sydney suburb of Darlinghurst, which he had bought in 1985 for $295,000 in cash. He drove a smart sports car and possessed a large collection of valuable Lalique crystal, said to be worth $1 million.

The Crown subsequently appealed to the NSW Court of Criminal Appeal which said that the sentence of weekend detention was 'manifestly inadequate', that Halabi had been in a position of trust and had taken advantage of that to engage in criminal activity. In February 1992 the sentence was converted to eighteen months' jail. Halabi had already completed six months in periodic detention, and would spend the next year at Long Bay jail. A *Four Corners* program, which went to air on 24 February 1992, filmed Halabi selling oil paintings outside Westpac's headquarters in Sydney's Martin Place, apparently to help pay his legal bills. According to journalist Ross Coulthart's narrative, Halabi, who claimed to be nearly bankrupt, saw himself 'as a scapegoat, a fall guy for the excesses of an industry which was never properly regulated'. Benny Choo's plea of guilty to the charge of improperly using his position to obtain an advantage brought him a fifteen-month sentence to be served by periodic detention. Ramzi Halabi was fined $200,000 and placed on a five-year good behaviour bond for aiding and abetting Choo.

Shortly after the criminal proceedings, in June 1991, Westpac opened an eight-week civil case in the commercial division of the Supreme Court against Naji and Ramzi Halabi, their brother Adli, their parents, Ramzi's ex-wife Christina as well as his companies Sonal Finance and Trans Pacific and other related companies, seeking to recover damages for financial loss. Charles Sweeney QC, for Westpac, said that Naji Halabi 'systematically plundered' $4.3 million from the bank through dishonest foreign-exchange deals between 1984 and early 1987 and the dollars found their way to the Halabis through a complex series of deals and an international network of compliant family members and friends. Ramzi Halabi, alleged to have master-minded the scheme, defended the civil suit. However, in an acrimonious marital separation, Christina had kept his Filofax which contained details of his dealings with Sonal Finance. These were critically useful to Westpac. Principal witnesses for Westpac were Rahoul Chowdry, who was in the witness box for two-and-a-half days, and Mike Eastaway. Judgment was reserved, and the parties went to mediation with Hal Wootten QC. Those involved had to travel to Hong Kong because Adli Halabi, aware that he was under suspicion for being instrumental in circulating the Westpac letters, was reluctant to enter Australia. The proceedings were settled in Hong Kong, in late January 1992, on confidential terms.

In a further action involving Naji Halabi and relating to the Westpac letters, Westpac won a ruling in the equity division of the Supreme Court in September 1991 that Halabi had infringed the bank's copyright and had disclosed and misused its confidential information. Mr Justice Powell awarded costs and unspecified damages against Halabi. He ordered that Halabi provide an affidavit identifying the persons who had supplied him with the Westpac documents and those to whom he had in turn given them. Halabi was also ordered to deliver all Westpac documents he held. Halabi continued to claim privilege against self-incrimination.

The long-running series of legal actions in civil proceedings between Westpac and the Halabis ended in April 1992 when Westpac received judgment that it was entitled to $13.4 million in damages and interest. There was an agreement to pay certain sums to Westpac, with the payments secured by certain assets of the Halabi family.

Foreign-currency loans

Foreign-currency loans and their associated problems, already in the headlines because of court cases involving the Commonwealth Bank and ANZ Bank as well as Westpac, received unprecedented prominence with the publication in newspapers of extracts from the Westpac letters, allegations of intimidation and gagging by Westpac of John McLennan and, to a lesser extent, the banking inquiry which was already under way in 1991.

Foreign-currency loans, where a client of a bank borrows in funds other than Australian dollars, were not new. Banks had been providing these loans for Australian companies and semi-government authorities since the 1960s. Borrowers tended to be large organisations, some with in-house expertise to manage their foreign-currency exposures. Before exchange controls were lifted in December 1983, banks could not lend foreign currencies in Australia so the loans were made through overseas offices, in Westpac's case usually through its Singapore branch. This practice continued after 1983, partly because the banks' procedures were well established in those offices, partly because there was no market in Swiss francs in Australia, partly because of the time-zone advantage over using, say, London or New York, and partly because a lower corporate tax rate applied in Singapore (although after the introduction of a foreign tax credit system in 1986 income was assessed at Australian marginal tax rates and a credit received for foreign tax paid). The appeal for borrowers of foreign-currency loans grew in the 1980s because of the lower interest rates applying to, say, Swiss francs, compared with the rates a borrower would have to pay for an Australian dollar loan. Westpac has esti-mated that close to 90 per cent of its foreign-currency loans were denominated in Swiss francs. The interest-rate differ-ential between Switzerland and Australia explains why. In December 1980 Australian interest rates were around 13 per cent compared with 7 per cent in Switzerland; the differential had widened by March 1982 when Australian rates were around 19 per cent and Swiss rates were unchanged. From then until 1986, when Australian rates were between 15 per cent and a high of 18 per cent in late 1985, Swiss rates were around 4 or 5 per cent. Such lower-cost financing enabled entrepreneurial developers to undertake projects that would not have been possible if funding had to be acquired at Aus-tralian rates. Foreign-currency loans were taken out for a range of purposes: to consolidate existing debt, expand a business or embark on a speculative venture, with property development a popular choice. The risk to a foreign-currency borrower was the possibility that the Australian dollar could fall in value against the Swiss franc to such an extent that the interest-rate advantage would be wiped out. But in many cases the 'greed factor' obscured the risk.

Banks started offering foreign-currency loans to 'retail' customers in 1981. It was a perilous business from the beginning: retail bank staff did not have the grasp of the intricacies and risks of foreign-currency lending that resided in the treasury and corporate banking areas. In an article in September 1990 in the *Journal of Banking and Finance Law and Practice*, Justice Andrew Rogers commented:

> ... the banks' front-line staff up to and including branch managers were substantially innocent of any real knowledge of the difficulties attaching to foreign currency borrowings. Whilst charged by higher management with the task of promoting such loans they were not equipped to explain to borrowers either the risks attaching to such loans or the measures that were available and required to contain the risk. Experience has shown that even when bank managers called in 'experts' from regional offices the difficulties continued. Higher management was advised that true expertise was restricted to staff of the banks' international branches.

In offering foreign-currency loans, banks have claimed that they were responding to customer demand and that if they had not obliged, the customers would take their business elsewhere. This assertion is supported by a view expressed in the *Manning River Times* by Ian Fisher, a northern NSW farmer who later became president of the Foreign Currency Borrowers Association and a forthright critic of the banks. In May 1985 he wrote to the paper in support of offshore loans as a solution to boosting farm incomes:

> The answer ... could well be foreign-currency loans. The term to be five years with no principal repayment, and an interest rate of about seven-and-a-half

per cent to be paid half-yearly in arrears ... It will
be found that the average bank manager knows little
of offshore lending. He knows that currencies fluc-
tuate and influence interest rates and is extremely
nervous of the whole deal. So he steers his clients
back to onshore loans, with 16–17–18 per cent interest rates, which he understands.

Competition was increasing, with the new, largely foreign-
owned merchant banks enthusiastically marketing foreign-
currency loans. Because of the risk of movements in
exchange rates, foreign-currency loans can involve a considerable element of gambling. This speculative aspect of
borrowing in foreign currencies can be removed, or at least
reduced, by taking out cover against exchange-rate movements, known as hedging, but the costs of hedging increase
the overall cost of a foreign-currency loan to a level that
approximates the cost of domestic finance, thus negating the
appeal. A handful of financial institutions, including Westpac's PPL, offered to manage foreign-currency loans on
clients' behalf to mitigate the risks involved, but in most
cases management of the currency exposure was the responsibility of the borrower.

261

Banks were aware from the outset of the risks of foreign
currency lending. A discussion paper delivered in August
1982 at a Wales managers' legal conference on offshore
lending argued for foreign-currency loans to be made to
companies, rather than trusts or individuals. The paper also
said: 'Potential borrowers should be made well aware of the
exchange risks involved and advised to seek hedging facility
available from the bank ... In many instances it may be
prudent to make such cover a prerequisite to the facility
being approved.'

The attitude of various judges towards foreign-currency
loans was by no means irrelevant to the fate of borrowers.

Justice Andrew Rogers was later to write, in his 1990 article, that the banks knew a foreign-currency borrowing was 'pregnant with the danger of large capital loss unless precautions were taken' and knew that staff was 'ill-equipped to explain the risk to the borrower'. Rogers went on to say:

> The documents . . . from a number of banks . . . reveal that for some years after 1982 the Australian banks operated under considerable constraints. There were, from time to time, restrictions on the local funds which were permitted to be lent. Local interest rates were high. In contrast there were almost unlimited funds available from overseas sources at rates eight to ten per cent lower than locally. The fees attaching to such loans were very attractive to banks. Nonetheless the difficulties confronting the banks in marketing such loans were indeed forbidding. Internal bank documents make clear that these difficulties were recognised at the higher levels of bank management. In my opinion the recognition of the difficulties and problems involved reflect on the duty of care owed by banks to borrowers.

Rogers bluntly criticised the foreign-currency loan to the particular plaintiff, and inferentially all foreign-currency loans in his judgment in the case of Mehta v Commonwealth Bank in 1990, saying: 'Nobody in his right mind, after being told that the possible loss was unlimited, that the necessary implementation of safeguards would be limited in their effect and would require continuous attention, which the bank refused to provide, would contemplate making the borrowing. Attractive as the borrowing may have been, the attraction could not survive a full and complete explanation.' In dealing with a proposition that foreign-currency loans, like some physical products, could come under a special principle relating to 'dangerous products', the Federal Court judgment in the David Securities case said:

> ... It *is* clear that the rule as to things dangerous in themselves can have no application here. Nor, in our view, can the rule as to things inherently dangerous provide an appropriate analogy in the case of a borrowing in a foreign currency.
>
> It may be interpreted that there will always be a risk of an adverse movement in the rate of exchange. But it does not follow that a foreign loan transaction is something 'dangerous', let alone 'dangerous in itself', or anything analogous to such a special thing ... all that can be said is that it is possible that such a transaction may result in some economic gain in certain events or in some economic loss if other contingencies occur. A foreign borrowing is not itself dangerous merely because opportunities for profit, or loss, may exist.

263

The claim of 'dangerous product' was also addressed in the NSW Court of Appeal in Mehta v Commonwealth Bank of Australia by Justice Roderick Meagher, who said:

> A foreign currency loan is largely a gamble; consequently, it would be unattractive to the timid and the prudent. Nonetheless, there are perfectly rational people who are prepared to gamble; and it is notorious that many borrowers did enter into such transactions at the time without suffering any damage, some of whom actually made a profit. All the experts agreed that it was reasonable for an informed borrower to enter into such transactions. One cannot but have an uneasy feeling that a dogmatic view that such loans are necessarily irrational

will lead to the imposition of liability on lenders
where justice does not require it.

Westpac arranged around 900 foreign-currency loans over a
three-year period to 1986. Few such loans were written after
1986. Westpac said in its evidence to the banking inquiry
that this averaged around 25 loans a month compared with
4,800 domestic commercial loan approvals each month.
Westpac was trying to hose down suggestions that the bank
had aggressively marketed the foreign-currency loans. It conceded that the product was advertised and information about
it provided in seminars. But Westpac gave evidence to the
banking inquiry that the bank had no centralised strategy for
marketing foreign-currency loans. Sometimes the enthusiasm
for foreign-currency lending stemmed from a handful of
individual bank officers, sometimes from outside advisers of
customers in a particular geographic area. Solicitors and
accountants, especially in some country centres, have been
blamed for encouraging clients into foreign-currency borrowings; for at least one bank, there was a noticeable pattern
of 'clusters' of foreign-currency loans in specific regions.

And Westpac's claim that it had no centralised strategy
sits oddly with some internal bank correspondence written in
the early 1980s which clearly set out the bank's ambitions
for selling foreign-currency loans. The memos also reveal
healthy internal debate about the pros and cons of foreign-
currency lending at the retail level and to a large extent
reflect the general ethos permeating Westpac in those years:
it was striving to become recognised as an international bank
capable of matching the competition in every way. A memo
dated October 1981 from H.P. Conway, state manager,
lending, NSW, said: 'We are anxious to have proposals to
expand offshore lending implemented as soon as possible'.
And an August 1982 note from Ken Richardson, chief
manager, NSW, concerning a business strategy meeting of

international managers reported that a decision had been taken

> to promote the availability of offshore currencies in relation to domestic lending and there is therefore need for all officers involved in offshore lending to corporate customers to be as well informed as possible. There are, for instance, problems in relation to documentation and we will be including information on the various functional aspects of offshore lending, eg, risk, taxation, legal, as well as on the marketing/ promotion side. For this purpose Mr A.G. Ayre, manager, Singapore branch, will be attending.

Memos written in 1985 by Frank Cass, chief manager, retail lending, and Frank Ward, general manager, credit policy and control, and revealed in the television program *Business Sunday* on 24 February 1991 showed that these executives had concerns about the foreign-currency loans. Cass's memo to Westpac's chief general manager, retail financial services, said: 'The escalation of unhedged offshore loans within retail banking, due to varying reasons has to my mind been a most unfortunate credit development. I feel strongly that we should now take definite steps to basically take the product off the shelf.' Ward's memo to Westpac's executive committee was blunt: 'The existing problems in the portfolio are a direct result of exchange rate volatility, depreciation, shortcomings in loan documentation and a lack of understanding of the complexities in the retail division.' In a memo to Ward, Cass later wrote: 'The basic question is whether it is prudent for a bank to lend unhedged which involves customers and speculating on currency, and as such speculation is not definable, must reflect through to the bank being involved in such speculation.' Cass ended with a comment from another Westpac executive: 'We prefer to be bookmakers, not punters.'

265

In his submission to the 1991 banking inquiry, John McLennan quoted a comment of Cass's, made in November 1985: 'Unhedged offshore loans were unheard of to most overseas bankers as they had enough difficulty with credit analysis without the added undefinable and uncontrollable risk of currency losses through exchange rate fluctuations.' McLennan commented in his submission that a 'prudent banker' would have 'undertaken a detailed analysis of the borrower's financial position to ensure they were of sufficient standing and had cash flow available to meet security top ups and increased cost of interest in the event the $A fell. We are aware that in 1981 the bank's guidelines contained very high security margins however these were later relaxed to meet competition.' In its supplementary submission to the banking inquiry, Westpac argued against that, stating that security margins were tighter for foreign-currency loans than for domestic borrowings, and were further tightened in late 1986. McLennan also said that a prudent banker would have assessed the ability of the potential borrower to manage an offshore exposure. 'It is clear that in fact virtually all "unsophisticated borrowers" could not manage an offshore exposure,' he wrote.

Foreign-currency borrowers

Foreign-currency borrowers were estimated in the mid-to-late 1980s to amount to close to 3,000, of whom almost one-third were Westpac customers. According to evidence presented to the banking inquiry, the foreign-currency borrowers from all banks tended to be small and medium-sized business operators, primary producers, property investors and developers. Many were in the finance and legal professions. Westpac estimated that about half of its borrowers were in finance, insurance, property and business services and included barristers, solicitors and accountants. In Westpac's case the minimum amount that could be borrowed in a foreign-currency loan varied between $250,000 and $500,000 and most bank foreign-currency loans ranged between $250,000 and $3 or $4 million, so the borrowers were not 'small' customers. Foreign-currency borrowers were described by a spokesperson for the Foreign Currency Borrowers Association in evidence to the banking inquiry as 'astute businessmen ... (who were) at the leading edge in the commercial field'. Giving evidence, one borrower stressed the high regard in which local bank managers were held:

> I and the majority of the borrowers that I have spoken to placed the bank manager in the same cat-egory as the parish priest and the local doctor. We would not do that now, we accept that, but back in the early 1980s we did ... The fact that we did place a lot of trust in our bank manager is not being clearly understood in the commercial realities of doing busi-ness out there. You have to deal with reliable, responsible people if you are going to run a success-ful business in Australia, and the bank manager back in the early 1980s was one of those people.

267

In a submission to the inquiry Westpac contended that while exceptions could be found, generally the foreign-currency borrowers were smart business people with access to inde-pendent financial advice, borrowing large sums of money, with assets to back the borrowings, trying to capitalise on 'cheap' finance and willing to accept the exchange-rate risk involved. In some cases, though, the borrowers became over-whelmed by mounting losses as the Australian dollar crashed in value against the Swiss franc, pushing up the Australian-dollar amount owed and raising the debt to a level that often dwarfed the value of security held by the lender. Borrowers and bankers alike were plunged into uncharted territory. For many borrowers, that led to the loss of businesses, homes and other assets and, as subsequent court cases showed, lives and lifestyles were ruined.

The problem

Foreign-currency loans did not create difficulties for borrowers in the 1980s until the sharp fall in the value of the $A in 1985 and during 1986, when some borrowers saw their debt increase by 100 per cent.

Fluctuations in currencies were not unknown. In a lengthy paper on eurocurrency (offshore or foreign-currency) lending at a national seminar on banking law in May 1979 Westpac's then chief legal officer, Bob Craigie, added a postscript pointing out that forward cover (in those days) was not available and 'even if it were, it might be far too expensive. The borrower is thus subject to a continuing exchange risk during the whole life of the loan.' Craigie went on to say that exchange rates were no longer stable: '... foreign exchange losses suffered recently by some major financiers have been staggering, especially for those who borrowed in Swiss francs. Over the past few years the Swiss franc has almost doubled in value in terms of the Australian currency.'

Things were to get much worse than that. At the start of 1985 the $A was worth slightly more than two Swiss francs; eighteen months later, in July 1986, it had halved in value to one. By late 1986 a number of foreign-currency borrowers were considering what to do about their deteriorating positions. Foreign-currency loans were generally for terms of five years and in many cases were non-amortising, with no principal repayment until the loan matured, so that the losses would not be realised until then. For many borrowers it was tempting to do nothing in the hope that the $A recovered. They knew they would have to meet higher interest-rate payments if they converted to an $A loan, a decision that was theirs; banks could not force borrowers to bring their loans onshore, and did not wish to advise them to do so.

The sharp fall in the $A took most economists and currency analysts by surprise. It certainly shocked the foreign-currency borrowers and disturbed their bankers. Concern at Westpac prompted an internal report early in 1986, prepared by Garvin Riley, chairman of the newly established offshore commercial (foreign-currency) loans task force established to determine the safety of the bank's foreign-currency loan portfolio in the wake of the weakening of the $A against other currencies. The report showed that at the end of 1985 Westpac's foreign-currency loans amounted to 6.6 per cent of total loans, and 'income from this source has been excellent'. The report noted that, given the volatile exchange rate environment, further substantial devaluations in the $A could not be ruled out. It went on:

269

> A major cause of concern is the lack of complete product knowledge by most people handling OCLs (this extends to administrative areas). Account managers appear uncertain as to the appropriate steps to take as losses caused by the $A depreciation is a relatively new situation, over which they have no power to manage or control (unlike an overdraft facility where cheques can be returned, and position crystallised). Most OCL borrowers are considered good customers of the bank—there appears to exist a high level of optimism by both customers and managers in that a solid $A appreciation is only a matter of time. Borrowers (and many managers) are of the view that if a loan is on a bullet repayment basis [payment on maturity] the only forex rate that matters is the one prevailing at the time of the maturity of the facility.

Westpac told the 1991 banking inquiry that because the fall in the value of the $A had been so underestimated, there was 'a tendency to let matters run on'.

The Riley report cited further problems, such as 'uncoordinated or inappropriate action in dealing with OCLs . . . increasing likelihood of litigation—extreme care is needed in discussing OCLs and proffering advice on forex movements, hedging etc . . . lack of information on Singapore branch files following approval of OCLs—this could contravene Monetary Authority of Singapore requirements; and inadequate or unreliable loan monitoring systems'. According to the report, Westpac had in May 1985 issued new policy guidelines which had been further tightened. For example, customers were required to have undoubted ability to 'top up' their security. Riley noted that, whether because of more stringent conditions or because of discouraging trends in the $A, new approvals had dropped from an average of 34 a month in the six months to the end of 1985 to eleven.

The report commented that only one case had been brought against a bank relating to offshore loans and this was settled out of court but it added:

> . . . we will be indeed fortunate if litigation is avoided entirely. Whilst the dangers attaching to these loans appear to have been explained to borrowers, records of such interviews are usually very brief. Additionally, we could be caught up with decisions handed down as a consequence of actions by litigants against other banks. Bank's solicitors [Allen Allen & Hemsley] are concerned that borrowers wishing to frustrate efforts for recovery by Bank could establish grounds for litigation by purposely encouraging an (inexperienced) account manager to proffer advice which may later prove to be inaccurate or ill-informed. It is clearly evident that extra care should

be taken by all personnel in discussing OCLs or responding to correspondence from borrowers.

An extract from an executive committee meeting held on 21 January 1986 stated that the committee was 'most concerned about the whole principle of offshore commercial loans, and decided that all such future advances could only be written in exceptional circumstances where the nature of the business completely supported offshore borrowings and its inherent risks'.

These matters came to be the subject of very public comment and complaint. In his evidence to the parliamentary banking inquiry, given at a public hearing in the NSW coastal town of Coffs Harbour on 20 March 1991, John McLennan said: 'The fear of litigation appears to have paralysed the bank's decision-making process and left the borrowers with no advice after further falls in the Australian dollar. It would appear that the chief manager, retail lending, Mr Frank Cass, general manager, retail banking, Mr McInnes, and general manager, credit policy and control, Mr Frank Ward, tried desperately to halt this type of lending. But the corporate and international division persisted until the potential losses and concern from chief manager, Europe, eventually forced a halt.'

Throughout 1988 McLennan became increasingly unsettled about the plight of the borrowers as their debts to the banks soared. He realised that alone they stood no chance against the banks, and in December he invited a group of twelve foreign-currency borrowers, customers of different banks, to a meeting in the NSW coastal resort of Port Macquarie. That was the start of the Foreign Currency Borrowers Association. The FCBA brought the borrowers mutual support, wide publicity and the exchange of information through letters and meetings. When a borrower won a case, the news spread rapidly, as borrowers hoped that a point that helped one might assist another in a case against a bank.

The FCBA claimed that the banks exploited the borrowers' captive and uncompetitive status by extracting excessive profit margins which were not explained to the borrowers. Giving evidence to the banking inquiry on 20 March 1991, McLennan said: 'Much has already been said about these documents [the Westpac letters] but it appears to me that no-one is willing to say what they really mean. The bank and/or its employees stole, yes, stole money from its clients. Whichever way you look at it, the taking of a secret commission incorporated in exchange rate is stealing; deal-switching is stealing. The bank used its trusted and privileged position to take secret profits and to make the borrowers' already tenuous position worse. I can think of no other worse example of corporate immorality.'

272

Banks charge a fee, in the form of a margin or spread above a wholesale foreign-exchange rate, to cover the costs of a transaction and make a profit. This is common business practice, and the margins vary according to the size of the deal. In the competitive interbank market, where multi-million dollar parcels of foreign currencies are traded, margins are very thin. At the retail end of the market, margins on very small parcels of foreign exchange are much fatter. Banks do not disclose a break-up of the components in an exchange rate, such as the margin. A bank keen to win a particular company's business might 'shave' a few points off the market rate when dealing with that favoured client, knowing it could recover the points in the rates charged to 'non-concessional' or 'captive' clients who did not have access to professional, wholesale rates or even to up-to-the-minute information about them. These clients also probably had little choice about the banks with which they could deal, often because their bank held whatever security was available against the borrowing. It was alleged by foreign-currency borrowers' expert witnesses that in some cases, especially those concerning managed foreign-currency loans, banks creamed off excessive points which cost borrowers thousands, and in at least one case millions, of dollars.

Litigation

For foreign-currency borrowers the costs of litigation and the sheer might of the banks were deterrents arguing against launching court cases. Lawyers did well out of the proceedings. It was estimated that it cost a borrower between $50,000 and $60,000 to bring a case to court, with expenses of between $10,000 and $15,000 a day. Borrowers who started out determined to fight soon were financially depleted, as well as emotionally exhausted. They had to be sufficiently well-informed and skilled to amass all the relevant information and they had to have the staying power to fight through a number of appeals. Overall, the hugely complex demands of litigation worked against them and in the banks' favour. Only a small number of foreign-currency loans went to litigation and most were settled. Of Westpac's nearly 900 foreign-currency loans, around 50 involved disputes, of which about half were negotiated and half litigated. Westpac told the banking inquiry that the cost and commitment of scarce management time made litigation 'a last resort', although the bank would defend its position where it considered that a borrower did not have a valid claim or persisted with what the bank regarded as an excessive claim.

Cases began to come before the courts in 1987. In one case, in June 1988, after only one day of evidence, a Gosford couple, real estate agent Raymond Hart and his wife, Beryl, who had decided to fight Westpac, withdrew their action. Legal costs already incurred gave them a taste of what lay ahead, with the Supreme Court hearing expected to last for ten days instead of the original estimate of three. They had taken out a Swiss franc loan of the equivalent of $A380,000 in 1985 and by February 1988 the loan had ballooned to $810,000 because of the drop in the $A against the Swiss franc. They had already sold their real estate business and liquidated other investments to meet the bank's demands to top up security against the loan. Costs were awarded against the couple and no judgment was made. Westpac claimed the case as a victory.

In a subsequent case, involving a Swiss franc loan of the equivalent of $A280,000 to a NSW farmer, the manager of the local Westpac branch who had organised the loan in 1984 admitted in court that he did not know how a foreign-currency loan hedge worked and that he had no experience with currency hedging. The farmer, Edward Downes, was suing Westpac for alleged breach of contract and negligence over the loan, which he had taken out to buy a dairy property. When the loan was taken out the Australian dollar was worth 2.2 Swiss francs but in the following two years it plunged to less than one Swiss franc, doubling the cost of the loan. The court was told that Westpac had organised seminars on foreign-currency loans in the area in 1984. Under cross-examination, the Westpac manager admitted that while he was enthusiastic about marketing foreign-currency loans he was not aware of a hedging market in Singapore, or concepts such as the trigger point of a stop-loss order. The manager told the court: 'I mentioned to him [Downes] that hedging was available and that in layman's terms it was an insurance against any loss. However, I never mentioned how it worked. I could not, because I did not know.' The case was settled on undisclosed terms on the third day of the hearing. Media reports that the farmer was 'very happy' with the outcome prompted a flood of telephone calls to legal firms from hopeful potential litigants anxious for advice on their chances in a fight against a bank. Concerned about the impact of a case where a borrower appeared to win, Westpac published advertisements in several newspapers stating that no payment had been made to the farmer; the bank paid for the advertisements, which were signed by Downes. In an article in *The Sydney Morning Herald* of 16 August 1988, Anne Lampe and Paul Cleary speculated that, while the bank made no outright payment, the terms of settlement could have included provisions favourable to the borrower, such as the bank renegotiating the loan agreement or agreeing that the loan be repaid at the original Australian dollar amount, or making another loan at a zero interest rate.

During 1989 a Sydney solicitor, Charles Spice, brought a case against Westpac claiming that the bank had been negligent in failing to advise him of the risks of taking out foreign-currency loans and the likelihood of losses after the $A fell in value against the Swiss franc. He alleged that Westpac employees had made untrue or misleading representations to him. In January 1985 Spice had approached the Liverpool Street branch of Westpac, in the centre of Sydney, to ask about the risks associated with foreign-currency loans. He claimed that the bank manager had told him that borrowing in a foreign currency at a low interest rate had 'no catch' and that Spice should consider Swiss francs because they offered the best interest rates. Spice alleged that another Westpac employee showed him a graph of the movements of the Swiss franc and the Australian dollar from 1979 to 1984 and said that was an example of their relative performance, with the franc a stable currency. Spice said that Westpac had a duty to take reasonable care to tender full, accurate and sound advice and that it failed to do so.

Spice launched action, seeking unspecified damages, costs and extinguishment of his liability to Westpac if he paid the bank $800,000 and interest. Spice alleged his liability on Swiss franc loans of up to $800,000, which he had taken up in February 1985, was greatly increased after the $A fell. By August 1986 it had blown out to $1,646,000, more than double the original amount. As the debt increased, Westpac requested that Spice top up security. When he refused, the bank deemed him in default. During the hearing in the Federal Court in March 1989, when Spice was suing Westpac under the Trade Practices Act, his counsel read out an internal Westpac memo compiled two years after the bank began to promote foreign-currency loans to borrowers. The memo suggested that all loan-offer letters should include advice that there was a considerable degree of risk in foreign-currency loans unless they were hedged and that borrowers should seek professional advice before committing themselves to such loans. Spice had received no such warning, his counsel said. Justice Foster found that Westpac had breached its duty of care, acted negligently and engaged in deceptive conduct when advising a client. The judge also found that Spice, although a retired solicitor, an importer and real estate investor, was an 'unsophisticated borrower' and that the bank was not entitled to assume that he had enough knowledge to be able to avoid the traps of foreign-currency borrowing. Spice was to repay only the original amount of the loan when it fell due, being $800,000 plus interest charged at the Australian interest rate prevailing when the borrowing was taken out, leaving him with the same liability he would have incurred had he borrowed in Australian dollars. Westpac had to pay all costs.

In July 1989, in a judgment described by legal experts as 'the key to the floodgates', the Federal Court ruled that Westpac acted negligently and deceptively in arranging a loan for a Brisbane-based foreign-currency borrower, Domenic Chiarabaglio, who was awarded unspecified damages and full costs. The ruling was an unambiguous win for a foreign-currency borrower on the point of whether a bank breaches its common law duty of care or the Trade Practices Act in promoting or arranging foreign-currency loans. In his decision, Justice Foster said: 'Westpac, a major financial institution in this country, was properly regarded by the applicant as an organisation that he could trust and whose advice he could follow with confidence.' The judge said that the bank had played down the risk associated with foreign-currency loans and referred to hedging only in the most cursory way. It had also arranged for the borrower to take out a loan for more than he required. The borrower's request for a loan of around $100,000 in 1982 had been met with a suggestion that he borrow the equivalent of $500,000 in yen, which offered an interest rate of less than 10 per cent. In 1985 the bank converted the six-year loan to Swiss francs. The $A plummeted and the loan doubled in value. The borrower claimed he had been 'improperly induced to enter into the foreign-currency borrowing in the first place'. Justice Foster said that if the substantial complexity and difficulty involved in monitoring and management had been brought to the borrower's attention he would have refrained from the offshore borrowing.

When the details revealed in Paddy Jones's letters became public, Westpac was hit by further claims and threats of lit-igation by angry borrowers, some former clients of PPL and some clients of the bank. Almost half of those claims were from borrowers who had had settlements in 1987 and 1988, when the Westpac board had instructed Paddy Jones and Ashley Ayre to ensure that all grievances were dealt with. But the revelations in Jones's letters motivated many to seek a second bite. Following the release of the letters in March 1991, Westpac published in several newspapers an 'open letter', signed by managing director Stuart Fowler, to former clients of PPL who had foreign-currency exposure manage-ment contracts between 1985 and 1987:

> The publication of the 'PPL confidential letters' and related media attention has raised questions about the impact of PPL's management of foreign currency exposures for individual clients.

Whilst Westpac believes it acted appropriately and attended to all known client concerns that arose in relation to this issue, Westpac invites former clients involved who may feel concerned to contact us with a view to discussing these matters. Westpac wishes to dispel any notion that these clients have in any way been inhibited from pursuing their concerns.

It would be our intention to resolve any concerns expeditiously and should it be necessary we will arrange for an independent mediator to assist. Sir Laurence Street, AC, KCMG (former chief justice of New South Wales) has agreed to undertake this role of independent mediator.

Westpac told the banking inquiry committee in 1991 that it had received sixteen responses to its letter, of which most were settled by negotiation. The committee considered that Westpac had provided 'reasonable mechanisms' to resolve the claims of former customers of PPL who had managed foreign-currency loans. However, the committee noted that the tabling of the 'Westpac letters' before it, and the committee's investigation of the issues, 'stimulated Westpac into a belated response to the problems that existed in PPL'.

Among the respondents to Westpac's open letter was Charles Spice, who mounted an action against PPL. Spice sued PPL for some $1.4 million in damages, allegedly lost through point-taking or deal-switching. His expert witness estimated that the cost to Spice of these alleged practices was $462,553. The case was mediated and settled in August 1994.

In January 1993 a memorandum of understanding was prepared between Westpac and the Foreign Currency Borrowers Association, based on a draft agreement devised during a five-hour meeting between representatives of the association and Westpac chief Frank Conroy and the bank's legal counsel,

Reg Barrett. Conroy was an enthusiastic supporter of mediation as a way of dealing with the foreign-currency loans and other problems. Terry Dunne and Barrett had already spent considerable time with the foreign-currency borrowers, to persuade them into the advantages of mediation and arbitration over court proceedings. Westpac won rare praise for the move. The FCBA president, Lionel Potts, who in 1992 had lost a foreign-currency loan court action against Westpac, said that the bank had done more than any other to try to speed up the settlement process. However, borrowers later said that Westpac had not delivered. Probably banks and borrowers would never see eye-to-eye on this issue: banks cited the difficulties of sifting through thousands of deal slips and other documents to find the relevant material, and would provide only what they regarded as documents to which the borrower was entitled. Borrowers claimed that it had been difficult to extract from the bank documents relating to transactions, and proceedings were generally being delayed, adding to borrowers' and the bank's costs.

279

A protracted court battle followed anxiously by borrowers and Westpac alike was the Drambo Pty Ltd case, involving resort developer Bob Porter. It was Westpac's largest disputed foreign-currency loan and the largest damages case involving foreign-currency lending brought against an Australian bank. Court hearings ran during September, October, November and December 1995 and into February and then July 1996 before a judgment was handed down in August 1996. The case in the end went against Drambo, but the story of the borrowing can be viewed as a sorry tale of incompetence on both sides.

In 1981 Porter and his father had acquired the shares of a shelf company which became known as Drambo. Drambo was developing the Whitsunday Terraces Resort with financial assistance of $7.5 million provided by the merchant bank Tricontinental Corporation Ltd. By the end of 1982 Drambo was in default in its Tricontinental loan and by 1984 the position had deteriorated further. Tricontinental was exerting pressure so Porter set about refinancing, which led him in late 1984 to the Brisbane branch of Westpac. Westpac provided 'in-principle' approval for $13.5 million, of which $13 million was to be in foreign currencies. A five-year loan for $12.9 million was arranged in January 1985 and Porter used nearly all the proceeds to pay out Tricontinental. Shortly after Porter had taken out his Swiss franc loan the $A began to fall rapidly, from 2.18 Swiss francs when the loan was drawn down to 1.81 some months later. Hedging was not an option because the cost would offset any interest-rate advantage in borrowing offshore, a cost that Drambo could not afford. The dollar continued to fall. In March 1985 the Whitsunday Terraces Resort and the Whitsunday Village Resort, the main assets securing the loan, were sold, generating almost $16 million for Drambo which it placed on deposit with Westpac as replacement security.

In August 1985, allegedly contrary to instructions from a Drambo director, Laurence Henderson, Westpac did not fulfil an order to hedge at 1.65 Swiss francs to the $A. Some compensation was paid by Westpac and a form of management agreement entered into with the objective of containing Drambo's exposure to an amount that would equal the security held by Westpac plus $500,000. The $A continued its slide against the Swiss franc, hitting 1.35 in June 1986. At that point Drambo entered into a more formal foreign-exchange management agreement with Westpac, with the bank assuming complete management of the loan. Westpac agreed not to charge Drambo a fee for managing the loan but it retained points above the interbank rate when undertaking trading on Drambo's behalf. Two years later, when the $A had slumped to 1.17 Swiss francs, the loan was brought onshore. Drambo now owed $25.2 million, a capital loss of $12 million. After offsetting the amount held on deposit the shortfall owed was $7.3 million.

In July 1991 Drambo sued Westpac for damages for the loss it had suffered. Westpac cross-claimed for $31.6 million plus interest due on the shortfall and on the alleged debt. Drambo contended that in 1984, in discussions about refinancing the Tricontinental facility, Westpac made representations that were misleading and deceptive in contravention of the Trade Practices Act and which involved a breach of duty of care. For example, Drambo claimed that the bank indicated that a Swiss franc borrowing was suitable and financially prudent, even lucrative, and that Westpac had expertise in dealing with foreign-currency borrowing. Drambo also alleged that in February 1985 Westpac made further representations that were misleading and that the company lost the opportunity to convert the loan to Australian dollars or to have it managed. The company claimed that contrary to the express terms of the agreement, Westpac failed to advise it on prudent management of the loan. Westpac was alleged to have again breached its duty of care in July 1988 when, contrary to instructions, it converted the loan to Australian dollars even though there were then reasonable grounds to expect the $A to improve against the Swiss franc. Drambo also claimed that Westpac breached section 261 of the Income Tax Assessment Act when it debited Drambo's account for more than half-a-million dollars due under Westpac's withholding tax obligations. Finally, Drambo alleged that Westpac had breached fiduciary duties owed to it by 'point-taking', ie, benefiting from the difference between the exchange rates at which the bank's interbank dealers sold foreign currency to the managers who controlled Drambo's facility, and the rates at which the foreign currency was available to managers in the market.

It was given in evidence in the court that Porter had often remarked, between 1982 and 1985, that if he took a foreign-currency loan he would be better able to meet his financial commitments because of the lower interest rates. Patrick Bradley, a former lending officer at Tricontinental, said he had told Porter that he should not borrow in foreign currency because of the risk involved and his lack of expertise in currency management. Bradley formed the view that Porter had almost no comprehension of foreign-currency loans, and no knowledge of margin calls, top-up clauses, security ratios, hedging or other matters relating to management of the loan but he agreed that Porter was capable of understanding these issues. In March 1983, when Tricontinental was threatening to appoint a receiver to the resort, Ian Johns, then Tricontinental's general manager, was appointed Drambo's 'adviser on construction of the Terraces'. Johns told Porter that borrowing in a foreign currency was not suitable.

When shopping for a refinancing deal in 1984, Porter received an offer of a Swiss franc loan from Citibank but he approached Westpac to see if Westpac would match or better the offer. For its part, Westpac was keen to have Porter's business.

After the fall in the value of the $A against the Swiss franc and problems in Drambo's loan, it ended up being managed in Westpac's foreign-currency risk management unit, established in July 1986 and run by Agnes Wong until she left Westpac in September 1987. Porter alleged he had been told that his loan would be in good hands with, first, Peter Chan, then head of Westpac's foreign-exchange operations and, after Chan left the bank in June 1987, with Wong. Wong said in a statement that her aim in risk-management was to try to unwind a hedge in whole or in part from time to time to take advantage of movements in exchange rates. That demanded constant and close monitoring. She also estimated that the cost of processing each deal slip for foreign-exchange transactions, given Westpac's 'extremely labour-intensive back office', was around $US75 (or at least $A100), costs which, she said, were absorbed by the bank.

In evidence, Peter Chan, now running the bank's operations in Hong Kong, said that the risk management unit was unable to provide monitoring and advice to all, or even most, foreign currency borrowers, because of inadequate resources. Chan admitted that had the Drambo loan been hedged at the outset, and monitored, and had stop-loss arrangements been in place, the losses would have been mitigated. Reflecting a general view among treasury operators that foreign-currency loans are just too hard to handle, Chan said he would not have taken out a foreign-currency loan himself. Drambo's counsel demanded to know why Drambo had consistently received a less competitive exchange rate than other foreign-currency loan clients and why Drambo's loan had incurred more than 500 transactions when another, much smaller loan, had involved only 34. In replying, Chan denied that Drambo had received a less competitive rate because it was regarded as a 'wood duck' or captive client which could not shift its business elsewhere.

Drambo's expert witness David Green estimated that the 'churning' involved in managing the Drambo loan, which led to 576 individual transactions, cost Porter slightly more than $3 million between October 1985 and July 1988. Giving evidence, another expert witness for Drambo, Gerhard Moser, who became the manager of the risk-management unit after Wong left Westpac in September 1987, said that in line with the advice given by Paddy Jones, recommending 'a policy of ruthless conservatism', borrowers were kept fully hedged, which prevented Drambo from recovering some losses on its loans in 1988 when the $A strengthened.

In a bizarre side-show to the lengthy trial, in November 1995 Westpac's Brisbane lawyers, Feez Ruthning, acting without specific instructions from Westpac, sent letters to a few Brisbane businessmen who, they believed, were funding Drambo's court battle, threatening to pursue them for the bank's legal costs should Drambo lose. The lawyers believed they were acting prudently in pointing out that, where a third party funds litigation and they are not told that they might be liable for the other side's costs, it might not be possible to recover costs from them. Westpac's legal costs were estimated at the time to be more than $1 million. Two weeks later Westpac's legal counsel, Bettie McNee, sent a further letter in which the bank withdrew the Feez Ruthning warning. Westpac was seen as backing off.

In August 1996 Justice Sundberg ordered that Drambo was entitled to recover the withholding tax of $577,732.15 plus interest and that Westpac was entitled to recover $37,882,975.07 from Drambo on its cross-claim, plus interest. Drambo lodged an appeal but did not pursue the matter. Westpac did not appeal against the withholding tax ruling.

Justice Sundberg was not the first to rule in this way on withholding tax. An earlier High Court decision had said that a clause in the Commonwealth Bank's foreign-currency loan agreement requiring the borrower to pay withholding tax on behalf of the bank was rendered void by section 261 of the Income Tax Assessment Act. The section dates from 1915 and, in a legal quirk, affects secured but not unsecured loans.

Australian banks were subject to a 10 per cent interest withholding tax on gross foreign-sourced income; that was one of the costs involved in providing a foreign-currency loan through an overseas centre. Banks claimed that it was uneconomic for them to bear the cost and so the tax impost was passed on to the borrowers. Whether banks were entitled to pass this on is a grey area that had been questioned for years. In his address to a national seminar on banking law in Melbourne in 1979, the Wales's chief legal officer Bob Craigie said: 'There is one other very awkward taxation provision that requires consideration. Section 261 of the Income

Tax Assessment Act 1936 provides that a stipulation in a mortgage which imposes on the mortgagor [borrower] an obligation to pay income tax shall be void. Thus any provision for grossing up withholding tax in a security document which comes within the wide definition of mortgage would be struck down by the words of Section 261. Withholding tax is income tax.' Westpac's group tax department was still wrestling with the issue in 1986 and noted in a memo: 'Westpac (the lender) is primarily liable for the withholding tax. Although the bank's standard loan agreement includes a provision requiring the borrower to meet interest withholding tax, legal view is that such covenant is unenforceable.'

Banks and other lenders found a way around the problem of section 261 by packaging loan documentation so that the obligation to pay the loan interest and principal is included in one document and the security is included in another, and for the relationship between the two to be beyond any 'collateral' link which might lead them to be treated as a single mortgage and caught by section 261. Westpac foreign-currency loans were written so that the loan agreement was the primary document and the mortgage (security) a secondary document. The issue of withholding tax was highlighted in 1994 when the ANZ Bank admitted an error and refunded $32 million in tax and interest to some 1,750 customers. In its media release, the ANZ said that in the early part of the 1980s interest withholding tax was due on many foreign-currency loans and was correctly passed on by the ANZ to its borrowers. 'Gradually, however, more loans were funded in a manner which did not attract withholding tax. Nonetheless, the bank continued automatically to pass a withholding tax charge on to its borrowers,' the ANZ said. Whether foreign-currency loans attract withholding tax depends on where the bank funded the loans; if the loans were funded domestically then there was no need to levy withholding tax. Westpac has claimed that there is no similarity between the manner in which ANZ funded the loans that did not attract withholding tax, and the way Westpac Singapore funded its loans.

Sundberg said in his judgment:

> Porter was not the foreign currency ignoramus he suggested he was. He had been interested in borrowing Swiss francs for months before he came to Westpac. What robbed his case of the attributes of the paradigm with which he sought to endow it was that he had spoken to and negotiated with other financiers about foreign currency loans, and came to Westpac with an offer of a Swiss franc loan from Citibank with which he was basically happy, and which he could then and there have accepted. In substance he said to Westpac's officers 'if you can better Citibank's terms, I'll borrow from you'. Westpac had a narrow brief. It was not asked for advice about the merits of borrowing offshore as opposed to domestically. All it had to do to win the account was to make the offshore borrowing cheaper than the Citibank offer. However, this case was pleaded and run as if this background and context did not exist. This led Porter to 'recall' statements by Westpac officers that in the circumstances are unlikely to have been made—how desirable offshore loans were, what interest savings were to be made by borrowing Swiss francs, and how little risk was involved. So gilded was the lily its stem snapped.

Some borrowers were luckier than others. One who borrowed in Swiss francs from Westpac in the mid-1980s was so pleased to have his interest costs halved that he gave his bank manager a luxury car believed to be valued at $80,000. The story goes that at first the manager refused, then he accepted the gift. The borrower's $3 million loan blew to $8 million as the $A crashed. A dispute arose over interest payments but the matter was settled with minimum fuss and minimal legal costs. The borrower remained happily in business.

Clive Alexander's reports return

Clive Alexander's investigations into the Halabi transactions in 1987 and 1988 had produced two handwritten reports. Unseen for four years, these contained allegations of questionable transactions in Westpac's foreign-exchange operations and implications of extremely favourable rates to favoured bank customers. Alexander's reports were leaked to ABC-TV's *Four Corners* some time in 1991 and the journalists began asking questions. Westpac, when asked to take part in the program early in 1992, made its former foreign-exchange head, Peter Chan, available and, after considerable debate, it was agreed that Frank Conroy would appear, live, provided he had seen the rest of the program in advance. The program was to conclude with his response. Clive Alexander was interviewed, and Peter Chan, both in pre-recorded sessions. The journalists travelled to the NSW central coast to contact Westpac's former head of global treasury, Stan Davis, but failed to locate him. Having decided he wanted to put his side of the story, Davis contacted the station but was told that he was too late. Eventually he was interviewed at length, in Sydney, for a segment deemed to add balance to the program. The *Four Corners* story went to air on 24 February. Davis's main points were that the allegations by Alexander had been the subject of a detailed investigation by Westpac a few years earlier and were not proven, and that he had not seen the handwritten reports until *Four Corners* had shown them to him that week. Davis, who had retired from Westpac in July 1989, shortly after Alexander left, claimed not to have received the reports while in his former role as global treasury head. His lip quivering with anger—he was clearly not enjoying the protracted interview and subsequently was critical of the program for what he said were unfair close-up shots—Davis was emphatic that he had never seen the reports, an assertion he later backed by saying that he initialled and dated everything he read, and the reports did not carry his idiosyncratic mark.

Alexander told *Four Corners* that he dreaded to think what he might have found if he had conducted a full audit into every deal transacted through Westpac's foreign-exchange dealing room from mid-1982 to 1987. His reports, with their allegations that some foreign-exchange customers received inexplicable profits at Westpac's expense, apparently lay unread somewhere in Westpac's files until the bank, sifting through documents in preparation for Naji Halabi's trial in 1991, found them. Halabi tried to subpoena the Alexander reports for his trial but Westpac's lawyers successfully argued that they were privileged. Chan told *Four Corners* that neither he nor his dealers, support staff or accounting staff had been approached by Alexander for their views. 'A lot of the conclusions made were based on assumption without the support of documentation,' he said, adding that without looking at a specific transaction he could not explain or elaborate on any discrepancy. Chan was adamant that no Westpac customers received profits to which they were not entitled.

Conroy, concluding the *Four Corners* program, announced that the bank had appointed Coopers & Lybrand to undertake a thorough independent investigation. Conroy had that afternoon received and read their interim report which, he said, 'does say there are some discrepancies in transactions that took place in 1985 and 1986—as outlined in Alexander's report—and on the one hand these could be totally innocent, they could be just errors or there could be something suspicious'. The matter was being pursued. If anything wrong was found to have been done, the bank would take action. Coopers & Lybrand spent several months going through Chan's bank accounts, receipts and financial affairs. They also examined transactions referred to in Alexander's reports, talked to staff who had been in the dealing room at the time and to several customers involved. Chan cooperated, and was meticulously grilled by the investigators. Coopers & Lybrand's report, although never made public, had the effect of clearing Chan of any suspicion. His friends at the bank threw a celebration party—and anyone who had avoided Chan during the investigation was not invited.

Because Coopers & Lybrand was reporting to Allen Allen & Hemsley, the details of that report are claimed to be subject to legal professional privilege and have not been made public. However, Conroy said in an address to the Securities Institute of Australia in August 1992 that the conclusions of the Coopers & Lybrand report were that there was no basis for a claim that any customer improperly profited from foreign-exchange dealings by some kind of collusion with Westpac officers, that there was no basis on which criminal charges could be laid against any employee, past or present, or any customers, and that the evidence brought to light would not support legal action by Westpac against any present or past employee.

In May 1992 Frank Conroy wrote a 'comfort' letter on behalf of Rob Douglass:

To whom it may concern

As managing director of Westpac, I write to clarify certain matters which pertain to the reputation of Mr R.H.V. Douglass and arise out of his position as managing director of Partnership Pacific

289

Limited ('PPL'), a wholly owned subsidiary of the bank.

The bank employed Mr Douglass between May 1983 and December 1986 as general manager, merchant banking. One of his duties was to take up the position of managing director of PPL from late 1984. That role involved responsibility for the seven divisions of PPL. The divisions reported to Mr Douglass through the general manager of PPL. The board of directors of PPL met on a monthly basis. It consisted of senior Westpac personnel, the chairman being the then deputy managing director of Westpac.

Mr Douglass had the ultimate responsibility within PPL for a foreign currency product which involved the management of clients' foreign currency exposures and was in vogue throughout the banking community during the 1980s. As is now well known, banks and their clients had difficulties in coping with the market environment which developed after deregulation of exchange controls in 1983 and gave rise to extraordinary volatility of the Australian dollar. PPL experienced its own internal difficulties, both with staff and computer systems. In 1985, Mr Douglass engaged the bank's solicitors, Allen Allen & Hemsley, to advise on the procedures to be established and documentation.

In 1987, the bank asked Allen Allen & Hemsley to carry out a review of the foreign currency product marketed by PPL. The result of the initial review is reported in what later became known as the 'Westpac Letters'. It is wrong that Mr Douglass has suffered as a result of being named in these 'Westpac Letters'. I believe that Mr Douglass, in his administration of PPL, acted as a reasonable person of integrity could be expected to have acted in the current state of knowledge of the market. The opinions of Mr Douglass and his version of events were not available to the author of the 'Westpac Letters', but have been made available to me. They cause me to think that the wholly negative assessment of Mr Douglass's performance in relation to the foreign currency product presented in the 'Westpac Letters' is not warranted.

It is my earnest wish, both personally and on behalf of the bank, that Mr Douglass should continue his career free from any negative associations arising out of his time with the bank or PPL.

Louise Jackson, unwilling to be tagged as a disgruntled ex-staffer, had avoided playing a key role as expert witness in any of the foreign-currency borrowers' cases. Nonetheless she felt aggrieved that her name had been associated with the 'Westpac letters' and allegations of bad management in PPL's foreign exchange department. Early in 1992 she met with Terry Dunne, at that time Westpac's chief legal officer, and his assistant, Barbara Filipowski. In 1994 she wrung out of Westpac a letter, signed by its legal division, confirming that the events described in Paddy Jones's letters related to a period at PPL after she had left the merchant bank.

CHAPTER ELEVEN

A Vision Launched, a Vision Abandoned: AMP and CS90

The AMP alliance: taking out insurance

The so-called strategic alliance between Westpac and the AMP Society, consummated in September 1991, brought together two enduring icons of the Australian corporate community. But behind the emotionally appealing symbolism of a union based on a natural synergy between the Sydney-based financial giants, one the country's oldest and biggest bank and the other its biggest life office, lay a pragmatic deal that gave Westpac desperately needed capital and brought the AMP a chance to secure a foothold in retail banking that had eluded it, despite its joint venture with Chase Manhattan.

Westpac was no stranger to investment and life products. A forerunner of the investment division was born in 1944 when the Bank of New South Wales Nominees Pty Ltd was set up to hold shares and securities and act as attorney for customers. The growth in staff superannuation led to the formal establishment of an investment division in 1960 to provide investment services such as unit trusts to the public and to manage the bank's investment portfolio. Jim Goldman, who had joined the Wales in 1944 in the NSW country town of Tenterfield, was the first manager of the investment division. Goldman left the Wales in 1970 to pursue a successful career in stockbroking.

He had left stockbroking in 1984 and was unsure what to do next when a call came from Westpac: would he care to return and again head the department he had once managed? Goldman was surprised. It was unusual, once having left the bank, to be invited back. Goldman returned to Westpac, ostensibly for four years.

Banks were recognising that people's savings did not just rest in bank accounts, and that banks had to offer a widening range of products that would appeal to those planning for retirement, seeking insurance or simply wanting to accumulate a nest-egg. Westpac identified growth potential in life insurance and, in 1986, established Westpac Life. A chief was needed. Westpac's advertisement for the post was answered by many, including Monty Hilkowitz, whom those who worked with him described as 'a rare creature, an actuary by training and a salesman by instinct'. In October 1986 Hilkowitz became managing director of Westpac Life. He and Goldman, as managing director of the bank's investment division, became two new members of the executive committee and reported directly to Stuart Fowler, who backed the new venture with his usual enthusiasm for innovation and growth. In 1988 Westpac Life and the investment division merged to form Westpac Financial Services Group (WFSG) and Goldman and Hilkowitz became joint managing directors. A potentially difficult situation was rendered reasonably workable because Goldman was planning to retire and the two complemented each other well in approach. Goldman understood bankers and their language and had a better rapport with senior bankers in Westpac who, by and large, did not feel at ease with the sometimes abrasive, sometimes charming, Hilkowitz. But Hilkowitz's background was immensely valuable to Westpac. A fellow of the London Institute of Actuaries with a wide background in life insurance, Hilkowitz was also a former managing director of Liberty Life in South Africa, a company which had successfully integrated life insurance and banking.

By 1989 WFSG had become the third-largest investment manager in Australia with close to $10 billion under management and $13 billion under its custodian services. Westpac's branch network was identified as a key advantage in distribution. Goldman had by now stayed well beyond his intended four years and was looking forward to retiring and leaving WFSG in the capable hands of Hilkowitz. But Hilkowitz was not enjoying the style of Westpac's chairman Sir Eric Neal, who had taken over at the start of the year and whose autocratic manner had proved capable of alienating some executives. Hilkowitz was therefore very receptive to a suggestion from fellow South African David Greatorex that he become head of Capita Financial Group Ltd, formerly the life office City Mutual, which Greatorex had steered through dramatic growth over the previous five years. Greatorex was now chairman of the promising company. Westpac lost the man credited with having pushed Westpac Life forward in a way that no-one in the bank could have done. Greatorex described his new colleague as 'the most outstanding life insurance executive in the country'. For Goldman, retirement receded again.

Coincidentally, Westpac was also seeking a replacement for Geoff Kimpton, who had succeeded Adrian Fletcher as head of group planning and was now being posted to Victoria as state general manager. Applicants for the post included Vern Harvey, with a background in consulting and planning, and David Morgan, senior deputy secretary of federal treasury. Harvey's experience was the more relevant of the two for the post advertised, but Neal, impressed with Morgan's economic background and political connections, was reluctant to turn him away. Morgan had played a central role in the development of the government's 1985 package of tax reforms and had been regarded as a serious contender for the position of treasury head, which had gone to Chris Higgins. Neal is remembered as being keen to employ him in the bank. Fowler and others had reservations about appointing someone who was not only a senior bureaucrat close to the then treasurer, Paul Keating, but who was also married to a Labor minister, Ros Kelly. But Fowler asked Goldman whether he had a successor in mind; Goldman had no-one in sight and was comfortable with the proposal that Morgan be appointed his deputy managing director and managing director designate. Morgan took up the role in January 1990, working with Goldman at Endeavour House in Pitt Street, down the hill from the bank's headquarters at 60 Martin Place. Despite the distance Morgan, unlike Goldman, attended Fowler's 7.15 am coffee sessions with senior executives. When Goldman retired, Morgan put in a bid for an office at 60 Martin Place.

Morgan became head of WFSG on Goldman's retirement in October 1990 and he took charge of the fastest-growing area of Westpac. He had under his control six business units: superannuation, life insurance, general insurance, unit trusts, custodian services and investment management. The group was mushrooming in terms of funds under management, sales force and annual premium income. Morgan says: 'Any objective reading of the facts shows that of the major banks, Westpac was further along the road than others in *allfinanz* [voguish industry jargon for the trend towards offering a wide range of financial services].' Morgan joined the seven-man executive committee which advised Fowler. His undisguised ambition and his ability to stage a good performance (a legacy of having been a child actor) led to his undertaking a series of public-speaking engagements in which he enthusiastically promoted WFSG and its achievements and aspirations. He rapidly became one of Westpac's high-profile executives.

AMP's plans

The AMP Society had been examining the potential of *bancassurance* (more industry-speak for packaged financial services) for some time. A former chief executive of AMP,

Alan Coates, had been a member of the landmark Campbell committee which had set out a blueprint for reforming Australia's financial system, and in the wake of that it was envisaged that banks would become more active in insurance and fund management. Without an alliance with a bank, AMP could be left out in the cold. Insurance companies had long envied banks their broad retail networks, a perfect distribution system which the insurers compared ruefully with the millions of dollars they had to shell out to their agents, who went cold-calling, knocking on doors to get their products to the investing public. In 1990 AMP had spent $390 million on agents' commissions; Westpac, admittedly with a fraction of AMP's life business, spent nothing on commissions because it sold to existing customers through its branch network, with branch staff able to pass on 'warm' leads to WFSG's financial consultants. A life company might have a strike rate of one out of ten prospective customers; in contrast, banks had millions of captive clients.

AMP had joined forces with the US giant Chase Manhattan Bank, one of the group of foreign banks admitted to Australia. Their joint creation, the Chase AMP Bank, was the first to open its doors, in September 1985, an event that helped crystallise Westpac's thinking about life insurance. But while the AMP had envisaged Chase AMP as a new avenue for cross-selling life products, the new bank veered off down a path of corporate lending and suffered badly from ill-fated loans to Australian entrepreneurs. AMP's vision of creating an enduring presence in bancassurance was evaporating. By the end of the 1980s AMP was keen to extricate itself from Chase AMP. Chase, unwilling to commit further resources to Australia, was happy to end the joint venture. AMP still hungered for a banking partner and began discussing opportunities with others, including the National Australia Bank, and made its first overture to Westpac in October 1990.

The story goes that the two chairmen, Sir Eric Neal and Sir James Balderstone, who enjoyed a longstanding relationship, hatched the idea of a grand alliance on the golf course. Frank Conroy and AMP's managing director Ian Salmon had more formal discussions which led to each company forming a three-man team to explore the feasibility of an alliance. Westpac's team comprised Conroy, Vern Harvey and David Morgan; on AMP's side the negotiators were Salmon, chief fund manager Ray Greenshields and strategic planner Ian Campbell. Taking pains to keep the project under wraps, the six held several meetings during October and November 1990, the first in Melbourne's Regent Hotel, deliberately chosen as a screen because they were less well known in Melbourne than in Sydney. Another clandestine meeting was held in a mid-city apartment in Sydney.

At the March 1991 Westpac board meeting, held in Melbourne, Harvey presented the case for the proposed alliance with the AMP Society. The chairman was enthusiastic. Conroy and Harvey were in favour, in Conroy's case largely because he was extremely fearful of a possible alliance between the AMP and National Australia Bank, although David Morgan was against it, as were a couple of directors who could not see any value in it for Westpac. Fowler and some others viewed the alliance as a convenient way of boosting Westpac's capital. However, the board decided not to proceed. Balderstone, who was also enthusiastic about the plan, was disappointed when he heard the verdict, and thought that was the end of it. He had underestimated Neal's powers of persuasion.

Immediately the meeting was over Morgan flew to London, where he was to speak at an international life insurance conference on 'Making *allfinanz* work'. He told his audience about the success of WFSG and explained why Westpac had chosen 'to grow a life company from within', saying: 'We believed that because the cultures between

banks and life companies are so markedly different, a tra-
ditional-style agent approach would not mix well with the
bank environment.' Morgan said that the move into life
insurance was ultimately a matter of extending the identity
of Westpac as a bank into financial services. 'We will continue to be the pioneer of *allfinanz* in Australia,' he said.
'We will continue to go it alone.'

But back in Australia, machinations over the alliance proposal had far from died. Over the weekend, telephone lines
between the Westpac chairman and various directors buzzed
with suggestions of a rethink. On the following Monday,
management was told that directors had now reviewed the
matter. At a subsequent board meeting management repeated
its presentation about the proposed alliance with the AMP
and the board voted in favour of it. Essentially, the AMP
Society would look after long-term savings and Westpac
would take care of shorter-term investments; each could sell
the other's products, ideally with mutual benefits in terms of
cost and distribution. AMP's life and superannuation products would be marketed through Westpac's 1,600 branches.
They complemented each other in other ways: Westpac was
well established in Asia and had a good base in the US, but
was weak in the UK and had no European penetration; AMP
had strong relations in the UK and was interested in Asia,
although less in the mature American market.

Under the alliance, Westpac Life became a wholly owned
subsidiary of AMP and was renamed AMPAC Life. AMP
paid $200 million for the business. The remainder of West-
pac's growing fund management activities—superannuation
and unit trust assets—remained under Westpac's wing in
Westpac Financial Services, so Westpac continued to sell
competing products. A new joint-venture company, Westpac
Financial Consultants Ltd (WFCL), staffed by former
Westpac employees and sales agents, was established to sell
AMP's retail life insurance and superannuation products

298

through Westpac's branch network. Westpac outlaid $30 million to buy the consumer banking business of Chase AMP Bank and AMP injected $24 million into BLE Capital, Westpac's venture-capital subsidiary.

Morgan was still of the view that the alliance made a great deal more sense for AMP than it did for Westpac. 'I didn't think that the strategic logic would endure because the major *quid pro quo* for Westpac at that time in the alliance was the capital strength of AMP when Westpac was heading into a time of capital weakness. But I was always confident of Westpac's ability to recover, so from Westpac's point of view the key reason for the alliance would evaporate. Also, we had developed considerable momentum in Westpac Financial Services. It was growing rapidly and profitably.' Morgan had been trying to effect a change in the thinking in Westpac's branch network, from a perception that Westpac Life was eating into a branch's deposits to one that a customer placing funds in a tax-efficient investment product rather than a bank deposit was beneficially transferring funds from one part of the Westpac group's balance sheet to another. That argument would not hold water when the funds were going to AMP's investment managers.

In selling Westpac Life the bank was hocking part of the crown jewels, even though the company had a voracious appetite for capital. It had been widely predicted that setting up a life company from scratch would be a huge drain on Westpac. Life companies soak up financial resources from a combination of the need to set aside capital against potential future risks associated with policies—claims and payouts—as well as the high selling costs of a traditional agency. Morgan rejects the suggestion that continuing with its own life office would have become an unsupportable strain for Westpac. 'Much of the cost-drain in traditional life company business stems from the agent distribution system. This would not apply in Westpac's case because the bank had the advantage of being able to distribute life office products to an existing customer base through its branches.'

The matter of the alliance had to be discussed with the federal treasurer and presented John Kerin with his first major decision in that role. He had taken over from Paul Keating who, having unsuccessfully challenged prime minister Bob Hawke for the leadership in June 1991, had for the time being retreated to the backbenches. The federal government had earlier quashed a proposed union between the ANZ Bank and National Mutual Life Association and would not give the nod to anything that smacked of a merger. Despite a forceful submission from AMP, Kerin rejected its application to buy 15 per cent of Westpac but gave approval for the AMP to lift its stake in the bank from 6.4 per cent to 10 per cent. He indicated he would consider an application to move to 15 per cent in twelve months, which subsequently happened. Salmon and others had wanted 20 per cent, which would have firmly cemented the alliance, but to secure that level AMP would have had to prove that the move was in the national interest.

There was pressure to complete the alliance before 30 June because Chase was keen to record the proceeds of the sale of its consumer banking business to Westpac in that reporting period. Sir Eric Neal, having presided over a string of disappointments at Westpac—mounting bad debts, falling profits and dividends—revelled in being able to deliver good news when, on 5 June 1991, he announced the union between Westpac and the AMP Society. AMP lifted its shareholding in Westpac to 10 per cent. Westpac got a net boost of $130 million. Sir James Balderstone, chairman of AMP, and board member Bob Johnston, a former governor of the Reserve Bank, were invited on to the Westpac board.

The 'strategic alliance' was approved by Westpac shareholders at a special general meeting in September 1991, at which a one-share, one-vote regime was introduced, a change to Westpac's deed of settlement which overturned a 174-year-old convention put in place to protect small share-holders from being outvoted by large proprietors. The media were excluded at the express wish of the chairman on the grounds that shareholders ought to be able to speak freely. It was a tactical mistake: one journalist objected and made something of a crusade out of the 'secrecy' issue. Westpac would have done better not to bar the media from the meeting. The adverse publicity the bank brought on itself overshadowed any kudos it might have expected over the AMP union.

Westpac Financial Services remained separate within Westpac, handling fund management, investment manage-ment and unit trusts. This was a victory for Morgan and a disappointment to AMP's Greenshields. 'Not getting Westpac Financial Services was a limitation to many people at AMP,' says Salmon. 'People found themselves competing with Westpac.' By some accounts there were Westpac people at ground level who acted deliberately to thwart AMP's ambitions. Over time, there were increasing tensions between AMPAC and Westpac Financial Services over their conflict-ing objectives. Looking back, many involved believe it was a good idea that was never given a chance to develop. Lack of enthusiasm among Westpac management ranks was evident from the outset, and probably helped seal the fate of the venture. And Westpac's own priorities and ambitions changed.

Later, as Westpac's share price slid and the bank increas-ingly became a target of criticism, AMP suffered a backlash from the media and policyholders over an investment that looked increasingly unattractive. Early in 1992 AMP's chief executive, Ian Salmon, was driven to say, during an inter-view with *Business Sunday*, that the alliance was 'never intended to be a rescue'. 'It was always intended to be an alliance,' he said. 'But in light of the financial performance during the year, the money that we provided would be of assistance to them. But it was never conceived to do that.' And AMP's stake was later anchored by a commitment to maintain the shareholding at 12–15 per cent. AMP's investment in Westpac had cost it $600 million. By the middle of 1996 that investment was worth $854 million. Ultimately, the deal was financially positive for AMP, but strategically it did not produce what the life office had hoped for. Westpac felt differently: the injection of funds in 1991 had saved the bank's neck.

Serious cracks began to appear in the alliance. In late 1993 Westpac and AMP had to pump $6.7 million into the joint venture company Westpac Financial Consultants Ltd, the main operating arm of the alliance, following a slump in its income. WFCL had lost many key executives since the alliance was formed, and sales had dropped. In March 1994, following a comprehensive joint review of progress, Westpac and AMP announced changes to the alliance's operating structure which reflected a considerable reduction in mutual commitment. In an acknowledgment that WFCL could not be made to work, Westpac took full control of the company, with WFCL's sales force and distribution activities fully integrated into the Westpac network. AMP resumed management of its approved deposit fund, previously managed by Westpac Financial Services, and AMP was no longer required to maintain a 12–15 per cent shareholding in Westpac. AMP stressed that it had no immediate intention of reducing its stake. David Morgan, at the time head of Westpac's retail banking, said that Westpac and AMP had been working to preserve the best features of the alliance. 'We recognised early on that joint ownership of Westpac Financial Consultants Ltd resulted in confusion and inefficiencies as staff tried to serve two masters. Now this has been remedied.' AMP's chief operating officer for Australia, Philip Twyman, said: 'This new, simplified arrangement means that AMP will wholly focus on the product and Westpac will wholly focus on the distribution channel, allowing both companies to benefit from each other's strengths.'

The spirit of the alliance, from AMP's point of view, had been sorely tested when, in 1993, Lend Lease had bought into Westpac, taken seats on the Westpac board and been given federal government approval to lift its shareholding, if it chose, to the maximum of 15 per cent permitted under banking legislation. Then, in 1995, AMP launched a home-lending subsidiary, Priority One, in competition with the banks. In 1996 Westpac and AMP divorced, with Westpac paying around $340 million to buy AMP's half share of AMPAC Life.

303

CS90: the computer crash

An early move by Frank Conroy, after becoming managing director in October 1991, was to take the shears to CS90, Westpac's computer system development which had begun in the mid-1980s. CS90 was conceived as a revolutionary banking tool that would become an industry in its own right—selling computer-based expertise to financial institutions around the world.

Technology in banking advanced exponentially during the 1980s and Westpac was keen to be at the forefront. In 1980 it had taken a giant step into electronic banking with the introduction of automatic teller machines, marketed as 'Handybank'. Electronic funds transfer at point-of-sale (EFTPOS) followed in 1984. Customers liked these new methods.

Westpac, with an estimated four million customers and about as many accounts, found that by the mid-1980s, when deregulation had encouraged a mushrooming in bank products, its existing computer system was under growing strain. Newer technologies enabled, among other advances, speedier access to account details and swifter processing of information. A thorough overhaul of the bank's computer system was approved in 1985 and started in earnest in 1986. By 1987 the scope and ambition of the project had grown and unforeseen technical difficulties emerged. Bob White, in a spirited defence of Westpac's investment in CS90, wrote in his memoirs:

> With a huge network of branches connected to a central computer, we envisaged a sophisticated communication system which could be used to transmit many kinds of information and instructions and which was related to more than just banking. I was all for it ... Core System 90 had the potential to revolutionise the delivery of financial products thereby increasing the bank's overall capacity to do business while holding down operating costs.

There were sceptics in Westpac, particularly at board level. CS90 lost two key supporters when Bob White retired at the end of 1987 and Peter Douglas, chief general manager of management services and an architect and visionary behind CS90, followed in March 1988.

By 1990 CS90's escalating costs and delayed delivery were causing concerns in the highest levels of Westpac. As work began on the bank's mid-year budget review, the team handling the process—Conroy, Derrick Heywood, Vern Harvey and group financial controller Malcolm Sandy—hit a brick wall when they asked the information technology division for a breakdown of costs and an explanation of why they had soared. Conroy enlisted Andersen Consulting to examine the project. Andersen, whose review began in the middle of 1991, delivered a damning report: CS90 was costing more than expected, its real costs were hidden and it was not delivering the results that had been promised. A large outlay on information technology had failed to give adequate value. Conroy lost confidence in those overseeing the project who, he believed, had known for some time that it was not going according to plan but had not shared this information. Andersen advised that the total cost of CS90 would escalate if the project were left unchecked and there was little prospect that it would deliver real benefits inside five years. Westpac's spending on information technology— all data-processing costs and not just CS90 development costs—was high by industry standards, estimated at between $300 and $400 million. In five years, CS90 had soaked up some $200 million and was continuing to run away from its original budget of $180 million over six years. Probably no-one really knows what CS90 ultimately cost Westpac. As a proportion of total operating expenses, Westpac at its peak spent 23 per cent on information technology, compared with an industry average of between 13 and 15 per cent. By 1991 Westpac had brought its spending down to 17 per cent, still questionably high. And CS90 had delivered only a fraction of its promises.

305

Conroy can take the credit for biting the bullet on CS90. The board did not like what he had to say; there had been strong questioning from the board about the computer system, with some directors very suspicious of the enthusiasm with which it was promoted. They blamed Conroy for not bringing better news.

Andersen's review resulted in some changes to the CS90 project. Bill McInnes, head of management services and information technology, retired, and Alan Hohne, who had been in charge of the project, left the bank. At the board meeting where Hohne's departure was announced, a director remarked that it was a pity that Sir Frank Espie was no longer on the board— Espie had consistently criticised CS90 and its architects over the years. In the October 1991 restructuring instituted by

Conroy, Tony Aveling was brought back from London and appointed head of information technology. Aveling, a line banker not trained in information systems, was nonetheless someone in whom Conroy had confidence. The managing director believed Aveling would improve the flow of information about the technology area to senior executives and the board so that they would be better placed to make decisions about its viability and effectiveness. Conroy had wanted to bring Aveling back to Sydney earlier but struck opposition from the chairman, who was thought to view the move as evidence of 'cronyism'. But Conroy was confident that Aveling would ask the right questions and reach the right conclusion: that Westpac had to radically scale down the effort being put into CS90.

Aveling, just finding his feet in the highly competitive London market with its hundreds of local and foreign financial institutions, was persuaded that the bigger problems back in Australia needed leadership and management. Apart from winding down CS90, he had to trim costs in the whole technology area. Staff was cut by some 25 per cent, and later by more. According to Aveling, the costs of CS90, the subject of much curiosity in the business community, were spread over a few years. 'We expensed it as we went along,' he says. 'That was the conservative accounting approach.' Certainly Westpac would not have wanted cumulative costs from CS90 to surface in 1991/92, when it had more than enough other problems.

Aveling says: 'CS90 was a great vision, and had excellent people working on it but the realisation came that it was never going to work out and it didn't. It was a huge, complex project for Westpac to undertake, there were big technical problems to be resolved and even with the help of IBM's best people, it was still not possible to crack some of those problems. The whole thing unravelled.' The ambitious system was driven by the fact that Westpac's core trading-bank system had been built over a long period and, as was the case with most banks, had become archaic. The longer change was delayed, the more expensive it would be. Westpac wanted to beat the future, to be the smartest bank. Aveling says that Westpac looked around the world, wondering if a suitable system could be bought off the shelf—but nothing of the size and scale required had been available. Westpac decided to build its own system, one that would do everything the bank and its customers needed.

Says Aveling: 'When CS90 was closed down not all the project was thrown away. Westpac used CS90 methodology and systems in an on-line account-opening process, in personal loans, term deposits and in particular in what is called CIS (customer information system).'

A combination of technical complexities and deficiencies, and management enthusiasm based on inadequate analysis, contributed to the death of CS90. Risks from the outset were that the database technology and advancing programming techniques required for the project were new and untried and the conceptual design was not clear-cut. The sheer size of the project suggested to the cautious that it could well get out of control. It did. Westpac saw as the greatest threat to CS90 the question of whether IBM could continue to produce the software necessary to ensure the project's success. IBM saw as the greater risk the bank's inability to define the business requirements of the system. Lengthy meetings addressed these issues and failed to find answers—a failure which, in the end, largely accounted for CS90's failure.

With the millstone of CS90 removed, Westpac's overall spending on information technology was trimmed to 14 per cent, with a further aim of 12 per cent. Supporters of the system continued to insist that, even at the time it was axed, no-one on the board or in senior management could have given a cogent and succinct account of what CS90 would have been capable of doing. The grandiose project joined Pollock in the Westpac elephants' graveyard.

307

CHAPTER TWELVE

WESTPAC'S *ANNUS HORRIBILIS* BEGINS

Throughout most of 1991, as it became increasingly clear that Westpac had very serious asset problems, senior management had spent a great deal of energy in devising a series of planning documents showing that it was essential to disengage the bank's strategy from the themes of growth, acquisition and expansion. Westpac was adequately provisioned according to its prevailing accounting policies: when a borrower was perceived as unlikely to be able to repay interest and principal, the debt was classified as doubtful and provisions were made; if it went bad, more provisions were made or it was written off. If there was a ready market for the security, realistic recovery value could be estimated. However, if there was no ready market or the market was depressed, recovery values were highly subjective. The problem in Westpac was a tardiness in recognising that a loan was doubtful, and an absence of realistic acknowledgment, in the face of relentlessly declining values, that security was woefully inadequate.

A bank has general and specific provisions. The appropriate level of specific provisioning is determined by examining every loan identified as 'impaired', ascertaining the principal outstanding, accrued interest and other charges or expenses, and deducting the projected realisable value of the security (thus provisioning and valuation are inextricably linked if the security is a building). If there is a shortfall then a provision is made. If security is adequate to cover the principal and accrued interest, there may not be a need to make a provision even if the bank is not receiving interest, although the loan would be classed as an impaired asset. Later, in January 1995, the Reserve Bank issued guidelines covering a bank's asset quality, specifically how to recognise and measure impaired assets, value securities and provision, and to grade loans for credit risk. No such official yardstick existed in Australia in the early 1990s, although banks listed in the US would normally comply with the US Securities and Exchange Commission regulations.

Over time, Westpac's expanding portfolio of property was looking increasingly sickly. While bad debts from corporates had been the problem in 1990, 1991 brought property problems. These were initially widely misunderstood. Westpac and AGC, deeply committed to property, misread the downturn in values as a temporary phenomenon. But the property market continued to sink. Unlisted property trusts had some $2 billion wiped off their values during 1990, with Aust-Wide and Westpac trusts recording declines of between 20 and 30 per cent. By October 1991 the worth of commercial buildings in central Sydney was down by 40 per cent compared with its peak in late 1989 and early 1990. Westpac was exposed to property through a range of entities: AGC (as a quasi-developer in joint ventures as well as a property lender), BAC and PPL, and the bank's own retail and commercial lending. Westpac's board had chosen as a valuation method 'intrinsic value'— that is, property values achievable in 'normal' times, possibly within three to four years and not taking into account the time value of money. With this method, a property that was well located, producing income and likely to recover in value over a 'reasonable' period was not marked down. However, the time-frame for the imputed recovery in the property market grew longer and longer, to the point where it became obvious that the bank was not taking a realistic view of its property exposure.

Westpac was fortunate in that it was well capitalised. One of Stuart Fowler's great accomplishments for Westpac was to ensure that its balance sheet was brimming with capital. Fowler did this in anticipation of making an acquisition, but in fact that capital was turned to a more critical use in carrying Westpac through hard times. Its strong capital position, and healthy profits, particularly in Australian retail banking, had differentiated Westpac from, say, US banks which had faced similar problems with their property assets. However, among banks worldwide, Westpac was holding one of the highest levels of problem assets, and had one of the lowest levels of provisioning. It was seen as being slow to recognise and admit mistakes, at a time when it was already being condemned for the difficulties with AGC's large property joint ventures, revelations in the 'Westpac letters', its declining credit ratings and its use of abnormals, such as the 1990 surplus in the super fund, to boost profits. Observers—investors, the Reserve Bank and the credit-rating agencies—believed that additional provisioning would be required because the non-accrual loans would continue for longer than had been thought. Westpac's $2.3 billion portfolio of highly leveraged transactions (HLTs), mainly in the United States, added to perceptions that it was on shaky ground. These were a source of constant questioning from the ratings agencies and a concern to analysts although, ultimately, the HLTs were not a cause of large write-offs. But they exacerbated Westpac's weakening image. The bank had lost industry leadership and one of its anchors, global financial markets, was under threat from the lower credit ratings.

In February 1991 Westpac's executive committee reluctantly concluded that the bank's weaknesses—AGC's joint ventures, the bad debts in the UK, the HLTs in the US and Westpac's own property exposures—could not be denied.

They forced a brake on further growth. Non-performing loans at 8 per cent of the total were already double the level regarded by ratings agencies as dangerous, while specific provisions to non-accrual loans remained well below 30 per cent, another threatening threshold. Corporate banking was underperforming in the Americas division and in Europe. Ratings agencies were quietly warning against an acquisition. Some banks had emerged from the giddy 1980s unscathed, and those would include Banc One and First Wachovia in the US, and possibly National Australia Bank in Australia, but Westpac was now indisputably a weak bank. Recovery, the committee agreed, lay in downsizing AGC, shrinking corporate banking in the US and Europe and selling poorly performing subsidiaries such as BLE Capital. The board was unconvinced, apparently believing that management was unduly pessimistic, and counselled incorporating more growth in the plans. Management maintained that Westpac had to get into better shape before it considered further expansion or an acquisition—that the ensuing two years should be devoted to setting its house in order and tightening corporate governance. At the March 1991 board meeting in Melbourne Frank Conroy was appointed deputy managing director and heir to Stuart Fowler, with all divisions in the bank except Westpac Financial Services reporting to him. The head of the Americas division, Tony Walton, was appointed to the board. It would be up to Conroy to set Westpac on its recovery path. Fowler told the assembled directors that recent months had driven home the seriousness of Westpac's problems, and that the bank was still vulnerable to further decline. Capital should be allocated only to activities which were creating value; Westpac had to turn its back on those which were not relevant to core business and review those that were underperforming.

The costs of explosive growth were becoming apparent: over the three years to September 1990, assets had jumped

311

by 52 per cent from $70 billion to $107 billion; over the same period, corporate banking assets had increased from $35 billion to $58 billion, a rise of 65 per cent. Corporate assets by now accounted for more than half of Westpac's total assets, a gradual climb from the early 1980s when they had accounted for just under one-third. But net profit after tax was declining, and would have plummeted were it not for transfers from pension fund surpluses. The bank's share price, which had been falling since the mid-1980s, and was now dipping more sharply, reflected the market's disenchantment with what it saw as Westpac's head-in-the-sand attitude, the continuing level of write-offs, interest forgone on the non-accrual loans and lost opportunities which were hard to quantify.

Westpac's global corporate banking review in June 1991, which analysed $30 billion of loans to almost 2,000 corporate customers, was conducted to measure their value and to indicate whether the bank should try to improve returns or get out of the business. Return on equity (ROE) for Australia was 21 per cent, on assets of $10 billion, employing capital of $551 million and with a cost of equity of 16.8 per cent. New Zealand was next with a healthy ROE of 19 per cent, on $2.4 billion of assets employing $132 million of capital and with an equity cost of 17.5 per cent. Europe and the Americas made a less robust showing: 8 per cent ROE for Europe on $3.2 billion of assets, using $176 million of capital and an equity cost of 16.2 per cent, while the Americas division had 6 per cent ROE, on $13.6 billion of assets, using $597 million of capital and with an equity cost of 14.6 per cent. It was becoming clear where the axe was going to fall.

Stuart Fowler had had enough. In July 1991 he surprised the market by announcing that he would retire in September, rather than wait, as was expected, for his 63rd birthday in March 1992. The board had asked him to stay until then to provide time to consider a successor but the succession was clearly in place. In recent months Fowler had borne the scalding publicity over the Westpac letters, and dedicated considerable time to the banking inquiry, increasingly leaving the day-to-day running of the bank to Conroy. A private retirement dinner for Fowler, held at one of Sydney's inner-city clubs, was attended by his close associates in the bank's senior management and two guests whom he had personally invited: Nick Greiner, then his local state member of parliament, and Paul Keating, former treasurer and at that point a backbencher but gearing up for a second and successful pounce at the prime ministership. Westpac executive David Morgan gave a brief speech. Keating delivered an impromptu talk, praising Fowler as a true Australian.

Fate had not been kind to Fowler when it placed him at the head of Westpac late in 1987. He came to the job lightly blessed, after protracted speculation about who would succeed the long-serving Bob White. He became head of a large, diffuse institution at a time when its corporate culture had fostered a view of itself as impregnable. He had been handed the problems of a previous era, although an era in which he had held a key role as head of corporate and international and then of retail, and as a member of the executive committee. Many believed Fowler was handed a poisoned chalice. His inheritance was a bloated cost structure, a corporate strategy bent on growth, particularly building corporate assets overseas, and a group of aggressive, independent-minded subsidiaries vigorously lending in the same market as the bank. Hindsight teaches that Westpac's strategy then should have been defensive: lowering costs, improving controls and management and information systems, and reviewing its business and credit policies in the light of a changing economic environment. Instead, Westpac launched itself on a trajectory of growth that took no account of changed market conditions. It was not alone. Despite the warnings of the sharemarket crash, banks continued to lend enthusiastically into a property boom that collapsed late in 1989. High interest rates snuffed out any lingering fire in the economy, which slid into a deep recession. During almost four years as chief executive Fowler was forced to react to a succession of events which were largely a consequence of earlier flaws in management and a failure to contain the unwieldy structure of the bank, compounded by an unforgiving economic environment. Fowler, intensely loyal to Westpac, a product of a system that rewarded activity but sometimes paid inadequate heed to its results, had fervently wished to see Westpac become bigger and better. But circumstances denied him that.

Cost-cutting measures continued. Westpac closed its executive dining room and sold the pleasure-boat *Tarquin* for a song. Chauffeurs were abolished except for the managing director and his deputy and first-class travel within Australia was restricted. Westpac's losses for the year to September 1991 were partly cushioned by the $130 million profit from the sale of Westpac Life to the AMP Society and the bank again used the superannuation fund to boost its reported results, this time by recognising a $685 million surplus in its staff superannuation funds as prepayments. Instead of inflating profit as the previous year's $325 million clawback had done, the amount was offset by a $700 million increase in the general provision for doubtful debts. Much was made in the press of the coincidence of the numbers. The Australian Stock Exchange suggested that Westpac's 1991 accounts were misleading, that the $700 million provision was a normal item and should have been charged against operating profit, which would then have become a loss, and that the super fund item was an abnormal. Westpac stood firm: a large loss would have been disastrous for its image. Derrick Heywood, Westpac's chief financial officer, had much correspondence with the ASX and the Accounting Practice

Group over the issue. The matter ended inconclusively after seven months of arguing. The only good news for Westpac in that reporting period came from New Zealand, where a substantial turnaround had produced an increased profit.

While the absence of harmony between Fowler and Neal was an open secret, a close relationship had developed between the chairman and Frank Conroy, Fowler's annointed heir. Conroy became managing director on 1 October—and was forced home at 10 am by a bout of flu. He had enjoyed solid support for his appointment from Neal who—mistakenly as it turned out—seemed to believe he could easily control the younger man. But, so far, their relationship had been successful.

One of Conroy's first decisions as chief executive was to abandon the executive committee; it was too slow a medium of action. This initiative was greeted enthusiastically by the board, particularly by Neal who had found the executive committee a thorn in his side. Conroy replaced the committee with a tight structure of executives who reported directly to him, which intensified accountability by function. Under a redistribution of control, Tony Walton was responsible for returns from business in Europe as well as the Americas division and David Morgan for the Asia–Pacific group, including New Zealand. Owen van der Wall became responsible for lifting returns on Westpac's corporate relationships in Australia as well as for global financial markets; Geoff Kimpton would have to answer for the effectiveness of Westpac's retail product range and marketing; John Chatterton, head of the branch network, assisted by Bill Paget and Helen Lynch, had to lower delivery costs and increase efficiencies; Barry Robertson's challenge was to get AGC back to profitability as quickly as possible; Darcy Ford was responsible for Westpac Financial Services Group, Keith Brown for personnel, Tony Aveling for technology, Harvey Garnett for credit policy and control, Derrick Heywood for financial control, internal audit, tax and group treasury, Vern Harvey for strategy and corporate development and Reg Barrett for compliance and legal matters.

When Conroy took over at Westpac, some three-quarters of the bank's capital supported businesses that were not meeting hurdle rates of return. His challenge was to secure board support for changes that would lift group performance. While still deputy managing director he had emphasised to the board over several months the extent of the problems Westpac faced, given the bank's own difficulties and the dismal economic conditions. As managing director, he now set about invigorating staff, many deeply demoralised by the censure the bank had received over the Westpac letters and, in some instances, alienated by Fowler's management style. Conroy, through more than 40 staff presentations around Australia and New Zealand, apologised for past mistakes and talked encouragingly about how the bank would cope better in the future.

Vern Harvey and Charles Littrell—who joined Westpac in Sydney in late 1990 from its Houston office—had begun discussions in mid-1991 with Conroy about how to lighten the burden of asset and property problems. This could be achieved, they argued, by devising a 'big hit', that is, making large—then considered impossibly large—write-offs and provisions for bad and doubtful debts so that credibility could be restored to its balance sheet. Littrell, who had previously worked for Bank of America, which struck a reef in the 1980s, had witnessed the collapse of major Texan institutions and had discerned a common cycle among troubled banks: first, a shift from denial of a problem to acceptance of a need for action, confession that wrong had been done and action initiated to correct it. The Westpac board needed to be coaxed beyond the denial stage. Discussions went on

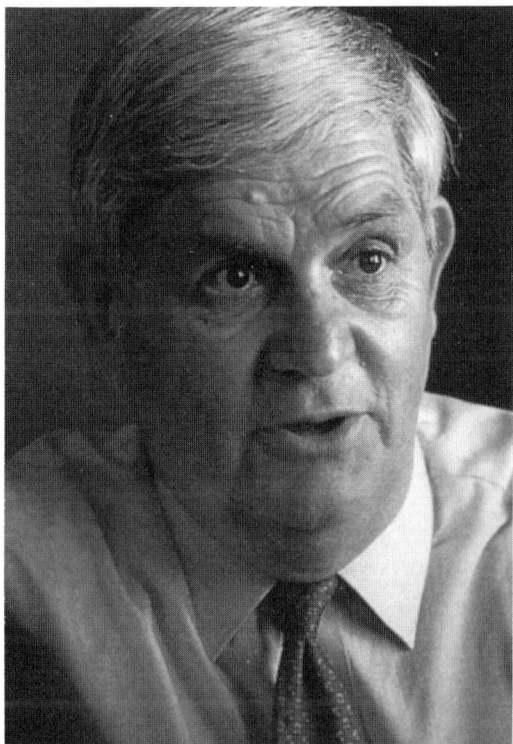

Jim Goldman, in 1989 managing director of Westpac Financial Services Group Ltd. With WFSG, Westpac was well on track to become more than a bank—to be a diversified international financial services group.

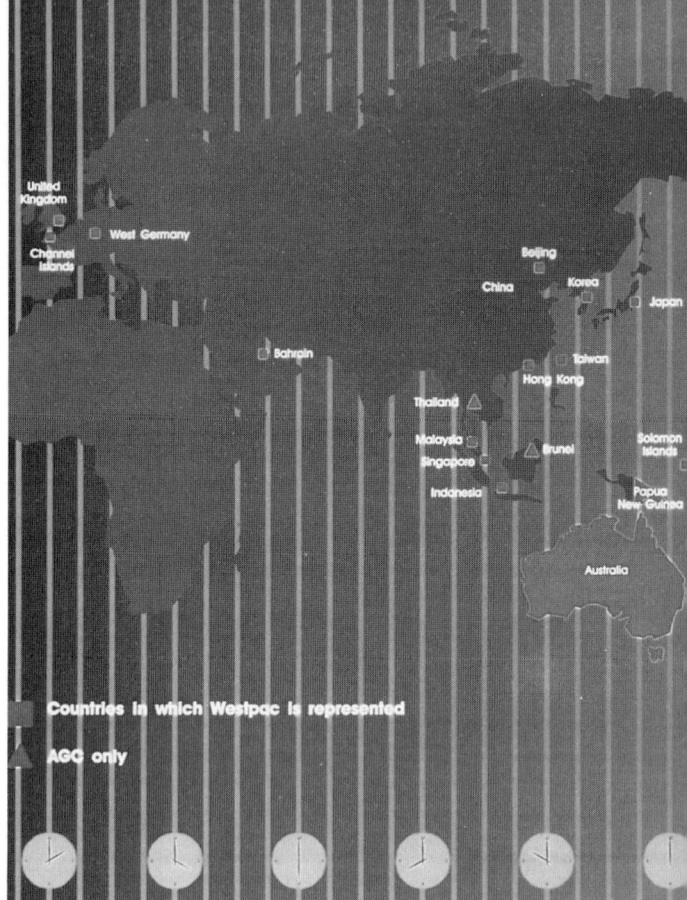

THE WORLD

United
Kingdom

West Germany

Channel
Islands

Beijing

China   Korea

Japan

Bahrain

Taiwan

Hong Kong

Thailand

Malaysia

Singapore   Brunei

Solomon
Islands

Indonesia

Papua
New Guinea

Australia

■ Countries in which Westpac is represented

▲ AGC only

1989: The World of Westpac—we never sleep.

Sir Eric Neal: autocratic chairman of an ailing bank.

In 1991 Frank Conroy was in the top job after more than 30 years with Westpac—and in 1992 he was gone. Conroy epitomised the Westpac lifer—and that cost him his job.

A relaxed-looking Westpac board in the 1991 annual report. But behind the scenes there was mounting awareness of problems confronting the bank and, as 1992 got under way, directors were to face their toughest decisions: (top, from left) Rod Cameron, Ian (Jock) Harper, Frank Conroy, Sir Eric Neal, Sir Neil Currie, Bruce Reid, Warren Hogan; (bottom, from left) Sir Llewellyn Edwards, Peter Baillieu, Sir Harold Aston, Tony Walton, John Uhrig, James Scully.

The 1992 board: different faces and coats off—the hard work continues as directors count the cost of the catastrophes of Westpac's *annus horribilis*. From left: Bruce Reid, Peter Baillieu, Warren Hogan, Reg Barrett, Frank Conroy, John Uhrig, Sir Llewellyn Edwards, Bob Johnston, Sir James Balderstone, Jock Harper.

John Uhrig: appointed chairman in 1992, his first job was to find a new chief for Westpac and then oversee the fixing of the image of a bank despised by its customers and share-holders.

The 1993 management team, some new faces, some old: could these people put the pieces back together? From left: Reg Barrett, Barry Robertson, Owen van der Wall, Robert Nimmo, Tony Aveling, David Morgan, Bob Joss, Helen Lynch, Derrick Heywood, Keith Brown, John Chatterton, Pat Handley.

Bob Joss: better, faster, cheaper, smarter . . .

through some two months of meetings, mostly among Westpac's upper echelon, on level 27 of the Sydney headquarters, including group financial controller Malcolm Sandy and chief financial officer Derrick Heywood. The executives sifted through the issues, debating how to classify them and how to compare Westpac's position with those of other banks, domestically and overseas.

This inner group of executives had become convinced that something had to be done to stem the damage from the bad debts. They knew that the bank faced an enduring downturn in the property market of a depth and gravity not seen since the 1890s. Credit-rating agencies had been sending out warning signals since December 1989. And the Reserve Bank was pointing out to Westpac that it was out of line in its treatment of problem assets; compared with other banks it appeared under-provisioned.

Problem assets fall into several categories including non-accrual loans (NALs), on which no interest is being accrued and the collection of principal and interest is in doubt; loans past 90 days due, where the payment of principal and interest is overdue but the bank continues to take interest to profit; and restructured loans, where changes have been made to the original terms and conditions and interest is less than prevailing market rates. A further category identified later by Westpac is 'other real estate owned', OREO, which includes all property assets and joint ventures which the bank acquired through a default by the mortgagee, often through AGC's joint ventures and PPL's property problems. A bank can have a high problem asset number but if it is 100 per cent provisioned then that is not a great threat, although it dilutes its earnings and so its returns to shareholders. But Westpac had a high level of problem assets, a substantial, if largely unintentional, group exposure to property, and low provisioning. The bank could not continue with a policy of just parking these bad assets on the balance sheet and hoping that the market would not notice while taking years to work them out. Another troublesome category was 'potential problem loans', loans which were not yet in default but known to have credit problems. These totalled $720 million in 1989, rising to $1.04 billion in the first half of 1990 and to $2.5 billion in March 1991, following which some were reclassified as NALs and restructured loans.

Westpac had made provisions for doubtful debts of $1.2 billion in 1990 and $1.7 billion in 1991, which had included $700 million in general provision. Frank Conroy's group of senior executives were convinced that this rate of annual charge was not adequate and that Westpac should undertake a painful but once-only adjustment to its balance sheet to reflect real values. This would restore its credibility in the eyes of the ratings agencies, analysts, customers and the media, they said. But it was not something a bank could undertake lightly; much discussion took place.

Since becoming chairman, Sir Eric Neal had been demanding an improved flow of information to the board to correct an earlier situation where getting information out of management was, said one director, 'like drawing teeth'. In 1991, as well as chairman Neal and two executive directors, Conroy and Walton, the board comprised: deputy chairman Sir Neil Currie, a former Australian ambassador to Japan and Westpac board member since 1987; industrialist Sir Harold Aston, a board member since 1988; Peter Baillieu, who had a longstanding involvement in the pastoral industry, was chairman of the investment bank Schroders Australia Ltd and had been a Westpac director since 1974; leading chartered accountant Rod Cameron, a director since 1987; Sir Llew Edwards, a former deputy premier and treasurer of Queensland and director of the bank since 1988; Allen Allen & Hemsley partner Ian (Jock) Harper, a board member since 1987; academic economist Professor Warren Hogan, who had joined the Westpac board in 1986; businessman

Bruce Reid, a board member since 1985; former public servant Jim Scully, a board member since 1984; and industrialist John Uhrig, a board member since 1989.

The board did not doubt the honesty of what management was telling them, but they did doubt whether management was giving, or even knew, the full story. Management, grappling with the consequences for business of a deep and protracted recession, often felt that the board had a tenuous grasp of how difficult life had become for banks and their customers. But a sense that they were not being given a comprehensive picture left the board very uneasy. Every time a problem had been uncovered, the board was assured that this was the last surprise. Problem loans were coming to light not so much through diligent analysis or foresight on Westpac's part as through shock realisations as companies fell over or were unable to repay loans. Westpac had been active in so many areas, and so deficient in adequate, centralised management systems, that ordinary scrutiny failed to reveal all flaws.

319

The board interpreted this failure as an intent by management to withhold detail. And the board members had difficulty following Vern Harvey's strategy presentations; some found his management philosophy impenetrable. Harvey had only recently arrived at the bank and was telling the directors things they did not want to believe. Initially, as information was still being gathered, Harvey was constantly refining the numbers and details, which probably added to the board's confusion. Seeking to add credibility, Conroy began to handle the presentations from group strategy. The content did not change, but it was hoped that the messages would carry more weight when delivered by Conroy as deputy, then as managing director, particularly as the chairman was known to regard the bank's strategic planning as an over-rated activity. Neal had often been heard to comment that, in his view, Westpac management needed to lift its game. The mutual distrust between board and management made a clear focus on the difficulties almost impossible.

The polarisation of views over the question of write-offs and provisions for bad and doubtful debts created a dilemma for Conroy as he found the executives' arguments increasingly persuasive. His own views firmed after a meeting with the ratings agencies in New York where, with Harvey, Heywood and Walton, he listened while the agencies pointed out again that Westpac was inadequately provisioned and, moreover, was still incapable of providing a sufficient explanation of its property exposures. After that session, Conroy was convinced that the way ahead to avert a crisis was to clear the decks and provide realistically for the debts. Reports of the ratings agencies' comments did not cut much ice with most of the board; not all members had a clear grasp of how ratings agencies' verdicts could affect a bank's position in equity and capital markets. Moreover, most of the board underestimated the experience and skills of staff in credit-rating agencies; the fact was that if an agency flagged a problem, there usually was indeed a problem. Further ammunition was provided for management's case when Alistair Walton, a bank analyst with CS First Boston in Sydney who when previously working with CSFB in the US had formed a good working relationship with Littrell, wrote a letter to Conroy emphasising that the arguments in favour of a substantial provisioning were overwhelming.

Management was making presentation after presentation to the board, showing assessments of the prevailing position, which operations produced value for Westpac, where profitability was coming from, where the bank was making an adequate return on assets and what action should be taken. In one presentation Heywood showed a slide to illustrate which entities were making an adequate return and which were not: he listed all Westpac's operations in descending order of return on assets and drew a line through the middle.

One director commented: 'You can't make it any plainer than that.' The verdict for those below the line was: either improve performance or face a reduction in assets or be prepared to be sold or shut down.

Adding weight to the arguments for action, and reinforcing management's conviction that Westpac could not continue with its problem loans and low provisioning, was a presentation in August 1991 by the investment bank Goldman Sachs which proposed dividing Westpac into a 'good bank' and a 'bad bank'. Goldman Sachs cited the example of Mellon Bank, historically a premier and AAA-rated US bank which, under a new chairman in the mid-to-late 1980s, experienced a sharp decline in asset quality. This dragged its credit rating down to BBB. Mellon Bank's response was to create a 'bad bank' which held the non-performing assets and worked on liquidating those while the 'good bank' concentrated on its positive business. The structure helped persuade the ratings agencies, the regulators, depositors and investors that the bank was dealing appropriately with its non-performing loans.

The Westpac directors found the notion of a 'bad bank' distasteful—but some of them were beginning to listen. Westpac called in analysts from Lend Lease to provide estimates of replacement costs for major properties acquired through AGC, such as Dockside, Oasis on Broadbeach and Como, and to advise on how and when to sell. Sir Eric Neal is remembered as taking the position that replacement cost was an absolute minimum value, an understandable approach given his background in manufacturing, where an asset can quite easily be valued at its acquisition cost. However, with many of Westpac's unfinished projects, poor controls and rising costs contributed to a 'cost to complete' that bore no relationship to prevailing market values. Neal took a long-term and fairly bullish view on commercial property. He was in favour of holding properties until the economy recovered,

321

demand returned and prices, fuelled by rising inflation, rose again. From this viewpoint, it would seem unfair to shareholders to sell a property which subsequently rose in value. Further, Westpac's underlying profitability should enable it to absorb the carrying costs. But banks also have to consider the earning capacity of an asset in the short term because they have to fund the asset. And pressure was mounting from various quarters—auditors, analysts and revamped corporations legislation—for assets to be in the balance sheet at a realistic value.

In August 1991, in the lead-up to finalising the 1991 accounts, management made a formal presentation to a small group of directors, showing estimates of how, in certain circumstances and given certain assumptions about the trend in property values, write-offs and provisions, Westpac's accounts might look and how markets and ratings agencies might respond. But the directors could not accept the principle that values should be written down to the 'realistic' selling prices prevailing in the depressed market. They were nervous that, if Westpac took a 'big hit' too soon, shareholders would be unforgiving because the bank would later be writing back what had been written off. The view was well-intentioned but, as it turned out, misguided. At that stage the data went no further. The papers for the presentation were ordered to be shredded.

The cloud of suspicion over Westpac was darkening. Shareholders were losing confidence and the bank was not seen as well managed. A background of instability in financial markets did not help. Estate Mortgage Trusts had collapsed in 1990, owing investors millions. The losses in the merchant bank Tricontinental Corporation Ltd crippled its parent, the State Bank of Victoria. Pyramid Building Society in Melbourne had gone to the wall. Early in 1991, State Bank South Australia, which had become more entrepreneurial under managing director Tim Marcus Clark, joined the list

322

of casualties. Energetic lending, much of it property-related, had played a part in all of these disasters and Westpac, with two-thirds of its problems in property, was seen as equally vulnerable. The market's view was that Westpac, sitting on grossly overvalued properties, had lost touch with reality. Bank analysts were making it plain that something had to be done about non-performing loans. But management attempts to convince Neal of the necessity for swift and radical surgery had failed. The issues at that stage were receiving closest attention from a small group which appeared to share the chairman's optimism. Management decided in December to defer the task until the new year. Littrell spent his Christmas break writing a report for Conroy on the issues confronting Westpac.

By now ragged patches were appearing in the relationship between Neal and Conroy, partly because Conroy, growing into his role as chief executive, was persistently pushing for a big write-off, which Neal did not feel was an acceptable solution. Conroy was increasingly frustrated at board interference in management, which he saw as unproductive, and at the chairman's unwillingness to curb growth in the Americas division. Conroy took a few days off over Christmas and New Year. Neal, never reluctant to pursue executives out of hours, kept up telephone contact until a fellow director suggested that he back off and allow Conroy more space.

The end of 1991 brought no relief from bad news: Westpac had to confirm its membership of a syndicate which had advanced funds to the now dead-and-disgraced British entrepreneur Robert Maxwell, resulting in an exposure of more than $130 million, one of the bank's largest. And in the US, where Westpac had to file the detailed annual Form 20-F required by the Securities and Exchange Commission, rumours were circulating that the bank was in serious financial strife. The whispers were filtering back to Australia where they mingled with home-grown speculation about the bank's position. Interviewed on Channel Nine's *Business Sunday* early in 1992 about Westpac's financial perform-ance, an ill-at-ease Frank Conroy said that Westpac was in a recovery phase. Asked if he believed the worst was over, Conroy said that he did not believe there were any skeletons in the cupboard. 'We believe we've identified all the issues, all the problems, we've been quite open and we're attacking all those problems,' he said. But the problems were not in retreat.

By early 1992 a few board members had been doing some homework of their own. The deputy chairman, Sir Neil Currie, had coincided with Heywood and Harvey in London in December 1991 when they were handling a presentation to fund managers and a separate presentation to bank ana-lysts of major broking houses. They invited Currie to sit in on the meeting with analysts. It opened his eyes to the issues that concern bank analysts, and the importance of their views to wider perceptions about a bank. Currie came away shaken by the degree to which the bankers were grilled, and impressed by their ability to handle it. It was a major break-through for management.

Sir Eric Neal summarised the year in his chairman's state-ment in the 1991 annual report. The statement, which had been furnished by management and written in a way that reflected what were known to be his views and attitudes, said:

> As foreshadowed in my last report to you, the 1990–91 year has been one of the most difficult Westpac has faced in its 174 years of operations. Australia's current recession has been longer and deeper than was expected and has seriously impacted the bank's operating results ... There are signs that the worst of the bad debt experience may

now be behind us ... Of particular significance to
the Westpac Group has been the downturn in the
commercial property market. Management of the
group's property portfolio has been strengthened
and the close involvement of the board property
committee provides additional assurance to proprietors that the group's property exposure is under
constant review ... Directors are satisfied that valuations of the group's major property exposures are
appropriate and that provisions have been established where necessary to reflect any potential loss
of value.

At the three-hour January 1992 annual general meeting,
shareholders complained about AGC's property lending and
Westpac's exposure to the bankrupt US retailer Macy's.
During the fiery meeting the board was attacked on issues
such as Westpac's poor management, excessive corporate
lending, foreign-currency loan problems and the falling share
price. In his address to shareholders Neal said: 'There is
some cause for optimism ... Despite continuing poor economic conditions our operating results for the first quarter
of this current trading year are encouraging and, if sustained,
offer tangible proof that the worst is behind us.' His words
echoed the sentiments of his chairman's statement in the
1991 annual report.

But even in early 1992 disagreement persisted between the
board and executives about how best to handle the bank's
property and problem asset portfolio. Against the view that
Westpac could ride out the property cycle was a mounting
concern about the impact of the impaired assets on its credit
rating, which in turn affected its ability to raise funds cheaply
in the international capital markets. A vicious circle was in
train which had to be broken. Had the substantial provisioning
suggested in August 1991 been made, Westpac's chairman

325

would not later have been in the embarrassing situation, in May 1992, of having to reverse positive statements made four months earlier.

For Conroy, 1992 began with the handing over by Harvey of the report that Littrell had composed during the holidays. There had been much discussion by Harvey, Littrell and Heywood about how best to frame the report to Conroy so that he would be fully equipped to present the facts to the board. On receiving Littrell's report, Conroy retreated to his office, closed the door, ordered that no phone calls were to be put through and sat down to focus his uninterrupted attention on the sobering document.

The Reserve Bank was by now expressing serious reservations about Westpac's provisioning and for some time had been prodding the bank to put a realistic value on its loans and properties. The central bank pointed out that market scepticism could further undermine confidence in the bank. Westpac had already been downgraded by Moody's and was now re-rated from AA to A by Standard & Poor's, reflecting a decline from a strong company to one that, while still well able to meet its commitments, was more susceptible to the adverse effects of changes in economic conditions than those in higher categories. Standard & Poor's commented: 'Westpac's ratings downgrade is due to the increased impact of problem loans and property investment exposures on the bank's current and future asset quality and earnings ... The Westpac group is relatively more exposed to larger corporate and commercial property problems than its peers ... a prolonged downturn in the commercial property sector would likely inhibit the recovery in asset quality and extend the impact on core earnings to a greater degree than previously expected.' Downgradings had an immediately damaging impact on Westpac's business because some major companies and state government authorities could not be counterparty to an entity rated less than AA; that is, they could not deal in Westpac's securities or make deposits with it, and those that could charged more to the lower-rated party. Westpac's depressed rating could cost millions in the financial markets, as well as being a psychological blow to staff. Central banks were already reducing the size of the bullion deposits they were prepared to place with Mase Westpac, and a further downgrading would badly affect the gold-trading subsidiary.

Not all of the board gave full weight to the RBA's warnings, some dismissing the central bank's opinion as being only that of officers of the bank. Those in regular contact with the RBA, though, knew that the reservations expressed were coming from the top. Besides having their own views, central bankers conferred with analysts and ratings agencies. They were well aware of Westpac's situation. Communication between Westpac and the RBA was taking place at various levels, with Conroy in discussions at governor level and management talking with an assistant governor, Graeme Thompson, and Les Austin, head of bank supervision. And lines of communication were strengthened by the presence on the Westpac board of a former RBA governor, Bob Johnston. In pushing their argument to directors, management cited overseas examples of how banks in a similar situation to Westpac's handled their problems, and the varying degrees of success that ensued. They also pointed out that were Westpac a US bank, it was not improbable that it would now be under formal supervision by the Federal Reserve, or forced into merger discussions. This was met by blank looks from several board members. Those directors who did understand the ramifications of the problem and powers of the RBA—which included replacing the board of a bank if it saw fit—realised that it was Westpac's survival that was under discussion, not just tactics for averting unwelcome bad publicity.

Breaking the CAMEL's back

It was traditional for the board and senior management to meet away from headquarters once a year and a strategy meeting was organised for early March 1992, at the Fairmont Resort at Leura in the Blue Mountains, west of Sydney. Ahead of the conference Conroy attended an annual prudential review meeting with the RBA and came away with a clear view that the RBA would support Westpac if it changed its approach to property valuations and how it provisioned. At the meeting, the central bank had formally raised its concerns about Westpac's level of provisioning. Harvey and Littrell, by now familiar with the Reserve Bank's delphic utterances, had urged the central bankers to speak plainly to Conroy, pointing out that the new managing director would be receptive to what they were saying. RBA support added greatly to Conroy's confidence in confronting the board with what he knew would be unpopular tidings. To set the scene, management circulated to the board, before the Leura conference, the minutes of the meeting with the RBA. That gave board members a clear picture of the regulator's preferred approach and, for many, legitimised Conroy's message.

Neal had additional warning that Conroy intended to present a watertight case for a large one-off provision. Following a management meeting in the boardroom on Wednesday 4 March, Conroy and fellow executive director Tony Walton, in Australia for the strategy meeting, briefed the chairman on what to expect. Conroy's case had the backing of most of the management team. Further groundwork was laid at the following day's regular board meeting when Westpac's chief economist Bill Evans gave a comprehensive rundown of his department's views on the property market, forecasting that it would be 2000 before the Sydney CBD vacancy rate returned to normal. The message that Conroy wanted to drum home to the board was that the collapse in the property market was of such dimensions that it would not be possible for the bank to sit it out. Driving up to the Leura conference that evening with fellow director John Uhrig, Neal was adamant that he would fight the proposal for major provisioning and a 'big hit'.

Conroy could draw on considerable support from analysts. James Capel Research commented: 'Westpac ... has been less than conservative in its provisioning (by not recognising the collapse in commercial property values); in its statement of income (by bringing to account income on loans that other banks would treat as non-performing) ... we can see this lack of conservatism manifesting itself in a series of disappointing results which will not stand up to analyst scrutiny.' CS First Boston predicted that the Westpac group's level of non-accrual loans and low earnings would not improve over the coming year or so and said: 'While some of the problems relate to economic conditions in Australia and the high level of unemployment, the credit control procedures and problem identification processes that have been employed in the past have also contributed.' Hambros emphasised that Westpac 'looks under provisioned, especially when its high exposure to property through AGC is taken into account'.

The Leura strategy meeting opened on Friday 6 March with Conroy's presentation. It was a confronting dissection of a disaster, detailing how problem loans had increased month by month, reaching about 12 per cent of total loans. These would be a drag on earnings for some time. By way of comparison, a bank rated AA would be expected to have non-performing loans of about 1 per cent of total, more than 4 per cent was regarded as a worry and more than 8 per cent critical. Few banks could survive once the ratio of non-performing loans to total loans hit double digits. Conroy ran through the implications for the bank's strategy, and showed how Westpac compared with overseas banks. Nowhere in the world did an equivalent bank have a similar level of problem loans to assets. Non-accrual and restructured loans had increased sixfold over three years, from $1.1 billion in 1989 to $2.5 billion in 1990, $6.2 billion in 1991 and $7.2 billion in early 1992 with AGC's joint ventures included, and higher again if potential problem and loans past 90 days were included. Over the same period specific provisioning had merely doubled from $400 million in 1989 to $800 million in 1991. Of the four major banks, Westpac and ANZ had the higher level of non-performing loans and were the least conservatively provisioned. Arguably the most worrying number, and one which unnerved ratings agencies, was Westpac's ratio of net problem assets to capital: in early 1992 its net problem loans of $7.2 billion matched its capital of $7.2 billion. The bank's entire capital was tied up in problem loans of doubtful value, half of which were earning no income. Westpac was a very weak bank.

Westpac had learned some unpleasant lessons, Conroy told the board: the growth and increasing complexity of the bank had not been matched by controls, core profits had been neglected and the bank needed to be more receptive to internal evaluations and external criticism. Conroy ran through the CAMEL model (capital, assets, management, earnings and liquidity). A good bank is strong in all five elements; let one element of CAMEL become weak, and a bank starts on a downward spiral. Westpac's capital was above average but its asset quality among the worst; management was not seen as a problem but earnings were below average while liquidity was well under control. Overall, Westpac's CAMEL was weak and it was no secret in the world's markets. Objectives for the 1990s must include restoring financial health, replenishing core businesses, especially retail, improving or discarding uncompetitive businesses, especially wholesale and international, and reconsidering growth from a stronger but smaller and more profit-efficient base. The alternative proposition that Westpac could ride out its problems without

330

radical change was not put to the board—management did not believe it was an option.

It was the first opportunity permitted to management to present comprehensively and formally to the full board not just the details of Westpac's parlous position but the implications of its problems and what ought to be done about them. The presentation ran for two hours before the chairman, who was growing visibly agitated, and some of the board members put a stop to it. The gist of their protest was: 'Stop right there—you have told us we are about the weakest bank in the English-speaking world so it is pointless to continue until we fix this.' Conroy persisted and resumed detailing the ratio of problem loans to assets (highest in the English-speaking world) and provisioning to loans (lowest). There was some scepticism about the numbers, with Neal leading the challenge to the property valuations and the level of provisions suggested. Bob Johnston, as a former Reserve Bank chief, was helpful in getting the key points across, painstakingly explaining the potential impact if the situation went unaddressed, and what steps the RBA could take.

At one point the management representatives were asked to leave while a board issue was discussed. Conroy and Walton, as directors, remained at the table. The other executives left, unsure how long they would be out of the meeting room; Tony Aveling is remembered as running a book on when they would be recalled. Conroy advised them at lunchtime that their further presence would not be needed that day. They went off to play golf or tennis, joining the board later for dinner. Before everyone gathered for the evening meal, Conroy briefed them on what had transpired in the room in their absence: the penny had dropped. The board had absorbed the bad news. It was the result many of the executives had been waiting for more than six months to hear.

This meeting was a turning point, but additional evidence was needed to shake off finally the conviction that Westpac,

Australia's oldest, largest and best bank, was infallible. The board instructed management to commission a major review of property exposures, to be conducted by Jones Lang Wootton and Baillieu Knight Frank. After the Leura meeting, Conroy paid a call on Bernie Fraser, governor of the Reserve Bank, to confirm that the valuation methods Westpac proposed to use were acceptable to the central bank.

Sir Eric Neal still seemed less than wholly convinced; he did not appear to be against the proposal to revalue the properties but had trouble believing the numbers put before him by management. Some executives perceived him as failing to grasp the urgency of the problems, nor fully appreciating the powers of the Reserve Bank. And he was unfamiliar with troubles of this nature or scale; he had always presided over successful industrial businesses. Mindful that management had frequently cited the experience of US banks as a guide, and to ensure that the Westpac board was getting the best possible advice and working with accurate figures, he called on James D. Wolfensohn Inc, the US consultancy now chaired by Paul Volcker, and it was agreed that the American firm would run through the numbers on bad loans and provisioning that Conroy had presented. It was not to be the only time the Westpac board called in expensive outsiders to check the work done by its own management, and was perhaps a sign of the mistrust between directors and executives. The team from James D. Wolfensohn Inc presented its data and conclusions in a report, *Project Sydney*, in May 1992. They verified the figures produced by Westpac management. The bank's plight was evident: its return on equity was 6.6 per cent compared with 15.5 per cent in 1988 and trailing NAB's 10.4 per cent although ahead of ANZ and Commonwealth Bank. Its problem loans as a proportion of total loans were 14 per cent, up from 12 per cent a year earlier, well above the international and

332

Australian peer-group average. The composition of West-pac's assets drew comment: its loans were almost one-third in real estate whereas ANZ had less than one-quarter in real estate and NAB less than one-fifth.

Volcker himself slipped into Australia for a few days. He was wholly supportive of the strategy of clearing the decks, telling Conroy, and later the board: 'You only get one chance at this.' It was essential to demonstrate that the bank had dealt with its problems; if, on the other hand, a perception lingered that Westpac had not gone far enough, the evidence suggested that the market would not allow it to survive. A bank had to get this kind of adjustment right first time. The case for taking a big hit, based on evidence put to the board and culled from overseas banks which had been through the process, was: substantially increase provisions and hold a capital issue to offset the effect of the provisions on the capital ratio. The market would applaud the directors; over a year or so the share price would recover and the bank would continue to trade with restored credibility. That was the experience in the US. With confirmation from this elite group, Neal's reservations were put to rest. Volcker subsequently sent Neal a note: 'You've survived your first banking crisis.'

JLW and Baillieu Knight Frank examined 470 properties (and took samples from a further 800), using two methods, current market value—the amount realisable in a sale between a willing buyer and willing seller within 24 months—and discounted cashflow analysis, which is based on the ability of the property to generate income over time, using supportable assumptions. Of the properties examined, 50 were classified as likely to be held for some time before disposal and were valued using the second method. The remainder were valued according to the current market value method. These valuations reflected the Westpac board's decision to dump the 'intrinsic value' methodology in favour of a more acceptable approach.

By April 1992 Westpac had an $11 billion real estate exposure in Australia. The bank also had a $1 billion property exposure in the UK and that, plus loans in the US and New Zealand, took group property exposure to $13.9 billion. Frank Conroy had commented in a recent interview with *The Australian Financial Review*: 'We had five separate entities—AGC, BAC, PPL and Westpac corporate and retail—lending to property at the same time. If you ask me what is the biggest mistake we've made during the decade, it was the governance of pulling all that together.' The atmosphere was less than conducive to celebration but Westpac marked its 175th birthday with tea and cake for staff around the country.

334   Credit-rating agencies continued to express concerns which echoed those of the analysts. But the bank's management was by now confident it was on the way to making some progress towards recovery. A capital raising was going to be necessary, and David Graupner, managing director of Ord Minnett, and fellow director Neville Miles, who had left Westpac to join the broking firm, were summoned to 60 Martin Place to discuss fundraising tactics with the bank's executives. Westpac could provide the brokers with only scant details because the proposal was still very much under wraps. However, the bank was planning a large rights issue to replenish capital. Vern Harvey explained in confidence that Westpac had decided to use a different basis of valuation of its property assets which involved writing them down considerably. As soon as the board formally adopted a revised valuation method to be used in the accounts, it would have to make an announcement to the market. Meanwhile, papers had to be prepared on a hypothetical basis. The Ords executives thought a sizeable write-down might be envisaged; but they were staggered to hear the amount being considered was

$2.2 billion. Armed with this information, Graupner and Miles returned to a long night's work, drafting a proposal. They concluded that Westpac would be best advised to go ahead with a plain 'vanilla' rights issue, with a deep discount (a low price of around $2.60/70, compared with Westpac's market price of around $4) to win support, and that the issue had to be underwritten.

The Westpac executives were not impressed with the verdict when it was relayed the following day: they regarded the discount as too deep, and feared it would reflect badly on the bank. And they did not want to appoint an underwriter because they were concerned about leaks—continuous disclosure requirements of the Australian Stock Exchange demanded that once Westpac formally decided to hold a rights issue because of a large loss it must disclose this to the exchange. Westpac was anxious to manage the impact of an announcement of such a change in valuation method. Ords stuck to its guns, insisting that a deep discount was essential if the issue was to attract investors—and Westpac had to raise the funds or risk breaching RBA capital adequacy requirements. This would be a disastrous blow to perceptions of the bank's strength. Ords put its views in a written submission and made a presentation to the full board. The brokers offered a choice: an ordinary rights issue, probably not requiring underwriting but definitely demanding a large discount of, say, 40 per cent to $2.40/50, or a domestic preference share issue, which would need shareholder approval. An acrimonious discussion about price ensued, with Ords and most management supporting $2.50 and the board insisting on $3. The board won. With a price at that level, management argued, the board would have to consider an underwriter. Ords' role had ended. Given that Westpac owned Ord Minnett, it was impossible for Ords to underwrite the issue and, despite its earlier advisory role, the company's name did not appear on the prospectus. This, given its views about the terms, was a considerable relief to Ord Minnett.

Analysts were still speaking out in favour of Westpac's acknowledging its weakened position. Potter Warburg commented early in May that the sentiment surrounding the bank remained bearish. 'The market is focusing on the unknown elements of asset quality problems ... We feel however that if management chose the "big bath" approach (even with an attendant rights issue) a move to a very positive sentiment would result.'

May 1992 was the 50th anniversary of the Battle of the Coral Sea, which in 1942 had turned the tide of the war in the Pacific against Japan. The significance of the occasion was flagged in January of that year when the US president, George Bush, addressed the Australian parliament. Australians and Americans had fought together in a number of engagements that contributed to Australia's security during the second world war. Sir Eric Neal, a naval history buff, had been appointed chairman of the Australia–United States Coral Sea Commemorative Council, and was orchestrating a program that would commemorate all significant events of 1942, with Westpac contributing a secretariat and staff to the council. A retired Westpac executive, Lindsay Hamilton, was brought back as the council's executive director to coordinate celebrations, seconded full-time as part of Westpac's contribution. The board had allocated $250,000 'in kind' but that was quickly absorbed in Hamilton's time, rents and secretarial services. Joint patrons of the council were the Australian prime minister, Paul Keating, and the US ambassador to Australia, Melvin Sembler. Luminaries on the council included several Westpac board members, managing director Frank Conroy, leading business figures such as Sir Arvi Parbo, BHP's John Prescott, MIM's Sir Bruce Watson, Rupert Murdoch and Kerry Packer.

As part of the ten days of events to commemorate the Coral Sea battle, several US navy ships visited Australian ports. On one occasion, a group of some 30 guests of the Coral Sea Commemorative Council were entertained aboard the giant aircraft carrier USS *Independence*, stationed off the New South Wales coast for the occasion. The guests, flown from Sydney's Mascot airport to the carrier in a spartan US navy transport plane, included Lindsay Hamilton, Westpac's acting chief manager of corporate communications, Alan Tippett, and media manager Rod Metcalfe. Aboard the aircraft, Metcalfe found himself seated across the aisle from Consolidated Press chief operating officer Al Dunlap, a graduate of the prestige US military academy West Point and a former US paratrooper. Dunlap seemed uninterested in making conversation so Metcalfe caught up on news, reading his copy of *The Australian*. The 90-minute flight was not particularly smooth, given that transport planes are designed for utility rather than comfort and passengers were seated with their backs to the cockpit. Shortly before landing, Dunlap broke his silence and demanded Metcalfe's paper, into which he promptly vomited. Once on the aircraft carrier, the guests toured the ship, participated in a memorial service and were treated to lunch in the captain's cabin.

Sir Eric Neal received several congratulatory letters for his labours in support of the commemoration, including accolades from the US secretary of defence, Dick Cheney, from Mel Sembler and from the White House. President Bush, who had met Neal during his earlier visit to Australia, said: 'I knew when we met in January that you were the energising force to bring this commemoration together. What was achieved was due, above all, to your vision, leadership and unstinting effort ...' In July 1992, Neal was awarded the US department of defence's medal for distinguished public service, the highest honour bestowed by the US government on a non-American.

CHAPTER THIRTEEN

FEAR AND LOATHING

A succession of shattering revelations had exposed the flaws in Westpac's dash for growth; they also laid bare deficiencies in its credit policy and control systems, and inadequacies in its control of subsidiaries. The confirmation of its level of problem loans blew apart any lingering complacency about the bank's strengths and position in the industry it had once dominated. More than a century of tradition was broken when, on 20 May 1992, Westpac announced a loss of $1.666 billion for the half-year to 31 March, following provisions for bad and doubtful debts of $2.65 billion; of that, $2.2 billion was property-related, $1 billion of it for AGC. While AGC's loss for the half-year was $719 million, its drain on Westpac's bottom line was higher because several AGC problems had been taken over by the bank and AGC's UK offshoot Westpac General Finance had produced losses. In all, AGC accounted for $1.1 billion of Westpac's $1.666 billion loss. The results were an unprecedented defeat for Westpac, reflecting the bank's belated acknowledgment of what had been building over previous years. The property write-downs included six major AGC joint ventures of which one was written down by $250 million and the others by more than $100 million each. Westpac's other real estate-owned (OREO) portfolio—mostly the property acquired by taking over AGC's joint ventures—of $1.7 billion had specific provisions of $1.1 billion, a sharp increase from $87 million six months earlier when OREOs totalled $1.3 billion. Half of the increase in OREOs, about $340 million, reflected the cost of taking out AGC's joint-venture partners. OREOs included non-accrual loans to

Southgate of $220 million, Australia on Collins $180 million, and Piccadilly Plaza $270 million, as well as restructured loans to Oasis on Broadbeach where the exposure was $110 million, Como $190 million, and Dockside and 270 Pitt Street around $100 million each. Valuation trends in Australian property remained crucial to the outcome for Australian banks' provisioning.

AGC's capital was restored by an $850 million equity injection from Westpac, and the risk participation and funding agreement ended. After the additional provisions, provisioning cover for Westpac's problem loans leaped from 28 to 47 per cent. The Americas division made provisions of $110 million, about 1 per cent of its assets, and produced a loss of $43 million, while in Europe Westpac made a provision of $296 million and recorded a loss of close to $400 million on assets of $8 billion. Westpac General Finance's property activities produced a further $73 million in losses. Most of the bad debts in the Americas division and in Europe resulted from three large loans, Macy's, Olympia & York, and Maxwell. Total problem loans for Westpac, including what had been called potential problem loans, increased by 21 per cent in six months to $9.7 billion by March 1992 compared with $8 billion in September 1991, itself an increase of 15 per cent on the $7 billion in March 1991. At the March half-year, after the write-offs, Westpac's shareholders' funds were $5.4 billion, less than its $6.2 billion of net problem loans. It had to raise fresh capital. After his first six months as managing director, Frank Conroy had nothing to celebrate. He said that the group's extensive exposure to property in Australia and, to a lesser extent in the UK, was the most pressing issue confronting it. He pointed out that in November, when announcing the full year results to September 1991, the bank had indicated that the group's property exposure would be under constant review.

The board was satisfied that, given expectations of recovery in the property market, the valuation bases being used for our major property exposures were then appropriate. More recently, there has been increasing evidence that the recession in the commercial property market has been more severe and that recovery is still a long way off. These conditions apply not only in Australia but in the United Kingdom and New Zealand.

Referring to the property review conducted by JLW and Baillieu Knight Frank, he said that, on average, valuations for all properties reviewed were 34 per cent below book value. 'The bank has taken these valuations, without amendment,' Conroy said. He emphasised the exceptional nature of Westpac's actions, and stressed that underlying performance was sound. Westpac's fresh approach to provisioning was more in line with that of its peers, although they did not have the same extent of property problems.

Conroy, at the end of a long session with analysts and the media, and the close of what had been a long week—he subsequently described it in a television interview with *Business Sunday* as the toughest in 32 years of banking life— boiled over into a public snipe at his arch rival, National Australia Bank. Quizzed about why NAB had performed so well, Conroy launched into a lengthy response, describing how the Big Four had set out much in line in the early 1980s, with the Commonwealth Bank then going on to focus on domestic banking, ANZ to make a major acquisition with Grindlays PLC and Westpac to concentrate on wholesale banking with operations in the US, Asia and the UK and significant merchant banking and corporate banking activities. NAB, through a large part of that time, said Conroy, was 'strategically sterile', before it crystallised its strategy in retail banking in English-speaking countries. In the end,

NAB had won. Conroy said later in the television interview that his words were a little unfortunate. 'I guess it proves at the end of the day I do have blood flowing through my veins and I am human,' he said. 'But I was responding to quite a few questions from media and analysts over the two days.' Conroy said he had immediately contacted NAB chief Don Argus and apologised 'for the way those comments had been conveyed in the media'.

Westpac shareholders were angry at the announcement of the losses, particularly given the promising verdict from the chairman at the January annual general meeting, only four months earlier. Inevitably there was a question in their minds as to whether Westpac was still putting a gloss on its figures. It was an issue of credibility. The shareholders were entitled to feel that Westpac could have written down its property more steadily over previous reporting periods; or it could have bitten the bullet and cut its losses eighteen months earlier, after the property market topped in late 1989 and early 1990. The AMP Society, having secured approval from the federal government to lift its shareholding from 10 to 15 per cent, had recently shelled out $300 million for Westpac shares, buying at $4.13 a share. It was appalled at the turn of events, and its policyholders were vocal in their complaints.

The Reserve Bank had been kept informed of Westpac's steps to strengthen the group's position, and supported them. Capital was not a pressing problem, although by 30 June Westpac was perilously close to the minimum level of 8 per cent capital adequacy. A more critical issue was its ability to pay dividends. The RBA's general view was that a bank making a loss could not pay a dividend because dividends can only be paid out of the current year's earnings and not out of retained earnings. However, Westpac management pushed the point that the bank was making an adjustment to its balance sheet rather than reporting a trading loss and that many small shareholders relied on the dividend for income. The central bank was prepared to be flexible.

At the 20 May press conference Westpac also announced its $1.2 billion 3-for-10 rights issue, the largest corporate issue in Australia. Initially the rights issue was not to be underwritten. Conroy was queried on this point and his reply was an emphatic no, the issue would not be underwritten. This would leave the bank bearing the risk of a shortfall in subscriptions. Views around the board table at that stage were not cohesive: some directors still believed Westpac was invincible. AMP saw the situation differently and its two representatives on the Westpac board were horrified. Its managing director Ian Salmon, in Canada on a business trip but in regular contact with his chairman and Westpac director Sir James Balderstone, was adamant that an underwriter was essential. Management agreed.

Two weeks later, on 4 June, Westpac announced that CSFB Australian Equities Ltd, the local offshoot of the giant New York investment bank Credit Suisse First Boston, would underwrite the $1.2 billion rights issue priced at $3 a share, a relatively slim discount to the market price of $3.94 on 20 May. Various groups had approached Westpac to win the underwriting of Australia's largest rights issue. CSFB was Conroy's choice; having identified them as leading contenders, he had secured the chairman's permission to have CSFB in the bank for a week to carry out due diligence in preparation for the issue. That, plus the work CSFB had carried out for Westpac earlier in the year, made it very familiar with the bank. Further, CSFB, backed by the balance sheet of its US parent, had made an underwriting offer that was a firm commitment of cash. Westpac would be assured of its $1.2 billion, with the underwriter then 'subbing' out the stock to sub-underwriters. A syndicate of, say, three smaller lead underwriters would have had to secure a spread of sub-underwriters before making a firm commitment. CSFB, well known in fixed-interest markets in Australia, was keen to lift its profile in underwriting equities. At a recent internal conference, CSFB management had been told unequivocally that it had to make underwriting a bank issue in Australia a primary objective; Australia was the only country where the CSFB group's name had not featured in a bank issue.

The appointment of CSFB caused considerable discontent among other potential underwriters who were critical of CSFB's approach. Several Westpac directors were concerned that getting the market offside was not an auspicious start to this crucial issue. The board had wanted local entities, with four or five players involved as joint underwriters to provide a more conventional structure which, they believed, would attract a greater spread of buyers and possibly wider support for the issue. But the bank's survival hinged on raising the capital and with CSFB Westpac had the money on the table. Many see that as Conroy's great gift to the bank. However, his victory over the board undoubtedly bruised his relationship with some directors.

Convincing them not so much of the need for an underwriter but of the wisdom of appointing CSFB had prolonged the June board meeting into a six-hour session including a long and bitter debate from which Conroy had emerged the winner. This was of considerable relief to management, and to the CSFB team which had been waiting for the nod to start subbing out the underwriting; anxious for an answer, they had become increasingly restless when the meeting broke for lunch without having reached a decision. CSFB finally got the go-ahead at 2.30 pm, and had the issue subbed out among 50 underwriters by 5.30 pm. For CSFB it had been a large but calculated risk. Westpac paid CSFB underwriting and co-ordinating fees of $16.5 million, out of which CSFB paid fees to sub-underwriters.

343

Why was the rights issue not underwritten from the outset? Partly because some of the board were startled at the notion that an underwriter was necessary for Westpac and partly because directors were paranoid about keeping the package (the write-offs, losses and the rights issue) confidential to avoid breaching ASC and stock-exchange disclosure requirements. Going out to the market to discuss a potential underwriting was out of the question because it would entail revealing details of Westpac's plans. Only a tight group within the bank knew the contents of the bombshell statement that was being constructed for 20 May. Management had alternative announcements drafted, depending on which way the board might decide. Overall, it was considered best to announce the loss and the proposed rights issue, let the market absorb the information, and consider the question of appointing an underwriter as soon as possible after that.

Within the bank, contingency plans had been made ahead of the announcements at the 20 May board meeting. The plans were not based on optimistic expectations. For example, Westpac's treasury arranged for wholesale funding to be available in case there was a run of panic withdrawals, and the bank made certain that there was plenty of cash at strategic branches, especially those near the major media outlets.

Speculation had been mounting and hints about the impending announcement of a rights issue were leaked in *The Australian* on the morning of 20 May. The Australian Stock Exchange, which had already queried Westpac's 1991 accounts, telephoned the bank just before the board meeting with a warning: if Westpac, as a listed company with obligations to comply with continuous disclosure, made a decision which the market was entitled to know about, the bank would have to make an immediate announcement or have its shares suspended. The prospect that it faced suspension of its shares, even for a matter of hours, was not attractive to

344

Westpac. Conroy rang Bernie Fraser at the Reserve Bank with an urgent request: Westpac needed support in keeping the ASX at bay. Westpac followed RBA advice and told the exchange in an interim announcement that while the position was not resolved, the matter of a rights issue was before the board and the market would be kept fully informed. That satisfied the ASX.

In the wake of the appointment of an underwriter, a due diligence committee was established, chaired by Westpac director Jock Harper with Warren Hogan as alternate chairman and including Westpac's secretary and legal counsel Reg Barrett. Other members were lawyers and auditors, investigating accountants and their legal advisers and US lawyers, because the rights issue was open in the US. Due diligence was a big process. The prospectus for the issue, drawn up under the 1991 Corporations Law, contained an unprecedented level of disclosure, driven in part by the demands of the US Securities and Exchange Commission, but chiefly by the revised requirements in Australia. It was a new experience for Westpac; before 1991 a prospectus was not required for a rights issue.

The backdrop to the share issue was darkening, with the sharemarket falling and taking the price of Westpac's shares with it. The sharemarket barometer, the ASX's All-Ordinaries index, fell from 1681 on 20 May to 1517 in August and by late September was 1485. Westpac's share price, $4 on 1 May, fell to $3.94 on 20 May and $3.20 in late July and continued to fall. ANZ's share price dipped from $4 in April to under $3 in September. The market's darling, NAB, hovered around $8. Adding to the gloom for Westpac, property analysts were revising earlier forecasts of when the property market might bottom and were now tipping a peak-to-trough fall in the Sydney CBD property market of some 54 per cent, considerably higher than the 29 per cent predicted a year earlier, with a recovery to

345

1989 levels unlikely before 2000. Melbourne was looking even bleaker.

Westpac was meanwhile rationalising and restructuring, trimming its European operations, departing from the eurobond market and selling the UK mortgage portfolio, and in the Americas division reviewing corporate banking relations with renewed emphasis on improving margins and profitability and reducing its level of assets. In July, as part of the plan to improve or close down non-profitable activities, Westpac slashed its European operations, closing the Paris branch which had opened only two years earlier. It also sold its 'strategic' holdings in Challenge Bank and in Advance Bank. To reinforce the message that Westpac was setting about fixing its problems, and to promote the rights issue, chairman Sir Eric Neal began granting more media interviews. A few days before Westpac's rights issue opened, Gavin Solomon, an activist Westpac shareholder and Sydney solicitor, spent $6,000 placing an advertisement in *The Sydney Morning Herald*, pointing out a 48 per cent drop in Westpac's share price since January 1990, the reduction in shareholders' funds following the write-offs and Westpac's request for new capital. 'It appears to me that Westpac shareholders have only two choices,' the text said. 'Either sell their shares (and why should they be forced to do that?) Or exercise their rights under the Westpac deed of settlement to rally at least 100 shareholders to call a special general meeting of shareholders to discuss these matters.' Solomon invited disaffected shareholders to contact him. He and a friend, investment banker Stephen Chapman, whose father was a longstanding Westpac shareholder, had devised a plan of action. Solomon emphasised in the advertisement's text that it was not a personal attack on board members, but said: 'Directors are entrusted to manage a company on behalf of shareholders.' There were overseas examples of directors taking accountability for a drop in a company's performance.

In 1991 the chairman of the UK's Midland Bank PLC, Sir Kit McMahon, resigned after the bank announced the first dividend cut by a major British bank in 50 years; earlier in 1992 shareholder dissatisfaction had forced the resignation of Sir John Quinton, chairman of another British clearer, Barclays Bank.

Westpac released the rights issue prospectus on Friday 31 July at a press conference attended by the chairman and several directors. It was a day of farce as well as tension. Westpac and Jones Lang Wootton had held lengthy discussions about the form of words to be used in the prospectus. The document was now finalised and awaiting signatures from the Westpac board when it was discovered that, despite the efforts of Reg Barrett, who had hounded JLW over previous days, a crucial JLW signature was still missing. The Westpac board was already assembled, pens poised, ready to sign off and now could not. A call to JLW elicited the information that the relevant person had gone to lunch and would not be back before 2.30 pm. An analysts' briefing and press conference scheduled for 12.30 pm had to be postponed until 2 pm. There was a further delay until 3 pm, by which time a roomful of media was growing restless and curious. The board was also still waiting. At 4 pm Westpac's media chief Graham Canning calmed the journalists by opening the bar. At 5.15 pm, when the JLW signature had finally been secured, the conference got under way. Conroy was furious at what he saw as a readily avoidable hitch created, in his view, by people who had failed to appreciate the urgency of the issue and who should have known better. It marred what was an important occasion for Westpac, given the enormous amount of work that had gone into preparing the prospectus. And once again the impression had been left that Westpac had bungled. Neal blamed an 'over-optimistic media unit' for the delay.

During the briefing, Neal and fellow director Jock Harper took the opportunity to emphasise the improvements that had been made in corporate governance in Westpac, with the appointment of board members to all main operating subsidiaries; for example, Warren Hogan had become chairman of Ord Minnett and Jock Harper chairman of Westpac Financial Services Group. This would help rectify a situation where, Neal said, certain subsidiaries of the bank did not have any direct links with the main board except through the profit reports provided by management. 'They were not reporting and being controlled as tightly as they should be,' he said.

In the prospectus, directors said the enormous half-year loss was 'a result of a decision to revalue all problem property assets to current market value', a stark contrast to the statement made only months earlier, in the 1991 annual report, that directors were satisfied that the valuation of the group's major property exposures were appropriate. The prospectus also cited 'other risks which will have a direct and potentially significant impact upon Westpac's future results ... [as] movements in property values and the resultant effects on proceeds of property realisations or variations in the credit loss provision; investment risk due to movements in the market value of Westpac's investments in listed shares; and movements in the actuarial surplus of its principal superannuation funds ...'

Conroy knew he had a challenge on his hands to change the perception of Westpac from an accident-prone, secretive and expedient organisation to one that was controlled, trustworthy and responsive. In an address to the Securities Institute in August 1992 he said that he was tackling these problems first and, possibly hardest of all, by 'standing up and accepting the criticisms ... and ... with large amounts of common sense and pragmatism, finding solutions to the problems'. Conroy also said that it was essential for Westpac's recovery that it reduce its problem asset portfolio; while these were now well provisioned by domestic and international standards, the problem portfolio was too large. And much of that related to property. Fifteen of Westpac's twenty largest problem loans, which totalled $3 billion in mid-1992, were to property developers. Its largest problem loan, $344 million, was to the diversified Adsteam/David Jones/Tooths group. Of the others, about $150 million was owed by Tugun Hospital, which ranked among the ten largest. So did Channel Ten, on which $150 million had been written off and a further $150 million was still owed. Herscu/Hooker accounted for close to $300 million. Westpac's exposure to Robert Maxwell was $130 million, and Macy's owed about the same.

Within weeks of the rights issue opening it was clear that it was not going well. There was no help from Westpac's share price, which by mid-August was below the rights price of $3. Solomon became vocal again, claiming support from 'hundreds' of shareholders for a board spill. The sharemarket in general was falling but the collapse in Westpac's share price was also blamed on some ill-willed offloading of the bank's shares. This put considerable pressure on the underwriters. When the market price of Westpac shares dipped below $3, at least one of the sub-underwriters expressed a desire to get out of its agreement. Many sub-underwriters, nervous of a shortfall, sold Westpac shares during the rights issue trading period to try to cover potential losses. The selling, plus speculation that Westpac had still not made sufficient provisions for its bad debts and was still guessing wrongly at the direction of the commercial property market, continued to push down the share price, virtually ensuring the issue's shortfall. Some analysts were critical of Westpac for its determination to pay a dividend at this point, arguably one of the worst moments in its history. James Capel Australia Ltd noted that Australian banks were facing their greatest problems since the 1890s and that Westpac's specific provisioning rate on non-accrual loans, at 44 per cent, was the highest of all the major banks and 'gives some comfort that Westpac is now facing up to its problems'. But National Australia Bank chief Don Argus inadvertently stirred the pot by publicly predicting that a second wave of property-related bad debts would hit the banking sector. It did not. NAB, less exposed than its peers before the property slump, had further reduced its exposure to commercial property.

During September 1992, Conroy undertook a roadshow in the US to help sell the share issue. He also flew to Chicago to attend the Westpac branch's ten-year anniversary. Given that the timing of his visit ran close to the annual International Monetary Fund and World Bank convention, held that year in Washington, Conroy had been enthusiastic about including that in his itinerary. It was his first chance to attend. However, that would have extended his absence from head office and the chairman believed that at the time, given the rights issue and the overhanging potential for bad and worse press, it was better to have the managing director at home to field questions. Solomon and his associate Chapman were constant and outspoken critics of the Westpac board and talk-back radio host Alan Jones was daily firing barbs at the bank. Conroy was also attempting to promote a $US250 million ($A340 million) subordinated debt raising in the euro-markets which would increase the bank's tier 2 capital. September 1992 went down in financial annals as a month of upheaval and wild trading in currencies, creating big gains for some and enormous losses for others. Amid growing apprehension over the Maastricht Treaty which formalised the European Monetary Union, European currencies and interest rates fluctuated dizzily. It was the worst kind of background for a debt issue. However, the bank ultimately raised $A500 million, indicating that US corporate investors were not troubled by the big hit Westpac had taken.

Late in September Westpac confirmed the appointment of management consultants McKinsey & Co as advisers in restructuring the bank, essentially to report on some initiatives suggested by Conroy. Andersen Consulting was already in AGC, reviewing how to cut costs and refine the business rather than strategy, which was McKinsey's specialty, but the announcement that they were now also to come under the McKinsey brief nonetheless left AGC staff speechless. Westpac's recovery plan incorporated the message that Conroy had been reiterating, externally as well as internally, for months and which centred on five points: forcefully reduce problem assets, refurbish retail banking to improve home-base earnings, improve or get out of under-performing businesses, plan future domestic growth and defer, or carefully consider, any international expansion. The bank established an asset management group, headed by Barry Robertson—some three years after it had first been suggested by an outside consultant that impaired loans should be quarantined and expertly managed. The issue had been debated internally for more than eighteen months before a decision was made to set up AMG. Some in the bank, and at board level, thought establishing a 'bad bank' would be an admission of defeat. After an unsuccessful advertising campaign for a head of AMG, Westpac appointed Robertson, its internal troubleshooter who headed an Australia-wide team of 140 at its peak, to work on the problems.

351

Debt collection: conduct unbecoming

Westpac's bad loans were quarantined into the asset management group which had a clear charter to manage and reduce major problem loans. A first step was to establish internal systems so that AMG could capture the extent of the problems. While the bank talked of working with customers to see them through their difficulties, to most of the clients in AMG it was a graveyard. What the customers had expected to be an exercise in loss minimisation appeared to them more as a single-minded determination by the bank to get its money back. With the departure late in 1991 of Iain Thompson, general manager corporate banking, who had overseen several big workouts with, it was considered, sensitivity, the bank seemed to have lost a voice of reason. To many of the customers in AMG, the bank appeared bloody-minded, bent on debt-collection, pressured by fear and obsessed with cutting problem assets rather than being guided by rational commercial considerations. They deemed it conduct unbecoming. Staff appeared traumatised by the uncertainties pervading the bank, to the point where the only course they could take safely was to say 'no'. Judgment was shunned, discretion not permitted; staff had a mechanical approach. If a loan proposal failed stringent criteria it would be rejected; some borrowers who got through were charged a punitive 5 per cent margin over the bank-bill rate of interest.

Many clients were dumbfounded by the bank's decision to put them into asset management; the decisions seemed to be made on the grounds that clients fell into what the bank deemed high-risk categories such as property or hotels, rather than on case-by-case assessments. While the bank claimed to be 'working with the clients', many felt that they were on opposing sides, with the bank showing little interest in helping a troubled customer get back on its feet.

In one instance, a longstanding business customer, owner/manager of his own business who had banked with Westpac for more than twenty years, found himself in asset management despite a faultless track record in meeting interest and principal repayments, operating a profitable business and holding a substantial cash deposit with the bank. Brown (a pseudonym) had recognised that the high interest rates of the late 1980s would be a pressure and he correctly identified further pressure on the hospitality sector, in which he operated, arising from the property crash. He advised the bank of his concerns. He attended an investment seminar held by the bank in late 1989 where a senior Westpac officer forecast that interest rates would rise. Influenced by this advice, Brown decided in 1990 to take a five-year, fixed-rate loan as protection against further interest-rate increases. Over the ensuing twelve months interest rates tumbled. In late 1991 he wrote to the bank, pointing out that, having followed their advice, he was now having to cope with a high fixed rate which was squeezing cashflow. He calculated that the difference between what he was paying under the fixed facility and the amount that would have been due at prevailing market rates ran into several thousand dollars a week. He felt that the bank, having given advice, should listen to the problem that had emerged and work with him to find a solution. The bank apparently did not agree with this point of view. The pressure of high interest rates had by then been compounded by the crash in property values, with values in the hospitality sector falling more sharply than in the rest of the property market. To alleviate financial pressure and repay debt, Brown sold several properties and he and his family moved into a one-bedroom unit in a property he owned, while he worked a 100-hour week in his business for nominal wages. Westpac had its head in the sand; it was to take two years of correspondence before the bank acknowledged Brown's problem.

Early in 1992, during a comprehensive revaluation of its property assets, Westpac slashed the valuation of Brown's property by nearly 50 per cent. Brown felt the bank's attitude reflected panic rather than commercial realism. Despite the bleak economic conditions, his business was trading well. However, the cut in its valuation meant that Brown was in a non-monetary breach of a loan covenant which stated that the loan could not exceed a certain percentage of valuation. This gave the bank considerable power.

Brown sought legal advice and the help of a banking consultant. He believed that, given the length of his relationship with the bank, the level at which he dealt and the profits of his business, he presented a reasonable case. But the bank had categorised him as a problem borrower. To emphasise its point, Westpac increased the interest margin it was charging him because of perceived higher risk. 'I engaged a lawyer and declared war,' Brown says. 'And Westpac made it very clear that you don't do that. Their attitude seemed to be: we are big, we have money and we'll keep litigating until you are broke.' By December 1992, because of the breach of loan covenant, Westpac had put Brown's loan into asset management. The business had still not defaulted on a single financial repayment and was trading positively.

Protracted discussions with the bank produced a solution of sorts: in March 1993 the bank agreed to allow Brown to break the expensive fixed-rate facility of several million dollars, which still had more than three years to run, although at a cost of more than $1 million to Brown. Westpac would lend further funds to cover this cost, which added to Brown's total debt. He felt he had no choice: if he did not pay the amount demanded to break the facility, Westpac could sell him up. It seemed to him that he was paying a penalty for being honest and alerting the bank to a potential problem, and that his profitable and successful business was being arbitrarily hurt. Further, in agreeing to a refinancing, Westpac insisted on an equity participation under which the bank would take one-third of the net proceeds of sale after full repayment of all money owed to it. The bank also insisted that, as part of the arrangement, a term insurance policy be taken over the customer, with Westpac as the beneficiary.

Brown had a surplus of assets over liabilities to repay the debt, even after the revaluation of his property portfolio. He could not avoid the suspicion that the bank, which was giving concessions to other, far more financially distressed customers, was cynically aware that, ultimately, it could sell him up and recoup all loan funds. The bank seemed unwilling to grasp the fact that its customer was a genuine businessman, trying to maintain the enterprise he had built up over twenty years. While fending off what appeared to him to be an unsympathetic, even vindictive, bank, where staff were mired in a culture of fear, he was endeavouring to run a business and maintain the morale of its staff. This last task was not made any easier by the bank's carelessness in sending highly confidential documents about financial negotiations to his business's general facsimile machine, where they were exposed to all eyes. Brown saw asset management as being not about rebuilding companies but about setting fires and grabbing whatever could be salvaged from the ashes for Westpac.

355

Brown was in asset management for some eighteen months, living, as he puts it, with Westpac controlling his life and appearing to be well aware of its power. He reflected occasionally that life might have been easier had he chosen to weather the high interest rate on the fixed facility. He would have been squeezed, but he could have coped, and a fight would not have arisen. Brown sold properties to pay out Westpac and then put his banking business out to tender. Five banks expressed interest. He quit Westpac in June 1995. 'Westpac had made me feel a failure and a loser,' he says. The hospitality industry improved, and his business went on to make greater profits.

Other customers with financial difficulties spoke of the 'culture of fear' that reigned at Westpac in the early 1990s. While other banks seemed prepared to help identify a problem and work with the customer to devise a solution palatable to both, Westpac appeared to be frozen in inactivity. Managers at several levels were terrified of making a wrong decision; it was more prudent, in their view, to make no decision at all. Customers knew that Westpac had problems but believed these were exacerbated by the bank itself. 'Its biggest problem was that the bank was gripped by total fear,' says one. 'And it panicked.'

Another instance involved a private (unlisted) but substantial company, ranked in the top 100 privately owned companies in Australia, employing several hundred people, which had a relationship with Westpac stretching over 30 or 40 years. The bank's approach to the company had been one of readily accommodating its needs and understanding the intricacies of its business. In the early 1990s that changed: the bank apparently became unable to grasp the company's finances and structure and was completely dismissive of the longstanding relationship.

356

A key factor in the mounting breakdown in communication was the different way that a private, as against a public, company runs its affairs. The private company often operates with a balance sheet that does not clearly reflect the current achievable value of its assets; it might write off an asset as rapidly as possible because that lowers the tax bill, or it might not write up the value of projects which are to be developed. Everything is held at the lowest possible value, whereas a public company tends to put forward the best possible interpretation of its performance for the benefit of shareholders and analysts. In 1992 the assets of this company were understated in its balance sheet by many millions. Another vital element in the company's deteriorating relationship with Westpac was that in the space of two years the company had seven different account managers—a costly burden, as each new manager had to be guided through its sites and its accounts and taught about the business. Increasingly, the company felt that it was dealing with account managers who misunderstood it, who perceived it as a highly geared company because the balance sheet did not fully reflect its wealth. Almost inevitably, one new account manager deemed the company a problem. It seemed to the customer that the Westpac staff were painfully conscious of the bank's weight of problem loans, and in such an environment no account manager was driven to defend a customer that might become a problem.

The customer received a phone call from a Westpac officer, saying that the company's account was being moved into a 'new division' which was being established with a view to giving superior service. This was the euphemistic description used for the new asset management group. A senior Westpac credit officer, who knew the company well, criticised the decision, saying it reflected a total lack of understanding of the company's accounts. As a placatory move, the company was promised a good loan manager, and one who would remain for at least two years. This it got. The manager confirmed that it had been a wrong decision to place the company in AMG; however, it remained there for three years. On being transferred out of AMG in 1996, the company lost the manager with whom it had developed an excellent relationship and months went by before it heard from its new manager.

While resentful of the move into AMG, the customer has nothing but praise for some of the talented people in that group. Its criticism of Westpac centres chiefly on three aspects: the bank's increasing tendency—and in this it is not alone—to treat customers as numbers rather than people, its constant 'restructuring' which results in loss of continuity as staff are peremptorily moved and replaced with others unfamiliar with a customer's business, and its apparent practice of favouring automatons rather than staff prepared to be accountable for their decisions.

Another business customer—an employer of a couple of thousand people—went through what he described as an

'expensive and terrible divorce' with Westpac after a relationship of more than ten years foundered in the bank's
asset management group. The company, already up to the
limit on its borrowings, needed bank guarantees to support
a large, new overseas project. Westpac would not provide
the support but fortunately the company, as is common, had
a relationship with another bank which proved a good ally.
However, the second bank required securities that were
already pledged with Westpac, which would not initially
release them. As others found, it was not easy to change
banks while in asset management but, fortunately, this company's existing alternative relationship cleared the way. The
move cost the company some $400,000 in legal charges and
stamp duty. Westpac lost a customer with complex, and
therefore lucrative, banking needs.

There were many dissatisfied customers who, when contacted, were trenchantly critical of Westpac's behaviour but
unwilling to elaborate for fear of repercussions. Westpac's
view is impossible to determine because the bank's policy
is not to discuss customer business. Westpac had lost business, big and small, some deliberately, some not, in the
name of shrinking the bank's assets to include only those
with an acceptable risk profile. In the process it had also
diminished its standing and acceptability in the corporate
community.

Packer circles

The miserable showing of Westpac's share price in September and October 1992 caught the eyes of a few bargain-
hunters, including Kerry Packer, who had been looking for
some time at buying into Westpac. He and Al Dunlap, Consolidated Press's chief operating officer, regarded Westpac
as big, fat and out of control, ripe for plucking. Packer
instructed Ord Minnett stockbroker Neville Miles to start

buying. Miles had worked with Packer on a number of projects, including Ords' underwriting of the float of Packer's Australian magazines earlier in the year. As a director of Ords, then a wholly owned subsidiary of Westpac, Miles took legal advice about the propriety of the association, but there was every likelihood that Packer's buying could salvage Westpac's share price. Over a period of weeks, Packer built up a position in the form of shares and options, gradually and quietly accumulating close to 5 per cent of the bank. This helped to keep a floor under Westpac's share price. Packer was keen to move to 10 per cent, the maximum permitted under the Banks (Shareholdings) Act and a level that would give him a say in what he viewed as a great asset that was being poorly managed.

Westpac's $1.2 billion rights issue closed on 23 September with an $883 million shortfall. Most of its 'proprietors' wanted nothing to do with it. Westpac got its money—CSFB and the sub-underwriters made up the difference—and pocketed $1.2 billion, after an outlay of $21.5 million in underwriting and coordinating fees, prospectus costs and fees to auditors, lawyers and an independent accounting firm. Without AMP's subscription for its entitlement as a 15 per cent shareholder—which had been a source of considerable comfort to the underwriters—the shortfall would have represented a rejection by more than 80 per cent of Westpac shareholders, even higher if Westpac directors' holdings were taken into account. In a final bid to offload some stock, CSFB on Thursday, 24 September, the day after the issue closed, held a one-day auction. It received no bids. The ASC was interested in how the shortfall was to be funded and immediately sent a request to CSFB for details of the sub-underwriters, to which the investment house responded that day. A Melbourne stockbroker, Trent Securities, closed its doors—not directly because of its involvement in the rights issue, but that was described as the last straw for the firm.

Speculation was growing about the extent of Packer's buying into the bank and his intentions. His acquiring stock had stabilised the share price—a reprieve for Westpac, just as the AMP's buying had provided much-needed capital in 1991. In the wake of the shortfall, coming on top of Westpac's earlier bad tidings, widespread media and shareholder calls continued for a board spill.

A crisis of confidence was mounting. The bank's share price hung obstinately under $3. Conroy was publicly vigorously defending the board and the chairman, although within the board there was a view that he was not sufficiently supportive of directors. Another view in the bank questioned why he should bother. Conroy felt hammered from all sides. Analysts were growing more and more critical of Neal's interventionist style. Conroy's public response was that given the serious nature of Westpac's problems, it was understandable that a chairman should be more involved than would otherwise be the case. Neal himself had previously defended his active role, saying: 'The increased emphasis on directors' responsibilities has caused most boards to take a more active interest in what is happening in their corporations than perhaps was the case in prior years.'

By the end of September 1992 rumours that Packer had bought 10 per cent of Westpac in return for two board seats were gathering such strength that Neal took the unusual step of issuing a denial, a response that was interpreted as evidence that this experienced boardroom player was becoming unnerved. In his statement, Neal pointed out that it was issued with the concurrence of Packer, with whom he had spoken that morning. Conroy also issued a statement that day, saying that clearly the bank was disappointed with the outcome of the rights issue, the absence of interest in the final auction and the level of the share price. He said that he was often asked if a bid for Westpac was looming. 'The bank's management and staff know that the threat is there.

We are doing our utmost on the one clear line of defence that we have, and that is our financial performance,' he said.

The bank's image was at its soiled worst. Discontent with the board continued to find a voice through the disgruntled Gavin Solomon, who pointed out that a board carries responsibility for a company's share price which, in Westpac's case, having hit a seven-year low of $2.40, was about half of its value in January 1990. However, Westpac offered the rumour-mill a crumb when it signalled that the board composition would be under review at the forthcoming board meeting. Five directors were due for retirement by normal rotation at the annual general meeting, which was to be brought forward from February to January. Behind the scenes, a decision had already been taken.

CHAPTER FOURTEEN

OUT OF AMERICA

Months of tension and speculation ended at the board meeting on 1 October 1992—coincidentally ten years to the day since the birth of Westpac Banking Corporation—when, in a day of high boardroom drama, Sir Eric Neal took responsibility for Westpac's stumblings and, with four other board members, resigned. They had taken the earliest opportunity after the end of Westpac's financial year and the close of the rights issue to make their *mea culpa* gesture. The directors, veterans of corporate and boardroom life, had never witnessed the like of this. Neal tendered his resignation shortly after the meeting opened. Those who left with him were deputy chairman Sir Neil Currie, Sir Harold Aston, Rod Cameron, chairman of the board audit committee, and Jim Scully, a board member since 1984—all identified as members of Neal's 'kitchen cabinet' and all members for several years of the AGC board. Sir Harold Aston had been an AGC board member since 1983, Rod Cameron since 1985, Jim Scully since October 1986, Currie and Neal since 1988. It has been suggested that at least two other directors should have taken the hint and fallen on their swords. The remaining eight non-executive directors and two executive directors voted into the chairmanship John Uhrig, a Westpac board member since 1989. Background manoeuvrings during the previous month had ensured that the nomination did not come as a surprise to Uhrig. Neal, on the other hand, was apparently rather taken aback by the degree of preparation that had evidently gone into settling on his successor. Long-standing board member Peter Baillieu in particular had been busy on the telephone, sounding out the likely reaction to a boardroom coup and to Neal's being replaced by Uhrig. Right up until the eleventh hour he was uncertain whether he had the numbers. But there was no coup: Neal anticipated the inevitable and quit.

The choice of Uhrig was generally popular in the investment community. Chairman of the mining giant CRA Ltd and deputy chairman of the Adelaide-based oil and gas group Santos, he was a down-to-earth, steely operator who had been chief of the Adelaide-based whitegoods group Simpson Holdings from 1975 to 1985, before it was taken over by Email Ltd. Uhrig had not been ambitious for the chairmanship of Westpac, but was persuaded into accepting it, largely by Sir James Balderstone, one of the two AMP Society directors on the Westpac board, who became deputy chairman.

No-one savoured what one director described as a thoroughly unpleasant day. Neal's supporters felt that, in chairing the bank through a uniquely traumatic period, he had heroically handled one of the most formidable tasks likely to confront any chairman. They saw his resignation as almost tragically symbolic—but necessary and inevitable. The shakeout would enable the bank to put its mistakes behind it and to start afresh. The bank's press statement said: 'The board accepts that recent events rightly involved questions of the traditional responsibilities of boards.'

The boardroom bloodletting was greeted positively by institutional shareholders and analysts anxious for evidence that Westpac was coming to grips with its problems. Within the bank, the release of tension was palpable; executives and staff felt they were facing, if not a sunny future, at least one in which they could see the way ahead.

The resignations and appointments, announced late morning, were the subject of a hurriedly arranged press conference held that afternoon. A solemn Graham Canning, head of external communications, introduced the new chairman and deputy chairman. Uhrig, presiding over his first media conference, opened by saying it had been a busy day at Westpac, and in many ways a sad one, with the bank losing five directors. 'I want to simply acknowledge that those people have done what they believe is best for the bank,' he said. 'They are to be admired for it and respected and we all do admire and respect them as honourable men.' He added that he would prefer to be asked questions about the future rather than the past, a fruitless suggestion, as he spent the following twenty minutes fielding a stream of questions about the day's events. He said the media had played a crucial role in adding to pressure on the board and appealed for Westpac to be given some 'elbow room', although he conceded that the pressure went beyond mere media criticism. 'To my knowledge, there has never been a case like this Westpac case, where there has been such pressure on a board of directors in any public company in Australia, ever,' said Uhrig. A first priority, said the new chairman, was for Westpac to improve its communications with its shareholders, the general public and depositors and all those taking an interest in the bank. Asked about his approach to the chairmanship, Uhrig responded that he had a 'simple view' of the role of chairman. 'The chief executive is captain and the chairman is the coach, providing counsel,' he said. 'The role of the board and of the chairman is to do what they can to make sure that the senior executive team is successful—not to do their job for them.'

The five departing directors did not attend the news conference. Questioned about their absence, Uhrig was blunt. 'That's their choice. They are free agents. They don't have to appear before you people any more. Perhaps they've decided that enough is enough. They don't owe the shareholders any further responsibility.'

Before he resigned, Neal had responded in writing to the chairman of the Australian Shareholders Association,

Brendan Birthistle, regarding four issues identified by the ASA as of particular concern: misleading information to Westpac shareholders in the 1991 annual report, Westpac's unrestrained asset growth, the surplus in the superannuation fund and failure to grant access to the share register. In recent months, Neal had been dogged by his statement in the 1991 annual report that 'there are signs that the worst of the bad debt experience may now be behind us'. Neal wrote to the ASA:

> These words were drafted by the management of the bank for inclusion in the annual report. The chairman's section of that report was reviewed by management, the chairman and the board. The directors did not change those particular words of the management of the bank. It is appropriate for me to express the view that, based upon the information provided by management to the board in the period leading up to the signing of the director's statement and the policy [of property provisioning] the non-executive directors would have had no reason to question the words referred to. You may therefore be assured that neither I, nor any of my fellow directors knowingly misled the bank's proprietors ... In conclusion, since I became chairman in late January 1989, my board colleagues and I have had the very unenviable task of resolving the many problems arising from the mid to late 80s and have devoted enormous effort to the task.

The knives had been out for Neal since earlier in the year. He had initially been seen as an architect of solutions for Westpac, but increasingly, as he became more interventionist, he came under more criticism. A Westpac executive told *The Australian*: 'He was the guiding force behind the bank.

And from about 1987, we suddenly became aware that he was taking a stronger role.' Neal is said to have got the board much more involved in management—'up to its elbows', according to one director, reflecting Neal's view that if the board is responsible, then it had better find out what is going on. And he clearly felt strongly that he had an obligation to respond to Westpac's problems. He revealed his attitude in Westpac's publication *Issues*: 'Previously, it was considered appropriate for directors to accept what they were told by management and only when things went bad would they seek to question further. But a lot of the recent court cases have asked directors why they didn't question management further, so I would say all directors now need to have in their make-up a healthy questioning and a healthy scepticism about things which may not seem quite right.'

He was not without his supporters. 'He's a bloody good bloke and doesn't deserve all this criticism,' a fellow director spluttered after Neal resigned. But he was more widely regarded as imperiously hands-on, an interventionist inclined to be dismissive of management but driven by a philosophy that all power is vested in the board. His comment in 1990, in a briefing to securities analysts, that 'as a non-banker I would hasten to say that the market-place for banking is like that for any other commodity, whether it be soft-drink, concrete or motor cars', also came back to haunt him. Banking is different from other industries because of the ever-present spectre of a run on deposits, and unrelenting outside criticism of the sort Westpac had endured could damage confidence and cause customers to walk away. Moreover, selling loans is not like selling bricks or soft-drinks. Sell a brick and you can forget about that particular brick, sell a loan and it keeps on occupying your attention until it is paid back. An industrial company monitors sales and growth; a bank must also monitor risk and maintain confidence.

Neal held obdurately to his belief that Westpac could have withstood the property downturn; his industrial experience had convinced him that business cycles can always be ridden out. Time has often shown this to be true. But an inescapable fact in Westpac's case was that the bank had been allowed to sink too far. It had been stonewalling for months as analysts called on it to recognise the depth and extent of its property problems, as credit-rating agencies punished it for not doing so and as shareholders and investors lost faith. The Reserve Bank had been quietly, and unavailingly, pressing Westpac to acknowledge its problems.

A week after resigning from the chairmanship of Westpac, Neal's short term as a director of the AMP Society ended. He had been one of two Westpac representatives appointed to the AMP board in April as part of the formalisation of the strategic alliance between the two companies. A proud man, he would have felt it a bitter blow to have a successful business career tainted by events at Westpac. But Neal did not stay down; he continued to hold board positions, including chairmanships of Metal Manufactures and of the private company Atlas Copco Australia Pty Ltd, as well as directorships of BHP and Coca-Cola Amatil Ltd, before resigning these in June 1996 when he was appointed governor of South Australia.

On 23 October the McKinsey consultants presented their strategy for Westpac's recovery at a management conference arranged by Conroy at the Ingleside training centre. With only one or two exceptions the board was in favour of McKinsey's approach, which added rigour and pace to management's recovery plan. About 30 people from Westpac senior management ranks were present and Conroy asked for their opinions. Several, including Derrick Heywood and Vern Harvey, were scathing, not of the objectives of the plan—management had already worked out what needed to be done—but of some of the methods and assumptions. However, many came away from the Ingleside conference with a clearer understanding of the magnitude of the task ahead. Westpac was on its knees. Then a further, unforeseen, hurdle arose.

About two weeks after John Uhrig became chairman, on 15 October, a matter came to light that was to unfold into a damaging drama for Westpac, at a time when the board and management were beginning to feel the bank had at last entered calmer waters. The first person in Australia to get word that a US tax accounting issue was crystallising as a problem was Malcolm Sandy, group financial controller, who was receiving daily profit updates from Westpac offices around the world. He discussed the issue with Heywood, who informed Conroy that there was a potentially significant tax problem in the Americas division. The tax issue had been noted earlier, in June, and was thought to have been resolved without any substantial impact on profit. This was apparently not the case. Conroy was preoccupied as he and Uhrig made the rounds of Sydney institutions, Conroy introducing the new chairman. Uhrig noticed that his managing director was unusually quiet.

Another board strategy conference had been planned for early November, at the Fairmont Resort in Leura, to review the proposed recovery plan. Westpac had gone through considerable pain, now the question was: where to next? On the day the conference was due to begin, 5 November—also the day of the monthly board meeting—Westpac made an announcement that again put its troubles into the headlines. The bank said that it had been obliged to set aside more than $100 million to cover a potential tax bill in the US.

Taxing problems

A fundamental difficulty was that, because of a quirk in US tax law, it was not possible to tax-effect interbranch transactions (that is, structure them to reduce tax). The issue of non-recognition of interbranch transactions had been bubbling since 1989, when it was raised with Westpac's external auditors in Australia, and had involved much correspondence between the Americas division and Westpac's group tax executives and chief financial officer in Sydney. It was a grey and untested area, where no-one was sure of the right path to take. Because of the uncertainties, further external advice was sought from tax experts and auditors in the US and Sydney.

The Institute of International Bankers in New York, of which Tony Walton was vice-chairman, had addressed the problem in an April 1991 paper submitted to the US Treasury and the Internal Revenue Service, and continued to raise the issue in meetings with Treasury and IRS staff. The institute noted:

> The key issue affecting international banks arises in the context of cross-border interbranch transactions. For example, a US branch of an international bank that has entered into an interest rate or currency swap with a customer will often enter into a cross-border interbranch swap, the terms of which mirror the terms of the swap with the customer. The US branch's counterparty in such a 'mirror' interbranch swap will often be the bank's head office or another branch responsible for managing worldwide swap risk. The result is that the US branch has hedged its position economically through the mirror interbranch swap, and the bank's head office will be in a position to hedge the bank's overall position.
>
> However, the IRS position is that US tax law does not recognise interbranch swaps or other interbranch transactions (although many countries treat branches

of American banks as separate entities). Accordingly, a US branch of an international bank that hedges its swap transactions in this way will be treated by the IRS as if it held an unhedged position for federal tax purposes, even though the US branch is fully hedged economically. As a result, the bank can have US taxable income far in excess of the bank's hedged economic income depending on the movements of interest or currency exchange rates. Likewise, depending on these market factors, a bank can generate a substantial tax loss in the United States, even though the bank has economic income on its hedged transaction.

The IRS has attempted to address the cross-border interbranch transactions arising from global trading operations by offering to enter into so-called 'advance pricing agreements' ... between the affected taxpayer, the IRS and the home country tax authority of the taxpayer.

The proposed advance pricing agreements were not acceptable to all tax authorities, though, so the problem was not solved. Mounting concern on the part of foreign banks operating in the US prompted the institute to hold a series of tax workshops to discuss steps for dealing with the issue. Walton's deputy, Gary Hett, said later: 'This was a very hot topic long before 1992. The institute had been on to this issue for a couple of years before that and the foreign banking community in the US was on to it. Internally, Westpac had been concerned about it and was trying to find some way through it. Tony had commissioned outside advisers to look at the matter so that whatever was available for Westpac to do, it could do, within ethical and legal boundaries. Against that background Westpac continued to do business in what it deemed to be the most prudent way, which was the way other foreign banks in the US were doing business.'

The advice Walton received involved assigning some swaps transactions to the London branch. In June 1992, about a year after the Americas division had assigned contracts to London, doubt was cast by outside advisers in the US on the tax-effect-iveness of the assignments. At that stage, though, the amounts involved were not large. Early in October 1992, after a further audit of the Americas division, additional potentially problem-atic transactions came to light. Westpac in the US concluded that the assignment of the contracts to London might not be recognised by the US tax regime (whose laws were written before the burst of activity in instruments such as swaps and did not specifically cover these transactions). In the second half of October some nineteen transactions came under doubt and the potential impact became far higher. Detailed analysis and investigation followed.

Back in Sydney, Westpac, while its rights issue was open in Australia and available to US shareholders, was critically sensitive to any development that might affect the profit and dividend projections in its prospectus. The bank was getting daily profit reports from Westpac offices around the world. If it significantly changed its year-end (30 September) profit and dividend projections from those outlined in the prospec-tus then the underwriters could have grounds to withdraw from the agreement.

The US tax matter had been recognised as an item to be considered during the due diligence investigation for the prospectus and in the period following its issue. Throughout that time, though, it had been treated as a modest amount which was not cause for alarm. When the due diligence process was terminated on 30 September there was no indi-cation that anything material was in the pipeline regarding US tax. In fact, the two issues that had been on the due diligence committee's 'watch list' and regularly reported on were the value of Westpac's ANZ shares and movements in the value of the bank's super fund surplus because any shift in such actuarially assessed surpluses is recognised as a credit or charge in the profit and loss account. There was no suggestion that US tax should be included on the watch list.

Extensive discussions took place during the second half of October about the tax matter. The Americas division, working with head office in Sydney, made an assessment of what taxes, interest and penalties might be payable. The potential worst-case liability was $US81.8 million. Hett says that the issue was quantified by the Americas division, under Walton's instructions, by an audit conducted in the US. 'That's how the full dimension of the potential problem was discovered,' he says. 'This was not unpaid tax. In a worst-case scenario, it was what taxes, interest and penalties might be. So what happened in mid-October 1992 was that after we had audited and scoped out the potential of the taxes, penalties and interest that might have to be paid, we went to our tax advisers and they recommended to us and to head office that, given the circumstances, a provision of $US15–25 million be made. They fervently believed that over the course of the next three to five years, no more than that would need to be paid.'

Based on the advice received in the US, Walton and Hett supported a recommendation that Westpac make a provision of between $US15 and $US25 million for the tax potentially owed. Derrick Heywood flew to New York for a meeting on 26 October with Walton and Hett and the bank's US tax advisers, the law firm Debevoise and Plimpton. He was adamant that Westpac's practice, in line with Australian disclosure requirements, was to provide fully for an amount in dispute and later, if the result were favourable, to make a write-back. He pointed out that Westpac had no wish to risk under-providing and then be forced, at a future time, to tell shareholders that it had to make another provision.

At a meeting in Sydney on the evening of Monday, 2 November, ahead of a scheduled meeting of Westpac's audit committee, a lengthy discussion focused on the appropriate amount of a provision, with the Americas division supporting the lesser amount its advisers had recommended and Westpac management proposing that the bank provide for the full amount. The full potential liability included a forward estimate of tax to be paid by the Americas division of around $A26 million but a substantial proportion of the remainder represented penalties that might never be imposed. The matter was again debated on the following day in the audit committee meeting, chaired by director Warren Hogan. It was Hogan's first audit committee meeting; he had been appointed chairman to replace Rod Cameron, one of the five directors who had resigned a month earlier. Hogan recalls that the meeting, held in Westpac's boardroom, was attended by eighteen people and included lawyers and accountants from New York as well as from Sydney. Issues stemming from the tax problem, such as responsibility, implications and amounts, were discussed for hours, in preparation for the matter to be taken to the forthcoming board meeting. Hogan recalls that Westpac management was firm in its rejection of the suggestion that the bank should provide for a lesser amount.

Having been joint chairman with fellow board member Jock Harper of the due diligence committee for the capital raising, Hogan was highly sensitive to any further provisions arising from the US tax matter. The stance of senior head office management on the scale of the provision was expressed firmly and repeatedly, despite the strong possibility of successful negotiations on the so-called pricing agreement and the substantial component of penalties and interest charges in the additional sum provided. After much discussion over two days, head office management secured the support of the auditors and other advisers for the maximum provision.

Walton, in Australia for the 5 November board meeting, asked Westpac chairman John Uhrig to meet him that morning. Both were staying at the Wentworth Hotel in Sydney and they met for breakfast and discussed the US tax question. Walton asked Uhrig to read the statement which he proposed to submit to the board during the day's meeting. The statement discussed the tax matter and contained Walton's offer to resign over the issue if necessary, although the statement also set out to establish that he was not personally at fault. Uhrig listened to what Walton said, read what he had written, and said it was a matter for the board to decide. Uhrig believed that he gave no indication of his views. However, Walton left that meeting reasonably confident that he had Uhrig's support. Uhrig believed that Walton was not to blame. In fact, says Uhrig, investigations found that no particular person was fully responsible for the outcome and there had been no wilful or deceptive conduct on anybody's part. He adds: 'One has to agree, though, that it was fairly unfortunate timing, coming after the rights issue and the resignation of five directors.'

A peculiarity of Westpac's deed of settlement is that no person can resign from being a director unless he or she does so in writing to the chairman and unless the resignation is accepted by the board. Walton had given the matter a great deal of thought during the previous night and considered the realities of his position: his second five-year contract would expire in the first quarter of 1993. He knew about the bank's property loans situation in Australia and about the McKinsey recommendations for shrinking assets and focusing on core business, so he essentially knew what the recommendation would be for the international business he headed—it would have to be significantly contracted. And, he says, since the tax mishap occurred under his watch, he felt it appropriate to take some heat on the issue. Walton read his prepared statement to the board, then left the room. After a discussion which took some time, Uhrig emerged and informed him that his resignation had been accepted. Walton's directorship ended.

Westpac's head office made a provision for the maximum potential liability, $US81.8 million ($A113.6 million, subsequently reduced to $106 million). The bank issued a press release outlining the tax issue and forecasting a reduced final dividend, possibly as low as six cents for the year to September 1992. 'The 12 cent dividend previously foreshadowed is no longer possible in light of a projected reduction in operating profit for the second half due to the emergence of an unanticipated year-end tax charge,' the bank stated. According to the press release, operating profit after tax was in line with earlier expectations, despite having to absorb a $77 million write-down in the value of its ANZ shares and a $90 million write-down following adverse movements in the actuarial value of the staff super fund surpluses. The impact of the US tax provision halved the financial result for the second half of 1992 from $210 million after tax to $104 million. Directors were said to have considered wholly eliminating the dividend, such was the psychological impact of the tax problem.

Westpac said:

> Although Westpac has effectively hedged [interest rate and currency] risks on a pre-tax basis, it is not able for US tax purposes (in contrast to the tax laws of other jurisdictions) to recognise gain or loss arising from transactions between its branches, although such gain or loss is recognised for transactions with customers ... The increase in tax liability relates to an area of US tax law that is not clearly defined and results from a reassessment of the appropriate treatment of interbranch transfers of

customer swaps and a review of transactions that might be subject to such treatment. Westpac is implementing changes in its interbranch hedging of global trading of swaps and foreign currency forward contracts to minimise future imbalance between different tax jurisdictions. Mr Anthony J. Walton, chief general manager, Americas and Europe group and a director of the bank, informed the board that he had relied on assurances from his senior management that all tax matters had been or were being addressed. He also said that, if the board wished, he would offer to leave. The board has asked Mr Walton to continue in his executive position into the first quarter of 1993 to work out an orderly transition. It has also accepted his resignation as a director and acknowledged his outstanding contribution to the bank.

According to a letter written on 16 November 1992 to Westpac's head office by Debevoise and Plimpton:

Westpac need not take a defensive attitude. Westpac's problems resulted from the fact that the US tax system is out of step with the tax regimes in other major countries in that the US does not recognise interbranch transactions.

The steps that Westpac took to ameliorate the harsh results of paying US taxes on far more than true economic income were reasonable attempts to correct this unfortunate situation. While its efforts might have been misguided, they were good faith efforts to bring US taxable income in line with true business income without any intent to disregard rules or regulations ... We believe that there is a good likelihood that Westpac will not have to pay the full amount of tax, penalties and interest that are being reserved.

Says Hett: 'There was a general market misperception in Australia, almost instantaneously, that Westpac, through the Americas division, had failed to pay all these taxes due and somehow at the last minute was making this huge tax payment. That was wrong. The bank did not fail to pay taxes, the bank did not make a huge tax payment, the bank made a worst-case tax provision.'

Walton adds: 'This topic was not one where we in the US were hiding anything. We had found it out ourselves, we were in direct dialogue with Sydney head office on this topic.' Hett says: 'The fickle finger of blame was not being spun here in the Americas division, because we were aware of the market perception of this problem, we were aware of what the institute was doing on this issue, we were aware that an exception had already been made in that an advance pricing agreement had been granted in at least one if not two cases, eg, for organisations to get around this issue in what was then the legal way to do it, with the IRS sanction.' John Brodie, Westpac's head of group taxation in Sydney, flew to the US to work as chief financial officer of the Americas division during 1993. Brodie succeeded in negotiating a resolution with the US and Australian revenue authorities in which Westpac's global profits from financial markets transactions were apportioned in a way that reflected the economic activity in each jurisdiction and eliminated the anomalies that gave rise to the tax accounting issue. Brodie also had a large hand in getting the amount of provision and payment back to a reasonable level, a process that took two years.

In 1995 Westpac wrote back $67 million, leaving the amount owed at $A39 million or around $US28 million. Recovery of the funds rated no more than a small-print mention in the 1995 and 1996 annual reports to the effect that the $67 million write-back of a $106 million tax provision followed settlement of prior years' US tax issues with the IRS. Shareholders might have been interested to read greater detail of how the bank had recouped $67 million. Says Walton: 'After recoveries, the actual amount was close to the recommendation that was made and disregarded.'

For a number of reasons—the disappointing rights issue, earlier image problems, unprecedented losses and write-offs, upheavals at board level—Westpac in 1992 had been determined to close the door on the US troubles. Hett says Westpac made the wrong decision, because of 'those reasons'. Moreover, the issue involved boardroom politics and personalities. By November 1992 Walton, regarded as something of a favourite of former chairman Sir Eric Neal, had lost some, though far from all, of his support around the board table. And Frank Conroy, who had earlier respected Walton's energy and drive, and his ability to build and hold a good team, had cooled towards him. The Americas division was destined to fall under the axe as Westpac strove to shrink assets and cut costs, and it was easier to dismantle the division without, rather than with, the presence of the man who had built it.

John Uhrig explains the significance of the position Westpac was in at that time. 'We felt that the tax matter could have been the straw that broke the camel's back,' he says:

> I won't reveal what I said when told about it but obviously I was shocked because I thought we were starting with a clean slate. We thought the dramas were behind us. It might be not unreasonable that for an organisation that had come to find itself in this position to feel that it was time to set signals regarding taking responsibility. The signal had to go to

everyone that things at Westpac are not going to be this way again. There is no sense in which Tony was personally responsible, other than that he was responsible for everything that happened in Westpac's business in the US. That was the signal that needed to be sent to everybody, that when you are responsible you must accept what responsibility means. The statement had to be made.

Uhrig agrees that it is understandable that those in the US would see the problem differently. But they did not have to face the shareholders. 'I'm not saying they were wrong, but they had a luxury Westpac at the time could not afford. On its own, the tax matter was no more than a business problem, but added to everything else that Westpac had endured, it was a big problem. Today, in 1997, with the bank stronger, it would be a hiccup but when it occurred, in the full context of the time, it was anything but.' A common comment was that if a potential tax liability in the US had been flagged in May, when Westpac was making a clean breast of its problems, it would have rated far less interest. Now Westpac had to confess to yet another sin.

379

Had Westpac known the full extent of the tax problem while the rights issue prospectus was open, it would have been required to issue a supplementary prospectus, which could have been a trigger for CSFB to terminate the underwriting agreement, throwing doubt on Westpac's ability to raise the required funds and possibly invoking an immediate reaction from the Reserve Bank. As it was, Westpac—acutely conscious of the significance of the announcement of an unexpected tax provision on the heels of the closure of an issue backed by a prospectus that talked of a 12-cent dividend that was now in doubt—informed the Australian Securities Commission by phone and fax immediately. The ASC shortly afterwards announced that it intended to re-open its post-prospectus review, which subsequently grew into a full-scale ASC investigation in which Westpac cooperated, providing the ASC with thousands of pages of documentation. Westpac conducted its own internal investigation, handled by Minter Ellison and headed by Professor Bob Austin, who had joined the legal firm after a career as a high-profile accounting academic. Minter Ellison sent a team to New York while Debevoise and Plimpton sent investigators to Sydney. Between the two groups 60 people were interviewed to establish the facts, then each gave advice. Everything Westpac's investigators discovered was shared with the ASC. Adding to pressure on Westpac, Ian Salmon, managing director of the bank's largest shareholder, the AMP Society, said that Westpac had six months to get its affairs in order. And it was 1994 before Westpac received notice from the ASC that no further action would be taken regarding the US tax matter.

Hett says the tax topic was a flashpoint for the foreign banking community in the US:

> The upshot was that Westpac made a business decision that was excessive. There was an element of senior head office management and boardroom panic. Moreover, the decision was reviled in the US market which deemed it stupid and excessive. As it turns out, through the good work of John Brodie and people in the Americas division, it was proven to be all those things because in a shorter period Westpac spent the amount that the US tax advisers said it would have to, by going through the proper channels and pointing out the ludicrousness of this entire arrangement. We shot ourselves in the foot then we wondered why we were in pain. I look back on that now and say, why was that?

380

From the time Westpac revealed its approach to the tax problem, Walton's and Hett's phones were ringing constantly with calls from foreign banking counterparts in the US market asking: 'What the hell did you guys do?' Many foreign banks had similar problems but Westpac was the only one that treated it this way. Other banks had exposures many times the amount involved at Westpac. Some said they had the same problem but told Hett they would go to the US Secretary of the Treasury before doing anything like Westpac had done because it did not make sense. Their view was, says Hett: 'The tax law is wrong. Why provision at the extreme end based on a tax law that doesn't make sense?'

Hett concedes he becomes passionate about this topic, partly because he was so involved, partly because of the provision level taken and because the subsequent recovery of funds was almost ignored. He well remembers 5 November, after a long night on the telephone from Sydney to New York, with no sleep. 'The Americas division went into shock,' he says. 'They were hearing reports that Frank Conroy and Derrick Heywood were fighting off a media feeding frenzy.' In Hett's view, the Australian media did not understand what they were being told; it was not made sufficiently clear that a provision, not a payment, was being made. The issue made headlines: 'Another day, another disaster', 'Tax shock rocks Westpac', 'Another Westpac bomb', 'Accident-prone Westpac'. Conroy said at the time: 'I can't explain too strongly how disappointing this is for the board and the bank.' A note of realism came from Perth businessman Kerry Stokes, a sub-underwriter to the rights issue: 'This is unfortunate ... but the $115 million involved is not a huge amount in terms of the bank's asset base, it's more the psychology of the thing as the market is pouncing on bad news.' Yet the timing made the issue crucial, particularly given the events that followed the

381

announcement of the tax problem—an immediate further dip in Westpac's share price, to a seven-year low of $2.40, prompting Kerry Packer to lift his stake in the bank, and ultimately a change in top management.

Staff in the Americas division were hurt by the way the tax issue was presented and handled. Apart from Walton's resignation, two others departed from the Americas division over the issue. Conroy, in the US for a roadshow in September 1992 to promote the rights issue, had visited the Chicago branch on 16 September to participate in its tenth anniversary. On the following day he called on major customers, even helping the branch win a large deal against competition from major US and foreign banks. That evening, by this stage joined by his wife, Jan, he attended a cocktail party for some 300 guests in Westpac's Chicago office and topped off the day with dinner with Walton and Barry Bint and his executive team. On the next day, Conroy flew to Detroit by private jet to call on other customers before leaving that night for Australia. Conroy was uneasy about the timing of the visit. He knew that a major contraction of Westpac's balance sheet was to be undertaken, although at that stage the details had not been finalised. Later, staff in the Americas division were left to wonder whether, as they celebrated, the wheels had already been set in motion for the dismantling of their business. That left more than just a bad taste.

Following the McKinsey review of Westpac and the advice that the bank had to shrink to recover, the Americas division was recognised as one of the options Westpac had to raise internal capital. Westpac's view was that while the Americas division had in many years far exceeded plan, the returns were still thin; the division had incurred few major losses, thanks to Walton's ruthless approach to credit, but the bottom line was that while positive returns were being generated, they were providing an insufficient return on capital at a time when Westpac needed to maximise every cent it used.

'What happened to the Americas division was in no way a reaction to, or punishment for, the tax issue,' says Hett. 'That is another bit of incorrect conventional wisdom. The Americas division was substantially reduced because McKinsey & Co said the bank needed to raise internal capital and the US was one of the few places where Westpac had a sufficiently healthy and substantial book, in a market where it could be done without exacerbating the bank's already poor position.' Also, in reviewing the performance of the Americas division, the following were taken into account: it was expensive; the last year's results had suffered as New York, in response to Sydney head office directives, made write-offs for the Macy's and Olympia & York loans as part of Westpac's large provisioning in 1992; and the Americas division shared the impact of Westpac's credit-rating being downgraded through having to pay higher interest rates—a cost of several million dollars a year.

383

Owen van der Wall was put in charge of cutting back the Americas division; he was the facilitator and Hett, who took charge after Walton's departure, was the executor, reporting to van der Wall. None of the team enjoyed the task but each had a job to do. Van der Wall travelled to the US in December 1992, to deliver the news that the biggest Australian bank in the US, and one of the country's largest foreign banks— whose assets stood at $US9.2 billion compared with the $600 million when Walton joined—was to be shrunk. The task was especially painful for van der Wall, who had worked in the division during the dynamic growth years of the 1980s. For Hett, who had worked closely with Walton in building the division, dismantling it was a dismal task. A projection by McKinsey had expressed a concern that shrinking the Americas division, moving nearly $US10 billion in assets, could cost 10 per cent of the face value in discount, or as much as $US1 billion; in fact, it cost $US60 million between 1993 and 1996. And a substantial part of the loan portfolio was sold to Canada's Toronto Dominion Bank in a single transaction, at par, which freed up around $A4 billion in risk-adjusted capital. Says Hett: 'The other banks in the US knew the quality of Westpac's portfolio, and saw this as a tremendous opportunity to leverage into relationships by buying Westpac's book. Westpac had good penetration in the US market. Also, the timing was in Westpac's favour: it was one of the first foreign banks to sell assets because of a repositioning strategy, so there was appetite.'

Out of the 500 or so staff, Westpac retained about 65 in the US, mostly in the New York-based financial markets division, still an essential part of the bank's international network. On an earnings and risk basis, a strong case could have been made for retaining Westpac's businesses in Chicago, particularly with the utilities but, in 1992, Westpac's focus was on its home base and on lifting returns to survive. Any business that did not fit with the strategy of repositioning and recovery was eliminated. Says Walton, who left the bank in March 1993:

384

> The people in Westpac's Americas division can all be justifiably proud of what they had achieved. It was a professional organisation, operating in a highly competitive environment at a time when many foreign banks faltered. The division consistently surpassed the performance measurements asked of it and stacked up well against its US-based peers. Most relevant, though, the division made an important profit and cultural contribution to the bank during a critical period in its history. It was a tightly knit group of individuals who, years later, remain in close touch.

Walton adds that, from a personal perspective, he looks back on his ten years at Westpac as the most professionally and personally satisfying of his career. 'Enduring friendships developed in the US and Australia for myself and my family,' he says. 'That being said, despite the record over the years, the lack of management support in the latter months of 1992 has always baffled me. Nonetheless, years later, a feeling of great personal pride remains in what the division accomplished.'

As for the criticism of Walton, Hett believes that both Walton and the Americas division fell victim to the Australian 'tall poppy syndrome'. He says: 'Many were jealous of the success of the Americas division, of the attention it was getting from the board and some senior management, and perhaps they were jealous of Tony as an individual because he's a smart, charismatic leader.'

CHAPTER FIFTEEN

BOARD GAMES

On Thursday 5 November—Guy Fawkes Day—the fuse continued to sputter towards the series of potential bombshells that were tormenting Westpac. Reg Barrett, the bank's legal counsel, spent most of it on the telephone, as he was to spend the next few days, talking to the Australian Stock Exchange, the Australian Securities Commission and Westpac's lawyers in the US. If litigation were to arise, it was thought more likely to come from the US than Australia. No writs emerged. Conroy and Heywood remained in Sydney to explain the dauntingly technical nature of the US tax problem to analysts and media, not arriving at the board strategy conference held at the Fairmont Resort in Leura until 10 pm. On the way, Conroy called CSFB, underwriters to the rights issue, to brief them on the tax question. It was a tense conversation. The other Westpac directors and executives had been at Leura since 5 pm. After dinner, a presentation about the new advertising agency had been shown—DMB & B/Weekes Morris Osborn had won the coveted $20 million Westpac account in a decision that ended three months of deliberations—but the board was restless, knowing that Westpac had a bigger problem on its hands. About halfway through the DMB presentation one board member demanded to know why they were watching this when more important issues demanded attention. Westpac's share price had plummeted to a new low. The tone of the media coverage suggested that the bank's name had become a byword for bungle.

Westpac's announcement of a large US tax provision eclipsed a revelation from the ANZ Banking Group that it had to pay $250 million to India's National Housing Bank to cover irregularities in government securities trading by its Indian subsidiary, ANZ Grindlays. This followed an earlier instruction from the Reserve Bank of India to ANZ Grindlays to make a provision to cover potential liabilities stemming from a transaction with Harshad Mehta, a Bombay stockbroker at the heart of the scandal. Two small Indian banks and several foreign banks were also involved. Westpac's media relations unit, coping with yet another frenzy of adverse publicity, sourly reflected that ANZ should have sent them a bouquet.

Before he arrived at Leura the absent Conroy came under fire, even though the board knew that he had organised the advertisers' presentation long before the tax crisis blew up. But he and management were on the back foot from then. For some weeks there had been speculation that Conroy would not last the distance. He had been under pressure for most of his short tenure at the top of Westpac and fate now seemed to be closing in on him. The mood at this conference was particularly black; Conroy had persuaded the board into a series of decisions during the year and the board wanted to know when it would see results. Its confidence in management, tested many times in the recent past, had hit a low point. The board also knew that it was going to have to face a difficult annual general meeting. No board member was comfortable in November 1992.

McKinsey's presentation absorbed most of the following day. John Uhrig, only a month into his chairmanship and running his first strategy conference, was very much in charge. After lunch on the Saturday, Conroy's top team was told their further presence was not required while the managing director explained a new executive structure. They spent the afternoon at golf. McKinsey's plan, which had been devised with Conroy, with its recommendations regarding downsizing the Americas division and other overseas activities, was accepted. The board was acting with a renewed sense of urgency. Chairman John Uhrig knew Westpac had to show results.

Conroy, too, was by now concerned about the pace of change; it was a year since he had announced a restructuring and he felt that progress was not as advanced as it should have been. Westpac's underlying profitability was satisfactory but the retail franchise was not managed tightly enough. Moreover, it had been wounded by the 'Westpac letters' revelations and a series of silly blunders that alienated customers, such as wrongly charging stamp duty on secured personal loans, which had forced Westpac to refund thousands of dollars to NSW customers, and earlier breaches of the Credit Act. Some deposits and some customers had been lost. Key points in the McKinsey plan were that Westpac had to reduce head-office costs and cut assets. Conroy expected, and got, resistance to this from some executives. McKinsey in particular drove home the message that head office had to be further pared back, with the head-office staff of 1,100 cut by up to 60 per cent, and that would entail drastic reductions in the economics and strategy units. The consultants were expensive, but persistent and persuasive. One expert, finding a Westpac executive resistant to cuts, said: 'We're not talking about whether the swimming pool is at the back of the house or at the front of the house. There is no swimming pool.' In the hope of gaining reassurance that his strategy was on track, Conroy took up an invitation from Al Dunlap at Consolidated Press (a long-standing Westpac client) to have a chat. 'Chainsaw' Dunlap owed his nickname to his ruthless approach to corporate downsizings to lift efficiencies. Listening to the expert—who had prepared for the meeting, with typed notes in front of him—Conroy was comforted by the knowledge that Westpac was doing everything Dunlap recommended. He could later report to Uhrig that Westpac was on the right path.

On 10 November Conroy, keen to win back investor confidence, announced a management restructure and the five-point recovery plan approved by the board at its meeting a few days earlier. The plan centred on slashing at least $10 billion in corporate loans from the bank's balance sheet by reducing assets in the US, Europe and Japan, cutting $300 million out of costs and boosting revenues, reducing staff and getting out of non-performing businesses. Westpac now had an ambitious target of cutting its cost-to-income ratio from 70 per cent to 58 per cent by 1995—a level, Conroy pointed out, that NAB had been achieving for years. Overseas, the bank would withdraw from corporate lending and instead focus on niche global financial markets centred in London, Tokyo, New York, Hong Kong and Singapore. More jobs would go as staff, already 7,000 down from the May 1990 peak of 46,600, was cut further. Westpac would restructure French Polynesian and New Caledonian branches, three years after it had paid $120 million to Banque Indosuez to acquire the business that propelled it to the position of the largest bank in the South Pacific. Branch networks and staff in the loss-producing businesses would be cut.

Conroy was outlining a new culture for Westpac. He said the bank was prepared to fall behind its three chief rivals if that was necessary to restore performance and dividends. Westpac's share price had clawed back to $2.67 but Conroy admitted that its level, a seven-year low, left the bank vulnerable to takeover. However, as one of the four major banks, Westpac was protected by restrictions in the government's competition policy. The management restructure placed Westpac in the hands of five group executives, reporting directly to the managing director and, unlike the earlier executive committee under Bob White and Stuart Fowler, sitting in on board meetings. The five were: David Morgan as head of retail, with a brief to accelerate change; Owen van der Wall, head of an enlarged institutional banking group encompassing corporate banking and financial markets operations in Australia, Europe, the US, Japan, Hong Kong and Singapore; Barry Robertson, head of asset management, the work-out group formed in September to manage and dispose of all problem exposures of more than $5 million; Derrick Heywood as chief financial officer; and Keith Brown as head of human resources.

A week later, Westpac announced its annual results. Shareholders who gagged at a full-year loss of $1.56 billion might have been comforted by a modest second-half profit of $104 million, which included good performances in Asia and New Zealand. The charge for bad and doubtful debts was lower, mostly because of a reversal of provisions made in the first half which were no longer required. The final dividend was cut, as forecast, to 6 cents a share. Westpac's results compared with a loss of $579 million for ANZ in the year to 30 September, and a $675 million profit for National Australia Bank.

On 26 November it was revealed that, over previous weeks, Kerry Packer had secured a strategic stake in Westpac. Packer had seized his chance when the bank's share price sank to a seven-year low of $2.40 in the wake of the revelations of Westpac's tax problems in the US. From Argentina, where he was playing polo, Packer had rung stockbroker Neville Miles in the middle of the night with instructions to build his stake in the bank. It was no secret who were unwilling holders of Westpac stock. Miles began buying both shares and call options over enough stock to bring Consolidated Press Holdings a 10 per cent stake in Westpac. Packer's stake cost him $500 million. His buying activity had lifted Westpac's share price from its low point to around $3 by late November, as disaffected holders

offloaded their stock. John Uhrig publicly welcomed Packer's presence on Westpac's share register, saying it showed
that Packer, an astute investor, had confidence in the bank's
long-term future.

Packer had bought well but at that stage had no detailed
plan of action. He was convinced, though, that Westpac's
recovery plan was not ambitious enough or swift enough.
His lieutenant, Al Dunlap, got things moving. Having earlier
turned around Packer's engineering group Australian
National Industries, Dunlap knew what Westpac needed:
lower costs, less staff. He flew in his own team of advisers
from the US, selected from the Wall Street investment bank
Salomon Brothers and accounting firm Coopers & Lybrand,
and secreted them at a Sydney city hotel to devise a plan of
action. Packer's confidantes, Miles and corporate lawyer
David Gonski, were sidelined. Dunlap had taken charge, and
was to take the strategy headlong in the wrong direction.

391

During November, Packer rang Uhrig to sound him out about
board seats for himself and Dunlap. Uhrig's view was that
Westpac ought to be fostering a good relationship with a
shareholder of such significance and he encouraged the
board to invite Packer and Dunlap to become directors. Early
in December Westpac announced that Packer and Dunlap
were joining the board, although they could not formally take
their seats until Westpac had completed the sale of Channel
Ten to CanWest (because of conflict of ownership, with
Packer owning the Nine network). Peter Ritchie, chairman
and managing director of the fast food chain McDonald's
Australia, was also confirmed as a director, with his appointment, too, subject to Westpac's selling Channel Ten, because
Ritchie was a director of the competing Channel Seven. The
three new appointees would have to stand for election at the
bank's annual general meeting, scheduled for 19 January,
and, assuming their success, would bring Westpac the

desired board complement of nine. Critics of the bank, Gavin Solomon and his associate Stephen Chapman, welcomed the new appointments because they would bring to the board 'successful and experienced individuals from service and customer-oriented industries'. Ritchie, one of the first appointments to fill the gap left by the resignations on 1 October, was a marketing enthusiast who had put the Big Mac on the map in Australia. A commerce graduate and trained accountant, he brought nineteen years' experience as head of Australia's largest franchise and a strong background in the services industry. Dunlap had restored Australian National Industries into profit through asset sales, then rationalised Packer's sprawling and debt-burdened empire by cutting Channel Nine's costs and generally refocusing Consolidated Press on its core media business. Dunlap set about his tasks with cold-blooded efficiency; the overhaul of Consolidated Press had led to the axing of more than one of Packer's longstanding relationships. Packer let Dunlap have his head. Despite his intimate knowledge of Consolidated Press, having grown up with the business he inherited from his father, publishing veteran Sir Frank Packer, when circumstances called for a radical revamp he had no hesitation in calling in the man whom British businessman Sir James Goldsmith described as 'Rambo in pinstripes'.

Packer, returned from his polo trip to Argentina, and having spent $500 million in a raid that netted him 10 per cent of Westpac at an average cost of about $2.75 a share, visited Uhrig during the afternoon of Wednesday 16 December. Uhrig said that the board was happy for Packer and Dunlap to attend the following day's meeting as observers. Conroy later asked Uhrig whether Packer had indicated he wanted the managing director's resignation. Uhrig said that was not the case, although Packer had been critical of management and had said that many changes had to be made. In fact Packer had rung Conroy from Argentina a few weeks earlier to say that there was no machiavellian manoeuvre behind his buying shares in Westpac. Uhrig told Conroy that Packer and Dunlap were serious about action and would want to talk to the board on the following morning, initially without Conroy's presence.

On the morning of 17 December Packer and Dunlap joined most of the board in the 28th floor boardroom. Ahead of the meeting's scheduled 9 am start, Conroy walked into the boardroom where everyone had assembled to wish Packer a happy 55th birthday. Conroy, who knew Packer as a client, shared in the greetings. Then he left the room. Urhig had asked him and legal counsel Reg Barrett to wait outside during a preliminary discussion while he 'made sure these people were on the same path'. Peter Ritchie, not yet formally on the board, was overseas. Another absentee was Jock Harper, a director since 1987 who was undergoing hip-replacement surgery. Harper and longstanding Westpac board member Peter Baillieu had been members of the Consolidated Press board but had recently resigned to clear the way for Packer and Dunlap to take up Westpac directorships.

Conroy and Barrett thought they would have perhaps a half-hour wait before the preliminaries were over. But their stay in the level 28 ante-room dragged on. Meanwhile, some senior executives had assembled in the office of Keith Brown, head of human resources, curious that their chief had been left out of the meeting for such a long time. Conroy, occasionally returning to his own office on level 27, was convinced his head was on the block. A further worry was that the chairman might also be asked to go. Something cataclysmic was clearly about to happen.

Conroy never did enter the boardroom that day. But he was again mounting the sweeping stair to level 28 when John Uhrig emerged from the boardroom and beckoned him into the chairman's office. Uhrig said: 'I should come straight to the point. The board wants you to resign.'

Conroy had been in the chief's role for a mere fourteen months, after a 32-year career at the bank. He had known that the task ahead was huge. He also knew that sitting in the Westpac boardroom was a man whose standard procedure in getting a company into shape was to start at the top and fire the managing director. Conroy knew how Dunlap operated. Part of Dunlap's creed is that, above all, a new boss must destroy the old culture. And, in his view, if a company cannot be turned around in twelve months then it cannot be turned around at all. One director had asked Uhrig how Conroy would react. Uhrig said he knew. In an earlier frank discussion between chairman and chief executive, Conroy had made clear his views that a chief executive could only operate effectively with the full confidence of the board. If the board no longer had confidence in him, he would go without trouble.

Conroy had received an unsettling hint of what lay ahead, following the chairman's cocktail party on the previous evening for the board, senior staff and retired directors. Packer and Dunlap had been invited, Dunlap attended. Traditionally, it had been the chairman's cocktail party but on this occasion Uhrig had decided that it was preferable to involve the managing director as a co-host to demonstrate the degree of harmony between the board and management. Uhrig and his wife, Shirley, and Frank and Jan Conroy stood as a receiving line of four, greeting their guests. It was obvious that Uhrig, chairman only since 1 October, was on less familiar terms with Westpac senior staff than Conroy. Driving home later, Jan Conroy said to her husband: 'We did the wrong thing tonight. You showed you were too friendly towards your executives.' Married to a man whose career had taken him up through the echelons of the bank, a former Wales employee herself and daughter and granddaughter of Wales men, Jan Conroy was instinctively attuned to the undercurrents of the evening. Only days before, she and her husband had been guests at a pre-Christmas party at Dunlap's Hunters Hill home. Now at the cocktail party, she had been studying Al Dunlap's abruptness when being introduced to executives and his stony expression during the speeches. The American's reaction to her husband's casual, off-the-cuff festive season comments was telling her something; Conroy was betraying his affection and protectiveness towards hard-working coal-face Westpac staff who had unwillingly been forced to share in the storm of criticism battering their employer. Her premonitions were confirmed when Conroy rang her at lunchtime on Thursday 17 December to tell her the news.

Uhrig is adamant that the move against Conroy was not premeditated. But it was a dramatic event, occurring as it did on the day after the two held their joint Christmas drinks party. 'At that stage there was internal boardroom dissatisfaction with Frank Conroy,' Uhrig says. 'But we did not go into that board meeting with such a plan [to get rid of Conroy] in mind.' Boardroom confidentiality constrains Uhrig from elaborating but he says: 'Westpac had come to the conclusion that the dimensions of what had to be done were so large that it was not practical for someone who'd spent his lifetime in the bank to do it in the time-scale in which it had to be done. While Frank Conroy would have done his best, the board came to the conclusion that it couldn't be done in the time. The board therefore asked him for his job.' Uhrig later said that Westpac's recovery plan remained in place, but the pace would be stepped up. Anxious to emphasise that the move against Conroy was not personal, Uhrig said at a shareholders' meeting in 1993 that Conroy did not cease being chief executive of Westpac because the board was dissatisfied with his ability to run the bank, or because he was not doing the best he could. He repeated in front of several thousand shareholders that the board had concluded that what had to be done was so difficult that it would be virtually impossible for it to be done, in the necessary time, by someone who had spent more than 30 years in the bank. Uhrig knew that Frank Conroy and his wife were among the audience, and he had deliberately said those words for Jan Conroy.

There is speculation that the directors were keen to show Packer and Dunlap that they called the shots, that they did not need 'Chainsaw' Dunlap to make the hard decisions. Several of the board had indeed harboured dissatisfaction about Conroy, based on their own preoccupations and prejudices. It had been Conroy who had pushed for a comprehensive review of the bank's property and for big write-offs, against the wishes of some directors. That had led to the rights issue, which had been spurned by shareholders, and a drop in the share price that signalled a huge loss of confidence in the bank, creating an opportunity for Packer to buy in. Some directors were still critical of Conroy's handling of the underwriting for the rights issue—in their view he was wrong in insisting on CSFB as underwriter, and they had not forgotten the bitter arguments. Others were critical of his lack of support for Walton over the US tax issue. Also, and possibly more significant, around the Westpac board table were representatives of the AMP Society, two sets of cross-directorships, with Westpac's John Uhrig and Peter Baillieu on the AMP board and Sir James Balderstone and Bob Johnston from the AMP on the Westpac board. AMP owned 15 per cent of Westpac, and it would be likely, given the paper losses it had sustained on its shareholding in the bank, that its directors would support a proposal for a change at the head of Westpac. AMP managing director Ian Salmon said of the move to find a new chief: 'What I think shareholders can take from this is that it's good evidence that the board is determined to see Westpac improved and improving quickly.'

Packer had made it clear in the earlier informal meeting that he thought management's progress was not adequate. He wanted more rapid results, and preferably under his own appointee. As they were only observers, neither he nor Dunlap was present when the vote was taken on Conroy's fate. But their influence was in the room. As it was, the board dumped Conroy without waiting to find a replacement as chief for the bank. John Uhrig, despite other commitments, took over the day-to-day running of Westpac.

By the time Uhrig had delivered his news to Conroy, the senior executives gathered in Keith Brown's office were anticipating a major announcement. The longer the meeting dragged on, the more evident it became that something serious was about to happen. Some thought the whole management team might be asked to go. More senior executives were called to the gathering. Conroy appeared and told the stunned group what had occurred. Then he left the room and Uhrig took his place to have a talk with the executives.

Graham Canning, Westpac's head of external communications, having checked with Reg Barrett that no news had come out of the boardroom, had snatched the opportunity to have a quiet pre-Christmas lunch out of the building with colleagues Rod Metcalfe and Alan Tippett. Morgan Williams, manager, media services, was left in charge of the media office as the trio adjourned to the nearby Celestial Chinese restaurant. Within an hour, Williams was frantically trying to contact them but their mobile phones did not respond. Williams was summoned to level 28, to help draft a press release announcing Conroy's departure. At the Celestial restaurant, Canning was restless; he had lived through too many dramas at Westpac to relax completely and, as they ordered coffee, he suggested that Metcalfe make a call to the office. Metcalfe went outside to ring. Normally pale-complexioned, Metcalfe was ashen when he returned. 'Conroy's gone,' he told Canning and Tippett, who initially thought he was joking. Another look at Metcalfe's face confirmed that he was not. Throwing enough money on the table to cover lunch, the three bolted back up the hill to 60 Martin Place. Chaos reigned on level 27.

Chris Hard, Conroy's personal assistant since his return in 1988 from Hong Kong, coped with the incessantly ringing telephone. Canning and Noel Purcell, briefly back in Sydney from Tokyo where he headed Westpac's office, strove to maintain a degree of calm in Conroy's outer office while Metcalfe and Williams helped Canning compose a press release based on words advised by the board. It was a brief announcement:

> The chairman of Westpac Banking Corporation, Mr John Uhrig, announced today that the managing director, Mr Frank Conroy, had resigned.
>
> This followed discussion by board members of the need for the leader of the bank's change program to be someone who comes fresh to the task.
>
> A new chief executive will be appointed from outside the bank. Mr Uhrig said the board anticipates that this will be achieved prior to the annual general meeting.
>
> Pending a new appointment, Mr Uhrig will act as executive chairman on an interim basis.

Canning took the draft to Uhrig for final approval. After reading it, Uhrig said to Canning: 'You don't agree with this, do you?' Canning asked if the chairman meant on a personal or professional level. Uhrig did not answer directly, but said: 'When you've been around as long as I have, you will understand what occurred.'

Word spread quickly around the bank. To most staff the news of Conroy's departure was devastating. It drove home the message that the old Bank of New South Wales, snuffed out in 1982, was truly buried. A different culture reigned. Ironically, one of Conroy's final tasks was to meet the chairman to discuss urgent changes to the annual report, which had already gone to print. Production was halted while Conroy's photograph was excised, although he remained in the report's picture of the board. Conroy also remained as a consultant to the Westpac chairman for several months after his departure.

Conroy was out of the Westpac building at 2 pm, driven home in a Westpac car, the 1988 Mercedes bought by his predecessor, Stuart Fowler. To ensure minimal public or media scrutiny, Conroy's driver took the car with its identifiable Westpac number plates—1817—out of the underground carpark by the entrance instead of the exit.

A career banker, Conroy had trained himself to remain cool in the worst possible circumstances, but this was numbing. Westpac represented his entire working life. At his home in Beauty Point, family and friends gathered in an atmosphere almost resembling a wake. The telephone rang constantly and hand-delivered letters began to arrive, including one from Rob Douglass, for whom Conroy had earlier in the year written a 'letter of comfort'. They watched the television news that evening, which gave wide coverage to Conroy's departure, with considerable speculation on the role of Packer, the alleged differences between his and Conroy's views about how best to set Westpac on a recovery path, and the likelihood of an American banker with experience in rapidly turning around a bank being chosen as a new chief for Westpac. On the following morning Conroy could indulge in a late sleep. His son Peter, returning with the newspapers, threw them on the bed. 'Well, Dad, you've gone out with a bang,' he said as he left for work. The headlines clamoured from every paper. 'Conroy quits Westpac', 'Westpac chief forced to quit', 'Banker victim of his own revolution'. Westpac had lost its seventh director in less than three months.

It had been made clear to Conroy that the vote against him had not been a personal matter, and he decided that, over the next day or so, he would ring all the directors, including Packer, to reaffirm that he understood this. He did not want a situation where people might be too embarrassed to speak to him. He was particularly anxious to make it plain to Packer that press reports of his opposition to Consolidated Press's presence in the Westpac share register were inaccurate; rather, he had taken the view that the new shareholder would bring some stability. Nor, he said, was he opposed to Packer and Dunlap being offered board seats, having been in Uhrig's office when the call was made to invite them on to the board. Packer, inured by years of unwelcome press coverage, set Conroy's mind at rest. During their conversation Packer offered the consolation that Conroy was a scapegoat and inquired if he was happy with the board determination of his payout. Apparently, during the previous day's deliberations, Packer had been insistent that Conroy should not suffer financially if he were forced to go. Aware that Conroy had become a regular user of the exclusive Consolidated Press-owned fitness centre, the Hyde Park Club, making thrice-weekly 6 am visits where he was put through his paces by a personal trainer, Packer said he would ensure the facilities remained open to him. Conroy never availed himself of the opportunity.

Conroy was out of Westpac, although his recovery plan, endorsed by the Westpac board a month earlier, endured. But it was the end of an era for Australia's oldest bank.

The esteem in which Frank Conroy was held by the Westpac community was evident at the farewell held for him at Sydney's Wentworth Hotel early in February 1993. Some 400 turned up, including three former chief executives—Sir Robert Norman, Bob White and Stuart Fowler. A further 100 invitees sent apologies and messages. Conroy, beer in hand

and appearing relaxed, accompanied by his wife, Jan, daughter, Brenda and son, Peter, greeted friends and former colleagues. John Chatterton, as master of ceremonies, read out many of the tributes which spoke of Conroy's energy and leadership, now lost to Westpac at a critical time, as well as the admiration and trust he engendered in staff. Representing 'the line' with which Conroy had been so closely associated was Queensland general manager Bill Brewer, who gave a speech that combined nostalgia, emotion, humour and straight-talking. In his response, Conroy said he had been overwhelmed by the volume of letters and calls of support in the aftermath of 17 December. He thanked everyone, from the committee who had organised the evening to the security guards and catering staff at Westpac, his personal driver, family and particularly the tight group of executives with whom he had worked closely during the testing times of 1991 and 1992. He candidly said he was leaving Westpac with deep regret, but with no anger or bitterness towards this 'great old institution'. And he reiterated his earlier advice to managers: not to be bowed by the constant barrage of media criticism, but somehow to rekindle pride in Westpac. The new managing director, he said, would need everyone's commitment to see Westpac on the path to recovery. His loyal audience, still equally loyal to the bank they had all served for most of their working lives, responded with prolonged and resounding applause. The Westpac family was together again.

401

Conroy took up several board positions, becoming a director, then in 1994 chairman, of Howard Smith Ltd, chairman of the Federal Airports Corporation and a member of various inquiries. He subsequently also became chairman of St George Bank and ORIX Australia Corporation Ltd, as well as a director of John Davids Holdings Ltd, Placer Pacific and Futuris Corporation. And he took up farming at Moss Vale, in the NSW Southern Highlands.

CHAPTER SIXTEEN

THE BIG SELL

No sooner in than out

Confident that he was clearing a way towards shaping
Westpac into a leaner and more profitable organisation, Al
Dunlap turned to the next step in his plan: to get rid of
chairman John Uhrig. Dunlap decided that he would write a
letter on Consolidated Press letterhead, signed by Packer, to
the members of the Westpac board, questioning Uhrig's abilities and calling for his resignation and replacement by
fellow director and former Reserve Bank governor Bob
Johnston. It is a measure of Dunlap's arrogance that he had
not consulted Johnston about this. Dunlap envisaged himself
overseeing strategy for the bank, with a suitable appointee
as nominal managing director in charge of day-to-day
operations. He had in mind Lindsay Pyne, who had turned
around the troubled Bank of New Zealand. Dunlap was
excited about the idea of clearing the decks, of having no
obstruction in his way. He felt he would not get a free rein
with Uhrig. It would appear that Dunlap, unfamiliar with the
Australian scene and with scant regard for local sensitivities,
underestimated the reaction of the Westpac board to an
attempt to dislodge the chairman.

The issue of the letter involved lengthy discussions
between Packer, his son, James, Dunlap and advisers
Neville Miles and David Gonski. Packer and James Packer
were well aware of the ramifications of such a move. Miles
and Gonski strongly advised against the letter being sent.
Numerous telephone calls between all parties failed to find

consensus, with Dunlap growing increasingly frustrated and furious. Packer backed his chief executive. The letter was sent in time to reach directors ahead of Westpac's January board meeting.

Packer and Dunlap arrived at 60 Martin Place to attend their first board meeting as directors of Westpac on 14 January. Each board member had the previous day received a copy of the letter, signed by Packer, calling for Uhrig's resignation and replacement by Bob Johnston. This was Johnston's first inkling of the plot. Deputy chairman Sir James Balderstone, on receiving the letter, had rung Packer to warn him that he would not be able to agree to this. Packer noted Balderstone's comments. At the meeting a couple of the directors suggested to Packer that the letter should be withdrawn, a view that was generally supported around the table. But when it became evident that this would not happen, John Uhrig pre-empted further discussion by calling for a vote of confidence in his chairmanship. As he went around the board table, it became clear that he had majority support.

First Balderstone spoke against Packer's proposal, then Bob Johnston, and by the time some five of those present had voiced a vote, Packer had had enough. Enraged at having misjudged the situation and apparently blaming Dunlap for this miscalculation, Packer announced: 'Al, we're out of here,' and stormed out of the boardroom, Dunlap in pursuit. Dunlap believed Packer was being impulsive and told him so. That sparked a loud argument that continued as the two marched into the lift and rode down. Dunlap could not contain his exasperation. Westpac staffers sharing the brief ride heard a furious Dunlap explode to Packer: 'I couldn't believe the excessive display of stupidity.' To this day, it is uncertain whose stupidity Dunlap meant.

Packer and Dunlap had formally but briefly attended their first and only Westpac board meeting. Packer blew the opportunity to increase his influence in the bank. Earlier indications among institutions and other interested parties, such as the major shareholder AMP, were that there was considerable support for Consolidated Press's holding an interest in Westpac. This was qualified in some quarters with apprehension about Dunlap's aggressive approach. The directors had thought that Packer was calling the shots, with Dunlap firing them. They were uncomfortable with what seemed to be the Dunlap plan, to install a nominal managing director reporting to him, with Dunlap virtually running the bank himself. The attack on Uhrig tipped the scales against Packer for several board members; they had no intention of being steamrollered. As Packer and Dunlap stormed out, not one of the remaining directors tried to persuade them to sit down and calmly talk things through.

404

Packer and Dunlap had been relying on boardroom support from Peter Baillieu, who was married to a cousin of Packer's, but Baillieu, attending the board meeting by telephone because he was out of the country, had supported the chairman. Later that month, Baillieu was cornered by Dunlap while having what was intended to be a relaxing massage at the Hyde Park Club. Dunlap hustled the masseur out of the room and subjected the prone Baillieu to a tirade of invective, castigating, among other things, Australia's 'inbred establishment'. There had been testing moments between Packer and Baillieu, too.

Back at his Park Street office after the aborted meeting on 14 January, Dunlap rang Neville Miles with instructions to sell Consolidated Press's Westpac shares. Miles rang Packer to point out that unloading such a large parcel of shares and options would be suicidal. Just as his buying had underpinned the bank's share price, if Packer were seen as a seller, Westpac shares would plummet. Packer agreed. A less impetuous approach paid off. A few months later he rolled over some options to protect the shares, and on 12 May sold his holding to Lend Lease for $608 million, netting a profit of more than $100 million.

Packer and Dunlap formally resigned from the Westpac board at 4 pm on 14 January. The day gave rise to further rifts. Balderstone and Packer have not spoken since, and within three months Dunlap had left Consolidated Press.

Fishing for talent

Westpac had ended 1992 under pressure to find a new chief executive as quickly as possible. The annual general meeting was looming and, given the events of the year, shareholders were likely to be particularly hostile and demanding. It was not uncommon for a search for a new chief executive to take as long as six months. The Westpac board did not have the luxury of even a few months. John Uhrig was keen to search not just in Australia but worldwide for the best possible person to head Westpac. However, he knew that there were not a great many people capable of handling the demands of the job.

Westpac engaged the headhunters Russell Reynolds Associates Inc and within 24 hours of Conroy's departure two managing directors of the firm, Lynn Anderson and Dennis McDonald, were in Uhrig's office discussing possibilities. The project had a sense of urgency from the outset. Russell Reynolds had a huge task ahead if they were to meet the deadline a mere month away. The headhunters came prepared; within hours of Uhrig's call they had been in contact with their offices overseas and had researchers checking their worldwide database, marking the start of a coordinated search by Russell Reynolds's global banking practice that would cover the US, Europe and Asia. Over the ensuing two weeks some 200 people were contacted. Russell Reynolds managing director Paul Murnane, who with Anderson handled the financial services side of the business in

Australia, interviewed several Australasian candidates, inside and outside Westpac. Each potential prospect was interviewed several times by two Russell Reynolds executives, in person or by telephone or video conference. Says Uhrig: 'Everyone of consequence in banking was considered, but we concluded that while there were one or two people we should consider most seriously, that was not going to provide enough potential. So we decided in a matter of days that the whole exercise had to be put on a global basis, covering the English-speaking world. There were approximately 30 names whom we thought could be possibilities in terms of preparedness to change and sufficient experience to do the job.'

The list was cut back to nineteen, of whom fifteen were in the US. Russell Reynolds interviewed those in Europe and Asia. Anderson flew to the US, where his colleagues had already been working on potential targets. Murnane continued interviewing and coordinating market research—checking and rechecking details such as education, employment and references. He liaised with the team overseas and with Anderson, who was in contact with Uhrig daily, by telephone. A number of people could not be contacted because they were on vacation, some did not want to make a move to Australia and others were eliminated for various reasons until the numbers were reduced to seven. Uhrig interviewed two who were not part of Russell Reynolds's research. Altogether, Uhrig was to talk with nine people from four countries.

Normally around Christmas John Uhrig would spend three weeks at the family's holiday home on Kangaroo Island, off the South Australian coast, where he enjoyed some relaxing fishing. That year he snatched no more than a few days. On New Year's Day he travelled to the mainland and interviewed a candidate who had flown from Europe for the day. They met at a hotel in Adelaide, discussed the matter and in the evening the applicant flew home and Uhrig returned to his Kangaroo Island fishing haven. He was there briefly before he left for the US on Friday, 8 January. He left Australia at 3.45 pm and, because of the time difference, was interviewing at 11 am on the same date in a Los Angeles hotel room. The first person he saw was Bob Joss, one of four vice-chairmen of Wells Fargo & Company, one of the US's best regional banks. Joss had received a call from Russell Reynolds's San Francisco office on Christmas Eve to tell him of an interesting assignment that he ought to consider. Australia and Westpac sounded a little far-fetched to Joss but the headhunters encouraged him to think about it. After mulling over the proposition and discussing it with his wife, Betty, Joss decided it sounded interesting and arranged to fly to Los Angeles to meet Uhrig at a hotel near the airport. Within twenty minutes Uhrig felt he had found someone who could do the job required at Westpac. What he did not know was whether Joss was prepared to do it—or if his additional interviewing would uncover someone else who could do it even better.

Uhrig conducted seven interviews in Los Angeles and New York and by the Sunday evening he was back at Los Angeles airport, from where he rang Joss and asked if he and his wife could be in Sydney by the following Friday, a holiday weekend in the US. Joss agreed. He and his wife arrived in Sydney on the day that *The Australian* carried a lead business article suggesting that Westpac had found a new chief executive. A few days later speculation named Joss. It gave the American his first taste of the high profile the bank carried in the community and the significance of its predicament.

Uhrig ensured that, through the auditors, Joss could have access to the bank's financial records and could familiarise himself with its accounts. The American spent several days holed up at the Park Hyatt at the Rocks, absorbing Westpac's financial details. As well as reading through annual reports, he rang contacts whom he trusted, talked to Westpac's auditors and accountants and tried to assess the real estate situation. He did not have a great deal of bank history to hand but, he says, the history was not so important; it was more a question of understanding where Westpac was and whether he thought the bank was financially sound and the situation salvageable. Uhrig, staying at the nearby Quay West apartments, was on hand to answer questions and Joss also had access to whomever he wanted to meet among senior Westpac ranks. Russell Reynolds had already provided him with public information and press cuttings to help with his crash familiarisation course.

Events moved quickly. Westpac was offering Joss the job but he and his wife had to decide whether this was something they really wanted to do. He knew the bank was keen for him to start as soon as possible, even to attend the annual general meeting a few days hence. Joss needed more time. He had been with Wells Fargo for 22 years, he had not been looking to move and he wanted to talk the matter over with his colleagues there. On the afternoon of Sunday 17 January Joss told Uhrig that he wanted to make the decision at home and was flying back to California. Uhrig rang deputy chairman Sir James Balderstone and said: 'I think I've lost him.' But telephone contact was maintained during the ensuing week and further negotiations continued over the following weekend, with Westpac's lawyer in Sydney discussing contractual details with a lawyer representing Joss.

Uhrig's hopes of being able to announce a new chief executive at the annual general meeting on 19 January were dashed. The marathon but inconclusive session in Sydney's vast Darling Harbour convention centre, attended by 5,000 angry and restless shareholders, lasted nearly eight hours and had to be continued the following week. Shareholders, disgruntled at the slide in the value of their holdings, came to vent their dissatisfaction with the bank. Some were demanding that the rest of the board should resign; others castigated the directors over issues such as the accounts and the US tax question in an overwhelming outpouring of resentment. Uhrig opened his chairman's address:

The large number of people present here today is an indication of the concern among proprietors about the problems the bank has been experiencing. The unusually large attendance is also a reflection of the intense focus of public scrutiny Westpac has had to contend with in dealing with an extremely difficult situation. There are proprietors, some of whom will be here today, whose primary interest is to seek vengeance because of poor profit performance. Others want to be able to feel more confident that the people currently responsible for ensuring improvement in performance can be relied upon to take that responsibility seriously.

Uhrig went on to talk of the bank's problems and the steps the bank was taking to deal with them, the degree of public scrutiny and the pressures this put on staff morale. His irritation with the level of information leaking out of Westpac had boiled over into an earlier remark to *The Australian Financial Review* that 'we might as well hold our board meetings in Hyde Park'. Uhrig pointed out that the five-point recovery plan, introduced in November 1992 by Frank Conroy, was under way. Westpac had sold more than $1 billion of problem assets in 1992. He also reported on progress in finding a new chief executive, saying discussions were incomplete. Uhrig was on his feet throughout the meeting; a few hours into the proceedings, a fellow director suggested he sit down for a while, but he replied that if he sat, he would not be able to get back on his feet. Besides, being seated would not have conveyed the correct image. Uhrig wanted to show he was alert and ready to deal with whatever arose. He outlasted many of the shareholders: only about 500 had the staying power to remain until the meeting adjourned at 6.30 pm.

409

Enter Bob Joss

At 2 pm on Sunday, 24 January, a deal was done. Uhrig could announce that Westpac had found a new chief. Within a few hours of their agreement, Joss telephoned many of the bank's senior executives from his home in San Franciso and talked to them. A press release was issued. The arrangements had been concluded 30 days from the first contact with Joss, and two weeks later he was in Sydney, at the helm of Westpac. At the second session of the annual meeting, this time attended by a mere 700, Uhrig was able to announce Joss's appointment and show a blown-up screen image of the new chief executive. It was less than five weeks since Conroy had left Westpac and there had been some scepticism about the bank's chance of finding a new chief in such a short time. 'We had luck on our side in that we found the right chief executive in that tight time-frame,' says Uhrig.

Robert Law Joss, a vice-chairman of Wells Fargo & Company since 1986, had joined the bank in 1971. At 51, he was the same age as the bank's chief executive, suggesting limited opportunity for the top job at Wells Fargo. To head Westpac he quit a job with an annual package of $US695,000, share rights and in-the-money share options and other long-term benefits. His income ranked him as the 56th-highest-paid executive in California. In deciding to move to Westpac, he sacrificed none of his earnings potential. He was recruited to Westpac on a salary of around $A1.9 million, with a significant proportion of his income performance-related. Uhrig, mindful that the bank was paying a generous salary to win Joss, apparently insisted that a percentage of Joss's salary be 'at risk'.

Incentive arrangements included granting Joss options over five million Westpac shares, enabling him to subscribe at $2.85 in three batches of 1.66 million shares staggered over subsequent years. The first batch was exercisable between January 1996 and January 1998, the second could be exercised only if Westpac's share price was at least $3.90 between January 1997 and January 1999, and a third exercisable only if the share price was at least $4.41 between January 1998 and January 2000. Such an option arrangement was common in the US. His contract with Westpac also included a condition that the bank provide him with appropriate accommodation. After a painstaking search, during which they lived in a $1.95 million three-bedroom penthouse at Sydney's Quay West apartments, Bob and Betty Joss settled in a house at Rose Bay. They already enjoyed a weekender at Palm Beach, where Westpac had purchased a $1.5 million cliff-top property.

Joss arrived at Westpac with a strong mandate to change the bank. His press conference on 21 February 1993, five days after he took up his position, was the first time that Joss had confronted the aggressive curiosity of the Australian media. It was an abrupt introduction to a level of scrutiny quite foreign to a man who came from a regional US bank which mailed out its quarterly results to analysts. Flanked by Westpac media chief, Graham Canning, and Geoff Kimpton, acting head of communications, the smiling and relaxed-looking Joss strode into a room crowded with representatives of every major Australian media organisation. His wife Betty was in the audience.

He had yet to become accustomed to the high profile accorded to Westpac in the Australian community. Banks in the US did not rate this level of attention. Big companies did. But in Australia, banks are big companies. Media fascination with Westpac had been at a peak for the past couple of years as the bank had dealt, not always skilfully, with a succession of crises that had left it a wounded and fearful institution. The bank had not enjoyed the spotlight. Nor did Joss now look completely at ease. His wide and cheerful smile faded and his initially easy manner grew more formal as he was grilled by an inquisitive and mildly hostile Australian media about his salary package, his plans for Westpac and his time-frame for achieving them.

Joss conceded that his strategy for Westpac was probably not very different in direction from that mapped out by his predecessor, Frank Conroy. What was more likely to be different was the execution. 'Most of what differentiates one bank from another is not so much the strategy but how well a bank executes and delivers,' he said. He had not considered that Westpac might become a takeover target. 'I can't control those things,' he said, adding:

> I only know the things I can control which is to work here and focus on what I know about the business and the people and about financial institutions and how they can be successful. Time is of the essence. I can tell you we have a great sense of urgency here about getting this right, and we'll be moving absolutely as fast as we can, as sensibly as we can. You can move too fast, you can cause great disruption to customers, and staff and systems if you move too fast in banking businesses. You can also move too slowly which is clearly what Westpac has done in the past. So that's part of the job, to find that pace of change, just how hard to push and how fast. But we'll be moving fast, I can assure you of that.

He said later that year that a fellow banker in California had tried to discourage him from taking up the post at Westpac, saying, 'It's a bloody awful mess ... You'll do all right by staying in California. Don't get involved.' Joss thought: 'What have I got to lose?' Joss's power stemmed from a mix of Westpac's dismal position, his own status as an outsider not hobbled by baggage and biases from the past and a recognition at board, management and staff level that Westpac had to change. He brought to the role a mix of laid-back Californian informality and the qualities of a steely US banker. With an economics degree, an MBA and PhD and experience in US Treasury before joining Wells Fargo, Joss could not have been further from the traditional Westpac chief executive. He had been one of a handful of executives who played leading roles in Wells Fargo's successes. In the early 1980s, when international expansion was the catch-cry in banking, Wells Fargo withdrew from global ambitions to focus on its home market in California. It carved out a successful business as a leader in trust account and mutual-fund business and gained a reputation as a bank obsessed with costs, with rigorous controls, a tight focus, low-cost deposits, high ATM use, healthy earnings and few under-performing businesses. It was not immune to downturns, though. A common criticism of Wells Fargo was that it had concentrated too much of its lending in California, particularly on real estate, which left it vulnerable when the property market collapsed and California went into recession. The impact on Wells Fargo's returns was savage; in 1990 its return on equity was an enviable 22.68 per cent and a year later it had crashed to 0.63 per cent, before recovering. In early 1993, when Joss moved to Westpac, Moody's rated Wells Fargo Baa1, while Westpac was a higher A2.

Joss quickly identified Westpac's two main flaws as problem loans and high costs. His vision for Westpac dismissed the 'universal bank' concept promoted in the 1980s. 'You start trying to be too many things to too many people,' he said in a magazine interview in 1993, providing a concise summary of how and where Westpac went wrong.

> You end up being mediocre to all of them and you lose out to the superior players in each niche. Perhaps where the bank went wrong was in trying

to do more things than it was capable of doing all at once. It grew extremely rapidly: between 1982 and 1989 it tripled in size, and that kind of very rapid growth is generally a potential warning signal of difficulty in financial services. Also, there was growth in a number of new areas—property development, overseas ventures, new territories, new parts of the world. The combination simply stretched the bank too thin in a financial and managerial sense.

However, in Joss's view Westpac was still active on the world scene, with global treasury and financial markets activities. 'We are a leader in treasury, derivatives, risk-management, interest-rate and currency products,' he said. 'We're driven by the needs of our customers and they're increasingly global.' As for Asia, he agreed that Australia was increasingly linked to Asia and economic ties were important, but emphasised that did not entail 'being on the ground in retail banking in Asia'.

Identifying Westpac's problems was easy. Implementing the changes necessary to correct them was the hard part. Not long after Joss arrived he decided a $500 million preference share issue was essential, arguing to the board that strongly capitalised banks have more opportunities open to them, are able to perform better and attract greater respect. While he cited the problem loans as Westpac's biggest financial burden, he declared that the bank's biggest strategic burden was the process of changing the organisation from one that was bureaucratic, high-cost and lagging its competitors in systems and processing to one that was more efficient, more sales-oriented and more cost-conscious. In the name of cost-cutting, middle management ranks at Westpac were remorselessly reduced, to the extent that market jokesters quickly circulated the nickname Job Loss. Joss, a highly disciplined individual, emphatic about the importance of being purposeful and focused, talked a great deal about 'more productivity and efficiency' and pointed out that people costs were half of Westpac's costs. Hardly surprisingly, staff morale suffered. Joss's pragmatic view was that in the longer term, staff spirits would rise when the bank's performance improved. Growth for Westpac was critical, he said in October 1993. 'Westpac could start to acquire. You always have to be looking at ways to grow. But you want to grow in areas where you think you have a chance to be successful. You don't want to keep trying to grow in things where you're killing yourself.'

During his early months Joss talked a few times with a good friend, Dick Rosenberg, then running Bank of America. When talking initially with Uhrig, it had struck Joss that there were considerable similarities between Westpac and Bank of America. He says:

> One factor that gave me confidence that Westpac could be turned around was that I had seen it done at Bank of America, just by getting back to basics and focusing on what it was that made the bank strong. Both had strong consumer franchises, good branch networks, good market positions and had gotten out of control from a credit quality and operational control point of view, and made some fairly serious financial mistakes and control mistakes. But they were fundamentally in a very strong position and could work their way out of it. And a lot of the people who turned around Bank of America were former Wells Fargo people and I knew a lot of them and their calibre, so I had a good sense of confidence about what could be done.

Shrinking for survival

Joss's impact on the five-point recovery plan devised in 1992, by Conroy was to speed up the process and intensify the focus. John Uhrig, while acting chief of the bank, had lost no time in putting pressure on senior executives to quicken the pace, so work was already under way in a number of areas. An area that felt the effect of significant change was the retail bank. David Morgan, head of retail, had been working on restructuring that side of the bank since late 1992 and in January 1993 he took to the board a proposal for a substantially more rapid makeover. By September 1993 its revenues had been increased and expenses trimmed to the tune of a $342 million pre-tax improvement in the bottom line. The shake-up included cutting retail staff by 5,000. Morgan says: 'The pressure was relentless. If the retail bank didn't succeed then Westpac wouldn't succeed. Those were the stakes.'

Progress was made in shaving the expense-to-income ratio towards the target of 58 per cent. Assets were sold. Westpac disposed of its stockbroking arm, Ord Minnett, ending nine years of ownership in a deal that brought Westpac around $36 million and saw the management and staff of Ord Minnett become equal partners in a joint venture with the leading Asian investment bank Jardine Fleming.

About a month after Joss had taken up the reins, a financial markets strategy meeting was held at the Ingleside training centre, attended by a few staff from Westpac's Asian network. In response to a question about Westpac's plans for its Asian operations, Joss said that at Wells Fargo the belief was that it was efficient to create alliances rather than have operations on the ground. It was clear that, despite considerable opposition in the bank to selling its Asian network, his mind was made up. Westpac's staff in Asia, having nurtured the business to the point where they believed it was on the cusp of a promising phase, were incensed. Westpac's spread of operations in Asia made it second only to ANZ Grindlays among Australian banks represented in the region. And Westpac's growing presence in Asia fitted nicely with Australia's policy of aiming for closer integration with its Asian trading partners, a flow of business of increasing economic importance to the country. Such was the angst in Canberra that Joss received a telephone call from a furious minister for trade, pointing out the potentially damaging fallout from Westpac's retreat. Many believed Westpac was burning a long-term opportunity. Staff in the Asian centres felt betrayed by the bank's pulling out. In Tokyo, where Westpac ran a large branch as well as a successful financial markets operation, staff were comforted by the fact that, so far, they were escaping the axe. The threat was elsewhere in Asia: 'the fire is on the other side of the river' as a Japanese saying goes. To those working in Asia it seemed that Bob Joss thought Westpac was like Wells Fargo, a regional Californian bank, whereas Westpac's presence in the region was more like an Australian version of a Citibank or a Chase Manhattan.

Westpac sold its branches in Taiwan and South Korea and its joint venture in Indonesia, as well as all the businesses of AGC in Hong Kong, where the company had eight branches, and Thailand, Singapore, Malaysia, Taiwan and Indonesia. The sales drew widespread interest from Asian banking and finance groups, and from several international institutions eager to expand in the region. Westpac's and AGC's businesses had been profitable, but were no longer central to Westpac's objectives.

Joss felt strongly that no bank could succeed in another market if it was not strong at home and, at that point, Westpac was weak at home. He said in 1996: 'Westpac is very focused around Asia, it's a fast-growing part of our business but we do feel strongly that you have to think through carefully what sort of capabilities to build, and whether you do it all yourself or with a partner. And Asian countries generally are overbanked, the markets controlled in terms of entry and what you can and cannot do so that you'd be lucky to open one branch in countries which mostly have larger populations than Australia. And what do you do with one branch when you don't know the language and the customers and don't have the staff?' By 1994 Westpac had only a New York office in the US and offshore activities of the bank were concentrated on financial markets operations in Tokyo, Hong Kong, Singapore, London and New York.

Joss's arguments for a preference share issue were successful: an issue in 1993 raised $600 million. Profit for the year to 30 September was a modest $39 million after tax and abnormals, although the bank reported that its underlying performance had improved slightly over that seen in 1992. The charge for bad and doubtful debts was more than halved, to $1.2 billion. In his first annual report as head of Westpac, Bob Joss talked of restoring the bank to 'a position of community leadership and respect', in the 'shortest possible time frame'. He ended his report with a homily on 'reforming our culture':

> Looking back in time, we created many of our own problems by allowing unproductive behaviour and attributes to become dominant inside the corporation. The result was a decline in customer service, quality control, staff morale and financial performance. All this must change, and change rapidly ... Changing corporate culture is not easy. It begins at the top ... You have today a management team that takes seriously its mission of financial stewardship over the affairs of a great institution. We are determined to remake Westpac

into a corporation that is disciplined about quality control and customer service; that is innovative, ethical and a rewarding place to work; and that is tightly focused on becoming the best, most efficient bank for our customers. To do so requires that we change people, change the behaviours that are recognised and encouraged, and change the values within the organisation.

Mase Westpac: an opportunity lost

Mase Westpac, Westpac's specialist bullion arm, fell under the hammer along with other so-called non-core assets. The decision to sell the gold dealer was taken before Joss arrived but, hopeful of a change of heart, Mase Westpac Ltd's London-based managing director, Dick Gazmararian, flew to Sydney in February 1993 to discuss the matter with the bank's new head. Gazmararian pointed out that Mase had well-established relationships with gold-mining companies in Australia and North America, that Australia was a major gold-producer and gold an integral part of the Australian economy. Surely, then, it was logical for an Australian bank to have a gold bullion subsidiary. Joss's response was reportedly: 'Australia is a big wheat producer but Westpac is not in wheat.' Gazmararian felt there was nothing more he could add. In June 1993, Mase Westpac was sold to a leading gold and silver bullion specialist, Republic National Bank of New York, for around $150 million, a substantial premium over net tangible assets, making it one of Westpac's more successful investments of the 1980s. Ironically, Republic National Bank of New York had been Westpac's competitor in 1986 in the bidding for Johnson Matthey Bankers in the UK.

419

Westpac's decision to take a position in the bullion industry through its investment in Mase and its subsequent purchase of JMB were bold moves at a time when the bank was testing the limits of its new power as a deregulated Australian institution with international aspirations. Ultimately, Westpac's inability to develop its gold business probably had its roots in the bank's having strayed too far too quickly from its cultural base—an assessment that can also be applied to its involvement in stockbroking through Ord Minnett. There were those in the bank who could see value in Mase Westpac, as there were those who wanted to retain Westpac's Asian network, but their voices were drowned out in the rising fervour to cut back to basics in the name of survival. In selling Mase, Westpac thought it was disposing of a cup that was half-empty; after Mase Westpac was sold, it realised the cup may have been half-full. Time would determine which assessment was the more correct.

420

CHAPTER SEVENTEEN

VALE, WALES

Joss took over a bank that had achieved the dubious distinction of having a 'world-class' ratio of problem loans to equity. He was alert to the difficulties of working through problem property loans: the operating costs of half-empty buildings, the maintenance, repairs and services, and the cost of carrying the loans with no compensating income. He had a few trends working in his favour: under Conroy, Westpac had been fighting a battle for survival, but by the time Joss arrived in the top job the war was over. A recovery plan had been mapped out. Further, the economy, which had been struggling to climb out of a recession, was again showing signs of life. But Joss had a great deal to learn about Westpac's place in the Australian psyche, and the depth of dislike in many sections of the community for banks in general and Westpac in particular.

About a year after he arrived, Joss and fellow American Pat Handley, the new chief financial officer who, during the 1980s, had been chief financial officer of Banc One Corporation in Ohio, an institution which grew rapidly by acquiring regional banks, attended a meeting with a market research company that gave them an insight into how Westpac was perceived in the community. Paul White, head of external affairs, thought it would be useful for them to hear what the average Australian consumer thought about banks. Questions were along the lines of: if your bank were a car, what model comes to mind? The Commonwealth was associated with Holden, Westpac a Volvo, not because of safety but because of its arrogance and slowness. Joss recalls that one of the techniques used was to ask people, if they could describe a bank as a person, who would that be? NAB was seen as someone successful who has let success go to his or her head, whereas Westpac's image was negative and aloof, a combination of fat cats and criminals, in the sense of the 1980s corporate cowboys. To Joss it was like a dash of cold water, and it reinforced how far they had to go in terms of winning back public acceptance and respectability.

White, one of the new faces in Westpac's media unit, had been recruited by Helen Lynch, who in September 1993 was appointed head of corporate affairs. White's appointment followed the departure of media chief Graham Canning who, with his assistant Rod Metcalfe, had handled Westpac's media relations for the previous two years, arguably the bank's worst period. They had dealt at times with a media call every two minutes. Canning and Metcalfe had navigated several reefs, coping with dozens of issues that ranged widely from foreign currency borrowers' claims to bank retrenchments, sexual harassment charges and complaints about fees and charges. In some instances they succeeded in avoiding bad publicity for Westpac, in others they tried to minimise the damage. However, they could not control either what the bank did or what the media wrote. During those years Westpac's image had taken a pounding, first from the aftermath of publication of the Westpac letters and court cases involving foreign currency borrowers, then from a seemingly relentless deterioration in its financial strength, culminating in a record loss and a rights issue shunned by shareholders. Over this time, Canning had forged a close working relationship with Conroy. However, there was a misguided view, particularly among some board members, that—even though the bank's financial performance was woeful, its public image enormously damaged, many customers unhappy with the treatment they were receiving and

its shareholders thoroughly dissatisfied—the bank's problems could be fixed if Canning and Metcalfe just took some
of their media 'mates' to lunch and told them to write favourably about Westpac. The approach of these directors was that
regardless of the mistakes the bank had made, it was the
media unit's role to achieve favourable coverage, either by
persuasion or heavy-handed negotiation. Joss, new to the
Australian scene and unaccustomed in his Wells Fargo role
to regular contact with journalists, was known to be happy
to keep media communication to a controlled minimum. In
contrast to his rapport with Conroy, Canning found himself
increasingly left out of consultations. After the constant
barrage of unwelcome publicity in 1992 and early 1993,
Uhrig felt it was a gift if a day went by and nothing appeared
in the media about Westpac. The shutters were pulled down.

Helen Lynch had worked in mainstream banking with
Westpac for 35 years, having started at the age of fifteen at
the Rockhampton, Queensland, branch of the Bank of New
South Wales. In 1984 she had become regional manager,
City South, in Sydney and in 1989 was appointed general
manager, South Australia and the Northern Territory. In
1990 she was nominated *Bulletin*/Qantas Businesswoman of
the Year. In 1992 she was chief general manager of Westpac's change program, overseeing several projects designed
to rebuild the problem-ridden bank. Joss had apparently been
receptive to the advice of an outside consultant that the communications job would be best handled by a woman. He
chose Lynch. The posting was a disappointment to Lynch,
who believed her experience merited a 'line' job such as
head of retail banking, and now saw herself stereotyped in
a 'soft' role in communications. A few months into the job,
she was certain that it ignored her skills and decided she
would leave. Paul White, with a background in current
affairs and electronic media, stayed with Lynch's department
for only a matter of months before being replaced by

Glenda Hewitt, a radio journalist who had specialised in financial reporting. In May 1994, shortly after recruiting Hewitt, Lynch left the bank. Westpac lost its most senior female executive. Lynch, at 50, struck out in a successful new career as a professional director, with positions on several major public company boards.

Helen Nugent, a director of the MBA program at the Australian Graduate School of Management, University of New South Wales, a specialist in corporate strategy and a former partner of the consultants McKinsey & Company, joined Westpac in June 1994 as director, strategy, and on arrival was told she would also have responsibility for communications, a role that lasted until early 1996 when Susan Brooks, former banking ombudsman and Australian Broadcasting Tribunal commissioner, was recruited as general manager, public and consumer affairs. As far as the media was concerned, Westpac had become impenetrable, defensive at best, hostile at worst.

John Uhrig, patriarchal and stern, was able to open the 1994 annual general meeting by saying that these were happier circumstances than had prevailed at the previous year's meeting. 'We can all take heart from the fact that Westpac is, once again, in profit,' he said. 'The significance of that return to profit, modest though it may be, should not be underestimated. A year ago, Westpac had recorded a large loss of $1.6 billion. It is not an exaggeration to say that the independence of the bank, Australia's oldest corporation, was at risk. It is not at risk today.' Discussing progress in Westpac's five-point recovery plan, Uhrig highlighted cost savings and revenue improvement in the retail banking group—the engine-room of Westpac—of $342 million, substantially above the initial target. The thrust for efficiency involved the closure of some 200 branches, about half of those in rural areas. The closure dismayed customers in the country where branches, as some pointed out in letters to newspapers, had not been responsible for the bank's massive losses. Risk-adjusted assets in institutional banking were reduced by $11 billion, most of that offshore. Staff had been pared from the 1990 peak of 46,600 to 33,000; more than 5,000 jobs had been abolished. When a shareholder suggested some words from Bob Joss would be welcomed, Uhrig said there was not a programmed segment for Joss but he was happy to have him talk about what he saw as the way forward for Westpac. Joss's approach to the microphone was greeted by resounding and prolonged applause from an audience who, at the previous year's meeting, had been able only to study his photograph. Joss, fluent as always, took the stand:

> Mr Chairman, you're right, I have nothing prepared but I'm always at the drop of a hat eager and anxious to talk about the bank. First of all I like what I've seen, I see an excellent franchise with, as the chairman says, a very solid customer relationship across the range of markets in which we operate, a very solid foundation of corporate customers, of middle-market customers, small business, households and consumers across Australia, across New Zealand. But we have a long way to go still in terms of catching up, in terms of delivering the kind of service and the kind of day-to-day quality that we know we have to do. But we're very focused on that ... We're a leader in a number of product areas—interest-rate management, derivatives, foreign exchange where we're a leading market-maker in the $A and $NZ ... The retail bank is the engine of our company ... we've done a lot to change the administrative structure over the past year to a more efficient, flatter and more productive approach.

> We're working very hard across all our lines of business to be more efficient and at the same time deliver a higher quality service. We believe we can do both.

Joss talked about being 'very focused' in the asset management group, selling properties and working out non-property problem loans, and of the disposal of what he called 'non-core, non-strategic activities, assets that did not relate to Westpac's strength'. Winding up his summary, Joss said that the aim was to return Westpac to 'where it belonged' which he believed was a position as Australia's best, number-one, bank:

> I think in a nutshell that's the summary I can give on strategy. Now, those things are easy to say, in many ways all banks might talk that way. I think the difference that hopefully you as shareholders will see in us is the way we activate and implement what we say. That's really the key in banking. Anybody can have the same idea, anybody can say the same words but the institutions that in a day-to-day way consistently deliver, execute, implement in ways that put them ahead of the pack [are the winners] ... We know where we have to go, we know we're at the back of the pack and closing but we want to catch the others and I can assure you there's nobody in the company that's not very very focused and dedicated on your behalf in that respect.

Having delivered his impromptu but stirring address, Joss sat down to thumping applause. Uhrig took the opportunity to ask for a show of hands to indicate if a rundown from the chief executive would be welcome at future annual meetings. Almost every hand in the room went up.

About a month after talking to the shareholders, Joss addressed a Trans-Tasman Business Circle luncheon in Sydney. He left no-one in any doubt about either his optimism for Australia and New Zealand's future or his belief in a bank's need for a tight focus on its market. Defending the winding back of Westpac's physical presence in the booming Asian markets, Joss said the combined Australian and New Zealand economies would be the equivalent of fourth ranking in the US after California, New York and Texas and so provided 'critical mass' and the promise of excellent economic growth. He conceded that the strategy of sticking to the local market might sound unimaginative but he was adamant that it did not preclude being well connected with the rest of the world— and being well connected did not necessitate having offices everywhere in the world. He pointed out that Westpac had substantial investments in offshore operations, through its global financial markets network. He emphasised:

> There is tremendous growth opportunity in my view right here at home, growth that comes because our home is linked to Asia and not because we might be able some day to open banks in Asia. In my experience, basic retail and commercial banking is a very difficult business to export and there are indeed very few examples of banks successfully operating retail and middle market banks across national boundaries. Citibank and National Australia Bank are among the very few successful cases. Recent banking history is littered with examples of banks not making it when they try to enter new high-growth markets.

Joss cited examples of four major UK clearing banks which made large investments in Californian banks, at the height of the Silicon Valley allure which made California the 'Golden State'. All four were praised for diversifying but all four eventually sold out and took sizeable losses on their investments.

Better, faster, cheaper, smarter

The pace of radical change intensified at Westpac during Joss's second year as the cost-cutting drive deepened and the institution underwent a traumatic shake-up in its senior management. Several key executives, apart from Helen Lynch, departed: Vern Harvey left to head Credit Union Services Corporation (Australia) Ltd, Derrick Heywood and Harvey Garnett retired. Americans, or Australians who had spent much of their working lives in US banks, replaced them. Joss chose Pat Handley as his chief financial officer, replacing Heywood; Robert Nimmo, an Australian who had worked with Citicorp in New York, joined Westpac as credit officer; Mary Carryer, a former senior vice-president from Wells Fargo, took up the new position of general manager, product management; Loran Fite, a former vice-president with Bank of America, became general manager, technology; and Sam Zweig from Chase Manhattan, became general manager, finance and administration. The list ran on. The invasion of American recruits prompted jokes that, in the rarefied upper echelons of 60 Martin Place, David Morgan's was the only Australian accent remaining. On a less flippant level, shareholders queried the wisdom of importing expensive newcomers, hard on the heels of having retrenched so many old hands, a 'restructuring' that also involved costs. And they were 'outsiders', perceived by staff, customers and long-time Westpac watchers as a disparate group with no long-term loyalty to Westpac, no interest in its history or culture or, for that matter, its future beyond the terms of their individual contracts.

Pat Handley had little time for anything that went before at Westpac. Confident and hard, he broadened the role of chief financial officer to the point where little seemed to happen at Westpac that did not involve him. He explained his philosophy to *CFO*, a magazine for chief financial officers, in July 1996: 'I look at finance not as a support role, but as a key role in the bank. It participates in the day-to-day running, it creates a discipline around the numbers and brings focus. The finance person has to understand the business ... Finance gets involved in negotiating the deals. And I am also involved intimately in the integration of the deal—making it work.' *CFO* quoted Michael Ullmer, chairman of Coopers & Lybrand's banking group, who shed further light on Handley's role: 'Whereas the Australian model is one which grows out of the chief accountant, keeping the books etc, Pat's role is more in line with the American model of the CFO, looking at macro financial initiatives, liaising with analysts, making sure fund managers understand the stock.' Others saw Handley more as Joss's henchman, implanting the new ideas, and using a sledgehammer if necessary.

429

Joss's response, in an interview for this book, was that the newcomers brought certain key technical skills in finance, credit and technology as well as good leadership and management skills. 'Good people attract other good people,' he says.

> Management skills are in short supply in Australia. That's a critical problem nationally and one thing that could prevent us from realising our national potential. No-one is taught how to be a good manager, no-one is held responsible for being a good manager, it's something you have to learn by doing and then people coaching you, getting feedback. It's a bit like swimming; you can read a book all about it but if you don't jump in the water, you don't learn. In Australia people have not been given management

WESTPAC: THE BANK THAT BROKE THE BANK

responsibility and then coached and taught and held accountable for hiring people, motivating them, getting results and managing performance, setting standards and living up to them. This is not just a cry in banking, you hear it everywhere. Companies tended to be structured and bureaucratic, human resources hired the people, some other area did something, unions decided certain things. No-one was ever responsible, everyone had an excuse if it didn't come out right.

At Westpac Joss was trying to lift the level of accountability, clarifying who is responsible for what and shedding committees.

430

The predominant area in Westpac where people had learned to manage was offshore. When they were sent to PNG or Fiji they had to figure it out. Out in the field, you have to decide what to do. That built the bank and made it great, but somehow it got away from that in the twentieth century and there was lots of structure and bureaucracy with everyone waiting to be told what to do. The culture was a bit like the army, and that's fine for the army ... but nobody questions, you don't get healthy debate and is that a good idea? In this day and age, you need people's minds, not just their bodies there at work. You need the whole person and you need everyone's intellectual input and ideas, you need them challenging and thinking and taking responsibility. They are the bank, they are Westpac, just as it was way back when they opened the bank in Sydney in 1817—there were just a few people and they were the bank, they had no-one to look to and tell them what to do.

Joss was also struck by the incestuousness of Australian banks, with a tradition of hiring school-leavers at sixteen who were with the bank for life, and not hiring staff from a rival bank. 'You train your own up in the bank, and you wear the consequences of that,' he says.

> And yet banking is a very complex business with a lot of risk, accountability and responsibility and it takes first-rate people to be responsible for it. When deregulation came in, and this applied in many countries whether you were deregulating the phone company or the banks, you go from that world of rules and policy manuals to one where people have to decide and act and take risks, you don't just flip the switch. Generally you get great difficulties. And we had financial deregulation then an economic boom where if you made bad decisions inflation bailed you out. Then at the end of the 1980s that all stopped and you could see what deregulation did. People were not really prepared for what life would be like in that real competitive jungle. It was like letting your house cat out in the jungle. It was not a fair fight. The people who understand that probably better than any are the Japanese. They see that, so they say we are not ready yet and they protect their market to give their people time to get stronger before they open and unleash. Australia did it all at once. It's a subtle thing, but people always underestimate the human side of any change—engineering, financial and physical elements are fairly easy to gear but it's that human side of change that really makes a culture.

431

Joss brought a pragmatic US attitude to the business which was in stark contrast to the traditions in Australian banking that had led people to expect a job for life. A highly disciplined operator, fitness fanatic and follower of the spartan Pritikin dietary regime, Joss was appalled by practices he viewed as indulgences, such as lavish media lunches complete with wine, and drivers for Westpac executives. Those disappeared, not so much because their abolition represented a major cost saving but because they conflicted with a new era of austerity. Joss will probably never escape the judgment that he followed a recovery plan already established when he arrived, but more generous observers credit him with bringing additional intellect and focus which helped implement the plan speedily and effectively.

Westpac might have broken many practices of the past but it had not lost its addiction to moving senior staff around. A reshuffle in October 1994 shifted David Morgan from head of retail banking to head of institutional and international, with Owen van der Wall moving from head of institutional to head of retail banking and Barry Robertson adding commercial banking to his existing responsibilities for asset management and property finance. Joss told *The Australian Financial Review* at the time that Westpac was moving from 'repair to consolidation' mode but added that the bank still had a long way to go. The changes sparked considerable speculation about who had emerged the winner but Joss, a firm believer in having executives move around to gain experience, would not be drawn on anointing any one executive. 'Like any coach I am trying to get the good players to work together as best they can,' he said.

By late 1994 Westpac had largely achieved its recovery objectives in terms of restoring financial strength. Backed by solid economic growth, the bank reported an after-tax profit of $705 million. It had reduced problem loans from 65 per cent to 30 per cent of shareholders' funds, increased its 'safe' assets such as home loans, with home lending up by 21 per cent, lifted dividends and cut its expense-to-income ratio to

432

59.5 per cent. It had also introduced a new approach to provisioning that was claimed to bring fresh rigour to credit management. Dynamic provisioning, as it was known in the US, had been used by Pat Handley's former employer Banc One since the late 1970s to avoid big swings in reported earnings and overweighting in certain types of credits. Handley and Robert Nimmo, head of credit, instigated the adoption of dynamic provisioning at Westpac. The method uses computer modelling to refine the process of estimating credit risks so that an appropriate level of provisioning is maintained. If a lender looks solely at the difference between the rate it can charge on a corporate loan and what it can earn from a consumer credit card, the slim margin on the corporate loan would make the business seem barely worthwhile. But when returns are calculated on a risk-adjusted basis, the corporate business looks attractive because it involves a lower risk, whereas credit card business, despite high interest rates, can involve significant losses. Dynamic provisioning helps a bank keep track of the risk in its balance sheet; consumer loans, such as those for home lending and personal finance, are analysed by product, and business loans are graded into different levels of risk. The longer the term of a loan, the greater the risk and so the higher the provision. If a bank lends to an AA-rated company it applies a certain amount to general provision at the outset; the loan is periodically evaluated and if AA becomes AA+ then a bank can lower the amount set aside to provision, while if AA becomes B then the charge to general provision is increased. A loan can be regraded because of a change in the economic cycle that has a good or bad impact on the borrower's industry. The idea is that a bank can develop a consistency of earnings that transcends credit cycles. Sceptics have dismissed dynamic provisioning as profit-smoothing under a new trendy label.

Joss said in November 1994 that for the first time in two years Westpac had the financial strength to consider an acquisition. In the 1994 annual report, chairman John Uhrig said:

'For the last two years Westpac has focused single-mindedly on survival, efficiency and plotting the right course for the future.' Joss commented that the bank was out of the 'stabilise and recover' phase and into 'improve performance and grow'. Internally, he said, 'we talk about doing things better, faster, cheaper' in every part of the organisation. Staff could expect further turmoil as Westpac continued its drive to become a 'world-class financial services organisation'.

The year 1995 opened with first a bouquet then a brickbat for Westpac. The bank had barely time to bask in the glory of having earned the title of top corporate loan arranger during the previous year when it was revealed that it had again committed the kind of public relations blunder for which it had already become famous. In October 1994 Westpac launched what was to be a six-month test on some 9,000 customers in the Hunter Valley district of NSW which involved offering them a range of fee structures on their accounts. Several thousand customers discovered that their accounts were 'upgraded' to qualify for a range of features which would be fee-free as long as their balances remained above $1,500; those with less were charged a monthly fee of $5. The customers had been sent information detailing the proposed fees but were not informed that they were participating in a trial. All banks were keen to test customer reaction to increased fees and Westpac had wanted to determine which structure they preferred. The controversial market research program raised a furore among customers and consumer groups, who cited the widely accepted code of professional behaviour which dictates that market research must be based on the 'willing cooperation of the public'. Westpac badly flatfooted by not letting people in on its secret trial. The experiment was called off. Customers who had been charged the monthly fee were reimbursed and offered free banking for the remainder of 1995. At the annual shareholders' meeting in January, John Uhrig said the research had been 'highly ethical' and 'well-intentioned' but it had been a mistake not to inform customers that they were participating in a test. Both he and Bob Joss apologised for the project and said it would never happen again. However, Joss did not rule out increases in bank fees. 'We are constantly reviewing the pricing and packaging we offer people on deposits and loans,' he said.

Joss was able to divert the shareholders' attention from the embarrassing gaffe by forecasting that Westpac would join those companies earning $1 billion in profits and confirming that it was interested in buying the State Bank of South Australia (BankSA), which was about to be privatised. Joss further fuelled speculation about Westpac's interest in BankSA in March when, addressing the Adelaide branch of the Institute of Company Directors, he made an uncharacteristic diversion from neutral topics and highlighted Westpac's involvement in South Australia and its eagerness to lend support to the state's economy. The bank's concentration on the economies of NSW and Queensland had by 1995 left the board asking where Westpac was going to achieve growth. Acquisition was one solution. Joss said at the time: 'I don't worry too much about growth, I think if you get the business strategy right, growth will come.' He rejected observations that Westpac had become overly narrow in its focus. But he agreed that the bank had been very cautious over the previous few years, saying it was a 'natural reaction ... but now Westpac is trying to get that balance right'. There was no doubt that Westpac's next recovery phase would be tougher than the first stage, which had relied on cost cutting and restructuring. Joss still had to rebut criticism that he had no more than implemented a plan already in place; he had to show that he had a long-term strategy. He had to reinvent Westpac.

Although by now thoroughly clear of the reefs that had threatened to sink it years earlier, Westpac was nonetheless seen as rather directionless. It had appeared to be the leading contender for BankSA, at a price between $600 and $700 million, but the state-based bank had been swallowed up by another regional, NSW's Advance Bank, which paid $730 million. Westpac looked left out in the cold. Joss and Pat Handley were determined that Westpac should emulate the strategy which had been a winner for Banc One: growth by acquisition, marketing itself under a different name in a different region. During his six years at Banc One, Handley had participated in 38 acquisitions. A regional acquisition in Australia would provide direction and momentum. And it would help bolster Westpac's defences against a larger predator, such as National Australia Bank. The federal government had made plain its position that it would not allow a merger of any of the big four—ANZ, Commonwealth Bank, NAB and Westpac—but that did not stop the weaker of them looking over their shoulders.

Westpac turned its sights to Western Australia's Challenge Bank, launching a formal offer in July 1995 based on $5 a share, which valued the target at $689 million or about fourteen times earnings. Westpac's proposal gazumped St George Bank, which had made a $580 million bid for Challenge a few days earlier. Under the terms of the offer, Challenge Bank would retain its own identity, and Westpac would fold its existing Western Australian retail operations into Challenge. This would mark the start of Westpac's policy of acquiring regional banks which would continue to trade under their own names—but with the Westpac logo figuring prominently—a policy intended to capitalise on the local popularity of the regional bank while also drawing on the strength of the nationally operating and far larger Westpac. Many regional banks had evolved from building societies and developed considerable strength in housing lending, good bread-and-butter business that any bank would welcome. The chief executive of Challenge Bank,

Tony Howarth, became managing director of the merged bank. Westpac learned how little goodwill its name carried: the new entity lost market share and staff, and the change-over from Challenge to Westpac systems diminished effi-ciencies. In January 1997 Westpac ran an advertisement in the WA media, pleading: 'Please bear with us', with the caption under a photograph of a baby. 'Bringing together two banks the size of Westpac and Challenge was bound to produce the odd teething problem,' the advertisement said. 'In just six weeks our staff have had to learn new systems and deal with a much bigger range of accounts, loans and investments. Misunderstandings are inevitable. But whatever the problem, we're investigating and solving each on an indi-vidual basis. While it may take a little longer, this personal approach is part of our commitment to creating a bank with a uniquely Western Australian focus. Rest assured the high standards you're accustomed to enjoying will return very soon.' The National Australia Bank's cheeky response was: 'At the National we give you the service you expect' in an advertisement that said: 'National Australia Bank is delighted to have provided banking services to the people of Western Australia for over 100 years. If you're not happy with the service your bank provides we welcome the opportunity to introduce you to the full range of financial and banking ser-vices available at any of our branches ...'

And by late 1995 there were rumours of a different kind, that Westpac, having substantially withdrawn from the world in 1993, was testing how to bridge gaps in its international network. David Morgan, now head of institutional and inter-national banking, confirmed that discussions were taking place about forming an alliance or partnership with a foreign bank. But negotiations would take at least a year.

Westpac reported an after-tax profit for 1995 up 34 per cent to $947 million, boosted by a decline in the charge for bad and doubtful debts to $330 million or half the previous

437

year's $695 million. Joss said the bank's running costs had been substantially reduced. However, underlying profit before charges for tax, bad and doubtful debts, abnormals and super fund adjustment was down marginally to $1,782 million from $1,799 million. Joss said that Westpac was still in transition but overall had more sustainable business, was less reliant on corporate banking or volatile trading business and was less asset-driven. The bank produced its highest return on equity, at 13.4 per cent, since 1987. Problem assets to equity, at 23 per cent, were the lowest since 1989. And it was again winning in the beauty parades: best banker of the year, according to the magazine *Personal Investment*, and fund manager of the year according to IPAC Securities in New Zealand; *BRW* voted it for the fifth consecutive year number one in financial markets for currency options and interest-rate risk management, and *Euromoney* ranked it number one in $A foreign exchange, interest-rate and currency swaps and loan-arranging for Australian borrowers.

During the year Joss had continued to strengthen the executive team, with former Lend Lease chief executive John Morschel joining the bank as an executive director, reporting directly to Joss. Although Morschel was not formally anointed as second-in-command, the appointment was seen as a rebuff to the ambitions of a select few in the bank with their eyes on Joss's job. Morschel had been on the Westpac board since 1993 when Lend Lease, now an 11 per cent shareholder in Westpac, had bought Kerry Packer's stake. And the infiltration of senior Westpac ranks by Citibank executives had continued: Michael Hawker, a former Australasian treasurer for Citibank, then head of its derivatives operations in Europe, joined Westpac as general manager, foreign exchange, money markets and derivatives. Hawker's appointment followed those of Jake Williams, who joined as general manager, corporate and institutional banking, and Michael Cannon-Brooks, as group executive, operations.

Westpac was climbing back up the ladder of financial respectability. Early in 1996 it won back the Aa credit-rating from Moody's, a ranking it had not held since June 1990. And the bank moved further into the modern era when, following the passing of the Westpac Banking Corporation Bill in the NSW parliament in December 1995, it was able to buy back up to 10 per cent of its own shares. This had not been possible under a state law which had been in effect since 1923. Westpac quickly moved to buy back some 5 per cent of its fully paid ordinary shares, an initiative described by Joss as an 'important part of an ongoing program of capital management' and which reflected Westpac's over-supply of capital, an expensive luxury for a bank. Reducing the excess capital would improve earnings per share. Westpac spent around $600 million buying the shares, which still left it with ample capital for another acquisition. That did not take long to find. In April Westpac announced that it was paying $1.1 billion for Trust Bank New Zealand, the country's fourth-largest bank. As had occurred in Western Australia with Challenge Bank, Trust Bank would retain its identity, trading as Westpac Trust and serving retail customers, with Westpac continuing in corporate and institutional banking.

A legacy of Westpac's enthusiastic push for a greater profile in South Australia was the opening in April 1996 of the bank's mortgage processing centre in the Adelaide suburb of Lockleys. During the previous year the governments of South Australia and NSW had lobbied keenly for the business. Westpac had identified nine suitable sites around Australia, with Campbelltown, west of Sydney, coming a close second to Lockleys. The Adelaide suburb won the contest because of ease of commuting and parking facilities. The experience of Pat Handley was again relevant in this initiative; Handley had earlier been chief financial officer of Banc One Mortgage Corporation, which he formed and ran. The centre at Lockleys was designed with the latest technology as a single-purpose national mortgage processor. Housed in a 24,000-square-metre warehouse, with some 250 workstations and nearly 1,000 staff, the centre would handle residential home loans, centralising and streamlining processes such as credit checking, loan documentation and customer inquiries. Centre staff would liaise with Westpac's 1,100 branches, mobile banking networks and electronic banking and telemarketing divisions. Another dimension for the centre was securitisation, where assets such as mortgages are pooled and sold so that the lender can reliquefy the asset. However, a prerequisite of efficient securitisation is standardisation of the assets—the centre would standardise mortgages in a form ready to be securitised.

Initially the centre was to handle Westpac business but the economics of the expensive project meant that eventually it would have to sell its services to other institutions and mortgage originators. It was an ambitious project, designed to bring considerable cost savings, but was dogged by disastrous teething problems. Some of these could have been avoided had the operations of the centre been phased in state by state; instead, the centre ambitiously attempted to service all states immediately. Problems reached such dimensions that the Law Society of New South Wales, on behalf of solicitors and conveyancers, formally complained to Westpac about delays, mistakes in documentation and bad communication. The bank invited conveyancing and legal industry representatives to a two-day session to demonstrate how the processing centre worked and to discuss concerns. Clearly offering the service to others would have to wait until the centre had learned to handle its own business effectively.

440

News of the centre's opening almost took a back seat to a revelation that Bob Joss had taken out permanent Australian residency, a necessary precursor to applying for citizenship should he choose that step. That, combined with John Morschel's acceptance of an outside board position with CSR Ltd, set off doubts about a succession that, only months earlier, had been taken for granted. Westpac played down the probability of Morschel's stepping into Joss's shoes, citing several executives who could fit into the top slot. Joss further dampened the succession theorists by suggesting that he might stay another term after his five-year contract expired in early 1998—and he later observed in an interview that the maximum life of a chief executive was ten years. He was clearly enjoying life in Australia and his wife, Betty, long rumoured not to be happy with the trans-Pacific move, according to her husband had settled down once they had found a harbourside home.

441

The remainder of 1996 was punctuated by a series of strategic moves in the financial sector, some prompted by expectations of change as institutions tried to guess what the Wallis inquiry into the financial system would recommend as a blueprint for the future. Chief among the concerns were the committee's views on bank mergers and possible changes to what constituted a 'bank'. Westpac sold the Victorian assets of Challenge Bank to Bank of Melbourne, a move explained by Joss as consistent with his bank's aim of concentrating on Challenge's strength in WA, but which would later be shown to be significant to Westpac's aspirations in Victoria. In the following month, the property and financial services giant Lend Lease, which had bought its stake in Westpac from Kerry Packer in 1993, turned its back on a ten-year ambition to buy a bank when it decided to cash in two-thirds of its holding, leaving the AMP again as Westpac's largest shareholder. As a result of its selldown to a 'portfolio' rather than 'strategic' investor, Lend Lease chairman Stuart Hornery resigned from the Westpac board. Westpac bought back its 50 per cent of AMPAC Life, its joint venture with the AMP Society, for around $340 million, finally enabling both parties to bury the corpse of the alliance. AMPAC, renamed Westpac Life Insurance Services Ltd, resumed life as an integrated part of the group.

Westpac announced a 19.5 per cent increase in after-tax profit to $1,132 million for the year to 30 September 1996. Bad and doubtful debts were down to $121 million compared with $330 million in 1995. However, Westpac's underlying performance, measured by profit before tax, bad and doubtful debts, abnormals and super fund adjustments, had dipped to $1,711 million from $1,737 million. Its headline profit figure had benefited substantially in 1994, 1995 and 1996 from the continuing drop in the charge for bad and doubtful debts. In his chairman's report to shareholders, Uhrig said that 1996 had been a 'year of considerable investment of capital and management effort in activity and innovation, aimed at building up the momentum of the business in a way which produces little or no immediate profit contribution, but improves the potential for a higher level of performance through the years to come'. Joss summed up the year as one of substantial achievement which, apart from the acquisitions and the new mortgage processing centre, included the completion of the branch back-office 're-engineering program'. During the year Joss had almost halved the number of executives reporting directly to him and restructured the retail bank into four regions to speed decision-making in top management and encourage closer contact with customers. Joss's 'inner circle' included Morschel, Pat Handley, David Morgan and credit chief Robert Nimmo. Owen van der Wall, formerly head of retail banking, moved to manage NSW in the reconfigured retail banking division. Barry Robertson moved from head of commercial banking and property finance to take charge of Victoria, Tasmania, South Australia and the Northern Territory. Tony Howarth retained responsibility for Western Australia and Challenge Bank, and David Liddy took over Queensland.

Back to the future

Speculation about Westpac forging an alliance to give it wider penetration in Asia bore fruit when, late in November 1996, three years after it had drastically slashed its Asian network to three branches and a string of representative offices, the bank confirmed it had formed a 'strategic relationship' with Standard Chartered Bank, which operated through 250 offices in 21 countries in Asia. Neither bank took an equity stake in the other but the two agreed to link electronic systems. Standard Chartered would provide cash management, local currency and trade services to Westpac's corporate clients operating in Asia, and Westpac would reciprocate for Standard Chartered customers in Australia. David Morgan said triumphantly that Westpac had secured an extensive Asian presence without spending a cent. Westpac retained its branches in Hong Kong, Singapore and Tokyo, and representative offices in Bangkok, Beijing, Jakarta and Kuala Lumpur, while Standard Chartered also kept its offices in Sydney and Melbourne. Predictably, the alliance drew cynical comments about its effectiveness and durability, particularly in the light of Westpac's notable lack of success in strategic alliances, having recently said goodbye to the AMP marketing partnership and seen the departure of Lend Lease as a major presence on its share registry.

Morgan, who says that the factors that make an alliance work or not are 'seared in my memory', counters that view. 'We have a relationship which is reciprocal, and we have made a mutual technological investment that will be enduring. These

443

are important contributors to the durability of this alliance.' He also emphasises that the alliance between Westpac and Standard Chartered goes far beyond a 'correspondent bank' role, where a bank merely acts as a point of contact for an overseas counterpart. 'We have spent months integrating the electronic banking systems of Standard Chartered and Westpac,' he says. 'This will provide enormous advantages for an Australasian-based corporate treasurer, covering local currency lending and integrated cash management. It's far in advance of a correspondent bank relationship.'

The deal between the two banks was at least eight months in the making, following a conversation between Morgan and Patrick Gillan, chairman of Standard Chartered, when the two coincided at Sydney airport. Formal meetings followed, culminating in a detailed study of customer needs and the options of how to implement the alliance. Says Morgan, widely regarded as the broker in the deal: 'It was a race against time, before another Australian bank could approach Standard Chartered. With nearly three-quarters of its business in Asia and a low banking profile in Australia, it is the only bank with genuine Pan-Asian capabilities which is not at the same time a domestic competitor for us.'

Morgan achieved such wide coverage over the deal with Standard Chartered that several Westpac executive egos were piqued. The outgoing and ambitious Morgan was told to subdue his public profile. Westpac, which for the past three years had orchestrated all press coverage through its tightly controlled media unit, had relented to the point of allowing Morgan his own media relations officer. Now she was told she had done her job too well. She left Westpac early in 1997.

At the annual general meeting in January 1997, a relaxed, jovial and plausible Bob Joss talked of Westpac's strategy of capitalising on its natural strength and of the importance of executing its business 'day in and day out with a sense of urgency, ownership and accountability'. Further cost cutting was much on his mind, and he would return to the theme in subsequent speeches. Later in the year, he said in an address to the Securities Institute of Australia that Westpac aimed to cut its operating costs by a third by offloading staff and closing branches. 'There's no point in us trying to protect yesterday's jobs,' he said. 'We need to bring value to our customers.' At the annual meeting he told shareholders that Westpac had increased its automatic teller machine (ATM) network by 21 per cent during the year; with a total of 1,030 ATM outlets it had for the first time more ATMs than branches. 'An interesting cross-over point in Westpac's history,' said Joss. Bob White, sitting in the audience, could recall Westpac making headlines only thirteen years earlier when it launched the world's first national electronic banking system. John Uhrig noted that Westpac's longest-serving director, Peter Baillieu, who had been on the board since 1974, had decided to retire. Uhrig, possibly with Baillieu's efforts in 1992 in mind, paid a brief tribute to his departing colleague: 'I would like to say personally that I know of no director in the modern history of the bank who had made a more important contribution to the outcome of the bank's work and its restoration to the improved situation we see today than has Mr Baillieu.' A small, private dinner was held later in the year, attended by the board, a few senior executives and a handful of former executives. Baillieu took the opportunity during his *vale* address to praise the former Bank of New South Wales, particularly for the way it looked after its customers.

Westpac fulfilled expectations that it had another regional acquisition in its sights when, early in April 1997 and only a week ahead of the long-awaited report on the financial system from the Wallis committee—widely expected to examine the rules applying to bank mergers—it launched a $1.4 million bid for the Bank of Melbourne. Such an acquisition was seen as essential if Westpac were to fulfil its strategy of building a strong state-based retail franchise. In particular, it would considerably strengthen the bank's flagging retail presence in Victoria. Selling Challenge's business in Victoria to Bank of Melbourne had clearly been preparation for catching the bigger fish. However, the takeover would be subject to scrutiny by the Australian Competition and Consumer Commission, which had already made clear that it regarded regional banks as crucial for competition. Federal treasurer Peter Costello wasted no time in issuing a response, saying: 'I want to stress this: that the treasurer has the ultimate discretion, and whether it was cleared by the ACCC or whether it wasn't, the treasurer retains the discretion to approve the merger. It's my decision and I won't be making any decision on this until the government as a whole has announced its policy.' Late in July, after a wait of nearly four months while the ACCC investigated the matter, Westpac received the go-ahead for the takeover.

Closing account

Westpac's retreat to its home market pulled the curtain down on its global ambitions in corporate banking which, overall, had failed to meet the bank's expectations. But it was Westpac's woeful handling of its affairs in its home market, including insufficient control of delinquent subsidiaries, particularly AGC, rather than its overseas operations, that brought the bank to its knees in the early 1990s. The losses to shareholders from ventures such as CS90 and Pollock, the loans that went sour, the support to AGC, Westpac General Finance in the UK and the assets sold at fire-sale prices added up to billions of dollars. Working in its favour, Westpac had a sound capital base and it had good businesses to sell, such as those in the US and Asia. But the bank's wealth had been wasted.

Joss took over a weakened and demoralised group which for 175 years had operated as a collegiate, family institution.

Retrenchments in the name of 'downsizing' tore that apart as thousands of employees went through the door in an exodus that caused widespread emotional, financial and marital stress. Westpac had recruited new people. But it had not rebuilt a team; rather, Joss was seen as being surrounded by skilled, ambitious individuals. Acknowledged as putting enormous effort into recruitment, he was nonetheless not considered a good judge of people and one of his weak spots was identified as a resolute blindness to flaws in those he had hired. And he was known as unwilling to confront difficult issues involving people. He preferred to present himself as the 'good guy', leaving Pat Handley to be the 'bad guy'. Time will judge whether Joss's faith in the Australian and New Zealand markets as adequate fields for expansion had curtailed Westpac's longterm growth possibilities. He was credited with bringing focus and discipline to the bank, and with having an excellent knowledge of banking and balance-sheet structure. But though affable and relaxed with people, he was seen as detached and unemotional—paradoxically, qualities initially regarded as strengths—and to be running an institution that had lost its soul and alienated many customers, large and small.

447

John Uhrig's reponse to those who say that Westpac's culture had changed was emphatic: 'We deliberately set out to change Westpac's culture,' he said in an interview for this book in March 1997. 'I would be disappointed if people were not saying that the culture has changed at Westpac. But the cultural changes we desire are not yet complete. We took a culture and changed it but we have not yet replaced it with a new one. We are still in transition.' Three years earlier, Joss told *The Sydney Morning Herald* that changing the culture of a big company is a 'long-term proposition'. He said: 'We've been moderately successful in making a start at it ... [but] you're talking almost about a decade in terms of a real fundamental change.' At halfway through that decade, some would say that Westpac was having a long transition. Uhrig, whose worldwide search for a new managing director had unearthed Bob Joss, and whose own fate was firmly yoked to that of his chosen chief, pointed out that Joss had produced real value for shareholders. Shareholders were enjoying a far higher level of dividend, 33 cents a share in 1996 compared with 18 cents in 1992, while the value of their shares had virtually trebled to around $7 since the low point of that year. Joss's options looked safe.

During the 1980s Westpac had run too fast in its anxiety to stay ahead of the rest of the pack, and it stumbled badly. Decades of hubris smothered recognition of its shortcomings and when reality caught up with it in the early 1990s it was almost too late to stop the rot. The consequences were that in the four years to 1992 it somersaulted from being Australia's leading bank to one of the world's weakest, a target of savage criticism with its reputation in tatters. The deterioration cannot be overstated. Joss and his fellow fixers pulled Westpac out of the financial mire. But, four years after his arrival, the jury was still out on whether he had restored Westpac to independence or merely smartened it up for sale. Joss spoke confidently of Westpac having a strategy that was working but many in his audience were yet to be convinced. They wondered whether it could ever fully recover. A major question was whether the strategy of state-based regional franchises under the Westpac umbrella could succeed. Or would it recreate state fiefdoms which, to be successful, demand unusually subtle management? Regionals do not like to be dictated to by head office, which has to allow them room to operate while keeping them under control. It is a management challenge at which Westpac failed abysmally in the past.

In 1997 Australia's 'world bank' was a mere memory. There was even talk that the bank's home-state branches would revert to the name 'Bank of New South Wales', in an attempt to draw a firm line in the sand between the past and the present. But that would be assuming a false identity; the bank had been irrevocably changed by what it did to itself in the 1980s and 1990s. It was unlikely that it could ever again meet the expectations of those who were the Wales's customers—the people who were loyal to the 'people's bank'.

What can be learned from Westpac's saga? The bank's aspirations in the 1980s ignored its management limitations; it did not, until it was too late, recognise that growth increases the complexity of the business and, in the absence of adequate controls, growth can run wild. In its drive to create an international presence Westpac neglected the wellspring of its vitality—its retail banking business in Australia—and its confidence, born of years of dominance in its industry, turned to arrogance and blinded it to criticism. Outsiders, ratings agencies, regulators and the sharemarket identified Westpac's flaws long before the bank publicly acknowledged them. It did so in 1992 and then, in the name of recovery, inflicted such savage surgery on itself that it has been left a pale version of the optimistic institution which set out to do so much in the 1980s. Surgery, it was said, was necessary for survival. In the process thousands lost their jobs and many customers were alienated. Westpac sacrificed promising businesses. The excitement of earlier years was replaced by the hard, unrelenting slog of cost cutting and repositioning. Much was given up in the name of survival.

Westpac's mistakes were not unique. Its blunders highlighted, though, the fact that banks are different from other companies. For a bank, soundness is perceived soundness. For a bank, its assets can be its biggest danger. Assessing credit quality, pricing for risk, correctly judging customers and markets, and being able to distinguish between reality and the popular view are key principles of banking that Westpac overlooked. It tried to build a behemoth—and broke a bank.

INDEX

452